Archival Insights into the Evolution of Economics

Series Editor
Robert Leeson
Stanford University
Stanford, CA, USA

This series provides unique insights into economics by providing archival evidence into the evolution of the subject. Each volume provides biographical information about key economists associated with the development of a key school, an overview of key controversies and gives unique insights provided by archival sources.

More information about this series at
http://www.palgrave.com/gp/series/14777

Elena Danescu

Pierre Werner and Europe

The Family Archives Behind the Werner Report

Foreword by Jean-Claude Juncker,
President of the European Commission

Preface by Harold James, Princeton University

palgrave
macmillan

Elena Danescu
Luxembourg Centre for Contemporary and
Digital History (C2DH)
University of Luxembourg
Esch-sur-Alzette, Luxembourg

Archival Insights into the Evolution of Economics
ISBN 978-3-030-40468-0 ISBN 978-3-319-96295-5 (eBook)
https://doi.org/10.1007/978-3-319-96295-5

Library of Congress Control Number: 2018951569

This Palgrave Macmillan imprint is published by the registered company Springer Nature Switzerland AG
The registered company address is: Gewerbestrasse 11, 6330 Cham, Switzerland

Pierre Werner (29 December 1913–24 June 2002)

Une oeuvre politique n'est jamais le produit de l'intelligence ou de la volonté d'un seul homme. Le chef politique doit être avant tout le catalyseur des énergies de ceux qui l'entourent et qui le secondent dans un grand dessein. Je crois à la grandeur du métier politique quand il est porté par la volonté d'unir les hommes.

[A political achievement is never the result of the intelligence or desire of a single person. A political leader must above all serve as a catalyst for the energies of those around him, those who assist him in the pursuit of a major goal. I believe in the greatness of politics when it is underpinned by the desire to bring people together.]

Pierre Werner, 1992

Acknowledgements

This study would not have been possible without the help of many people, to whom I wish to express my gratitude—even if I realise that the few words which follow cannot do justice to the valuable support that I have received.

I would firstly like to extend my sincere thanks to the Werner family, especially Marie-Anne Werner and Henri Werner, for opening up their father's personal archives, for their kind permission to publish several of the documents unearthed from them and for their constant support throughout my research on Pierre Werner's philosophy and achievements.

My heartfelt gratitude also goes to European Commission President Jean-Claude Juncker and Professor Harold James (Princeton University), who kindly accepted to preface this volume and generously share their personal thoughts, ideas and recollections.

I greatly benefited from discussions with the academic steering committee of the 'Pierre Werner and Europe' research project (2011–2016), composed of Professors René Leboutte (University of Luxembourg), Ivo Maes (National Bank of Belgium and Université catholique de Louvain) and Sylvain Schirmann (University of Strasbourg and Sciences Po Strasbourg), and with the members of the 'Architects of the Euro' research project (2013–2016), coordinated by Professors Ivo Maes and Kenneth Dyson (Cardiff University and British Academy). Significant insights also emerged during exchanges at a number of conferences and debates held by the European Society for the History of Economic Thought (ESHET), the University Association for Contemporary European Studies (UACES), the European Union Studies Association (EUSA), the Italian Association for the Study of Economic Thought (AISPE) and the Network for European Studies (NES), and also within Robert Triffin International and the Pierre Werner Foundation.

I was privileged to receive much helpful advice and constructive criticism of my writings in their various stages of development from many other contacts, both academics and officials, especially Alain Alcouffe, Matthew Broad, Michel Camdessus, Armand Clesse, Philippe Duvieusart, Marie-Claude Esposito, Giovanni Farese, Luc Frieden, Christian Ghymers, Pierre Gramegna, Albert Hansen, Erna Hennicot-Schoepges, David Howarth, Harold James, Jean-Claude Juncker, Antoine Kasel, Koen Lenaerts, Astrid Lulling, Yves Mersch, Xu Mingqi, Guy de Muyser, Charles-Ferdinand Nothomb, Ion Popescu, Viviane Reding, Charles Ruppert, Jacques Santer, André Sapir, Hanspeter Scheller, Bernard Snoy et d'Oppuers, Blanche Sousi, René Steichen, Alfred Steinherr, Niels Thygesen, Jean-Claude Trichet, Sir Brian Unwin, Amy Verdun, Andreas Wilkens and Léon Zeches, as well as the late Josette Elvinger, André Heiderscheid, Edmond Israel, Raymond Kirsch, Jean-Claude Koeune, Philippe Maystadt, Jean Mischo, Michael Palmer and Hans Tietmeyer. I am also grateful to the publisher Palgrave Macmillan, particularly Rachel Sangster and Joseph Johnson, and to its anonymous academic peer reviewers.

Finally, a special mention should go to all those who were involved in diverse capacities throughout my research process, including my collaborators and colleagues at the Centre Virtuel de la Connaissance sur l'Europe (CVCE), the Luxembourg Centre for Contemporary and Digital History (C²DH) and the University of Luxembourg, particularly Victoria Mouton, François Klein and Isabelle Vaillant, who shared their expert opinions with me, and Sarah Cooper, for contributing her linguistic expertise to the quality of this publication.

It goes without saying that I take full responsibility for the views and interpretations expressed in this volume.

The usual disclaimers apply.

Elena Danescu

Foreword

The first time I saw Pierre Werner face to face was 1974, during the Parliamentary election campaign which ushered him into political opposition for the only time in his distinguished governmental career. '*What do you do in life?*' he asked me. '*I'm preparing my Baccaulaureat*', was the humble reply I gave to this man who would play a greater role in my life than I could have imagined possible in that fleeting moment.

My next memories of Pierre Werner are from my University days, when I found myself studying in Strasbourg, and where I attended two or three meetings at which he explained the Plan that carried his name. This would have been several years after the Werner Plan was published, and without very much progress having been made on its recommendations. And yet what I noticed in this man's lectures, and remembered about him, was his faultless engagement and a complete lack of discouragement about the slow start to the Plan which he had launched. I was also struck by the fact that Werner did not stop pleading for Europe and for a common currency, even during his time in political opposition, when many politicians naturally have doubts about the path which they have chosen.

Our paths crossed again a few years later, and began to intertwine. I was a 22-year old candidate in the next Parliamentary elections in 1979, which took Pierre Werner back into the office of Prime Minister of Luxembourg. I cannot claim that my fate in those elections was key to his victory however, as I waited until the next elections in 1984 to claim my seat in the Chamber of Deputies for the first time.

But it was in that year, 1979, that we first began to work together, or rather when I first began to work for him, as Parliamentary Secretary of the Christian Social Party which he led and represented as the head of the Government. I took another step forward under his patronage in 1982, becoming Secretary of State in his Government, and that was the moment when I truly got to know this esteemed man, whose chair I would one day fill. He was an extremely demanding Prime Minister, who did not tolerate any indiscipline or ignorance on the dossiers which we worked on. He was a man who taught me a certain way of working, with seriousness and rigour.

Pierre Werner never let you forget your privileged position, and its ultimate fragility. He sent me to see the Grand Duke for the first time with a stern warning ringing in my ears. As I set off to be formally sworn in as Secretary of State for Labour and Social Security, on a proud morning in 1982, he said these words to me: '*Do not think yourself too important. You are a Minister but you are too young. You must tell yourself, every morning when you shave, that you might not be a Minister tomorrow*'. Those words stayed with me for my 30 years as a Minister. They are the wise words which every political father should utter to his young charges.

During the 20 years of my friendship with Pierre Werner, we spoke often and in great depth about Europe. Already when I was a young party activist he was the man who represented a certain idea of Europe in the eyes of my colleagues and I. And when I became Secretary of State I had many opportunities to speak with him during meetings of the Council of Ministers and of our party, and when I would travel abroad with him to take part in negotiations with our neighbours in the Dutch, Belgian and German Governments. When we first worked together it was the height of the steel crisis, and we focused a lot of our energies on addressing the social elements of our response to the issue.

Werner is rightly remembered for his work in the field of economics, but this was always underpinned by a quest for social justice. This was one of the guiding principles of his leadership, set out in his first budget speech in the Chamber of Deputies, as Dr. Elena Danescu notes in this impeccably researched book which I have the honour to introduce. Werner also brought this spirit to the European level, writing the social chapter of the EPP's electoral manifesto for the first European Parliament elections in 1979.

My overriding memory of Pierre Werner is that he was a man who believed passionately in the European vocation of Luxembourg, and in making sure that his people became and remained pro-European. He taught me that Luxembourg must always be a champion of European integration, and must always be among the leaders and initiators when European questions are brought to the table. He taught me this and I followed faithfully his guidance and European ideology.

For Werner, and for all the men and women of his generation, Europe was above all else a question of peace over war. He had seen the disaster of non-Europe, and so he played his role in the creation of Europe. As a Minister of Finance, he worked on the creation of the Coal and Steel Community and of the Common Market. He also contributed to the development of the common agricultural policy, putting in place the foundations for a programme which is still at the heart of our Union today. And of course, most importantly, he was one of the fathers of our economic and monetary union.

So when we talk about Europe, and when we talk about Pierre Werner, the connection is indisputable. One cannot discuss Werner without discussing Europe, and one cannot discuss Europe without discussing Werner.

Werner passed on this dedication to me. If Europe is in my heart, it is thanks to Pierre Werner, as well as to my own personal family history. In politics, I learnt from him that in case of any doubts, I should always play the European card over the national card. For Werner, if you pursued only a national path, eventually you would cut yourself off from the European path. And he also taught me that the European path is a more virtuous path to follow, and that it is the path that can best guide and benefit your national path. Werner also taught me how to negotiate in Europe. He showed me the value of compromise, and sometimes of concession.

Nothing that I have done in my European journey would have been possible without the lessons which Pierre Werner had the kindness to pass on to me. This pro-European tradition was not just anchored in Werner and I by our nationality, but also by our Christian Democratic political family. In Luxembourg, at least, no one can expect to lead the Christian Democrats without first being a fervent pro-European who believes that we must fight each day to construct and mould our continent and help it to evolve towards a stronger common future.

The euro and our economic and monetary union are part of that future. And Pierre Werner was ahead of most others with his ideas for monetary union. As Minister of Finance, with deep knowledge of the world of international finance, he saw very early in his political career the benefits of pursuing an idea which had already stuck with him from a young age, to give Europe a real monetary firepower. Before he was asked to develop the Werner Report, his most famous and lasting work, he had already insisted many times during the 1960s, in international forums and in the Chamber of Deputies, on the necessity of turning the Common Market into a common currency.

Pierre Werner's most famous contribution to the birth of the euro zone was of course the Werner Plan, also known as the Werner Report. One has to be very cautious when a plan is given your name. It usually means somebody expects it to fail. From my own more humble experience, I note that the Juncker Plan, which has now generated around €300 billion of investment in the EU, has lost its original nomenclature now that it has become a success, whereas it was widely known as the Juncker Plan when people thought that it would not work. The Werner Plan was also given Pierre's name when the national leaders who asked him to prepare it were not sure what end it would meet. As his successor in several functions, and as a long-time President of the Eurogroup, it is only right that I make sure his name is associated with our economic and monetary union in these days of success, as much as it was in those early moments of doubt and darkness.

On the day when we introduced the euro, on 1 January 1999, it was therefore only natural that it was to Pierre Werner that I addressed my speech from Brussels. It felt almost like the duty of a son to his father. It was the moment when I should thank Werner, praise Werner, and congratulate Werner. For he was one of the founding fathers of the euro, if not *the* founding father. And after that speech in Brussels, I returned the same evening to Luxembourg to celebrate the moment together with him.

The currency which Pierre Werner imagined and nurtured has come a long way since the Werner Plan of 1970, and the launch of the euro in January 1999. I am delighted that Pierre Werner was still with us to see the euro notes and coins enter into circulation on 1 January 2002, though it saddens me deeply that he is not still with us now, when the euro has become the common currency for 19 of our 28 EU Member States, and is used by over 330 million people every day.

When I took over the Presidency of the European Commission in November 2014, I put the completion of the Economic and Monetary Union at the top of my list of priorities, which I hope Pierre Werner would have approved of. Our single currency is a valuable tool for creating jobs, growth, investment, social fairness, and stability. We have overcome a period of turmoil in the euro zone, and now that it has stopped raining, it is time for us to repair the roof and to strengthen our foundations.

The economic crisis of 2008 brought difficult times to Europe, even if this turmoil did not have its roots in Europe. If Pierre Werner had seen our adventures of the past few years, I expect he would have smiled. In a funny way, he would have liked the difficulties we faced. Because he would have known that they would have been even greater, and even harder to overcome, if it were not for the common currency which tied us together, and which he fathered.

I have always considered it my great privilege to have shared part of my European journey with Pierre Werner, and I am honoured that this great man shared part of his wisdom, grace and guidance with me. For many years to come, Europeans will benefit from the work of Pierre Werner. And I want to congratulate the author of this book, Dr. Elena Danescu, for her role in telling his story, and for ensuring that more of our fellow Europeans know his name and can honour his work. Pierre Werner is already known as a great Luxembourger. He should also be known as a great European.

Brussels, Belgium
August 2018

Jean-Claude Juncker
European Commission President

Jean-Claude Juncker is a Luxembourg statesman who is the current President of the European Commission; he began his five-year term on 1 November 2014. From 1995 to 2013 he was Luxembourg's 23rd Prime Minister, becoming the longest-serving head of any national government in the EU and one of the longest-serving democratically elected leaders in the world. Between 2005 and 2013 he was the first permanent President of the Eurogroup (the informal body for the Finance Ministers of the euro area Member States), playing a major role during the height of the European financial and sovereign debt crises.

Jean-Claude Juncker was Luxembourg Minister of Labour from 1984 to 1999, Minister of Finance from 1989 to 2009 and Minister for the Treasury from 2009 to 2013. In this period he was also a Governor of the World Bank (1989–1995), a Governor of the International Monetary Fund (1995–2013) and a Governor of the European Bank for Reconstruction and Development (1995–2013). He entered the Luxembourg Government in 1982 as State Secretary for Labour and Social Security. After joining the Christian Social People's Party (CSV) in 1974, he served as the party's leader from 1990 to 1995 and subsequently became its honorary president.

He has received many prestigious international awards and honours, including the Charlemagne Prize in 2006 for his outstanding European achievements. He has also been conferred a number of Doctorates Honoris Causa from prestigious international universities (including Munster, Bucharest, Thrace, Strasbourg, Pittsburgh, Thessaloniki and Salamanca). In 2009 he became a foreign associate member at the Académie des Sciences morales et politiques of the Institut de France and an Honorary Senator of the European Academy of Sciences and Arts.

Jean-Claude Juncker was the European People's Party's *Spitzenkandidat* for the European Commission Presidency in the 2014 European Parliament election. After the party won the most seats, he was officially nominated to the post of President of the European Commission by the European Council, and the nomination was confirmed by the European Parliament. He is the third Luxembourger to serve as President of the European Commission, after Gaston Thorn (1981–1985) and Jacques Santer (1995–1999).

Preface

This important study by Dr. Elena Danescu analyses the work and influence of the long-standing Luxembourg Prime Minister Pierre Werner on the basis of family papers, and concentrates in particular on his work designing the blueprint for European monetary integration. Werner's contributions lay in modernising his country's economic and industrial structure, within a European context. Pierre Werner can be seen in particular as the father of the euro. He chaired the European Economic Community 'Committee of Presidents of Committee', whose 1970 blueprint for closer European integration was originally intended as a response to the travails of the international monetary order. Wernerism is in fact a synonym for European integration.

Luxembourg has a peculiar role as a melting pot for different traditions, which Werner experienced personally. In terms of traditional Great Power politics, it was situated uneasily between France and Germany—and was susceptible to the power plays of those Great Powers. It is also situated between different French and German ways of thinking about economics. But it is also a mediator for smaller states—initially for Belgium and the Netherlands—and their role in the integration process. Europe won't work if it just depends on the visions of the large and powerful countries.

Rereading the debates in the Werner Committee, and the responses to its report, gives a sense of the timelessness of many of the discussions about European integration. First, European integration from Werner's perspective is a response to global issues and challenges. The fixed but adjustable par value system of Bretton Woods was under increasing strain at the end of the 1960s. The Bretton Woods order centred on the dollar looked as strained and crisis-prone as the modern dollar-based financialised monetary order. The dollar is still at the centre, and US policy is still the dominant driver, even under very idiosyncratic Presidents. Werner sometimes observed that the EEC should develop a 'personality' in respect to debates on global monetary policy.

Second, Werner saw that national policies are limited by the development of the international economy (though the term globalisation was not then in widespread use). That limitation is of course particularly obvious in the case of very small countries like Luxembourg. As the report put it: 'The increasing interpenetration of the economies has entailed a weakening of autonomy for national economic policies. The control of economic policy has become all the more difficult because the loss of autonomy at the national level has not been compensated by the inauguration of Community policies. The inadequacies and disequilibrium that have occurred in the process of realization of the Common Market are thus thrown into relief.'

Third, monetary union on its own is not enough. It would give rise to new issues, and would demand some sort of transfers—but those would be politically contentious. Werner seems to have imagined large-scale fiscal operations, but those would encounter suspicions in the countries (notably Germany) that might be expected to be net contributors. 'The realization of global economic equilibrium may be dangerously threatened by differences of structure. Cooperation between the partners in the Community in the matter of *structural and regional policies* will help to surmount these difficulties, just as it will make it possible to eliminate the distortions of competition. The solution of the big problems in this field will be facilitated by financial measures of compensation.'

The 1970 report's most striking and most lasting feature was the sharp delineation of a final objective, of monetary union. 'Economic and monetary union will make it possible to realize an area within which goods and services, people and capital will circulate freely and without competitive distortions, without thereby giving rise to structural, or regional disequilibrium. [...] The implementation of such a union will effect a lasting improvement in welfare in the Community and will reinforce the contribution of the Community to economic and monetary equilibrium in the world.'

The debates of the Werner Committee looked rapidly outdated when the international monetary system collapsed in August 1971—but it is a testimony to the strength of the underlying analysis that the idea kept returning, especially at moments of great strain in the international system. The vision was essentially revived by the Delors Report of April 1989. That too might have been filed away like the Werner Report had it not been for the geopolitical revolution that followed the publication of the report, as communism collapsed in Eastern Europe and the Soviet Union.

The three points central to Werner's contribution, globalisation, national insufficiency, and the inadequacy of a monetary solution on its own, have been consistent features of the European debate. So have the fears that they conjure up: on the part of France that Germany might be too powerful, or that Europe was becoming too 'centralised'; and on the part of Germany that France was trying to launch a grab for German resources. Even in 2018, the underlying issues have not really been solved.

Princeton, USA
July 2018

Professor Harold James
Princeton University

Harold James is Claude and Lore Kelly Professor in European Studies, Professor of History and International Affairs and the Director of the Programme in Contemporary European Politics and Society at Princeton University. He is a Senior Fellow of the Centre for International Governance Innovation, Ontario, and a Senior Fellow of the Global Governance Programme at the European University Institute, Florence. He completed studies at the University of Cambridge and was a Fellow of Peterhouse for eight years before coming to Princeton University in

1986. His specialist research fields are economic and financial history and modern European history, and his current work is concerned with the history of European monetary union.

In 2004 he was awarded the Helmut Schmidt Prize for Economic History, and in 2005 the Ludwig Erhard Prize for writing about economics. His early books include a study of the interwar depression in Germany, *The German Slump* (1986); an analysis of the changing character of national identity in Germany, *A German Identity 1770–1990* (1989); and *International Monetary Cooperation Since Bretton Woods* (1996). He was also coauthor of a history of Deutsche Bank (1995), which won the Financial Times Global Business Book Award in 1996. He went on to write *The End of Globalization: Lessons from the Great Depression* (2001); *Europe Reborn: A History 1914–2000* (2003); *Family Capitalism* (2006); *The Roman Predicament: How the Rules of International Order Create the Politics of Empire* (2006); and *The Creation and Destruction of Value: The Globalization Cycle* (2009). His study *Making the European Monetary Union* was published by Harvard University Press in 2012, and his recent work *The Euro and the Battle of Economic Ideas* (with Markus K. Brunnermeier and Jean-Pierre Landau) by Princeton University Press in 2016.

Contents

Acknowledgements vii

Foreword xi

Preface xvii

List of Abbreviations xxvii

Terminology xxxi

1 Introduction 1
- 1.1 A Man Committed to the European Ideal 3
- 1.2 A Man as Seen Through His Archives 6
- 1.3 A Man and His Report: A Brief Overview of the Narrative 9

2 *Itinéraires luxembourgeois et européens*: **Pierre Werner's Biographical Highlights** 19

3 The Werner Committee in Context: Monetary Unification and European Integration 33

3.1 The Post-War International Monetary Environment 35

3.2 Pierre Werner's Monetary Thinking and Political Action in the 1960s 40

3.2.1 Monetary Innovation Through the Luxembourg Financial Centre 52

3.3 A Turbulent Economic and Monetary Climate 53

3.3.1 The First and Second Barre Plans 56

3.3.2 The Hague Summit 61

3.3.3 Belgium, Germany and Luxembourg Present Their Plans (January–February 1970) 69

4 Formation of the Werner Committee and an Overview of Its Work (March–October 1970) 93

4.1 Pierre Werner's Appointment as Chairman—Three Different Accounts 94

4.2 The Work of the Werner Committee—An Ambitious Task 100

4.2.1 Preliminary Meeting (Luxembourg, 11 March 1970) 100

4.2.2 First Meeting (Luxembourg, 20 March 1970) 102

4.2.3 Second Meeting (Brussels, 7 April 1970) 104

4.2.4 Third Meeting (Rome, 30 April 1970) 108

4.2.5 Fourth and Fifth Meetings (Luxembourg, 14 May and 20 May 1970) 110

4.2.6 Further Work by the Werner Committee 112

4.2.7 Sixth Meeting (Luxembourg, 24 June 1970) 119

4.2.8 Seventh Meeting (Paris, 7 July 1970) 121

4.2.9 Eighth Meeting (Luxembourg, 27 July 1970) 122

4.2.10 Ninth Meeting (Luxembourg, 10 and 11 September 1970) 124
4.2.11 Tenth Meeting (Copenhagen, 23 and 24 September 1970) 125
4.2.12 Eleventh Meeting (Luxembourg, 7 October 1970) 126

5 The Werner Report 161
5.1 The Interim Report 163
5.1.1 The Start Point of EMU 164
5.1.2 The Final Goal 166
5.1.3 An Irreversible Process by Stages 169
5.1.4 The First Stage 170
5.1.5 An Exchange Stabilisation Fund in the First Stage? 171
5.1.6 Conclusions 173
5.2 The Final Report 175
5.2.1 Final Objective and Institutional Aspects of EMU 175
5.2.2 Key Features of the First Stage 178
5.2.3 Transition to the Final Objective 181
5.3 Input from the Committee of Governors of the Central Banks 182
5.4 Economists vs. Monetarists: Towards a Balanced Approach to EMU 189

6 Reactions to the Werner Report 203
6.1 The European Parliament 205
6.1.1 Debate by the Special Committees of the EP 205
6.1.2 Enlargement of the Community and the Outlook for EMU: What Role Should the Pound Sterling Play? 214
6.1.3 Debates During the Plenary Sittings of the EP 217

6.2 The European Commission and the Werner Report—Agreement and Discord 225
6.3 The Council 234
6.4 Political Reactions in the Member States 242
6.5 Representative Economic, Social and Civic Organisations 262
6.5.1 The Economic and Social Committee 262
6.5.2 Professional, Trade Union and Civic Organisations 266
6.6 Reception by the International Media 271

7 The Implementation of the Werner Report 305
7.1 The First Stage Under Pressure 306
7.2 The Monetary Snake and the EMCF in Trouble 311
7.3 The Report Is Shelved 318

8 The Werner Report: A Blueprint for EMU? 331
8.1 Plans and Studies Drawn up After the Werner Report 331
8.2 The Werner Report and the Delors Report 334

9 Pierre Werner and the Werner Report 345
9.1 A Three-Point Method 345
9.2 Deepening of the Werner Group's Work for the Final Report 346
9.3 The Role of the Central Bankers in Shaping EMU 346
9.4 The External Dimension of EMU 347
9.5 Consensus Building Through Network Diplomacy 348
9.6 A Parallel Approach to a Symmetrical EMU 349

10 Conclusion 355

Appendix A: Archival Insights 359
Part I: Photo Album 359
Part II: Selected Documents 389

Appendix B: Chronology 399

Appendix C: Index of Key Figures 441

Appendix D: Luxembourg in a Nutshell 469

Sources and Bibliography 479

Index 491

List of Abbreviations

ACUSE	Action Committee for the United States of Europe (the Monnet Committee)
AV (ALUC)	Association of Catholic University Students (*Akademikerverein*/*Association Luxembourgeoise des Universitaires Catholiques*)
BENELUX	Belgian-the Netherlands-Luxembourg Economic Union/ Benelux Union
BIS	Bank for International Settlements
BGL	Banque Générale de Luxembourg
BLEU	Belgium–Luxembourg Economic Union
CAP	Common Agricultural Policy
CCB	Banking Control Commission
CFB	Committee for Finance and Budgets
CGCB	Committee of Governors of Central Banks
CLT	*Compagnie Luxembourgeoise de Télédiffusion*
COREPER	Committee of Permanent Representatives (*Comité des Représentants permanents*)
CSV	Christian Social People's Party (Luxembourg)
DB	Deutsche Bank
DGII	Directorate General II (Economic and Financial Affairs)
DM	Deutschmark (D-Mark)

DP	Democratic Party (Luxembourg)
EAC	Economic Affairs Committee
EBF	European Banking Federation
EC	European Community
ECB	European Central Bank
ECFTU	European Confederation of Free Trade Unions
ECOFIN	Economic and Financial Affairs Council
ECSC	European Coal and Steel Community
ECU	European Currency Unit
EDC	European Defence Community
EEC	European Economic Community
EIB	European Investment Bank
EFTA	European Free Trade Association
ELEC	European League for Economic Cooperation
EMCF	European Monetary Cooperation Fund
EMF	European Monetary Fund
EMI	European Monetary Institute
EMS	European Monetary System
EMU	Economic and Monetary Union
EOWCL	European Organisation of the World Confederation of Labour
EP	European Parliament
EPP	European People's Party
EPU	European Payments Union
ERM	Exchange Rate Mechanism
ERP	European Recovery Programme (Marshall Plan)
ESC	Economic and Social Committee
ESCB	European Sytem of Central Banks
EU	European Union
EUA	European Unit of Account
EURATOM	European Atomic Energy Community
G-5	Group of Five (USA, Japan, Germany, France, UK)
G-7	Group of Seven (USA, Japan, Germany, France, UK, Italy, Canada)
G-10	Group of Ten (USA, Japan, Germany, France, UK, Italy, Canada, Belgium, the Netherlands, Sweden)
GATT	General Agreement on Tariffs and Trade
IBRD	International Bank for Reconstruction and Development
IFSE	International Federation of Stock Exchanges

IGC	intergovernmental conference
IMF	International Monetary Fund
IML	Luxembourg Monetary Institute (*Institut Monétaire Luxembourgeois*)
IMS	International Monetary System
KBL	Kredietbank Luxembourgeoise S.A.
LSAP	Luxembourg Socialist Workers' Party
LSE	Luxembourg Stock Exchange
MTFA	medium-term financial assistance
NATO	North Atlantic Treaty Organisation
NBB	National Bank of Belgium
OEEC	Organisation for European Economic Cooperation
OPOCE	Office for Official Publications of the European Communities
PAC	Political Affairs Committee
SDRs	Special Drawing Rights
SES	*Société Européenne des Satellites*
SNCI	National Credit and Investment Company (*Société Nationale de Crédit et d'Investissement*)
STMS	short-term monetary support
UNICE	Union of Industries of the European Community
WEU	Western European Union

Terminology

Given the many changes and adaptations that have occurred throughout the development of the European institutions, the terminology used to describe them can sometimes lead to confusion. It is therefore useful to clarify the following terms:

'European Community', 'European Communities' and 'European Union'

The European Economic Community (EEC or Common Market) was established in 1957 by the *Treaty of Rome* (or Treaty Establishing the European Community), which was signed on 25 March 1957 and came into force on 1 January 1958.

The term 'European Communities' described the three Communities that were set up under three separate treaties:

- the European Coal and Steel Community (ECSC), established by the *Treaty of Paris* (which was signed on 18 April 1951 and expired on 23 July 2002)

- the EEC, established by the Treaty of Rome 'for an unlimited period' (Article 312)
- the European Atomic Energy Community (EAEC or Euratom), established by the Euratom Treaty (signed, along with the EEC Treaty, in Rome, 'for an unlimited period' [Article 208])

After the adoption of the *Merger Treaty* (or *Brussels Treaty*, which was signed on 18 April 1965 and came into force on 1 July 1967), the three Communities shared the same institutions, although they remained legally separate. The Treaty provided that the Commission and Council of the EEC should replace the Commission and Council of Euratom and the High Authority and Council of the ECSC. Prior to this Treaty, they already shared a Parliamentary Assembly and Court of Justice. They always had the same membership.

The European Community (EC) was the successor to the EEC. The *Maastricht Treaty* (which was signed on 7 February 1992 and came into force on 1 November 1993) stipulates that the EC formally replaces the EEC, although the term 'EC' had already been widely used for several years. The EC formed one part of the European Union (EU), which was the overarching structure, comprising the Community (together with ECSC and Euratom) and two intergovernmental 'Pillars' (Common Foreign and Security Policy (CFSP) and Justice and Home Affairs (JHA), subsequently renamed Police and Judicial Cooperation in Criminal Matters (PJCC)).

The *Treaty of Lisbon* (which was signed on 13 December 2007 and came into force on 1 December 2009) changed this structure, and now we are left with the EU.

European Council, Council of the European Union, Council of Europe

Only the European Council and the Council are EU bodies. The Council of Europe is a different organisation altogether, albeit with an overlapping membership.

The European Council

This is the meeting of Heads of State or Government, which meets formally at least twice a year (June and December), informally in spring and autumn, and whenever necessary. The Lisbon Treaty made the European Council an 'EU institution' and introduced the position of President of the European Council. The European Council does not exercise legislative functions, but it makes certain decisions based on the Treaties, including establishing the broad direction of EU policy-making.

The Council of the European Union

The Council of the EU (formerly the Council of Ministers) is the main decision-making body in the EU. It has both executive and legislative powers and is composed of government ministers from each EU country, according to the policy area to be discussed. The Council of the EU negotiates and adopts EU laws, together with the European Parliament, based on proposals from the European Commission; coordinates the policies of EU countries; develops the EU's foreign and security policy based on European Council guidelines; concludes agreements between the EU and other countries or international organisations; and adopts the annual EU budget, jointly with the European Parliament.

There are no fixed members of the EU Council. Instead, the Council meets in ten different configurations, each corresponding to the policy area being discussed (Agriculture and Fisheries; Competitiveness; Economic and Financial Affairs; Education, Youth, Culture, and Sport; Employment, Social Policy, Health and Consumer Affairs; Environment; Foreign Affairs; General Affairs; Justice and Home Affairs; Transport, Telecommunications, and Energy). There is no hierarchy among the Council configurations, although the General Affairs Council (GAC) has a special coordination role and is responsible for institutional, administrative, and horizontal matters. The Foreign Affairs Council (FAC) has a permanent chairperson, the EU High Representative for Foreign Affairs and Security Policy. Countries in the euro area coordinate their economic policy through the Eurogroup, which is composed of their economics and finance ministers.

The Presidency of Council configurations other than GAC and FAC is held by groups of three Member States for a period of 18 months. The groups are made up on a basis of equal rotation among the Member States, which each hold the Council Presidency for a six-month period.

The Council of Europe

This is a post-World War II intergovernmental consultative organisation, founded by the *Treaty of London* (signed on 5 May 1949). It comprises 47 Member States and its main achievement is the *European Convention on Human Rights* (which was signed on 4 November 1950 and came into force on 3 September 1953). The (intergovernmental) Council of Europe is completely separate from the (Community-based) European Union, although the two organisations use the same European flag (twelve gold stars on a blue background) and the same anthem (based on the 'Ode to Joy' from Beethoven's 9th Symphony). Ratification of the European Convention, or the intention to ratify it, is a pre-requisite for EU membership.

1
Introduction

Twenty years already! Twenty years since the euro opened a new chapter in contemporary history and in the daily lives of hundreds of millions of people. With the irrevocable fixing of parities between the currencies of the participating countries, which took place overnight on 31 December 1998 with an official ceremony in Luxembourg, Europe embarked on the third stage of Economic and Monetary Union (EMU), resulting in the creation of the single currency. The euro was used as a 'book currency' from 1999 onwards by the financial markets, before the introduction of banknotes and coins on 1 January 2002 in the twelve euro area Member States. This led to new opportunities in terms of growth, employment, prosperity, and competitiveness for Europe, within a globalised environment.

While the euro initially seemed to deliver on its promises—reassuring the people of Europe that they had made the right choice in both political and economic terms—the spark lit by the US subprime crisis in 2008, which soon spread across the world with an inexorable domino effect, triggered the European debt crisis, making the euro area a key target for the financial markets and jeopardising the very existence of monetary union. Even beyond the impact of the global recession, the

E. Danescu, *Pierre Werner and Europe*,
Archival Insights into the Evolution of Economics,
https://doi.org/10.1007/978-3-319-96295-5_1

euro suffered from its intrinsic weaknesses, its incomplete design in the context of an asymmetrical EMU and shortcomings in its governance.

Europe is currently in a phase of post-crisis convalescence and is facing a number of uncertainties: the implementation of Brexit, the management of the refugee crisis, the breakdown of solidarity among the Member States and the growth of populism and nationalism are giving rise to fragmentation and division, which in turn are fostering Euroscepticism and even Europhobia. It is a time for introspection, for self-examination. But it is also a time to look back at the lessons that can be drawn from an analysis of the past, to explore what can be learned from the lessons of history about the strengths and weaknesses of EMU and heed the concerns raised by the architects of this process, who for the past 70 years have been involved in a unique intellectual effort of reflection, political action, and European engagement with the aim of bringing it to reality.

There are some public figures who leave a lasting legacy on the lives of their contemporaries and remain firmly etched in the collective memory. Pierre Werner (29 December 1913–24 June 2002) was one such figure.

As Prime Minister and Finance Minister of Luxembourg for many decades, this prominent Christian Democratic intellectual and committed federalist was a true statesman whose life spanned the twentieth century. Driven by a deep humanism firmly rooted in tradition and by a forward-thinking attitude, he worked with courage and tenacity to set his country on a path that embraced democracy, freedom, solidarity, and dialogue, laying the foundations for a promising future that would be realised in a spirit of unity.

Many of the bold initiatives he pioneered—including promoting Luxembourg to the status of an international financial centre, developing the audiovisual industry via the satellite project, paving the way for an economic and monetary union in Europe and fostering a climate of social dialogue and consensus—resulted in economic and cultural growth and were subsequently taken up by his successors. Pierre Werner worked tirelessly to bring his ideas to fruition, becoming a mentor and a source of inspiration for future generations.

1.1 A Man Committed to the European Ideal

Pierre Werner was one of the rare politicians to be associated with all the major milestones in the building of a united Europe, from the 1950 Schuman Plan to the Fontainebleau European Council in 1984.

He placed the European integration process at the centre of Luxembourg domestic policy, convinced of the need to preserve national identity and sovereignty by adopting an international outlook. Determined to set the country on a forward-looking path, he pursued a pragmatic yet ambitious approach to economic diversification, focusing in particular on consolidating the international financial centre from the 1960s onwards, nurturing the idea for a national shipping flag, developing the audiovisual sector and launching the innovative satellite project.

Before rising to the highest ranks of EEC policy-making, Pierre Werner played a major role in regional integration, especially in the Belgium–Luxembourg Economic Union (BLEU) and Benelux, and was a staunch advocate of small-state diplomacy. Werner was unanimously recognised for his skill in forging political consensus: between larger powers, above all Germany and France (as illustrated by the Luxembourg Compromise in 1966), between diametrically opposed positions—including among political authorities, where his approach ultimately led to the Luxembourg model of social consultation—and between contrasting doctrinal views (as epitomised by the 'economists' vs 'monetarists' debate on European monetary integration, a chasm successfully bridged by the Werner Report in 1970). In this way he effectively defended Luxembourg's vital long-term interests, from the steel industry to the seats of the European institutions and the development of the financial centre.

Werner's talent for mediation went hand in hand with a thorough understanding of key issues and an unswerving, fervent commitment. From his early years, he developed a keen interest in economic and monetary questions. Inspired by the unique situation of Luxembourg—a country which did not have its own central bank or currency and had therefore always favoured currency unions—Werner developed his own ideas and way of thinking by drawing on academic and scholarly expertise in Europe and the United States. He became a key figure in the major intellectual debates of his time and in influential networks set up to establish transnational guidelines and consensus on monetary and financial matters, together with other instigators of monetary innovation, especially Jean Monnet's Action Committee for the United States of Europe (ACUSE).

Above all, Werner's name is associated with the *Report on the realisation by stages of economic and monetary union in the community*. From the early 1950s onwards, he called for the establishment of a European monetary system based on a unit of account (for both official and private usage) and a clearing house for central banks. He made monetary policy a pivotal part of his government's action, and the burgeoning Luxembourg financial centre, which experienced major growth in the early 1960s, served as a vanguard for a European currency unit. In 1968, this balanced monetarist began to advocate the 'effective parallelism' principle between economic integration and monetary unification. For Werner, economic union and monetary union had to work in tandem, with political union as the ultimate aim and with the social dimension as an intrinsic element. The careful balance he imagined reappeared in the Werner Report of 1970, which was offered as a blueprint for EMU in the EU.

'Pierre Werner had a vision of Europe as a structured ensemble. That vision was unquestionably inspired by his experience in *Pax Romana*, the international movement for Catholic intellectuals, during his youth. He saw the great wealth of human potential in that organisation and no doubt wondered how one might create structures which would allow all that promise to be released. [...] For him, the main problem of Europe was to channel the strengths of diversity into effective structures that would provide a basis for action. He liked to say that while minorities have rights, they also have duties, namely accepting and making a positive contribution to viable structures at national and European level. [...] He also wanted a social Europe. This approach, grounded in his Christian convictions, was inspired by his wife, Henriette, who was a pillar for him throughout all his challenges. My parents shared an appreciation for people that were straightforward, and I remember long periods during which Pierre Werner listened to the grievances of those who came to speak to him, even during his leisure time, when he was visiting a museum, for example.'[1]

All the accounts of those who came into contact with Werner describe a man of great simplicity and humility, who drew on his faith in humankind to find the inspiration and motivation for his involvement in politics, which he saw as serving the common good. Nurtured by his artistic sensibilities (he was a gifted pianist with a passion for literature), his spirituality served as a solid basis for his inner convictions and freedom of thought. A desire for social justice and for a unity that recognised the importance of diversity, as well as the refusal of any culture of dogmatism, would shape his thoughts and actions.

Werner was discreet and unassuming, virtually never writing about his deep-seated beliefs and only briefly touching on them in his memoirs, *Itinéraires luxembourgeois et européens. Évolutions et souvenirs: 1945–1985*, published in the latter years of his life. In his many political, doctrinal, and socio-economic writings, his reserved nature and altruism meant that he was very sparing and restrained when it came to revealing details about himself; he preferred to shine a light on others. His contemporaries therefore found themselves in a somewhat paradoxical situation: here was a man whose work had such a profound impact but about whom very little was actually known. Some of his achievements, including the Werner Report, seem to have been shaped by a deep alchemy as well as by the upheavals of the era.

This is the challenge that the book attempts to tackle, namely to reveal more about Pierre Werner's personal and intellectual achievements and to shed new light on the development of his vision of Europe—based on a thorough exploration of his private papers, opened for the first time for research purposes, on many other previously unpublished sources, and on a series of original interviews with key figures and family members. Drawing on this rich collection of material, my aim is to offer a 'rereading' of the Werner Report, a new perspective on this document that represents a milestone in the history of European integration.

1.2 A Man as Seen Through His Archives

I never thought that I would have the chance to meet Pierre Werner one day. But I was indeed privileged to meet him in the early 1990s, just as I was embarking on my Ph.D. At the time, the focus of my research as an economist and historian was the transition to democracy and to a market economy after the fall of the Berlin Wall, looking ahead to the future of the Eastern European countries within a united Europe. I soon realised the importance of developing a thorough understanding of the various successful post-war European ventures, in which Luxembourg played a key role, and also gathering accounts from figures who shaped the future of their countries at this time.

Pierre Werner agreed to grant me several interviews, speaking to me at length alongside his daughter Marie-Anne Werner. I was of course already familiar with the Werner Report, having studied it at university, and my lecturers were full of praise for its subtleties, its succinctness, and the delicate balance between the position of 'economists' and 'monetarists'. But during these interviews I began to discover the man behind the report—a person full of charisma, steeped in wisdom, extremely courteous and unfailingly honest. He displayed a contagious yet controlled passion and he weighed each word carefully, while remaining constantly attentive to his interviewer. In his accounts, backed up with several documents from his personal archives, he spoke in detail about the origins of Economic and Monetary Union and its architects, describing how the idea for a single currency gradually took shape and began to become a reality. It was of course an economic venture, but Pierre Werner saw it as one with significant political implications and also a clear social dimension. He considered currency (a common currency to start with, then a single currency) to be the tangible expression of the shared destiny and conscience of the people of Europe—a Europe which should be more socially and economically balanced, more closely aligned to the values of democracy and solidarity. He also recognised the responsibility of the politicians involved in these new processes—both the transition to democracy and the development of the single currency—for whom strong ethical values and a sense of integrity were an intrinsic part of their mission to 'serve others'. They had to be capable of listening to and understanding citizens, of bringing them together by means of dialogue, discussions, and exchanges, around a shared project and a common future.

Pierre Werner gave me precious advice on how to analyse and interpret socio-political phenomena from a long-term perspective; his guidance shaped my intellectual reasoning, and I have continued to apply his approach ever since. I subsequently decided to shift the focus of my thesis—and the majority of my research since—to the Luxembourg development model and the achievements of Pierre Werner. And it so happened that I defended my thesis the very day that Pierre Werner celebrated his 85th birthday, which gave me an unexpected but perfect opportunity to pay him a special tribute.[2]

From 1996 to 1998 I remained in contact with Pierre Werner. While writing my thesis, with his gracious consent, I was able to translate his *Itinéraires* into Romanian (my translation is the first and currently the only foreign translation of his memoirs). Pierre Werner himself selected the texts (which focused on Luxembourg's European and international policy), wrote the preface and attended, together with Marie-Anne Werner and Erna Hennicot-Schoepges (a famous musician, at that time Minister of Culture), the official launch of the book on 18 May 1998 in Bucharest.[3] Since by that time the country had applied for accession to the European Union, the Romanian publisher kindly agreed to donate copies of the book to the main public libraries so that as many people as possible, especially the younger generation, could familiarise themselves with the milestones in European history via the direct account of one of the EU's main architects. After being republished in 2004, a third Romanian edition of the *Itinéraires* (reviewed and extended) is now available.

A few years later, I was given the opportunity to delve deeply into the private archives of the eminent Luxembourg statesman when the Werner family agreed to open them for the first time for research purposes and gave me exclusive access to the collection. The focus of this archival research was the interdisciplinary 'Pierre Werner and Europe' research project, which I developed, together with a number of colleagues, from 2011 onwards, initially at the Centre Virtuel de la Connaissance sur l'Europe (CVCE) and then at the University of Luxembourg.[4] I discovered that Pierre Werner's private archives—which after his death were carefully organised, classified, and inventoried by his son Henri Werner—contain thousands of documents carefully gathered from the 1950s onwards, including manuscripts, handwritten notes and comments on official documents, exchanges of letters with various figures, diplomatic correspondence, institutional texts, graphs, diagrams, and statistics, as well as a large number of press articles from all over the world on the European integration process and on economic and monetary questions. This material is accompanied by reports, speeches, and public statements on a range of subjects made by Pierre Werner or published during his career. It also includes an extensive collection of photographs and a series of audio and video recordings.

Of course, like all personal archives, this collection has inevitably been shaped by any prior selection and processing that Pierre Werner himself or others may have performed. But this is largely compensated by the three major strengths of the archives: their originality, their diversity, their consistency, their remarkably exhaustive nature, and the lengthy historical period they address, since they cover virtually the entire life of Pierre Werner—in other words almost the whole of the twentieth century.

The structure and thematic variety of these private papers, which include numerous handwritten documents (notes, draft speeches, sketches for articles and commentaries, letters, background papers and scribbled ideas or thoughts), reveal Werner's intellectual world, giving us a glimpse of the reflection process that took place in his mental 'workshop' as he looked ahead and prepared his political action. Werner's writings are characterised by their relevance, their carefully constructed arguments, their concise style and textual fluidity, all of which go a long way to explaining his persuasive capabilities. His texts were meticulously prepared, drafted, and refined over several successive versions, with an eye to detail and a great deal of attention paid to the clarity of the message. When it came to the spoken word, contrary to appearances, Werner's oral style was therefore in no way improvised or 'off the cuff', since his words were inevitably based on a thoughtfully prepared written text.

The rich nature of these archives, when compared and contrasted with other sources and with the scientific and historiographical literature, enables us to place this thinker, politician and European in the context of his time and of the institutional, human, and technical framework within which he worked. We can even follow the way in which his public image developed and was portrayed over time in the media, while piecing together his biographical background.

1.3 A Man and His Report: A Brief Overview of the Narrative

Werner's private archives yielded a host of original documents that shed new light on various aspects of European integration history and also on the role of Luxembourg and its elites in forging European policy. My selection—as you will have grasped by now—focuses on the Werner Report, which after 1970 served as the benchmark for all discussions on EMU and ensured that Werner's name will forever be associated with the single European currency.

My ambition was not to conduct a critical analysis, in the strict sense of the term, of the Werner Report itself, whether from a theoretical, methodological or conceptual viewpoint. For nearly 50 years now, the report has captured the interest of experts from all fields—economists, political scientists, legal practitioners, sociologists, and historians—and has been the focus of a wealth of specialised literature, which is largely cited and referenced in this book. The aim instead is to offer a new narrative of the underlying events and ideas, the relationships between the main players involved (individuals, institutions, and Member States) and the mindset in which the Werner Report was developed, as revealed by new and previously unpublished primary sources, considered by means of a bottom-up, interdisciplinary approach. This choice is justified by the absence of sufficient archives describing the debates within the Werner Committee, identifying the balances of power between its members (including areas of agreement and points of contention) and explaining how the plan by stages was drafted, how the crucial political compromise was progressively secured and how the Werner Report was received in the Member States.

This approach has inevitably led us to focus on the pivotal year of 1970, but for reasons of historical context, the analysis provides an overview of events over a longer period which stretches from the immediate post-war years to the present day.

The book is structured around several themes, which it explores in detail. It starts by looking at Pierre Werner's personality, career and achievements, outlining the theoretical and political background of his vision, his various spheres of action, the mentors, peers, and networks with which he had intellectual discussions and the delicate balance that he managed to strike between his European vocation and his commitment to his native Luxembourg (Chapter 2).

It then turns to the alchemy of the 1970 Werner Report, examining the historical background of the ideas and challenges involved in a Europe built through currency. It offers a comparative analysis of a wide variety of concepts and players—organisations, institutions, Member States, individuals, and civil society—in order to determine the role of the Werner Report in major monetary debates and in the history of European integration (Chapter 3). The formation of the committee of experts after the Hague Summit (1–2 December 1970) and the appointment of Pierre Werner as chairman, the committee's intensive work and the many hurdles and tensions it faced—about which little was previously known—are explored, and the exchanges of ideas, clashes between different doctrines and political views, the balance of power between the Member States and Community institutions and the role played by different figures and networks are all highlighted. The Werner Report produced by the committee of experts is placed in context alongside the subsequent proposals from the Commission, which were inspired by the report without openly acknowledging this influence (Chapter 4).

The method, principles, and concepts of the Werner Report are then analysed, with an examination of how they emerged and developed from the interim report to the final report. In this context, new light is shed on the clashes between 'economists' and 'monetarists' that characterised the work on the plan by stages, and also on the input of the Committee of Governors of the Central Banks in favour of a symmetrical EMU and a politically independent central bank (Chapter 5). The reception of the Werner Report by the Community institutions (Parliament, the Commission, and the Council of Ministers) and the repercussions and impact of the plan in the Member States (Germany, France, the Netherlands, Belgium, and Italy) and in various economic, social, and civil circles, as well as its portrayal in the media, are then discussed, alongside its influence on the negotiations for British accession (Chapter 6).

The volume also looks at how the implementation of the Werner Report was shaped by economic and monetary difficulties in Europe and across the world, and how this led—after the problems experienced by the currency snake and the establishment of the EMCF—to its de facto suspension in 1974 (Chapter 7). Taking the Werner Report and the Delors Report as points of reference, this section focuses on the path travelled by EMU from its early form in the 1970s to its enshrinement in the 1992 Maastricht Treaty. Although the Werner Plan was ultimately put on hold, it proved to be a source of inspiration for European monetary integration. The relationship between the Werner Report and the European Monetary System (EMS) introduced in 1979 is examined, with a particular focus on the impact on future monetary cooperation. A comparative analysis of the Werner and Delors Reports is made so as to identify areas of convergence and continuity in the definition of EMU and pinpoint the reasons why one report was shelved while the other was successfully implemented (Chapter 8).

Finally, the book highlights Pierre Werner's work in favour of EMU in the context of his European achievements as a whole, by highlighting his contribution to the method and substance of the plan by stages and his role in securing a political consensus. Emphasis is particularly placed on his commitment to the underlying principles of the report: 'parallel movement in the economic and monetary fields', the democratic strength of EMU and the social dimension (Chapter 9).

Drawing on the thorough exploration of Pierre Werner's previously unpublished personal archives, the original interviews[5] and the extensive research in many other archives (public and private, Luxembourg and European),[6] and with the aim of offering specific academic added value and providing new resources for the research community, at the end of the book readers will find an album of previously unpublished photos and selected documents; a comprehensive bibliography about the Werner Report and EMU, including, for each chapter, an exhaustive list of works by Pierre Werner; a chronology illustrating Pierre Werner's role in the creation of a monetary Europe; and an index of key figures with short biographies. Some terminological clarifications about the European institutions have also been provided, as well as an overview of Luxembourg.

When writing a book, the author makes a number of personal choices and has to take responsibility for any associated pitfalls. This book is no different. The first stumbling block I ran into was that of the overall approach. Standing at a crossroads and faced with many alternative routes, my personal choice was for a study that would take the form of a triptych, with a chronological background and thematic context supporting a central focus on Pierre Werner's thought and achievements. I therefore set out to explore what really took place in this vital period for European integration and, based on a vast collection of previously unpublished documents, to offer readers a narrative that covers the origins of Pierre Werner's work, his intellectual development, his public and personal life, and his encounters with key figures, with the concomitant aim of revealing the complex historical evolution of a country—Luxembourg—and of an entire era. I ultimately ended up with an 'event-based biography' of Pierre Werner, which is not intended to serve as a dry description of his life but rather to follow the journey of a man through his work and key actions.[7] The book therefore falls into a niche that has developed in recent years; it is one of a number of non-conventional volumes that reflect the history of EMU through the lens of the biographies of its architects.[8]

Piecing together a life story is a major challenge, first and foremost because of the need to identify and select sources—and this was the second hurdle that had to be navigated. Carrying out one's own enquiry to pinpoint documents based on various analytical criteria, finding the right balance between archives from different sources (private and public, institutional and non-institutional, from Luxembourg and abroad) and of different types (written documents, images, photos, audio and video archives, etc.), correctly evaluating their relevance and making the 'right' choices will always inevitably reflect the author's subjective approach. This is compounded by a number of external factors (the geographical distance of some archives, access difficulties, the lack of archival catalogues, etc.), which even the exchange of ideas and information and the adoption of a heuristic approach involving several research networks can only partly overcome. This inevitably leads to an unbalanced, limited and incomplete coverage of subjects, which will always result in dissatisfaction and debate. At any event, my choice of sources does not deliberately favour any particular legal, economic or historiographical doctrine or school of thought and is intended to represent as broad a range of views as possible.

The third potential pitfall relates to historical criticism. The biographical portrait of Pierre Werner offered by this book is open to question. Determined to maintain a suitable distance from the focus of my research, I tackled the task with an objective, critical approach honed from my experience of the historical discipline, underpinned by the code of ethics that all researchers impose on themselves and the rigour of a serious analytical study—but also, unavoidably, by my own subjectivity, since historians are, by definition, subjective individuals. My personal view necessarily influenced the way in which I examined events, the questions I asked, the supporting arguments I drew on, the nuances I perceived and my interpretative understanding. So I would invite readers, based on the numerous archives and original sources presented here, to make their own judgment of the key issues that characterised this era, of the forward-looking vision and challenges that drove the plan for an economic and monetary union for Europe; in short, of the version of Pierre Werner's 'personal equation'[9] that this book proposes.

Notes

1. See 'Témoignage d'Henri Werner, Fils de Pierre Werner' (2014), in E. Danescu (ed.), *Pierre Werner, témoignages d'une vocation européenne. Actes de la table ronde des grands témoins (Luxembourg, 23 novembre 2013)* (Luxembourg: CVCE), pp. 42–43.
2. E. Danescu, *Le retour progressif et l'élargissement à l'économie de marché dans l'oeuvre de Pierre Werner. Le modèle luxembourgeois de développement* (The increasing emphasis on a market economy in the work of Pierre Werner. The Luxembourg development model) Ph.D. thesis in political economics, supervised by Prof. Tudorel Postolache (a member of the Romanian Academy), Bucharest, National Institute for Economic Research of the Romanian Academy, defended 29 December 1998.

3. P. Werner (1991) *Itinéraires luxembourgeois et européens. Évolutions et souvenirs: 1945–1985* (Luxembourg: Saint-Paul). Translation from French to Romanian and addenda by E. Danescu (1998) *Itinerarii luxemburgheze si europene. Evolutii si amintiri 1945–1985*. International Academy for Research into the History of Culture and Religions: Editions Gnosis, 398 pages.
4. E. Danescu (2011–2016) *Pierre Werner and Europe*. Research project. Luxembourg: Centre Virtuel de la Connaissance sur l'Europe (CVCE) and University of Luxembourg. https://www.cvce.eu/project/werner/ (home page), accessed on 6 March 2018.
5. A series of historical interviews conducted with members of Pierre Werner's family and key figures from Luxembourg and the international community (more than 55 hours of footage in total) complement the extensive research carried out in these and other archives, offering added value and new resources for the research community. The figures that have been interviewed thus far are as follows (in alphabetical order): Michel Camdessus, Honorary Governor of the Banque de France, Managing Director of the IMF (1987–2000); Luc Frieden, Luxembourg Finance Minister (2009–2013); Albert Hansen, Secretary-General of the Luxembourg Government (1979–1998); Edmond Israel (1924–2011), Luxembourg banker, President of the Board of Directors of Cedel International (1970–1999); Jean-Claude Juncker, President of the European Commission since 2014, Prime Minister of Luxembourg (1995–2013), first permanent President of the Eurogroup (2005–2013); Helmut Kohl (1930–2017), Chancellor of the FRG (1982–1998); Philippe Maystadt (1948–2017), Belgian Finance Minister (1988–1998), President of the European Investment Bank (2000–2011); Yves Mersch, Member of the Executive Board of the European Central Bank (since 2012), President of the Banque centrale du Luxembourg (1998–2012); Guy de Muyser, Marshal of the Grand Ducal Court (1971–1981); Charles-Ferdinand Nothomb, President of the Belgian Chamber of Representatives (1979–1980, 1988–1995), Honorary President of the Pierre Werner European Circle; Viviane Reding, Member of the European Commission (1999–2010), Vice-President of the European Commission with responsibility for Justice, Fundamental Rights and Citizenship (2010–2014), Member of the European Parliament (since 2014); Lex Roth, Director of the Information and Press Service of the Luxembourg Government (1988–1993); Charles Ruppert, Chairman of the Luxembourg Bankers' Association (1992–1995), Chairman of the Pierre Werner Foundation; Fabrizio Saccomanni, Vice President of the European Bank for Reconstruction and Development (EBRD) (2003–2006), Italian

Minister for Economic Affairs and Finance (2013–2014); Jacques Santer, Prime Minister of Luxembourg (1984–1995), President of the European Commission (1995–1999); Bernard Snoy et d'Oppuers, International President of the European League for Economic Cooperation, President of Robert Triffin International; Gaston Thorn (1928–2007), Prime Minister of Luxembourg (1974–1979), President of the European Commission (1981–1985); Hans Tietmeyer (1930–2017), President of the Deutsche Bundesbank (1993–1999), Member of the Werner Committee (1970); Niels Thygesen, Member of the Delors Committee (1988–1989), Chairman of the European Fiscal Board (since 2016), Professor at the Institute for New Economic Thinking; Sir Brian Unwin, President of the European Investment Bank (1993–1999), Governor of the European Bank for Reconstruction and Development (1993–1999), Chairman of the Supervisory Board of the European Investment Fund (1994–1999); Henri Werner, son of Pierre Werner; Marie-Anne Werner, daughter of Pierre Werner. Other accounts concerning the personality and European achievements of Pierre Werner emerged during interviews conducted by several of my colleagues for the CVCE's project 'Accounts by Luxembourg Ambassadors' (Jean-Jacques Kasel, Adrien Meisch, Jean Mischo) as well as interviews with Étienne Davignon, Member of the European Commission (1977–1981) and Vice-President of the European Commission (1981–1985); Jacques de Larosière, Assistant Director (1967–1974) then Director of the French Treasury (1974–1978), Managing Director of the IMF (1978–1987); Jacques Delors, President of the European Commission (1985–1995); Mark Eyskens, Belgian Finance Minister (1980–1981) and Prime Minister (1981); Wilfried Martens, Prime Minister of Belgium (1979–1981/1981–1992). All these interviews, their transcriptions and translations into English, French, and German are published in E. Danescu, *The Werner Report of 8 October 1970 in the Light of the Pierre Werner Family Archives* (research corpus). https://www.cvce.eu/project/werner/ (home page), accessed on 6 March 2018.

6. The Luxembourg-based sources include the Luxembourg National Archives (those of the Ministry of State and the Ministry of Finance), the diplomatic archives (Ministry of Foreign Affairs), the archives of the Banque Centrale du Luxembourg (particularly those of the Luxembourg Monetary Institute), archive material from the Government's Information and Press Service, the documentary collection of the National Library of Luxembourg, documents from the Luxembourg City Photo Library, archives from the Société Européenne des Satellites (SES) and the Compagnie Luxembourgeoise de Télédiffusion (CLT),

and a range of press and audiovisual archives. Documents from the Ernest Michels private collection were also consulted.

With regard to the European sources used, we should mention the documentary collections of the European institutions such as the Historical Archives of the European Union (Florence); the Historical Archives of the European Commission (Brussels) (including the archives of the Monetary Committee, the Committee of Governors of the Central Banks, the Conjunctural Policy Committee, the Medium-Term Economic Policy Committee, and the Budgetary Policy Committee); the Historical Archives of the Council of the European Union (Brussels); the Historical Archives of the European Parliament (Luxembourg); the archives of the European Central Bank (ECB); the archives of the Bank for International Settlements (BIS); and the archives of the European Commission Audiovisual Library. The archives of the Jean Monnet Foundation for Europe (Lausanne), the private archives of Tommaso Padoa-Schioppa (currently in the process of being inventoried at the Historical Archives of the European Union) and the Robert Triffin Archives (Université catholique de Louvain) were also explored.

Diplomatic documents from the archives of the Belgian Foreign Ministry, the Netherlands Foreign Ministry, the French Ministry of Foreign and European Affairs (La Courneuve), the German Federal Archives (Koblenz), the Italian Historical Diplomatic Archives (Rome), and various BLEU and Benelux documentary collections were also consulted. The archives of the central banks of the six Member States that made up the European Community in 1970, along with various other public and private archives, have not yet been explored.

7. For a critical summary of this approach, see P. Bourdieu (1986) 'L'illustration biographique', in *Actes de la recherche en sciences sociales* (62–63), pp. 69–72; and S. Loriga (1996), 'La biographie comme problème', in J. Revel (ed.), *Jeux d'échelle. La micro-analyse à l'expérience* (Paris: Seuil-Gallimard), pp. 209–231.
8. See K. Dyson, I. Maes (eds.) 'Intellectuals as Policy-Makers. The Value of Biography in the History of European Monetary Union', in *Architects of the Euro: Intellectuals in the Making of European Monetary Union* (London: Oxford University Press), pp. 1–29.
9. Concept used by François Perroux in reference to Joseph Schumpeter, meaning all the factors that come together to define his personality, in *La pensée économique de Joseph Schumpeter* (Paris–Geneva: Librairie Droz), 1965, p. 15.

Elena Danescu is a Research Scientist in the Contemporary History of Europe Department at the Luxembourg Centre for Contemporary and Digital History (C²DH), University of Luxembourg. She holds a Ph.D. in Political Economics (1998) from the National Institute of Economic Research of the Romanian Academy, with a thesis on the Luxembourg development model and the achievements of Pierre Werner. She previously completed a DEA post-graduate diploma in international, diplomatic and strategic relations at Paris III University and a Master's degree in Economics. She began her career as a researcher and guest lecturer before becoming involved in cultural diplomacy and international cooperation. She has played an active role in several international projects and networks, initially focusing on the European integration and transition to democracy of Central and Eastern European countries and then turning to the part played by Luxembourg and its elites in the European integration process, in Economic and Monetary Union and in EU governance. Before joining the C²DH she was a researcher at the Centre Virtuel de la Connaissance sur l'Europe, where she developed the interdisciplinary 'Pierre Werner and Europe' research project (2011–2017) based on an exploration of the Werner family archives, opened for the first time for research purposes. She is an active member of several professional associations, including the University Association for Contemporary European Studies (UACES), the European Union Studies Association-USA (EUSA), the European Society for History of Economic Thought (ESHET), the Italian Association for the History of Economic Thought (AISPE), Robert Triffin International and the Pierre Werner European Circle. Elena Danescu translated and published the memoirs of Pierre Werner in Romanian (first edition in 1998, second edition in 2004 and third edition in 2010). She has authored various academic publications in her specialist areas.

2

Itinéraires luxembourgeois et européens: Pierre Werner's Biographical Highlights

Pierre Werner was born of Luxembourgish parents in Saint-André, near Lille, France, on 29 December 1913. A few months later, following the start of the First World War, the family returned to Luxembourg.[1]

After primary school, he attended a secondary school that prepared him for a career in industry and business so that he would be able to take over the family business from his father. Pupils at this school received intensive English lessons, which was unusual at that time. Werner continued his education in a multicultural environment that was typical for Luxembourg, and in addition to the country's three languages (Luxembourgish, French and German), he also learnt Italian. His extensive language skills opened up new intellectual horizons, enabled him to structure his thoughts clearly and gave him a good understanding of the language and culture of those he came into contact with. Encouraged by his teachers, who were keen to see this gifted pupil devote more time to the humanities side of his studies, he then spent a year studying Latin and obtained his baccalaureate at the prestigious *Athénée* in Luxembourg City, the same Lycée classique that Robert Schuman had attended in the late nineteenth century. In 1934, he enrolled in the higher preparatory course in law in Luxembourg. One year later, he joined the Faculty of

E. Danescu, *Pierre Werner and Europe*,
Archival Insights into the Evolution of Economics,
https://doi.org/10.1007/978-3-319-96295-5_2

Law in Paris, at the same time attending courses at the École libre des sciences politiques (1935–1937). In January 1938, Werner successfully submitted his thesis in law in Luxembourg.

From early on, Pierre Werner was an active member of student associations, taking on major responsibilities. In Luxembourg, he was elected as president of the Association of Catholic University Students ('Akademikerverein') from 1935 to 1937, and in 1937 he became the Vice-president of the international 'Pax Romana' movement. During his time in Paris, Werner lived at the Biermans-Lapôtre Foundation, where he was involved in the activities of the 'Cercle historique' (History Club) run by fellow Luxembourgers Joseph Guill and Georges Bourg with the aim of encouraging students from Luxembourg to learn about the history of their country. It was here that Werner joined the European ranks of Catholic thinkers and forged useful links with several prominent figures. He regularly attended lectures by Jacques Maritain and became very familiar with the ideas of this mentor of the Christian Democracy movement. His humanist beliefs also spurred him to offer practical help to those in need, and he joined the 'Équipes sociales' run by Robert Garric.

In his studies, Werner was particularly interested in company management and private finance. He forged strong ties with his teachers Jacques Rueff and Wilfrid Baumgartner (both future French Finance Ministers), Charles Rist and André Siegfried, all of whom influenced his intellectual development and sparked his interest in the study of economic and monetary phenomena. In Paris he met another Luxembourg native, Robert Schuman, who at that time was a member of the French National Assembly and who was to become an iconic figure in the launch of post-war European integration. Schuman showed him round the Palais Bourbon and tried to give him a taste for politics. Werner did not yet feel that he was ready, because

> if a young man wants to be more than just an average politician, he needs to be all the more conscientious and hard-working in preparing for his political career.[2]

As a young barrister in Luxembourg, in 1938 Pierre Werner secured a six-month internship at the Banque Générale de Luxembourg (BGL).

With the outbreak of the Second World War, he ended up staying there until 1944, receiving on-the-job training in the banking profession. His work in the general secretariat of the BGL gave him the opportunity to closely monitor developments in the legislation introduced by the German occupiers and the effects it had on Luxembourg society. Approached by the Martin network of the French Resistance, Werner managed to pass on a range of information to the Luxembourg government in exile in London, including a report on the monetary, financial and banking situation in the country in 1942.[3] As he revealed in his memoirs, he escaped Nazi persecution both because of Deutsche Bank's financial interests in the Luxembourg bank and also thanks to the efforts of Hermann J. Abs, a banker and Chairman of the Board of Directors, who ensured that Luxembourgers who refused to enrol in Nazi organisations would avoid the worst consequences of their actions.[4] The Werner family was not spared by the war, however: Pierre's younger brother, who was forcibly recruited in the *Wehrmacht*, died at a labour camp in Eastern Prussia on 15 January 1945.

After the Liberation, the Secretary-general of the government, Léon Schaus, recruited Werner as an attaché to the Ministry of Finance. Prime Minister and Finance Minister Pierre Dupong involved this young expert in the major issues of the time. In 1945, he was tasked with carrying out a study of the reorganisation of the banking system in Luxembourg. Subsequently he was appointed banking Commissioner. In this capacity he was involved in the creation of an authority to organise and regulate the credit market and contributed to the establishment of international financial relations. He was associated with the operations for the reintroduction of the franc, the refloating of banking activities, and the reestablishment of the main Luxembourg state bank, the Banque et Caisse d'Épargne de l'État. He represented Luxembourg in international negotiations, particularly in Switzerland and within the BLEU and the Benelux. As adviser to Prime Minister Pierre Dupong on financial affairs, Werner also took part in multilateral dealings relating to defence, including NATO, the abortive European Defence Community (EDC), and Western European Union (WEU). At a very early stage he became familiar with the International Monetary Fund (IMF).

In 1947, the government gave him the task of negotiating a $12.7 million loan from the International Bank for Reconstruction and Development (IBRD) to rebuild the country. Luxembourg was one of the first four applicants for aid, despite the fact that at this time, the IBRD (which had not yet established any real rules of operation) had intended these loans to go towards relieving balance-of-payments difficulties rather than internal budget expenses. Nevertheless, following three months of intense negotiations in Washington, Werner, with the support of Ambassador Hugues Le Gallais, successfully secured the loan.[5]

Werner had been aware of the importance of European issues since his university days, and his commitment to European unification gradually began to take firm shape. From 1949 he became convinced

> of the urgent need for the countries of Western Europe to undertake the economic and political construction of a united Europe. His experience of working in the international arena, particularly an awareness of the weakness and the divided state of Europe, made it almost an intellectual obligation.

He later took an active role alongside Jean Monnet in the Action Committee for the United States of Europe (ACUSE).[6]

In 1949, as government adviser and acting Secretary to the Council of Ministers, Werner was brought into direct contact with the country's general affairs and European integration strategy. He worked closely with the Prime Minister, who increasingly regarded this competent, meticulous expert as the best person to succeed him as Minister for Finance. This duly came about on 29 December 1953, the day of Werner's 40th birthday, when he was appointed Minister for Finance (and the Armed Forces) in the government formed by Joseph Bech following the unexpected death of Pierre Dupong.

This was the beginning of a long career as a statesman, in which public finance played a prominent role. In his first budget speech to the Chamber of Deputies, he outlined the principles underpinning his political approach, to which he would remain committed for his entire life: for Werner, safeguarding Luxembourg's financial stability and budget equilibrium, adding a human dimension to law enforcement and guaranteeing social justice were vital for the creation of solid foundations on which to build the country's independence.[7]

Werner headed the list of candidates for the Christian Social People's Party (CSV) in the parliamentary election on 1 February 1959 and was duly elected Minister of State (Prime Minister). For twenty years—from 1959 to 1974 and from 1979 to 1984—he led the coalition cabinets that his party formed with either the Liberals or the Socialists. His role as Prime Minister was also combined with other ministerial portfolios in what were seen as priority areas for a country that was constantly innovating and developing. He served as Minister for Finance (1959–1964 and 1969–1974), for the Treasury (1964–1969 and 1979–1984) and for Foreign affairs and Justice (1964–1967), as well as for the Civil Service (1967–1969) and for Cultural affairs (1969–1974 and 1979–1984).

Werner turned his attention to major projects with a view to making Luxembourg a forward-looking country and a true international platform. The development programme for the 'European quarter' on the Kirchberg (1961) was a major trump card in the country's hand during the 'battle for the seats' in 1965. He worked hard to diversify the economy, especially focusing on consolidating Luxembourg's transformation from a banking centre to an international financial centre from the 1960s onwards, nurturing the idea for a Luxembourg shipping flag, developing the audiovisual sector and, in particular, setting up the satellite project.

For Luxembourg, European political and economic integration took precedence over all other international concerns and Werner was associated from the very outset with the major issues. The merger of the executive bodies of the ECSC, Euratom and the EEC in 1965, the choice of Luxembourg as one of the permanent capitals of the Community institutions, the development of the Kirchberg European quarter, the 1966 Luxembourg Compromise and the 1970 Werner Report that sketched the outlines of EMU are just some of the achievements to which Werner made a vital contribution.[8] In the mid-1960s, in his efforts to affirm Luxembourg's position of leadership on the international stage, Werner played, alongside the eminent legal expert Pierre

Pescatore, Secretary-general of the Foreign Ministry, a part in developing an independent diplomatic service based on national intellectual elites, continuing the work begun by Joseph Bech at the dawn of the Second World War.[9]

As a proponent of dialogue and rapprochement, Werner was also involved in other issues—the strengthening of the institutions, political cooperation, enlargement, the reform of the common agricultural policy (CAP) and international relations—when Luxembourg held the rotating presidency of the Council of the EC.[10] When Europe experienced difficulties, this little country was able to make a decisive contribution to breaking deadlocks and proved to be an essential mediator, facilitating dialogue between its larger neighbours and partners. The 1966 'Luxembourg Compromise', which brought an end to the empty chair crisis, is a clear illustration of this role. He adopted an approach which he saw in theoretical terms as a method for any fruitful presidency:

> I regarded my presidency as an opportunity, primarily, for creating an atmosphere and a climate of negotiation which took account of the delicate sensitivities of partners aspiring to reach agreement. The agreement must not leave any losers in a squabble over minutiae of language which may disguise a persistent underlying disagreement.[11]

At that time, Werner's European commitment and mastery of the art of consensus gave rise to the idea that he might one day stand for the post of President of the Commission of the Communities. It was only a rumour, as the Luxembourg Prime Minister never really considered giving up his national elected office.[12]

The election on 26 May 1974 resulted in a new coalition formed by the Democratic Party (DP) and the Luxembourg Socialist Workers' Party (LSAP), under the premiership of Gaston Thorn. The CSV, which had led all the country's post-war governments, went into opposition. This political upheaval coincided with the beginnings of the painful steel crisis. Werner was elected as chairman of the CSV party's group in the Chamber of Deputies. He worked to rebuild his party and encouraged it to pursue an approach inspired

> to some extent by the British tradition of 'Her Majesty's loyal opposition' – respecting any ministerial management driven by concern for the welfare of all Luxembourgers, and proposing original solutions (using watertight legislative techniques) as alternatives to the options put forward by the government and the majority.[13]

As leader of the opposition, Werner focused on key issues for domestic policy. He pushed the CSV to play an active role in the consensus-based management of the steel crisis and worked for social dialogue. One of the results of this approach was the establishment of the 'steel tripartite', which subsequently developed into the 'Luxembourg model for social consultation'. The government also adopted two mechanisms—for economic diversification and for the creation of the Société nationale de crédit et d'investissement (National Credit and Investment Company, SNCI)—which Werner had recommended years before to boost the country's competitiveness.[14] At the same time, renowned for his expertise, Werner remained a reference for politicians of all stripes.[15] Finance Minister Raymond Vouel (Socialist) consulted him on budget issues such as the crisis budget and public spending, and Prime Minister and Foreign Minister Gaston Thorn (Liberal) discussed strategic issues and international policy questions with him.

Werner's longevity in power and his European commitment enabled him to forge lasting relationships with many eminent figures and to be involved in various transnational governance networks, communities of experts, and influential groups. He also took an active role, alongside Jean Monnet and Robert Triffin, in the Action Committee for the United States of Europe (ACUSE), the European League for Economic Cooperation (ELEC) and the Christian Democrat International, via conferences run by universities and banking organisations and in the media. His favourite subjects remained EMU and political union. Together with Jacques Santer, Werner also played a part in the establishment of the European People's Party (EPP), which was founded on 8 July 1976 in Luxembourg. He wrote the economic and social chapters of the EPP's electoral manifesto for the first European Parliament elections by direct universal suffrage in 1979.

The parliamentary election on 10 June 1979 saw Pierre Werner return to power as leader of a coalition government between the CSV and the Liberals. The new Minister of State received more individual votes than his predecessor, Gaston Thorn, who became Deputy Prime Minister and Foreign Minister and would soon become the first Luxembourger to serve as President of the European Commission (1981–1985). The CSV also won the European elections and secured three of the six seats allocated to Luxembourg.

From 1979 to 1984, the Werner government faced major challenges, including the resolution of the steel crisis with its major social consequences, economic diversification and societal reforms. Realising that as Prime Minister he would have to be closely involved in balancing conflicting interests, Werner gave up the time-consuming portfolio of Finance. He retained his role as Treasury Minister, however (responsible for monetary and credit policy), thereby continuing a tradition that held true until the most recent Government took office (December 2013): Luxembourg Prime Ministers always had monetary issues as part of their responsibilities. He also chose the portfolio of Cultural affairs. His main achievements in this field were the creation of a National Cultural Fund and the Language Law, which enshrined the three-language model as the basis of Luxembourg's national identity.[16] Jacques Santer, Werner's long-standing colleague and leader of the country's main political party, was appointed Minister for Finance. During the 1979–1984 term, several reshuffles took place, including the entry into government of Jean-Claude Juncker, then aged just 28, as Junior Minister for Employment.

Halfway through its term, the Werner government was faced with a serious and unexpected crisis. On 22 February 1982, the Belgian government took the unilateral decision to devalue its currency. This had a major impact on Luxembourg's fiscal policy, which was designed to combat inflation and promote full employment. Although the idea of withdrawing from the monetary union with Belgium was raised in some quarters, Luxembourg chose a more moderate course of action.

> Monetary decisions are always taken on the spot and depending on the economic, social and financial conditions of a national community at a given time. The main thing in a monetary union is that the interests of

> one of the partners should not be sacrificed. [...] Discussions on a monetary proposal are always tricky since they can give rise to positive or negative evaluations which, by implication, can have a negative impact on the very aim of a monetary policy, which is stability.[17]

In these circumstances, the Werner government successfully redefined the economic and monetary doctrine of the BLEU, and in May 1983 it adopted the Act establishing the Luxembourg Monetary Institute (IML), which had been on the agenda of the Chamber of Deputies for several years.[18] The IML operated until 1998, when Luxembourg opened a full central bank as a member of Economic and Monetary Union.

The Luxembourg government focused its diversification strategy on two innovative areas that would become the country's key drivers for growth: the financial centre and the audiovisual industry.[19] Werner had a thorough knowledge of the financial centre, which had gradually taken shape since the 1960s under the leadership of his successive governments. Ongoing improvements to its legislative and institutional infrastructure and a policy of specialisation (in insurance and reinsurance, consultancy firms and training) strengthened its international competitiveness. Over time, the financial centre became a real-world laboratory for the single currency, with the first Eurobond issue and the implementation of the public and private European unit of account. When the Werner Report was published in 1970, Pierre Werner set up an informal think tank for the financial centre, composed of well-known experts from Luxembourg and abroad (including Robert Triffin, Fernand Collin, Edmond Israel, Raymond Kirsch and Jean Blondeel), which anticipated future trends and sketched out various development scenarios.[20]

Bolstered by the success of the Compagnie Luxembourgeoise de Télédiffusion (CLT) since the 1950s, the Werner government decided to target what appeared to be a promising niche market: satellites and telecommunications. Given that the European audiovisual sector was only just beginning to gain momentum, this was a significant challenge, with considerable economic implications (the advertising market) and cultural implications (the broadcast language and the culture portrayed). To guarantee Luxembourg's long-term position in this sector, the

Werner government was of the view that 'only a Luxembourg-run satellite would be satisfactory'. This firm condition gave rise to a bitter political and diplomatic clash with France and Germany doing their utmost to block the plan. The excessive demands of some US technological and financial partners also created an obstacle to the implementation of the plan. Ultimately this initiative only came to fruition during Santer's first premiership in 1985, with the creation of the Société Européenne des Satellites (SES), which has now become the world's second leading satellite operator.

In July 1984, despite his party's victory in the parliamentary election and his own popularity with the electorate, Pierre Werner chose to withdraw from political life.

> Seeing politics as a sacred calling, Pierre Werner fully embodied a sense of personal and political integrity that was never questioned by anyone, including his fiercest opponents.[21]

He remained active in public affairs, particularly focusing his energies on the promotion of EMU and the euro, notably as joint chair, alongside Raymond Barre, of the Lyon-based ECU Institute, a think tank composed of international economic and financial experts that was set up in 1992 to promote the European currency. He also retained an active interest in the development of the media and the audiovisual sector, especially through the project for the SES, whose board he chaired from 1989 to 1996 and of which he subsequently became honorary president. In 1992, he published his memoirs, entitled 'Itinéraires luxembourgeois et européens'.

His wife Henriette Pescatore, together with their five children (Marie-Anne, Jean, Charles, Henri, and Elisabeth), provided invaluable support for Pierre Werner throughout his lengthy career. With discretion and efficiency, she was closely involved throughout her life in a number of causes that were particularly important to her, including the provision of schooling for the children of Luxembourg's fairground workers and, alongside the famous banker Edmond Israel, encouraging multicultural, ecumenical and inter-religious dialogue between Jews and Christians.[22]

In recognition of Werner's lifelong commitment to a united Europe, he received the Robert Schuman Gold Medal in 1971 and the Prince of Asturias Award in 1998, sharing the latter award with his disciple Jacques Santer for their 'contribution to the process of European monetary integration that has culminated in the creation of the euro'.

Pierre Werner passed away in Luxembourg City on 24 June 2002.

The former EU Commission President Jacques Santer—a long time collaborator of Pierre Werner and his successor as Prime Minister of Luxembourg in 1984—said of him:

> It is rare to find politicians that can rightly claim to have left a decisive mark on the country they were called to serve and therefore successfully steered the course of events.[23]

Notes

1. *Itinéraires luxembourgeois et européens. Évolutions et souvenirs: 1945–1985* is the title of the memoirs published by Pierre Werner in 1992 with Éditions Saint-Paul de Luxembourg [roughly translated in English as 'Routes through Luxembourg and Europe. Developments and memories: 1945–1985'].
2. P. Werner (1934) 'AV et la politique', in *Association catholique des étudiants luxembourgeois* [Catholic Association of Luxembourg Students] (ed.) *Revue Academia* (national issue), p. 25.
3. 'Rapport sur la situation monétaire, financière et bancaire luxembourgeoise de 1942' drawn up by Pierre Werner in 1943 and sent to the government in exile in London through the Martin network. Centre for Documentation and Research into the Resistance, Luxembourg. Subsequently published in *Rappel—Organe de la Ligue luxembourgeoise des prisonniers et déportés politiques, Luxembourg*, 1 (1994).
4. 'Thanks to my job at the Banque Générale, in which the Deutsche Bank had taken a major holding, I was able to escape Nazi persecution. Mr. Weicker and I refused to join the "Heim ins Reich" movement despite the insistent urgings of a director who had been seconded by the German bank' [our translation]. P. Werner (1992, I) *Itinéraires*, pp. 15–16.

5. Telegram from Pierre Werner to Pierre Dupong (New York, 22 July 1947). Archives Nationales de Luxembourg (ANLux)/AE-09283.
6. The Action Committee for the United States of Europe (ACUSE) (also known as the Monnet Committee), founded on 13 October 1955 by Jean Monnet, assembled trade union and political forces in the six Community countries (representing over 10 million unionised workers). The committee held its first session in Paris on 18 January 1956. Its overriding objective was to help bring the treaties for the Common Market and Euratom to a successful conclusion. The treaties signed in Rome on 25 March 1957 were voted by the six parliaments in the same year.
7. P. Werner (1954) 'Le discours budgétaire de 1954 prononcé le 11 février 1954', in *Les discours budgétaires de 1954 à 1963. Recueil publié à l'occasion du dixième anniversaire de la nomination de M. Pierre Werner aux fonctions de Ministre des Finances.* 29 December 1953–29 December 1963 (Luxembourg: Ministry of Finance), p. 6.
8. On these matters see especially: N. P. Ludlow (2001) 'The Eclipse of the Extremes: Demythologising the Luxembourg Compromise', in W. Loth (ed.), *Crises and Compromises: The European Project 1963–9* (Baden-Baden: Nomos), pp. 260–264; C. Barthel (2017) 'Trois chefs de la diplomatie, un défi commun. Joseph Bech, Eugène Schaus et Pierre Werner face à la question du siège européen à Luxembourg (1952–1965/67)' *Nos cahiers* (3/4), pp. 29–151; J.-M. Majerus (2011) 'Pierre Werner & Gaston Thorn. La perception de la politique européenne au Luxembourg dans les années 1970', in S. Schirmann (ed.), *Quelle architecture pour quelle Europe? Des projets d'une Europe unie à l'Union européenne (1945–1992)* (Brussels: P.I.E. - Peter Lang), pp. 145–163; and C. Barthel (2008) 'Le difficile transfert de la BEI vers le Grand-Duché de Luxembourg', in É. Bussière, M. Dumoulin, É. Willaert (eds.), *La banque de l'Union européenne. La BEI, 1958–2008* (Luxembourg: Imp. Centrale), pp. 261–286.
9. See C. Schroeder (2014) *L'émergence de la politique étrangère du Grand-Duché de Luxembourg vue à travers le Ministère des Affaires étrangères (1945–1973)*, PhD Thesis (unpublished), University of Louvain-la-Neuve (Belgium).
10. Since the signing of the Treaty of Rome Luxembourg has held the rotating presidency of the Council of Ministers on twelve occasions: in the first half of 1960, 1963, 1966, 1969, 1972 and 1976, in the second

half of 1980 and 1985, in the first half of 1991, in the second half of 1997, in the first half of 2005 and in the second half of 2015. Between 1960 and 1972, and in 1980, these presidencies were exclusively managed by various Werner governments.

11. P. Werner (1992, II) *Itinéraires*, p. 79. See also J. Delors (1993) 'Le Luxembourg et ses présidences du Conseil européen', in R. Kirt, A. Meisch (eds.), *Innovation-Integration, Festschrift für Pierre Werner/ Mélanges pour Pierre Werner* (Luxembourg: Éditions Saint-Paul), p. 327.
12. K. Dyson (2015) 'Mastering Small-State Diplomacy: Pierre Werner in the History of European Monetary Union' in E. Danescu, S. Muñoz (eds.), *Pierre Werner and Europe: His Approach, Action and Legacy* (Brussels: P.I.E. - Peter Lang), pp. 19–26; G. Trausch (dir.) (2003) *Histoire du Luxembourg. Le destin européen d'un 'petit pays'* (Toulouse: Privat).
13. P. Werner (1992, I) *Itinéraires*, p. 300.
14. G. Trausch (2000) *L'Arbed dans la société luxembourgeoise* (Luxembourg: Arbed SA Communications and Imp. V. Buck), p. 73 sqq.
15. It is also worth noting that during his time in opposition, Pierre Werner served as a member of Luxembourg City Council, where he saw the realisation of one of the plans he had put forward in the early 1950s, when he first stood for election—the Grund lift, linking the lower and upper districts of Luxembourg City.
16. 'Loi du 24 février 1984 sur le régime des langues' in *Mémorial*, 27 February 1984. According to the law 'the national language of the Luxembourg people is Luxembourgish. The administrative and legal languages are French, German and Luxembourgish'.
17. 'Statement by Prime Minister Pierre Werner on Luxembourg Monetary Policy', *Documentation Bulletin*, 3 (1983) (Luxembourg: Information and Press Service, Ministry of State), pp. 8–9, here p. 9.
18. On 15 March 1979, the monetary status of Luxembourg was clearly laid down for the first time in law. The new Act provided for the participation of the Luxembourg franc in the definition of the ECU and gave the government the prerogative to set applicable exchange mechanisms. The Act also provided for the creation of a new institution, known as the Luxembourg Monetary Institute, responsible for monetary and credit policy in the country and for representing Luxembourg within the newly created EMS. The proposal for the creation of this new institution was submitted to the Chamber of Deputies in November 1981

but was delayed because of disputes over the status (public or private) of its staff.

19. L. Moyse, M. Meiers, M. Maquil (2014) *The Architects of Luxembourg's Financial Industry: Personal Accounts on the Origins and Growth of the International Financial Centers* (Luxembourg: Éditions Saint-Paul, Luxembourg); S. Döry (2016) 'The Role of Elites in the Co-evolution of International Financial Markets and Financial Centres: The Case of Luxembourg', *Competition & Change*, 1, pp. 21–36; C. Forrestier (2011) *The Untold Story of Astra, Europe's Leading Satellite Company* (Berlin: Springer). See also Interview with Edmond Israel (Luxembourg, 27 August 2010) and Interview with Luc Frieden (Luxembourg, 28 July 2010), https://www.cvce.eu/project/werner/ (home page) and http://www.cvce.eu/en/oral-history (main page), accessed on 6 March 2018.
20. See E. Danescu (2016) 'Pierre Werner, a Visionary European and Consensus Builder', in K. Dyson, I. Maes (eds.), *Architects of the Euro. Intellectuals in the Making of European Monetary Union* (London: Oxford University Press), pp. 93–116. See also E. Danescu (2018) 'Through a century of change: portrait of a pragmatic visionary', *Journal of European Integration History*, 20, pp. 9–30.
21. E. Hennicot-Schoepges (2003) *Le discours de la ministre de la Culture, de l'Enseignement supérieur et de la Recherche lors de l'inauguration de l'Institut Pierre Werner*, Luxembourg, 12 October 2003 at http://www.gouvernement.lu (home page), accessed on 6 March 2018.
22. See particularly Interviews with: Albert Hanesn (Sanem, 31 May 2010), Henri Werner (Sanem, 1 June 2010), Marie-Anne Werner (Sanem, 1 July 2010), Edmond Israel (Luxembourg, 27 August 2010), https://www.cvce.eu/project/werner/ (home page) and http://www.cvce.eu/en/oral-history (main page), accessed on 6 March 2018.
23. J. Santer (1993) 'Vorwort', in R. Kirt, A. Meisch (eds.), *Innovation-Integration. Festschrift für Pierre Werner. Mélanges pour Pierre Werner* (Luxembourg: Éditions Saint-Paul), p. 15.

3

The Werner Committee in Context: Monetary Unification and European Integration

After the Second World War, as efforts were being made to rebuild a Europe devastated by war, the question of monetary unification in the continent came increasingly to the forefront at a time when major changes were taking place within the international monetary system (IMS).

These changes mainly took the shape of deep national monetary reforms. This was the case for West Germany, where wide-ranging, radical monetary reform resulted in the creation of the Deutsche Mark (German mark) on 20 June 1948. At the same time, the volume of money in circulation was reduced by a factor of ten, public and private debts were consolidated and a new bank was set up, independent from public authorities, to guarantee currency stability. This was the Bank Deutscher Länder, the forerunner of the Bundesbank.[1] This was followed by liberal economic policy measures implemented by the Federal Minister for the Economy, Ludwig Erhard, which led to the establishment of a social market economy (high growth, reduced inflation, low unemployment, and a social protection system), the basis of the 'German economic miracle'.

E. Danescu, *Pierre Werner and Europe*,
Archival Insights into the Evolution of Economics,
https://doi.org/10.1007/978-3-319-96295-5_3

A few years later it was France's turn to introduce major reforms. When General de Gaulle returned to power in May 1958, the French economy was in the throes of financial and monetary instability, further worsened by the crisis of the political regime. The economy was very inward-looking, and foreign trade was governed by a strict protection mechanism (high quantitative and tariff restrictions, distorted competition, etc.). To deal with the imbalances in the domestic budget and foreign trade, a committee of experts was set up, chaired by economist Jacques Rueff. The committee's work to find solutions to stabilise the economy on a lasting basis led to the Rueff Plan.[2] This orthodox, liberal plan contained four major areas for action: restoring competitiveness, reducing inflation, opening up the economy, and stimulating investment. It was successfully implemented by General de Gaulle's Government in late 1958. Public finances were restored, the franc became convertible (the new franc or 'heavy franc' came into force on 1 January 1960) and exchange controls were loosened. Rueff continued his work and, in a second report that he published in July 1960,[3] he recommended opening the economy up to competition, despite the fact that the Common Market was only in its early days.

Other countries—Belgium, Luxembourg and the Netherlands, as well as Austria and Norway—also tried to restore order to their respective monetary policies, carrying out monetary and fiscal reforms during the period 1945–1948. Although the countries had various specific difficulties, they all displayed similar symptoms: destruction of the economic order, elimination of stimuli, increase of the volume of money in circulation and curbing of price mechanisms. The specific measures implemented varied from country to country, but they ran along similar lines: reducing the volume of money in circulation, freezing assets (deposits and bank accounts), issuing new banknotes and coins and introducing new instruments (reserve requirements, discount rates, selective credit policy, fiscal penalties, etc.).[4] Faced with increasingly difficult situations, other countries pursued more lax policies. In Italy, where inflation was causing major problems, the government chose not to introduce convertibility to prevent mass purchases of foreign currency and foreign goods. The deep economic and monetary reforms in Germany and France, as in other countries, were based on certain key principles (fixed exchange rates, price stability, and curbing inflation, the independence of the issuing body/central bank, etc.) that were at the basis of monetary Europe.

From the 1960s onwards, efforts in favour of a monetary Europe were stepped up by national authorities, Community institutions, European activists, academic bodies, and various key figures. In this historical context, the year 1970 was particularly important as it saw the development of the plan for the stage-by-stage establishment of economic and monetary union in the Community, also known as the Werner Report.

3.1 The Post-War International Monetary Environment

While Europe was still in the throes of the Second World War, the United Nations convened a major conference in Bretton Woods (in New Hampshire) from 1 to 22 July 1944, with the aim of creating a monetary system that could serve as a solid framework for the reconstruction and economic expansion of the free world.

The aims of the principles established by the Bretton Woods Agreements[5] were to restore the freedom of international payments in order to revitalise international trade, and to guarantee exchange rate stability. In Europe, the main currencies were not freely interconvertible (until 1958), which created huge problems for trade multilateralism. The second aim was to be achieved by introducing the Gold Exchange Standard, under which the US dollar acted as a means of reserve and of international payment[6] and which presupposed parities that were fixed, but adjustable, between participating countries' currencies. A new international body designed to promote monetary cooperation, guarantee financial stability and facilitate international trade came into being — the International Monetary Fund (IMF). Its purpose was to lend currency to its member states in order to make up temporary deficits in their balances of payment. The IMF intervened by means of reserves created from the quotas paid by member countries. A second major institution was set up, the International Bank for Reconstruction and Development (IBRD),[7] with the aim of contributing to the reconstruction and development of the countries devastated by war.

The United States played a decisive role in establishing this new order, whose early days proved difficult. Immediately after the war, Europe was on the brink of economic collapse and trade was extremely asymmetric. With a view to protecting their rare gold reserves, the European countries very soon erected trade barriers, which led to a decline in intra-continental trade. American exports to Europe produced a balance of payments surplus, together with massive gold and currency revenue for the United States, which generated a shortage of means for international payment. There was a 'dollar gap' in the international economy, as demand for dollars substantially exceeded supply. The solution lay in the outflow of US dollars beyond US borders and the Americans therefore sought means of boosting the European economy by means of an ambitious structural programme. That is how the Marshall Plan[8] came to be implemented. That programme led to the establishment of the Organisation for European Economic Cooperation (OEEC), which was designed to improve multilateral trade and promote the closer integration of European economies, in particular by liberalising capital movements, coordinating economic policies and preventing trade reprisals.

The OEEC also set monetary objectives. Pursuant to Articles 6 and 7 of the Convention for European Economic Cooperation (CEEC), each participating state is required to monitor the stability of its currency and ensure sound trade relations. Yet the OEEC remained an intergovernmental cooperation body and did not manage to create a customs union. The French, Italians, and Americans, who were in favour of this option, came up against the formal refusal of the UK, which was more concerned with maintaining its special bilateral relations with its colonies on the one hand and the United States on the other. The European countries were encouraged gradually to remove their quantitative restrictions on trade and to buy among themselves, in order to reduce their imports in dollars. A few improvements emerged in regard to customs barriers, but in the event of economic difficulties, member countries could always opt out: a reservation clause in the CEEC provides that members declaring themselves not interested in an OEEC measure may abstain from decisions. Initially, they concluded intra-European payment and compensation agreements, eventually leading to the European Payments Union (EPU).[9] This new institution gave them a financial instrument to promote the liberalisation of trade among themselves. It created a multilateral, obligatory and automatic monetary clearing system in place of the network of bilateral agreements member countries had formerly concluded. Given that this agreement provided for the full transferability of currencies participating in the system, some were of the view that the EPU served as a 'regional monetary union' and also paved the way for organised European monetary cooperation, raising the question of a Western European monetary identity.[10]

The EPU,[11] which was regarded from the outset as a temporary solution, helped ensure complete stability of exchange rates in post-war Europe and promoted the liberalisation of trade among its member states. Yet it fell victim to successive crises, particularly because of opposition to price developments and the interchangeability of European currencies among issuing banks but not at individual bank level, and it was therefore dissolved on 27 December 1958. It was replaced that same day by the European Monetary Agreement (EMA),[12] which postulated the collective return to monetary convertibility in Europe, accompanied by closer involvement in international economic trade movements.

Although the Bretton Woods system and the mechanisms based on it—the EPU followed by the EMA—helped stabilise monetary relations among participating countries, its foundations remained fragile: the United States was not bound by any economic and monetary policy obligations, even though its capacity to guarantee the gold parity of its currency lay at the heart of the Bretton Woods Agreements. The system was centred around and promoted the US dollar, which benefited from a high level of confidence in its capacity as the international currency. Confidence in the dollar was based on three main elements: the US' economic power, the convertibility of the dollar into gold, and the country's large gold reserves. Following the US economic aid that had enabled

Europe to restore its productive potential, and in the wake of a number of devaluations in relation to the dollar that made European exporters more competitive, the American balance of payments found itself almost permanently in a state of imbalance. To fund the deficit in its external payments, the United States issued debt in dollars, which helped bolster international reserves. Central banks across the world, including those in Europe, were accumulating increasing quantities of dollars in their reserves, without, however, calling for them to be converted into gold, because of their confidence in the American currency.[13] There was a sort of tacit agreement between the United States and some European countries under which the latter agreed not to request conversion of all their dollar surpluses into gold. Germany, the Netherlands, Belgium, and the UK, as well as Japan, all toed this line. But France refused to go along with this principle, and in 1964, it converted its surplus dollars into gold to fund its own unmatured debt to the United States. This French attitude was harshly criticised by the US Administration.

It was therefore as if, by accumulating dollar reserves, the central banks in the rest of the world were lending the United States some of the money required for US companies to buy companies in their own countries. This 'exorbitant privilege' was criticised by General de Gaulle in the mid-1960s, and he called, in vain, for a return to the principles of the gold standard. But this source of international liquidity was soon to be supplemented, then replaced, by the Eurodollar market, which became a key element of the international financial system.

In the late 1950s, the system gradually deteriorated and the dollar rate declined on the markets in relation to gold, whose price rose substantially.

The resulting surplus of dollars led to an erosion of confidence in the American currency. Foreign assets in dollars rapidly began to exceed the American gold stock, a situation that was incompatible with the US obligation to convert dollars into gold at the request of the central banks. On 15 August 1971, President Richard Nixon suspended the convertibility into gold of the US dollar, heralding the end of the Bretton Woods system. The crisis of confidence in the dollar created a climate of speculation. At the dawn of the 1960s, Robert Triffin foresaw the gradual disintegration of the International Monetary System (IMS) and the need to create a European monetary union with a common currency.[14]

The monetary issue arose very early on in the debate on European monetary integration after the Second World War. At their 1947 conference in Montreux, the European federalists tabled a motion on economic policy calling for the European Federation to have the right to 'regulate monetary conditions', without prejudice to the powers and responsibilities exercised by universal organisations. Two years later, the Pan-Europa Congress called for Europe to be equipped with 'a sound monetary instrument, managed independently of any strictly national economic policy'. During the 1950s and 1960s, study groups such as the Bellagio Group and the Bilderberg Group began to look at European monetary integration.[15] The idea came up of creating a European central bank. The Action Committee for the United States of Europe (ACUSE) that Jean Monnet founded in 1955 set European monetary integration as the key objective.[16]

Driven by a voluntarist approach and the efforts of some key figures—including visionaries (Jean Monnet and Altiero Spinelli) and leaders (Robert Schuman, Konrad Adenauer, Paul-Henri Spaak, and Alcide de Gasperi)—and following initiatives implemented by their governments, the European integration process got under way. It began during the early days of the 'thirty glorious years' (1945–1975), a period of exceptional economic growth in Europe, the USA, and Japan.[17] Sustainable growth, virtually full employment, and monetary stability were accompanied by improved living conditions and general modernisation in these societies, even if their growth was not uniform. Twenty-five years later, the two oil shocks and the collapse of the IMS brought this era of prosperity to an end. The golden age was followed by a period of crisis (1975–1984) and eurosclerosis.

The initial stage of European integration, inspired more by politics than economics, eventually led to the European Coal and Steel Community (ECSC),[18] followed, seven years later, by the European Economic Community (EEC) and the European Atomic Energy Community (Euratom) established by the Rome Treaty of 25 March 1957.[19] Based on the principle of the free movement of goods, persons, services, and capital, these treaties aimed to establish an internal market among Member States (more widely known as the 'common market') and thereby boost regional trade within a customs union.

The trading activity resulting from the elimination of barriers to trade highlighted the need to go beyond mere economic integration and to drive the signatory countries towards monetary cooperation. The only way to safeguard the Common Market was by an internal system of stable exchange rates, given that, within this framework, 'it is possible and necessary [...] to ensure at the same time the external balance and the internal balance of the economies governed by a system of exchange rates closely linked among themselves'.[20] European monetary union was on its way.

3.2 Pierre Werner's Monetary Thinking and Political Action in the 1960s

Pierre Werner's years as a university student in Paris and the contacts he made with eminent teachers, among them Jacques Rueff, Charles Rist, Wilfrid Baumgartner, and Fernand Collin, gave him a taste for the study of economic and monetary developments, which was reinforced when he joined the world of banking in Luxembourg, where he started his professional life. As soon as he moved into government posts, he was given responsibility for setting up the banking control commission. Thereafter, his career in the Ministry of Finance brought him into European and international negotiations, particularly in the context of the IMF and the World Bank as soon as those institutions were set up. His background as an economist and his training in the world of finance enabled him to grasp the essence of the problems brought up for discussion. The political posts he held gave him the means of action, and his skill in bringing people together elicited commitment from those of his associates whose task it was to implement practical solutions. His constant presence in the closed circle of the Finance Ministry over a period of 25 years and his dealings with experts always kept that interest alive, even though, by the force of circumstances, his political work often enjoyed greater prominence and visibility in the eyes of the public.[21]

Going beyond the official side, though, had a real passion for economic and monetary questions, as his private archives amply demonstrate. They contain detailed, amazingly rich files of documentation, which he himself methodically compiled and filed from 1950 onwards. They contain texts, most of them in manuscript, on the subject of European monetary integration, along with many articles, often with his comments, from the Luxembourg, European and international press. Werner had a way of thinking about economic and monetary affairs which was quite his own and was built up from personal ideas and the contributions of others. He was inspired by the unique situation of Luxembourg, a country which did not have its own central bank or national currency and had therefore always favoured currency unions. This thinking developed in interaction with the European academic and university worlds, to which he remained linked, and was expounded, in particular, at the political forums to which he was invited by virtue of his official duties and functions.

It was thus in a lecture entitled 'What monetary integration means', given in Strasbourg on 21 November 1960, that Werner set out his first thoughts on European monetary integration. Looking for his inspiration to the lessons learned from the Benelux Union (which was based on a monetary agreement), Werner stressed that 'economic cooperation and integration come about more directly through the instrument of monetary policy', but that unilateral and therefore brutal decisions were not desirable.

> Between sovereign countries, monetary rapprochement can only be gradual and concomitant with the rapprochement of economic policies [...] and monetary unification comes at the end rather than the beginning of the integration process.

A common market requires not just a financial order within the Community but a financial order on a broader international, continental or world scale. As for the financial order of the Six, it was not enough for it to join a broader monetary system, but 'a stronger Community slant should be given to their financial policies'.

To meet these objectives, he proposed 'the progressive introduction of a European currency of account' capable of lessening the risks caused by speculative movements of capital in connection with currency devaluations and revaluations. The use of such a unit of account could be extended without necessarily requiring a revision of the Treaties. In the EEC's international relations, this European currency 'would supply a benchmark for value shielded from ups and downs in the national currencies, facilitate the expansion of international trade and encourage the development of savings'. Private use could be introduced gradually—for loans and travel tickets, for instance—to 'accustom people, little by little, to this collective currency'. On the basis of the dollar-equivalent unit of account to be adopted as a 'currency of account' by the EPU, known as 'Epunit', Werner put forward several proposals for names: 'Euror', 'Goldeur', and 'Gramor', with a preference for the first of these. Why 'Euror'? 'The fact that it sounds like both "aurore" (dawn) and "or" (gold) would be bound to inspire confidence'.

Pierre Werner was, therefore, in tune with the ideas of Robert Triffin—which, inspired by the dollar and the American deficit, looked ahead to a gradual disintegration of the and argues for the setting up of a European monetary with a single currency—as well as with those of his Belgian opposite number, Pierre Wigny, or indeed those of Fernand Collin. The latter, a Belgian university teacher and banker, famous for having been one of the pioneers of the establishment of a European currency and known to Werner since 1956, greatly encouraged him to continue with his own thinking on monetary problems and to expound it publicly. It was he who stimulated him to play a regular part in conferences and congresses of economists. The intellectual exchanges between them were to continue as a constant feature, reaching particular heights of intensity during the work of the Werner Group. Fernand Collin was actively involved in setting up some of the special features of Luxembourg as a financial centre and his suggestions regarding the accounting currency and exchange clauses took place largely in the Luxembourg subsidiary of Kredietbank Luxembourgeoise S.A., which for a long time was a pioneer in the use of these new forms of cash.

Although he was not yet a member of the—and without having had, in that framework, any structured exchanges with the prominent personalities involved in it, despite being in touch with its chairman, Jean Monnet—Pierre Werner, as early as the summer of 1961, was familiar with the Committee's proposal for the establishment of a European Union of the monetary reserves of the Six—the prelude to a common monetary policy and a common currency. Werner kept up to date with developments in economic and monetary thinking, testing some of his ideas and initiatives in a wide range of settings. Pride of place went to regular meetings with European heads of state and government, especially when affiliation to Christian Democracy gave him an added kinship with them; to the discussions which took place within the BLEU and the Benelux; and to the meetings of the EEC finance ministers, in which he was involved for many years. He established relations of trust with his EEC counterparts, particularly with Raymond Barre and Valéry Giscard d'Estaing in France, Baron Jean-Charles Snoy et d'Oppuers in Belgium, Karl Schiller and Franz Etzel in Germany, and Emilio Colombo in Italy; with central bank governors including Baron Hubert Ansiaux in Belgium, Guido Carli in Italy, Jelle Zylstra in the Netherlands, Bernard Clappier in France, and Karl Blessing in Germany; and with other bankers, especially Collin and Abs of the Deutsche Bank. They held regular exchanges over a long period. Werner enjoyed very close relations with his Belgian and German partners. He also had cordial relations with the British, especially with Edward Heath, taking a close interest in Britain's moves towards membership of the EEC and the problems raised by the pound sterling in the context of a European monetary identity.[22] The good connections he had long maintained with US political and business circles added the requisite global dimension to his views, especially as regards the conclusions to be drawn from American economic liberalism and the role of the dollar as both a national and an international currency.

The idea of a common monetary policy was implicit in the Treaty of Rome of 1957.[23] The concept of a unit of account actually appears in it, but there was no provision for a single currency for all the EC Member States. Almost at the same time (1958), free convertibility between the currencies of the major industrial countries was restored, but the illusory monetary peace which relied on trust in the Bretton Woods system was no inducement to the partners in Europe to embark on the road to monetary integration, even though that would be tantamount to independence vis-à-vis the dollar. This idea made its first official breakthrough in the Action Programme for the Second Stage of the EEC (1962–1965), which proposed reforming the Treaty of Rome and working towards a 'real economic and monetary union'.[24]

To plug the gaps in the Treaty of Rome, three specialist committees were set up: the Committee of Governors of the Central Banks (CGCB), whose main aim was to coordinate the Member States' monetary policies; the Budgetary Policy Committee and the Medium-Term Economic Policy Committee. The Monetary Committee established by Article 105 of the EEC Treaty, tasked with monitoring the monetary and financial situation of Member States and of the Community as well as the general payments system of Member States, had become operational in 1958.

This initiative took into account the growing economic integration of European countries, which were having to stabilise their exchange rates more than ever before, as a common trade policy could not properly be implemented without a common monetary policy. The programme was co-authored by Robert Marjolin and Robert Triffin, who were renowned for their advanced ideas on the subject, and followed on from a proposal by them advocating the creation of a 'European reserve fund' and the establishment of a new European unit of account.[25] In 1962, a European unit of account was actually set up to act as a common denominator for farm prices and to express the amounts in the Community budget.

Some central bankers, however, were already warning against a premature monetary union. As early as 1962, the President of the Bundesbank, Karl Blessing, was already taking the view that

> monetary union could be envisaged only in the context of a European federal state constituted prior to it. He was also opposed to a pooling of part of the monetary reserves in the state of the Community at that time. The Dutch monetary authorities were of more or less the same opinion.[26]

Baron Hubert Ansiaux, President of the National Bank of Belgium, whom Pierre Werner met regularly in the context of the BLEU and with whom he had regular discussions on monetary questions, was very chary when the idea of a European currency emerged. A few years later, when he was on the Werner Committee, his viewpoint was to change radically.

In November 1962, Werner was the first EEC head of government to react favourably to the Action Programme for the Second Stage of the EEC, which European Commissioner Robert Marjolin had presented one month earlier. In a lecture given in Brussels on 27 November 1962, Werner once again asserted the relevance of a European unit of account defined in relation to gold as a means of 'giving a kick start to a European monetary system'. He emphasised the need for having fixed exchange rates, common monetary discipline and solidarity in a specific institutional framework, that is to say a 'Monetary Institute which could concomitantly develop its role as a Clearing House between the central banks'. Werner went on to say that

> the method recommended here would enable monetary integration to proceed along the lines of development of the Community's tasks without impinging on national responsibilities and without premature dispossession [...] The unification of economic policies will never be absolute: at specific times, short-term economic measures may be imposed in this or that country.[27]

It was only in 1964 that some of the European Commission's recommendations in terms of monetary policy started to take practical shape, in particular with the creation of the CGCB, which was set up in June 1963, and the establishment of collaboration between the Member States on international monetary relations in 1964. They reflected a growing concern to make further progress in European monetary integration.[28]

In February 1965, as the idea of a regional monetary system in Europe was increasingly coming to the forefront, the French President came out in favour of a reform of the IMS, which he deemed unbalanced and fragile. He was strongly critical of the imperialism of the dollar and was opposed to the US' position on whether and how the IMS should be reformed. General de Gaulle's proposals were firmly in line with a clearly defined view of international relations and European integration that he began to develop on becoming President in 1958, alongside a policy of national independence and identity ('a certain idea of France').[29] By advocating a 'European Europe' with its own political and military identity, independent from the United States and with a strong influence in the world, and above all a 'Europe of states', in which each country would retain its sovereignty, he hoped to curb any move towards supranationality.[30] This standpoint caused a good deal of friction between France and its partners (as demonstrated by France's withdrawal from NATO's integrated military command and its ambivalent attitude towards the Atlantic Alliance, the 'empty chair' crisis and the second veto to British accession).

In 1965, Werner was the first head of government, whilst president-in-office of the EEC Council, to emphasise the importance of monetary integration as part of the Community's internal and external policy. In the wake of the proposals from General de Gaulle, Werner reiterated the need

> to lay down, as soon as possible, the foundations for closer monetary cooperation between the six EEC Member States, to protect the Common Market from uncoordinated financial and monetary operations.[31]

This official statement before the Luxembourg Parliament by the Prime Minister, Finance Minister, and Foreign Minister—the speaker held all three posts simultaneously at the time—was an indication of the priorities of the Grand Duchy's foreign, and particularly its European, policy, in which economic integration occupied a prominent place. Monetary policy as the vehicle for this—with Werner as a committed defender of it—became one of the fundamental pillars of long-term government action, and the international money market which was just then emerging in Luxembourg was gradually associated with it, employing its own particular methods. Loans in European units of account (and in foreign exchange) were floated on the money market in 1964, and later to an increasing extent. Although the public displayed great curiosity regarding European monetary union, economic and financial circles remained sceptical—with the monetary authorities in the lead.

In the first half of 1966 it was Luxembourg's turn to hold the presidency of the Council of the European Communities, and Pierre Werner, who conducted the business, contributed to the securing of the 'Luxembourg Compromise', which put an end to the 'empty chair' crisis.[32] In his speech to the European Parliament in Strasbourg summing up what had been achieved, and referring to the key issues which had focused the Luxembourg Presidency's energies (the crisis in Europe and the finding of a solution to it, the entry into force of the Treaty establishing a single Council and a single Commission of the Communities, the financing of the common agricultural policy, and the multilateral negotiations within the GATT), Werner stressed 'the need to set up [...] common monetary procedures and [...] the need to enshrine fixed exchange rates in a set of monetary rules'.[33] This position, as well as the idea of a generally adopted European unit of account and the need for common monetary discipline, together with moves to coordinate the economic policies of the Six, had been supported some days earlier in a lecture to American businessmen and politicians in which Werner gave his views as the 'spokesman for European monetary policy'.[34] He did the same from the IMF and World Bank podium at the annual meeting of governors in 1966, where he spoke as acting President of the Council of the European Communities.

In May 1967, the 20th Benelux Economic Congress, meeting in Luxembourg, gave Werner a fresh opportunity for setting forth his vision of the urgent need for European monetary solidarity through a European currency, of which one of the chief virtues would be that 'it would resolve the problem of fixed exchange rates'. There had to be solidarity of action in this field, which was still dominated by a very strong sense of national identity. Even though he thought that 'the creation of a single European currency by a bank of issue would be premature', he believed that a tightening of monetary discipline was not only necessary but possible, since the Common Market countries worked so closely together in the pursuit of their economic objectives. From the same podium, Fernand Collin, President of Kredietbank Luxembourgeoise S.A., called for the establishment of a European currency and defined its characteristics.[35]

Until 1967–1968, European monetary cooperation was clearly an extension of the integration of Europe's markets and the establishment of a true common market in industrial and agricultural products. The rules of the common agricultural policy—particularly through the fixing of common farm prices, in terms of units of account—had de facto imposed monetary discipline. 'The functioning of the Common Agricultural Policy has thereby sustained the illusion of a European monetary union secured as if by magic'.[36] But an external factor which dispelled that illusion was to appear turbulence in the IMS and the weakening of the Bretton Woods system. 'As soon as doubts as to the viability of the system began to emerge and the first signs of destabilisation appeared (particularly with the crisis of the pound sterling in 1967), the idea of setting up an area of monetary stability in Europe and thereby protecting the European economies from the upheavals which the dismantling of the Bretton Woods system would cause was able to gain strength'.[37] With Britain's application for accession, it became necessary to give detailed thought to the question of currencies and monetary solidarity.

Taking these new circumstances into consideration, Werner threw further light on his ideas for monetary solidarity in Europe, which he discussed on 26 January 1968 from the podium of the Europaforum congress, alongside Jean Monnet and Walter Hallstein. He started by arguing for British membership, since Britain would bring into the Community a reserve currency and one of the currencies of account used in world trade, and since its application for membership '[…] would require the institutions of the Six to take stock of their monetary policy objectives'.[38] In his speech, which dealt with the prospects for Europe's financial and monetary policy in an increasingly unpredictable international context, he set out a theoretical structure for the means and instruments of practical action, in the spirit of the plan adopted by the Commission in 1962. Six months before the entry into force of the Customs Union between the EEC Member States, Werner therefore put forward a roadmap to European monetary integration. His action plan for European monetary integration was based on five pillars: the creation of a European unit of account, prior consultation between national authorities, fixed exchange rates between the Member States, internal and external solidarity (particularly within the IMF), and the creation of a Community reserve fund.

> I am not arguing for us to rush headlong into action on this matter without giving it due thought, but for progressive, organic action in keeping with what our Community actually needs in order to function. Of course, the use of the unit of account and various institutionalised measures to bring about solidarity will bring us closer to the ideal, final system based on a European reserve fund and a European currency.[39]

He emphasised the consequences of liberalising capital flows and of the development of the Euromarkets, subjects that he had been able to analyse within the Luxembourg financial centre.[40] Werner thereby anticipated the set of questions that the EC Commission set before the meeting of Finance Ministers in the 'Barre memorandum' of 1969, with a proposal for carrying out research into certain issues which might intensify monetary solidarity.

Throughout 1968, Werner played an increasingly active role in Monnet's ACUSE and enjoyed fruitful exchanges with Monnet, Triffin, and Carli. The governor of the Banca d'Italia praised the pioneering nature of this 'first Werner Plan' and circulated it in international financial circles and within the to the central bankers community.

> 'The prospects for European financial and monetary policy' were published and disseminated under the auspices of the Italian banking association, giving Werner's proposals extra publicity and visibility and stimulating discussion of the issues in specialist circles.[41]

The German economics minister, Karl Schiller, wanted to see the Community progress in the direction sketched out by Werner.[42]

The five-point action plan aroused interest and was well-received in political and banking circles, and a few months later Werner was invited to explain it to the Benelux colleagues.[43] His monetary thinking did, in fact, draw its inspiration from the lessons learned from cooperation in the Benelux context, and he pointed out that the success of such a plan, in the form of 'guaranteed stability of financial relations between the Member States' of the Community, would be assured by the giving of undertakings similar to those given in the Benelux framework. The plan he put forward was in the same form as it had been in January, but an important condition was added as regards the consultation procedure: 'changes to exchange rates may be made only by common agreement'.

At the meeting of of the Community Member Statesin Rotterdam (9–10 September 1968), Werner reiterated his five-point action plan, which he supported and qualified—placing the emphasis on commitment and political will—in the official address which he gave before his colleagues from the other Member States. What drew attention was the focus placed on the need for economic policies to be coordinated in parallel with monetary integration.

> Monetary solidarity will only be established laboriously in line with the strengthening of economic policy, and is dependent on it. On the other hand, the establishment of legal procedures and instruments directed towards a common monetary policy will be a powerful lever for bringing national economies closer together.[44]

The careful balance he imagined reappeared in the plan for economic and monetary union by stages (the Werner Report) of which he was to coordinate the drafting a few months later.

Werner's 'five-point plan' received undreamed-of levels of publicity in Europe and elsewhere, as it came from a member of the Council of Ministers and responded to the concerns of the time. But he was no longer the only person advocating action. He was on the same wavelength with's proposals linked monetary integration to a reform of the IMF, by imagining a European unit of account independent of the dollar and convertible into European currencies, followed by the establishment of a European monetary authority and, later, by a common monetary policy.[45]

The origins and development of Werner's monetary thinking up to 1968 show that he was an early activist for a single European currency, which he saw as being not just for use (including private use) within Europe but also internationally, in a way that would stimulate trade.

Such a currency, springing from the solidarity of a monetary policy common to the Six, would be immune to national weaknesses. As an advocate of the need for fixed exchange rates between European currencies, as compared to foreign exchange, he proposed that a monetary institute should be set up to take responsibility for such a policy. Werner was among the first to stress the need to take the role of the pound sterling in a common European currency into account, looking ahead to the inevitability of British membership of the Community, which he supported and for which he worked hard.

Sticking faithfully to the line he always followed, that of balance and moderation, he believed that the gradual building of monetary solidarity should be conducted in parallel with the coordination of the Member States' economic policies, which went against the views—and the political line—of the Germans and the Dutch. His own views on the matter already placed him in a median position in the dispute between the various trends in monetary and economic thinking, between which it fell to him to arbitrate in order to bring the work of the Werner Committee to a successful conclusion.

Pierre Werner was categorically opposed to monetary solidarity secured by means of a unilateral (and inevitably brutal) decision, which he regarded as undesirable and unacceptable. He had in mind the experience Luxembourg had had to go through with the forced introduction of the Reichsmark and, later, the franc after the Liberation.

> [...] Everyone knows how many severances and imbalances, how much human and social suffering such a radical process would bring in its wake. Twenty years ago, Alsace, like Luxembourg, underwent the experiment of headlong integration under the aegis of the Reichsmark ... Normally, such a course of action would practically mean a return to the economic liberalism of the 19th century or, if there is a wish to alleviate the pain of adjustment, the imposition of a monstrously complicated set of regulations.[46]

It was, in fact, that succession of switches which he had lived through from the inside, as a banker at the KBL and then as a government official in the Finance Ministry, which had prompted him to give thought to the currency question and the monetary processes of conversion and reconversion—in a context where there was no specific national currency and no bank of issue.

Events at the end of 1969—the revaluation of the DM, the devaluation of the French franc and events on the international currency markets which marked the end of the Bretton Woods system—highlighted the lack of coordination on monetary questions among the Six and gave a fresh impetus to European integration.

3.2.1 Monetary Innovation Through the Luxembourg Financial Centre

As finance minister and later prime minister, Werner was well aware of the potential of the banking sector for the diversification of an economy that was entirely dominated by the steel industry. Luxembourg had several distinguishing features which gave it a competitive advantage. They resulted in part from action taken by the government and in part from various external factors, including the interest equalisation tax introduced in the United States in 1963 and the German securities transfer tax (*Kuponsteuer*) introduced in 1965. In particular, the absence of a central bank meant that Luxembourg-based banking establishments were not obliged to set aside compulsory minimum reserves. Furthermore, the dual Belgium–Luxembourg exchange market, which was managed by the Institut belgo-luxembourgeois du change (the Belgium and Luxembourg Exchange Institute), created a separation between commercial and financial transactions and facilitated international activities. The supervisory authority, the Commissariat au contrôle des banques (Banking Control Commission or CCB), was a small structure, with a dynamic decision-making process and a Commissioner with extensive powers, making it particularly responsive to opportunities as they arose.

Finally, the presence of the ECSC was followed by the relocation to Luxembourg of the Community's financial institutions, including the European Investment Bank (EIB), which established its headquarters there in 1968. Their presence gave the Luxembourg financial centre a European dimension, placing it in a strong position to become an 'incubator' for monetary integration. The monetary association with Belgium meant that Luxembourg had only a 'virtual monetary authority', exercised by the CCB. However, this did not stop the country from playing an active role in international monetary debates, with its representatives regularly invited to participate, alongside the experts of National Bank of Belgium, in the Basel Committee of Banking Supervision and the Group of Ten.

The proactive policy of the successive Werner governments in the decade from 1960 to 1970 led to the development and specialisation of Luxembourg as an international financial centre. It became a pillar of the economy and served as a 'laboratory' for a common European currency. In 1959 the first US bank opened in Luxembourg as Crédit Européen, followed by the first Luxembourg investment fund, Eurunion. In 1961, the Luxembourg Stock Exchange (LSE) became a founding member of the International Federation of Stock Exchanges. In 1965, the legal status of 'financial holding company' was created to attract long-term capital by eliminating double taxation. In 1967, the first branches of German, Swiss and Portuguese banks arrived in Luxembourg. Subsequently, in 1969 Werner set up an informal think-tank on the financial centre, including Robert Triffin, Jean Blondeel, Fernand Collin, Constant Franssens, Edmond Israel and Raymond Kirsch, to analyse future trends with a view to the identifying the prospects for Luxembourg with EMU.

3.3 A Turbulent Economic and Monetary Climate

At the end of the 1960s, the deterioration in the international monetary climate threatened the Bretton Woods system, particularly as a result of the balance of payments policy pursued by the United States. The EEC Member States felt these tensions and had to face the risks that currency speculation posed to their economic stability. The coordination and joint consultations that there had to be among the Six had been undermined by growing differences between prices and costs, which sparked off several foreign exchange and balance of payments crises. There was a risk of these threatening to disrupt the customs union and the common market in agricultural products, which had been operating more or less satisfactorily up to that point.

Turbulence on the money market in Europe increased after the devaluation of the pound sterling. On 18 November 1967, the UK devaluated its currency by 14.3%, which delivered a severe jolt to the system. The pound at that time was the world's second reserve currency and was involved in a quarter of monetary transactions in world trade. Sterling's exchange rate value was the outcome of both European and international factors: some researchers therefore took the view 'that it is no exaggeration to see in it [in the tension surrounding the pound] the beginning of the end of the Bretton Woods system'.[47] The weakness of the British currency and the effects of its devaluation on the exchange rate of the pound were used as justification for the veto imposed by General de Gaulle on 11 November 1967 to British membership of the Common Market.

In 1968, the dissolving of the 'gold pool' was followed by serious monetary disturbances.[48] In May 1968, uprisings by dissident French students plunged the country into a difficult political situation, which led to disruptions to the currency. In this connection, Werner wrote:

> From 14 to 21 November 1968, fierce speculation broke out regarding a revaluation of the Deutschmark and a devaluation of the French franc [...] The underlying economic realities called for a widening of the exchange rate disparity between the DM and the French franc [...] The German refusal to allow this was motivated primarily by the drop in German farmers' incomes which would occur if the principles of the common agricultural policy were strictly applied on the basis of price unity as expressed in units of account[49]

The French franc duly came under attack from speculators and on 8 August 1969 the government devalued it by 11.1%. The German currency then fell victim to speculative dealing and was revalued by 9.3% on 24 October 1969. As there was a risk that the imbalance between a strong DM and a weak franc would destabilise the common agricultural policy, monetary compensatory amounts were introduced in order to preserve both farm price stability on the French market and German farmers' incomes. These amounts, which were temporary but which lasted for a decade, were a distortion of the philosophy behind the common agricultural policy and were later to poison intra-Community relations at the annual fixing of farm prices. Despite the customs union, which entered into force on 1 July 1968 and was designed to eliminate all forms of quantitative limits on trade between the Member States, in practice Europe carried on being compartmentalised and fragmented, owing to divergent economic policies, differing taxation systems and the monetary compensatory amounts.

But the split went even deeper: consultation between the partners was not working. The decisions to devalue the French franc and let the DM float were taken unilaterally. Community solidarity was seriously weakened by the diametrically opposed interests of France and Germany. There was not just a threat to the functioning of the common agricultural policy, where the need for stable prices dictated urgent adjustments, but above all monetary questions were dependent on very deep-seated national interests and, in reality, fell exclusively within the remit of national sovereignty. Notwithstanding the major progress made by the EEC in the area of the customs union and the common agricultural policy, the advances by the Six in relation to the coordination of macroeconomic policies and monetary cooperation were unsatisfactory and illusory.

At the international level, monetary relations were based on national currencies at fixed, though adjustable, exchange rates and anchored to the dollar in the gold standard. During 1968, the IMS began to run into difficulties and its stability was threatened. On the other side of the Atlantic, persistent pressure on the dollar, for macroeconomic policy reasons, and then exacerbated by the Vietnam War, gradually exhausted the US Treasury's gold reserves. The constant growth of dollar reserves outside the United States ('eurodollars') made it difficult to convert them to gold at the official rate.

In August 1969, to support the Bretton Woods fixed exchange rate system and promote its role in the world economy, the IMF established the Special Drawing Right (SDR), an international reserve asset whose main function was to replace the national reserve currencies, primarily the US dollar. Exchange rates would continue to be stable, though adjustable, and the IMF would monitor the quantity of SDRs so as to meet world requirements for liquidity. This instrument was only able to palliate the short-term weaknesses in the system. Speculation by a fixed exchange rate system on the one hand, and, on the other, the systematic shortcomings of international authorities such as the IMF in relation to the coordination and adjustment of national policies, could only lead to the collapse of the Bretton Woods system.

The monetary turmoil experienced by the Six from the mid-1960s onwards, as well as the difficulties facing the pound sterling—which only highlighted the considerable discrepancies between the countries of Europe—had wide-ranging consequences. At Community level, it had an impact on the coordination of European policies, particularly the common agricultural policy, which was governed by the principle of single prices. To correct the distortions of competition caused by currency fluctuations, compensatory amounts were introduced, but they proved difficult to implement. Since the Treaty of Rome contained only rudimentary provisions in terms of monetary cooperation, close collaboration in this area was not a priority for the Member States; this was reflected by their unilateral approach to devaluation/revaluation measures. The EC countries were part of the IMS, which was characterised by fixed but adjustable exchange rates between currencies that were pegged to the dollar and the gold standard. But the increasing instability of the dollar, the weakening of the Bretton Woods system—which was on the verge of collapse—and the 'fear of seeing the European Community endangered by a disorderly revaluation of the European currencies' prompted the Member States to start working towards economic and monetary union.[50]

3.3.1 The First and Second Barre Plans

Alerted by the breach in Community solidarity, the Commission—prompted by Raymond Barre, Vice-President responsible for economic and financial questions—drew up a confidential paper which it submitted to the European Finance Ministers at their meeting in Rome on 28 February 1968. Inspired by the 1962 Marjolin's Action Programme, albeit less ambitious, this 'Memorandum on Community action in the monetary field' looked ahead to the development of closer monetary relations between the Member States. It proposed, inter alia, obliging

'Member States to adjust exchange rates only by prior mutual accord', abolishing the margins of fluctuation and setting up a mutual aid system. There was also provision for the adoption of concerted stances in international monetary institutions and the defining of 'a unit of account to be used in all fields of Community action requiring a common denominator'. Barre's approach was cautious and pragmatic. Not wishing to go too far, he excluded any provision for introducing a European reserve currency. 'Personally, I do not think anything would be gained by adding a new reserve currency, which would be a European reserve currency, to the old reserve currencies', he declared.[51] In the short term, the Commission paper called for research into certain themes which might make for closer European monetary solidarity.

The Commission's proposals were criticised by Germany and the Netherlands, which felt that there was no point in a unilateral monetary approach of this kind. The central bankers, meanwhile, had reservations as to the possibility of establishing closer monetary cooperation in the Community. The territory of the Community was too small; what is more, it was only a customs union, not an economic and political union.[52]

In October 1968, Barre was sceptical as regards economic and monetary union and adopted somewhat 'economist' positions. His view was that the priority should be given to more effective economic policy coordination and that monetary union would be the culmination of economic union. In a speech to the European Parliament, he maintained that there would need to be a European political authority to guarantee the success of economic and monetary union.[53]

This memorandum marks the emergence of a real awareness on the part of the Member States' governments.[54] Thus, in the final communiqué from their meeting of 13 December 1968, the EC Finance Ministers once again stated the need for increased convergence of their economic policies, as well as greater monetary cooperation between them.

The Commission's proposals followed those Werner had made earlier in his 'five-point action programme'. Laying out a practical path towards European monetary integration, the Luxembourg paper already made provision for the principle of prior consultation, bolstered at a later stage by the need for unanimity and the avoidance of any unilateral action. Joint monetary consultation was a matter of concern to the Benelux partners.

On 15 January 1968, the Foreign Ministers of the three countries agreed on a common work programme and decided to act in concert in pursuing their work within the Six, including their work on monetary cooperation.

On 12 February 1969, the Commission, prompted by Barre, submitted to the Council a 'Memorandum on the coordination of economic policies and monetary cooperation within the Community', which was seen as 'an original and complex economic entity' consisting of national and Community elements. Because of the growing interdependence between the Member States' economies, incompatibility between policies or strategies could jeopardise the customs union.[55]

Known as the first Barre Plan, this paper called for increasing integration of Europe's economies and recognised the need for an alignment of economic policies and monetary cooperation. The preamble to the memorandum was devoted to an inventory of the provisions on economic and monetary policy adopted by the Council on 15 April 1964, which made it possible, at the time, to set up the CGCB and the Medium-Term Economic Policy Committee. The failure of the mutual assistance clause mechanism was noted.[56] The plan, which incorporated the main lines of the 1968 memorandum, then proposed stepping up Community action on a number of fronts. The first area related to bringing about the convergence of medium-term economic policy guidelines (especially in respect of production, employment, wages and salaries, and the balance of payments). The second stipulated the coordination of short-term economic policies, such that the economies could develop in accordance with the medium-term objectives. There were also proposals for a mechanism for 'compulsory prior consultation on short-term policies', and an 'early warning' indicators system. The third area involved the establishment of European monetary policy instruments. For real monetary solidarity, the memorandum advocated a short-term monetary support mechanism, to go hand in hand with medium-term financial assistance. 'The mechanism for Community monetary cooperation will not take the place of the mechanisms for international monetary cooperation but, as envisaged, it can be incorporated into them without difficulty'. The plan also looked ahead to the possibility of abolishing the margins for fluctuation between European currencies and a jointly agreed 1% flotation as against outside currencies. On 17 July 1969, the Council gave approval to the setting up of a Community short-term monetary support system.

> The characteristic feature of the Barre Plan is a particular association of traditional German and French concepts, particularly as regards the convergence of medium-term national guidelines. [...] At this level, a French-inspired medium-term analysis was applied to the German idea of economic convergence.[57]

The ideas expressed in this paper were less ambitious than those put forward in Rome in February 1968. At the time, it was a question of abolishing the margins of fluctuation between exchange rates, giving a commitment by joint agreement in the event of a parity change and establishing a European unit of account. The explanation for this backward movement could be the lack of political will on the part of the Community partners (particularly France) and the disparities between national economic positions.

Werner anticipated some of the proposals in the first Barre Plan when, as early as the autumn of 1967, at a meeting of the Finance Ministers, he suggested recognition of

> the need for a revision of the margins for fluctuation between European currencies, the creation of a support network to fight against speculative movements, and the establishment of uniform units of account.

The Commission Memorandum was ratified by the decision of the Council of Ministers of 17 July 1969, but was, nevertheless, greeted with some reserve. The discussions were enlivened by two different ways of looking at monetary solidarity, pitting the 'economists' against the 'monetarists'. For the hard currency countries—whose standard-bearers were Germany and the Netherlands—the priority had to be given to economic policy, the coordination of which should make it possible to strengthen the weaker economies, resulting eventually in less recourse being had to monetary solidarity. They also supported broader powers for the Community institutions. The countries with weak currencies, on the other hand, with France in the lead, regarded monetary solidarity as fundamental. Monetary integration must entail economic integration, and convergence of the economies was no longer a preliminary to, but a consequence of, monetary union. To their way of thinking, too, setting a timetable for monetary integration would be bound to have a positive effect on the economic players involved in it. The Germans therefore recommended that medium-term policies be developed systematically and in parallel, and coordinated. The Belgians, the Dutch, the Italians, and the Germans agreed on short-term, non-automatic support. The Luxembourgers took a balanced position and the representatives of the central banks were very reserved as regards monetary cooperation. The Benelux countries adopted a common position, hoping that the veto on British accession would be lifted before any negotiations on further European integration.

The Commission wanted specific measures to be adopted by the autumn of 1969, but the monetary disturbances provoked by the floating of the French franc and the Deutsche Mark stopped the first Barre Plan going into action. However, gauging the consequences of their lack of cohesion and the risks that currency speculation posed to their economies, the Six committed themselves firmly to progress towards monetary integration and made it a priority matter.

Once fresh impetus had been given to the building of a united Europe by the summit conference in The Hague on 1 and 2 December 1969, the Vice-President of the Commission for economic and financial affairs presented the 'second Barre Plan' on 4 March 1970.

The new document, which followed the broad lines of the first Barre Memorandum, laid down specifically that the convergence of national guidelines should go hand in hand with concerted action in the field of economic policy. From that point on, economic coordination and monetary solidarity were inseparable from each other.

> While it is true that monetary union, if it is to last, needs to be soundly based on economies evolving on compatible lines, with convergent economic policies, it is equally true that closer monetary solidarity enhances the prospects for both such compatibility and such convergence. The interaction of the economic and monetary sides is a powerful factor for greater Community cohesion.[58]

A ten-year working calendar for the move to economic and monetary union was also outlined, emphasising that 'the measures to be adopted will need to be decided in the light of a concept of 'common interest' combining and going further than the mere addition of national interests. This was despite the fact that the plan 'attempts to offset the imbalances created by separate action by Governments and to make for some degree of coordination, but does not yet supply the permanent instruments for a common policy'.[59]

3.3.2 The Hague Summit

The Hague Summit, a decisive moment in the process of European integration, took place on 1 and 2 December 1969 under the auspices of the 'completion, enlargement, deepening' triptych.

Completion (of the Common Market) meant resolving the differences over the common agricultural policy. A compromise was found which allowed for the adoption of the financial regulations relating to agriculture, as requested by France, and an increase in the European Parliament's budgetary powers, which the other parties, especially Italy, wanted. The Six also agreed in principle to a financial regulation on the Community's own resources.

Under the heading of Community deepening, two aspects stand out: economic and monetary cooperation and political cooperation.

> [The Heads of State or Government and the Foreign Ministers of the Member States of the European Communities] reaffirmed their readiness to further the more rapid progress of the later development needed to strengthen the Community and promote its development into an

> economic union. They are of the opinion that the integration process should result in a Community of stability and growth. To this end they agreed that within the Council, on the basis of the Memorandum presented by the Commission on 12 February 1969 and in close collaboration with the latter, a plan in stages should be worked out during 1970 with a view to the creation of an economic and monetary union. The development of monetary cooperation should depend on the harmonisation of economic policies. [They agreed] to arrange for the investigation of the possibility of setting up a European reserve fund in which a joint economic and monetary policy would have to result.[60]

Why did economic and monetary integration occupy such a prominent place at the Hague Summit?

There could be various factors to account for it, starting with the completion of the Common Market, which, after a 12-year transitional period, was preparing to move into its final stage on 1 January 1970. That result, and especially that positive momentum, had to be safeguarded and consolidated. It thus became clear that on top of the customs union there had to be an economic and monetary union.[61] Then, because of the monetary disturbances in 1969, monetary cooperation began to seem both absolutely essential and virtually impossible.[62] First came the sterling crisis, then that of the French franc, which, after ten years of stability, had been weakened by the effects of the events of May and June 1968. Its devaluation (by 11.2%), followed by the revaluation of the Deutschmark (by 9.29%), caused widespread anxiety. These currency adjustments affected the common agricultural policy, based as it was on single prices expressed in units of account which presupposed monetary stability. Other monetary upheavals and fresh exchange rate instability put the balance of the Common Market at risk and could have led to the dissolution of the customs union and the end of the common agricultural policy. Lastly, considering the role of the US dollar and its pivotal position in the Bretton Woods system, the idea of asserting the Community's external personality more forcefully took an increasing hold. The Member States considered equipping themselves with a European monetary entity in international relations.

The aim of the second aspect was to define the progress which could be made in the area of political unification.[63] Thus, a committee began to take shape, consisting of the political directors of the six foreign ministries, chaired by Étienne Davignon of Belgium; its task was to hammer out proposals on foreign policy issues. These diplomats worked to bring the Member States' points of view closer together and, if possible, to define common standpoints. Their proposals, which were very cautious, were imbued with the sensitivities of France, which, unlike its five other partners, championed the intergovernmental method.

The Davignon Report, adopted by the Council of Ministers of the European Communities on 27 October 1970, recommended the setting up of a mechanism for political information and consultation through half-yearly meetings of the Foreign Ministers (the first of which was held in Munich on 19 November 1970) and quarterly meetings of the political directors. A European correspondent was appointed in each ministry to ensure that information circulated more effectively between the Member States' administrations. In other words, there was provision for political cooperation outside the Community framework. To ensure that political union was properly grounded in democracy, there was to be an informal symposium every six months attended by the ministers and the European Parliament's Political Affairs Committee. Once a year, the Presidency of the EC Council would send the European Parliament a communication on the state of political cooperation. The Commission, in turn, could be consulted on certain matters.[64] There was also provision for a special institution for political cooperation. This would be a political secretariat (based in Brussels) vested with the right of initiative and intended to contribute to the drafting of general guidelines. This endeavour came to nothing owing to France's refusal to step outside the intergovernmental framework.

The Member States agreed to the enlargement of the Community through the accession of four candidate countries: Denmark, the UK, Ireland, and Norway. Compulsory conditions for admission were attached to this principle: the candidates had to accept the Treaties and their political finality, the decisions taken since the entry into force of the Treaties and the options made in the sphere of development.

Following the Hague Summit, the Six agreed on a transitional period (of five years) during which the candidates had to progressively adopt the existing body of Community legislation in all fields (with the possibility of variations in respect of more difficult issues). A calendar was drawn up with the dates for implementation of the adaptation measures (the abolition, in several stages, of customs duties, the gradual adoption of common agricultural prices, etc.). The role the new members were to be given in the Community institutions was still to be defined.

The link between deepening and enlargement was stated in the following terms: before any enlargement of the Community, integration must first be stepped up, to facilitate governance. The Commission thought of deepening in a broader way, looking ahead to the development of powers and the strengthening of the Community institutions. But the Five were not keen to expand the areas of cooperation in the short term, in order not to place more difficulties in the way of British accession.

There is no doubt that two figures who came to power almost at the same time left their mark on moves to relaunch European integration at the end of 1969: Georges Pompidou in France and Willy Brandt in Germany.[65]

Pompidou, who was close to the UK and to financial and industrial circles and had a much more flexible view of Atlantic questions than that of his predecessor, wanted to break France for good out of its diplomatic isolation within the Community and thereby give a fresh impetus to European integration. 'While defending France's national interests was the priority, he showed himself to be a sincere champion of Europe'.[66] To keep his election promises and return to a consistent dialogue with his European partners, Pompidou proposed 'a summit meeting of Heads of State of the Europe of Six, to hold a debate on the triptych of completion, deepening and enlargement'. The summit was held on 1 and 2 December 1969 at the invitation of the Netherlands Government, which held the Presidency of the Community at the time.

In France's view, 'completion' meant the need to establish a stable financial settlement to perpetuate the common agricultural policy. For the French President, 'enlargement'—and particularly the opening of accession negotiations with the UK—would not only counterbalance the considerable economic and political influence of Germany, but also protect Europe from any moves towards federalism, to which the British were traditionally hostile, and would reaffirm Europe's political vocation. In return, Britain had to show that it was sincere in joining the European Community and comply with everything that had so far been achieved in the building of a united Europe. British accession was essentially based on the resolution of five major issues: the international role of the pound sterling; the British contribution to the Community budget; the common agricultural policy; Britain's exit from the European Free Trade Association (EFTA); and the Commonwealth.

This initiative by France initially aroused scepticism from the other Member States—particularly the Belgian, Dutch, and Italian Governments—and from the Commission and Parliament. France was suspected of wanting to delay enlargement by creating numerous prerequisites. The fact that the meeting was a summit, with its Gaullist connotations, made the Member States even more wary that France was trying to replace the Community institutions with an intergovernmental structure. President Pompidou finally suggested inviting the Commission to give a presentation on Community issues as part of a technical working session. This would satisfy the Commission but would keep it in the background. The Commission was not in favour of the holding of a summit, but once the Council adopted this principle (by its decision of 22 July 1969). It said that it wanted to be involved and contributed to the preparations. To this end, it set out its own vision of the 'completion, deepening and enlargement' triptych and reflected on how to complete the customs union by establishing an economic and monetary union.[67] Finally, the Commission was invited to the discussions only on 2 December, the second day of the summit. At the end, Paris agreed to the Commission's representing the Six at the negotiations on British accession. The securing of own resources for the EC, too, was a step forward for the drive to supranationalism. However, the Commission's voice at the summit did not carry the day, and it found itself sidelined by this intergovernmental way of proceeding which was institutionalised in 1974.

The German Chancellor was keen to go down the path of active diplomacy, and punctilious cooperation with France was a vital element in his foreign policy, particularly since the assumption of the French Presidency by Pompidou appeared to favour such a prospect. This being the case, Brandt returned to the belief that a Franco-German understanding would constitute the critical basis for the further development of the Community. In a letter dated 27 November 1969, Brandt informed Pompidou of the objectives which he believed should take priority with a view to the forthcoming conference and which, it seemed, could perfectly well be attained [...]: agreement in principle on a final settlement of the question of financing the agricultural policy, a common decision on the negotiations over British accession, and the setting up of a 'European Reserve Fund'[68] Brandt believed that the fund was vital to stability and solidarity in the Community and that setting up a genuine monetary dimension was a way of deepening the process of Community integration. Germany's Minister for Economic Affairs had a different view of the matter and did not share the Chancellor's enthusiasm.

What lay behind this personal initiative was the fact that 'Brandt was a staunch European federalist and very much in favour of economic and monetary union, just like Gaston Eyskens of Belgium and Pierre Werner of Luxembourg. He was a member of Monnet's Action Committee and consulted him before preparing for the Hague Summit, and Monnet called on Triffin, who drew up the proposal for a European monetary fund'.[69]

This idea actually came from Monnet, and that Brandt took it over as his own. On 31 October 1969, when the Chancellor had only just taken office, Monnet sent him a detailed memorandum on the advantages and the practical operation of the European Fund. A week later, on 7 November, Brandt and Monnet had a long discussion in Bonn, in the course of which Monnet was at pains to dispel a number of doubts the Chancellor had regarding the reaction from German experts, the consequences the project would have for the British accession process and the probable attitude of the United States. On 9 November, in a handwritten note, Brandt himself summarised the purposes and aims of the European Fund and the controversy it would certainly set in motion.[70] As Raymond Barre put it:

> This decision by the Heads of State and Government ... was the outcome of an agreement between Mr Pompidou and the German Chancellor Mr Willy Brandt, and Mr Monnet, whom I had seen before the summit. He had told me that he was intervening personally to ensure that the monetary question would be raised at the summit.[71]

In the programme that he presented from the podium at the Hague Summit, Brandt emphasised the 'political end-purpose' of European moves towards integration and stressed that economic and monetary union, to begin with, had to start with 'effective coordination of short-term economic policies', followed later by a common economic policy which must lead 'to a Community of stability which is open to the world'.[72]

Before the Hague Summit opened, Werner, who saw the monetary aspect as a priority for European integration, set out the official position of Luxembourg. Progress was expected on the completion of the Communities, on their geographical enlargement and their reinforcement, materially and institutionally. The central focus of his statement and of Luxembourg's view was, however, monetary cooperation.

> The conditions for economic union cannot be met unless economic planning and short-time economic policy planning are developed. The achievement of these goals is often seen as preceding monetary integration. [...] If we refuse to accept a measure of monetary discipline at the Community level, it is highly probable that coordinated short-term economic policy will never come about. [...] Economic and monetary union, far from attempting to impose uniformity and rules on all the practicalities of a defined policy, should essentially be based on an acceptance of fundamental forms of discipline which ensure that the interests which all partners share are taken into account.[73]

As far as Werner was concerned, making positive progress towards monetary union would not mean that the national sovereignty of the Community countries would have to be encroached on, since, as 'the history of confederations and federations has amply demonstrated, the last bastion of national sovereignty is not the currency but tax, as the distributor of national income'.[74]

Until the objective of a European reserve currency was attained, quasi-fixed exchange rates between the European currencies should be maintained. Changes could only be made by following the Community's approval procedures, where prior consultation would be obligatory. At the same time, the European unit of account enshrined in the Treaty must come into general use as a common denominator for transactions among the Six. Werner went still further, suggesting a concerted Community stance at the international level. Thus, he proposed the setting up of a European monetary fund to manage mutual assistance operations and monetary credit granted to non-Community countries. A common stance and common management of SDRs on the IMF were also promised, as was the merging of quotas. Ten years seemed to the President of the Government in Luxembourg a long time for achieving these goals, but it felt premature to set an actual period.

> However that may be, the Luxembourg delegation would be happy to see a reference made in our communiqué to our wish to establish monetary union within a period of time to be determined, by successively setting up the appropriate understandings, mechanisms and bodies, relying on coordination of the economic policies which it will be their task to stimulate.[75]

The final outcome of the Hague Summit was positive and it opened up new prospects for the building of a united Europe which gave the forward march of the Community new momentum. The decision was taken to explore ways of making progress towards economic and monetary union by stages and to set up an ad hoc committee of experts in the field to carry out this work. Raymond Barre warned against the difficulty of the road ahead, emphasising that

> even though we can be pleased that we are ready to display greater political will, we mustn't get carried away; we must realise exactly what the gradual creation of economic and monetary union actually entails.[76]

3.3.3 Belgium, Germany and Luxembourg Present Their Plans (January–February 1970)

Before the committee of experts started its work, several governments put forward proposals for the implementation of economic and monetary union and Memoranda came out from Belgium (published on 27 January 1970), Germany (published on 17 February 1970), and Luxembourg (published on 23 February 1970). After being named after their promoters, in this case the finance ministers from the respective countries (the Snoy Plan, the Schiller Plan, and the Luxembourg Plan, also known as the 'first Werner Plan'), these three government proposals were discussed at the meeting of the Council of Finance Ministers held in Paris on 24 February 1970, with Valéry Giscard d'Estaing in the chair.[77]

3.3.3.1 The German Monetary Plan (the Schiller Plan)

While the Werner Group was still to be set up, Germany's official position on monetary integration was made public in a memorandum which the Minister for Economic Affairs, Karl Schiller, publicly presented on 12 February 1970.[78]

The focus of this plan was the establishment of economic and monetary union in four stages of unspecified length, though the final phase was to begin in 1978. The first two stages (1970–1975) were the most important, their objective being the harmonisation of economic, monetary, and fiscal policy and the establishment of a system of medium-term assistance in the event of a serious disequilibrium in the balance of payments. Only during the third stage, when the European economies were converging towards common objectives, were Community elements to be gradually brought into being. These involved, in particular, reduced margins for fluctuation between the currencies concerned, changes in parity to be submitted to the partners for agreement, and the setting up of the European Reserve Fund.

The transition from one stage to the next was dependent on the main measures planned for the preceding step having actually been brought into effect. The final target—the fixing of definitive exchange rates, or even the introduction of a European currency unit, and the conversion of the committee of governors into a European Central Bank—was only sketched out vaguely, with no indication of the practicalities of achieving it or a timetable. 'Concerted action by the Member States on international monetary questions' was suggested, but without further details.

3.3.3.2 The Belgian Monetary Plan (the Snoy Plan)

The Belgian plan was drawn up at the instigation of Jean-Charles Snoy et d'Oppuers, the then Finance Minister.[79]

By his own account, when he was drafting the document, he referred extensively to the work of the National Bank of Belgium and its governor, Hubert Ansiaux. The exchange of proposals on a personal, confidential basis with Raymond Barre, was also especially valuable to him. The first Barre Plan, indeed, not only influenced his ideas but was to a large extent carried over into the Belgian document. The plan takes its inspiration from certain positive conclusions drawn from the Benelux experiment which could be extrapolated and applied to action by the Community, including the adoption of uniform rules for the presentation of national budgets, official currency parities fixed in relation to the other Community countries and tolerance for certain variations only by common consent.[80]

The Belgian monetary plan comprised three stages, which were to begin in 1971. It set out to be a flexible plan, open to amendments, and laid down the lines for the achievement of monetary union by 1977.

The first stage (1971–1973) covered five points, including three taken from the Barre Plan. The first point involved the coordination of medium- and short-term economic policies on the basis of Council decisions, to be taken, possibly, by qualified majority.

The second concerned the need to allow any variation of official currency parity vis-à-vis the Community countries only by common agreement (this was already the rule in the Benelux countries). The third point aimed to establish mutual assistance through the setting up of an automatic short-term credit system. If needed, medium-term mutual assistance would help rectify any imbalances which might occur. There was already provision at this first stage for a common stance by the Six in international monetary organisations. It was up to the Council, deciding by qualified majority, to define what this stance would be.

The second stage (1973–1975) set out four priority measures: the alignment of the partners' medium- and short-term economic policies (under supervision by the Community institutions), the abolition of the margin for fluctuation of currencies and standard ratings against the dollar, the review of automatic short-term credit, and the definition of a single, common monetary value in each of the currency areas of the Community.

The third stage (1975–1977) was to lead to European monetary union. During this final stage, a single European policy on medium- and short-term economic objectives would have to be adopted and pursued rigorously. A Community banking system, similar to a federal reserve system (such as that of the United States), would be set up for the Member States' central banks. It was to be in charge of the Community's credit and exchange policies and would be under the control of the Council of Ministers acting by qualified majority.

Although it confirmed the need for full commitment to economic and monetary union, the Snoy Plan barely touched on the idea of a common currency, instead favouring intergovernmental cooperation.

> During the final stage there would be an authority that would act at the level of the Community as a whole. The decisions of this body would set binding limits on the autonomy of national decisions.

3.3.3.3 The Luxembourg Monetary Plan (the 'First Werner Plan')

The Luxembourg document entitled 'L'union monétaire par étapes—esquisse d'un plan d'action' ['Monetary union by stages—outline of a plan of action'] was based on the address given by Werner in Saarbrücken on 26 January 1968, as well as on the main advances achieved by the Commission (the first Barre Plan) and the guidelines laid down by the Council of Ministers.[81]

The 'five-point plan' submitted two years earlier had been expanded and adapted to take account of developments in collaboration among the Six, including the inevitable prospect of Community enlargement. True to the idea that the UK could not long be left out of the Community structure, Werner, in his various proposals and public statements from the early 1960s onwards, had taken account of the political and economic role of the UK and its currency, seen as potentially bolstering the Community's future monetary policy. The chief factor in the shaping of the Luxembourg Plan, though, was the deterioration in the international monetary environment and the weakening of the world's reserve and safe currencies: the US dollar and the pound sterling. Werner believed that incompatibility between the principle of stability and exchange rate flexibility, at both European and international level, should drive the Community partners towards real cohesion, and in monetary questions first and foremost. A single currency would bring stability by putting a permanent seal on the interdependence of mutual interests and would make it possible to institutionalise the personality of the Community more effectively.

In the Luxembourg Plan, Werner set out seven stages spread over a seven- to ten-year period. The order in which they were taken and the impetus put into them could be modified in accordance with changes in the economic and financial situation over time. The overall political framework should be fairly flexible, avoiding an overly restrictive number of political thresholds which would necessarily be condensed and difficult to cross.

The first stage (regarded as being 'under way' in 1970) was designed to establish reciprocal, compulsory consultation on certain operations relating to monetary matters or the economy in general. The trend should also be towards 'concerted action, designed to be preventive', particularly as regards international monetary relations. The plan also recommended the allocation 'of SDRs on the IMF in part to the Community' as a 'first step towards the establishment of a Reserve Fund'.

In the second stage, there would be a mechanism to reduce exchange rates between partners, which would make for increasingly synchronised development of the exchange rates of the currencies of the Six against the dollar. 'The instruments for creating and circulating money, i.e. the lending instruments allowed or used by central banks, should be compared'. Ways of concerting the amounts of credit granted and the credit procedures followed by central banks, and general guidelines for budgetary policies, should be worked out.

In the third stage, 'a European unit of account would be defined, its use to remain optional and pragmatic to begin with', to encourage the setting of fixed exchange rates between the national currencies. It would stimulate greater interpenetration of European money markets and the emergence of an independent European financial market. The European unit of account would be introduced gradually for private use, which would have a positive impact on European thinking and public opinion in general.

In the fourth stage, any changes in parity would be subject to Community approval procedures, with voting methods to be defined.

The fifth stage would involve harmonisation of short- and medium-term assistance between Community partners and the setting up of a Community organisation (a European Monetary Cooperation Fund) run by a management body to be defined. This organisation would keep its accounts in European units of account. It would be up to the Commission, on proposals from the competent bodies—the partners' central banks and the Monetary Committee—to decide how this mutual assistance organisation would operate.

The sixth stage would see the European Monetary Cooperation Fund extended to cover certain categories of short-term credit granted by the Community in the context of international monetary relations. This would speed up the harmonisation of the economic policies of the Six and would give the partners greater weight in international monetary negotiations. The fund could also act as a financing instrument in the Community's trade agreements. 'To facilitate such operations, the central banks of the Six would entrust the management of part of their gold and currency reserves to the Fund, as follows: SDRs in total: 100 per cent; foreign exchange and gold up to percentages to be defined (e.g. 25 per cent and 15 per cent)'.

In the seventh and last stage, the European Monetary Cooperation Fund would be turned into a European Reserve Fund.

> In accordance with Professor Triffin's plan, sponsored by the Monnet Committee, central banks would hold a specific proportion of their global monetary reserves in the form of deposits [...]. The deposits would be denominated in European units of account [...]. The defining and use of the unit of account would bring us close to the last stage, the definitive centralisation of monetary policy and the replacement of the national currencies by a European currency, for accounting and circulation purposes. This will most probably not be achieved unless political integration is taken further forward.[82]

In the speech he delivered when presenting the Luxembourg Plan, Werner pointed to the political vision and the method to be adopted in order to reach the desired result: a gradual approach, by stages, with assessments, corrections, and adjustments after each stage, but against the background of a real, shared commitment in monetary matters, though without preventing the Member States from attaining their national economic policy objectives.

> Any common policy is at risk of instability at any time as long as the Member States have not taken the decisive step towards monetary cooperation and the harmonisation of their financial policies. Bringing about the conditions for monetary union presupposes development

> of economic planning in parallel and the coordination of short-term economic policies. The achievement of these aims is often seen as having to take place prior to monetary integration. That is not necessarily so, however. If we reject some measure of Community monetary discipline, it is quite likely that a coordinated policy will never come about.[83]

Werner's vision was very close to that of the French Finance Minister, Valéry Giscard d'Estaing, and that of the Vice-President of the Commission, Raymond Barre, who put forward his own second Barre Plan at the beginning of March 1970.

On 18 March 1970, the EC Commission drew up a paper comparing the proposals set out in the four monetary plans mentioned above in relation to the coordination of economic policies, the money market, the fiscal domain, and the monetary domain.[84]

An overall table summarising all the steps to be taken in the various fields was also produced. The institutional aspect, on which the various plans were not very specific, was not analysed separately, as the Commission felt 'that it would be premature to determine what reforms should be carried out in that area before the content of the plans by stages has been specified'.

In these four monetary plans, the number, duration, and sequence of the stages are different but two basic stages are to be found in all of them: a preparatory stage, regarded as ending in 1975, and a final stage, during which the Community structures vital to the smooth running of an economic and monetary union would come into being.

> We should point out here that because of the way this is presented, it has been necessary to make some fairly arbitrary choices: thus, for example, as regards the Werner Plan, one might say that the fifth stage could be incorporated just as well into the first stage as into the second, which is the solution we have adopted.[85]

The four plans all viewed the issue from a different standpoint, but the Commission defined two landmark positions: firstly, the Werner Plan, which took the most purely monetary approach, and, secondly, the Schiller Plan, which put most stress on the role of the measures to be undertaken in the various spheres of economic policy. The other plans displayed intermediate features.

To complete the task of establishing economic and monetary union, a period of eight to ten years was put forward. The Schiller Plan was the only one which did not provide for automatic transition from one stage to the next but required a Council decision each time.

None of the various plans dealt in any detail with the problems which would arise simultaneously because of the enlargement of the Community.

Notes

1. The Deutsche Bundesbank (German federal bank) was created by the law of 26 July 1957 (the *Bundesbankgesetz*), which came into force on 1 August of the same year. See O. Issing (1984) *Geschichte der Nationalökonomie* (München: Vahlen); M. Mitzakis (1950) 'La réforme monétaire en Allemagne occidentale', in *Revue économique*, I/3, pp. 311–340; C. Pengalou, T. Guggenheim (1966) 'Le problème de la réforme monétaire après la deuxième guerre mondiale, et la solution en Allemagne occidentale, en Autriche, en Belgique et aux Pays-Bas', in *Revue économique*, 17/6, pp. 1030–1031.
2. This is sometimes referred to as the 'Pinay–Rueff Plan', after French politician and statesman Antoine Pinay (1891–1994). In 1952, he served as President of the Council of Ministers for several months before becoming Finance Minister in the early days of the Fifth Republic under President de Gaulle. In this capacity he played an important role in the implementation of the Rueff Plan.
3. 'Rapport du Comité pour la suppression des obstacles à l'expansion économique' [Report on suppressing barriers to economic growth], known as the 'Rueff–Armand Plan', drafted by a committee of experts chaired by Jacques Rueff and Louis Armand (1905–1971), a senior official and company director.
4. See L. H. Dupriez (1978) *Les réformes monétaires en Belgique* (Brussels: Office international de librairie); M. Pohl (1994) *Handbook on the History of European Banks*, European Association for Banking History (ed.) (Aldershot: Edward Elgar).

5. See M. Bordo, B. Eichengreen (1984) *A Retrospective on the Bretton Woods System: Lessons for International Monetary Reform*, National Bureau of Economic Research (ed.) (Chicago and London: The University of Chicago Press); T. Padoa-Schioppa (1994) 'L'influence de Bretton Woods sur l'intégration monétaire en Europe', in *Revue d'économie financière* (Hors-série Bretton Woods: mélanges pour un cinquantenaire) (Paris: Association d'économie financière), pp. 217–227.
6. The purpose of the Gold Exchange Standard was to ensure that each currency could be defined in relation to gold and, at the same time, in US dollar-gold, according to the value in gold of the US dollar on 1 July 1944. That is how the US dollar became the reference currency, for at the end of the war only the United States had sufficient gold reserves (approximately 2/3 of the world stock), and therefore only the US dollar could take on this position of gold convertibility outside its borders. At that time, the official definition of the dollar in relation to gold was 35 dollars an ounce. The system was equivalent to a dollar standard.
7. The agreements establishing the IMF and the IBRD are known as the 'Bretton Woods twins'. Thirty-five states signed the Articles of Agreement for the IMF in Washington on 27 December 1945 and they entered into force that same day. The IMF became operational on 1 March 1947. See O. Kirschner (ed.) (1994) *The Bretton Woods-GATT System: Retrospect and Prospect After Fifty Years* (New York: M. E. Sharpe).
8. The European Recovery Program took shape on the initiative of General George Marshall, US Secretary of State. In a speech given at Harvard University on 5 June 1947 he declared that the US Government wished to contribute to the economic and social recovery of Europe. The plan to assist Europe encompassed \$35 billion, of which \$11.5 billion took the form of military aid, \$17 billion was a grant and \$6.5 billion was in long-term loans. President Harry Truman signed the Foreign Assistance Act (the Marshall Plan) on 3 April 1948. See M. Hogan (1987) *The Marshall Plan: America, Britain and the Reconstruction of Western Europe, 1947–1952* (Cambridge: Cambridge University Press).
9. The specific object of the European Payments Union (EPU) created on 19 September 1950 by the 18 OEEC member countries with retroactive effect to 1 July 1950, was to make European currencies interchangeable on the basis of estimated rates corresponding to the respective national economic situation. Henceforth, the EPU was to serve as an international clearing system for making up and balancing

the accounts of each European country with its neighbours. In practice, every EPU member country fixed a parity between its currency and the unit of account (fixed in grams of fine gold on the basis of the dollar value in gold), and a single exchange rate. At the end of each month, exchange regulations were effected partly in gold and partly by granting credits to the EPU. Subscribed by the United States., the initial EPU capital enabled it to regulate, and therefore cover, the creditors as soon as the debtors made their payments. Under that system, the national central banks also placed their currency 'at the disposal' of their partners, while the Bank for International Settlements (BIS) in Basel was responsible for the technical execution of compensation operations. Each month the EPU determined the net assets and liabilities of each member state vis-à-vis the other Union countries as a whole. A quota was fixed per member state, representing the maximum amount its balance of accounts could achieve.

10. É. Bussière, M. Dumoulin, S. Schirmann (2009) 'Le développement de l'intégration économique', in G. Bossuat, É. Bussière, R. Frank, W. Loth (dirs.), *L'expérience européenne, 50 ans de construction de l'Europe, 1957–2007* (Bruxelles: Bruylant).
11. R. Triffin (1957) *Europe and the Money Muddle: From Bilateralism to Near Convertibility* (New Haven: Yale University Press).
12. The 17 EPU member states concluded the EMA on 5 August 1955. This set up a European reserve fund for countries whose balance of payments was in deficit, together with a multilateral system of settlements and compensation on the basis of exchange rates that were as stable as possible. The BIS was in charge of carrying out the financial operations resulting from the agreement. 'Accord monétaire européen et protocole d'application provisoire de l'Accord monétaire européen (Paris, 5 août 1955)', in *Notes et études documentaires: Accord monétaire européen et protocoles additionnels* (5 août 1955–27 juin 1958), 2.514 (1959) (Paris: La Documentation française).
13. M. Friedman (1969) 'The Euro-Dollar Market: Some First Principles' *Selected Papers*, 34 (Chicago: University of Chicago). These were known as 'Eurodollars', dollars acquired by banks outside US territory and outside the scope of US regulations and used during loan operations to non-bank clients.
14. In his book of 1960 *Gold and the Dollar Crisis: The Future of Convertibility* (Yale: Yale University Press), Robert Triffin shows that the IMS based on the US dollar was bound to fail. According to the 'Triffin paradox' or

'Triffin dilemma', a national currency cannot serve as an international currency on an enduring basis. Either the global balance of the country using the international currency is in deficit, giving other countries payment instruments but eventually sapping confidence in that currency, or its global balance is in surplus, which leads to a lack of international liquidity and thereby slows down the growth of international trade.

15. J. Wilson (2004) 'Le groupe de Bellagio: origines et premiers pas (1960–1964)' and V. Aubourg (2004) 'Le groupe de Bilderberg et l'intégration européenne jusqu'au milieu des années 1960', in M. Dumoulin (ed.), *Réseaux économiques et construction européenne (Economic Networks and European Integration)* (Brussels: P.I.E. - Peter Lang), pp. 391–410, respectively pp. 411–429.
16. 'The objective would be to create a European financial market, with a bank and a European reserve fund, the common use of national reserves, convertibility of European currencies, the free movement of capital among the Community countries, and finally the establishment of a common financial policy'. J. Monnet (1976) *Mémoires* (Paris: Éditions Fayard), p. 502.
17. J. Fourastié (1979) *Les Trente Glorieuses ou la révolution invisible de 1946 à 1975* (Paris: Fayard). See A. Carrerass (2006) 'The Twentieth Century', in A. Di Vittorio (ed.), *An Economic History of Europe: From Expansion to Development* (London: Routledge), pp. 239–353; B. Eichengreen (1996) 'Institutions and Economic Growth: Europe After World War II', in N. Crafts, G. Toniolo (eds.), *Economic Growth in Europe Since 1945* (Cambridge: Cambridge University Press), pp. 38–72.
18. On 9 May 1950, on the initiative of the first Commissioner-General of the French National Planning Board, Jean Monnet, French Foreign Minister Robert Schuman proposed the creation of a European organisation responsible for pooling French and German coal and steel production. The Schuman Declaration, which took place in the Salon de l'Horloge at the Quai d'Orsay in Paris, is regarded as the founding text of European integration. https://www.robert-schuman.eu/en/doc/questions-d-europe/qe-204-en.pdf, accessed on 6 March 2018. It was to result in the signing, on 18 April 1951, of the Treaty of Paris which established the ECSC of six European states.
19. On 25 March 1957 two treaties were signed in Rome: the Treaty establishing the EEC and the Treaty establishing the European Atomic Energy Community (EAEC or Euratom). https://eur-lex.europa.eu/legal-content/EN/TXT/, accessed on 6 March 2018. Following

ratification by the six signatory states (West Germany, Belgium, France, Italy, Luxembourg and the Netherlands), the treaties of Rome entered into force on 1 January 1958 and marked the symbolic birth of the European Union (EU).

20. H. Ansiaux, M. Dessart (1975) *Dossier pour l'histoire de l'Europe monétaire 1958–1973* (Bruxelles: Vander), p. 44.
21. See E. Danescu (2016) 'Pierre Werner: A Visionary European and Consensus Builder', in K. Dyson, I. Maes (eds.), *Architects of the Euro: Intelletuals in the Making of European Monetary Union* (Oxford: Oxford University Press), pp. 93–116; E. Danescu (2015) 'Pierre Werner: l'homme et son œuvre', in E. Danescu, S. Muñoz (eds.), *Pierre Werner, une vision pour l'Europe: pensée, action, enseignements* (Bruxelles: P.I.E. - Peter Lang), pp. 117–140; E. Danescu (2011) 'Le Comité Werner: Nouvelles Archives', in F.Clavert, O. Feiertag (eds.), *Histoire, économie et société. La revue d'histoire économique et sociale du XVIe au XXe siècle*, 30/4 (Paris: Armand Colin), pp. 29–38.
22. In the negotiations for British accession to the European Community, monetary questions had been a major issue and one which came up time and again. In 1967 General de Gaulle vetoed the opening of negotiations on the grounds of the economic, financial, and monetary situation of the UK following the devaluation of the pound sterling—the world's second reserve currency—a few days before. During the 1970s, the question of the pound sterling hampered the plan for economic and monetary union and the financing of the Community budget, with speculation over the ending of the Bretton Woods system constantly in the background.
23. Part III, Title VII (ex-Title VI), Chapter 2, entitled 'Economic and monetary policy', Articles 103 to 108. The main provisions of these articles are as follows: Article 104—Each Member State was responsible for pursuing 'the economic policy necessary to ensure the equilibrium of its overall balance of payments and to maintain confidence in its currency, while ensuring a high level of employment and the stability of the level of prices'; Article 105 provided for the establishment of a 'Monetary Committee' with 'consultative status'; Article 107 laid down that 'Each Member State shall treat its policy with regard to exchange rates as a matter of common interest'; Article 108 brought in supranational financial measures, laying down that where a Member State is 'seriously threatened with difficulties as regards its balance of payments

[...] and where such difficulties are likely, in particular, to prejudice the functioning of the Common Market [...] the Commission shall [...] examine the situation of such State and [...] indicate the measures which it recommends to the State concerned to adopt'. Should these not prove sufficient, it 'shall, after consulting the Monetary Committee, recommend to the Council the granting of mutual assistance and the appropriate methods therefor' and the Council, 'acting by means of a qualified majority vote, shall grant mutual assistance'.

24. The Action Programme (24 October 1962) proposed to reform especially the Article 108 of the Rome Treaties. This, the second stage (1962–1965) introduced the requirement to hold prior consultations before any major monetary operation, and the third stage (1965–1969) set out the main lines of economic and monetary union with fixed exchange rates between the currencies and a monetary policy coordinated between the Member States. http://www.ec.europa.eu (front page), accessed on 6 March 2018.
25. In 1962, shortly before the submission of the Action Programme, Robert Triffin and Robert Marjolin made public their joint proposal for the establishment of a 'European reserve fund', the resources of which would consist of 10% of the central banks' reserves, and which would be intended to give the Commission a financial role independent of, and supranational in relation to, the Member States. In his book *Europe and the Money Muddle: From Bilateralism to Near-Convertibility, 1947–1956* published in 1957, Triffin, economic adviser to Monnet's Action Committee was already urging Europeans to move towards economic and monetary union, before the Common Market even existed. See G. Bossuat (1996) 'Jean Monnet. La mesure d'une influence', in *Vingtième Siècle. Revue d'histoire*, 51, pp. 68–84.
26. P. Werner (1992, II) *Itinéraires*, p. 119.
27. P. Werner (1962) *Problèmes de l'intégration financière de l'Europe*. Talk given in Brussels by Pierre Werner, Minister of State, President of the Luxembourg Government and Finance Minister, to the members of the Association des Amitiés Belgo-Luxembourgeoises and the Cercle Royal Gaulois (Brussels: Cercle Royal Gaulois). Pierre Werner Family archives.
28. Set up in June 1963, the CGCB met for the first time on 6 July 1964 at the Bank for International Settlements in Basel. 'Monetary and Financial Cooperation in the European Economic Community, EEC Commission, Brussels', in *Bulletin of the European Communities*,

6/7 (24 July 1963), pp. 33–40. See also Council Decision of 8 May 1964, on co-operation between Member States in the field of international monetary relations (OJ of the EC No. 77 of 21 May 1964, pp. 1207–1208).

29. The French believed that the status of the US dollar as the principal currency in the IMS gave the United States special privileges. Firstly, the Americans could accumulate debt freely thanks to the dollar reserves held abroad, particularly in the European central banks. Secondly, to guarantee the 'cohesion of the system', they exerted pressure on these banks, which soon became unable to make use of these reserves. For de Gaulle, this privilege was tantamount to a form of imperialism, facilitating the US' external political commitments and also investments in the country's companies abroad. The French position on the reform of the IMS can be summarised as follows. Initially, the system should be maintained in its current form, although steps should be taken to improve its operation. The countries with reserve currencies—first and foremost the United States—should eliminate their balance of payments deficits. At this stage, there was no need for additional liquidity in the international system. If new reserve or credit instruments were set up in the future, their neutrality should be guaranteed by establishing a link between these new instruments and gold, and by introducing specific controls. On these matters see particularly: Institut Charles de Gaulle (ed.) (1992) *De Gaulle en son siècle, tome III: Moderniser la France* (Paris: Plon); Comité pour l'Histoire Économique et Financière de la France (ed.) (1998) *La France et les institutions de Bretton Woods, 1944–1994. Colloque tenu à Bercy les 30 juin et le 1er juillet 1994* (Paris: Ministry of the Economy, Finance and Industry); A. Prate (1995) *Les batailles économiques du Général de Gaulle* (Paris: Omnibus).
30. In 1960, General de Gaulle asked Alain Peyrefitte to draw up 'a note on the practical ways of stifling supranationality'. For de Gaulle, Europe could only ever be a confederation, with power exercised not by an independent body but by the representatives of the Member States (ministers or representatives at the highest level), who had a right of veto. See J.-M. Palayret (1994) 'Le Mouvement européen, 1954–1969. Histoire d'un groupe de pression', in R. Girault, G. Bossuat (eds.), *L'Europe brisée. L'Europe retrouvée. Nouvelles réflexions sur l'unité européenne au XXe siècle* (Paris: Publications de la Sorbonne), pp. 374–377.

31. P. Werner (1965) *La politique étrangère du Grand-Duché de Luxembourg*. Address by Pierre Werner, Minister of State, President of the Luxembourg Government, Foreign Minister, Minister for the Treasury and Minister for Justice, to the Chamber of Deputies of the Grand Duchy of Luxembourg, in *Documentation Bulletin*, 1 (1965) (Luxembourg: Information and Press Service, Ministry of State), pp. 1–11. Pierre Werner Family archive.
32. The 'empty chair policy' refers to the strategy pursued by the French Government under General de Gaulle from 30 June 1965 to 30 January 1966. Refusing any extension to the role of the European Parliament or to the European Agricultural Guidance and Guarantee Fund (EAGGF), which had been set up to implement the common agricultural policy, and above all opposing the replacement of the unanimity principle for decision-making by the majority rule, de Gaulle suspended France's participation in the meetings of the EC Council of Ministers, effectively blocking any decisions. The agreement signed in Luxembourg on 29 January 1966 granted concessions to France in terms of voting procedure. These were phrased as follows: 'Where, in the case of decisions which may be taken by majority vote on a proposal of the Commission, very important interests of one or more partners are at stake, the Members of the Council will endeavour, within a reasonable time, to reach solutions which can be adopted by all the Members of the Council while respecting their mutual interests and those of the Community'. See 'Final Communiqué of the Extraordinary Session of the Council (Luxembourg, 29 January 1966)', in *Bulletin of the European Economic Community* (Luxembourg: Office for Official Publications of the European Communities), 3 (1966), pp. 5–11.
33. 'Address by Pierre Werner, President of the Council of the European Communities, to the European Parliament in Strasbourg, 28 June 1966', in *Documentation Bulletin*, 9 (1966) (Luxembourg: Information and Press Service, Ministry of State), pp. 8–12. Pierre Werner Family archive.
34. P. Werner (1966) 'Exposé sur la politique monétaire européenne. A lecture given in Brussels by Pierre Werner, Minister of State, President of the Government and Minister for the Treasury and the Civil Service, at the invitation of the American and Common Market Club, Brussels, 5 June 1966', in *La Libre Belgique*, 6 June 1966, p. 3. Pierre Werner Family archive.

35. 'Speech by Fernand Collin, President of Kredietbank, 27 May 1967', in *Problèmes économiques*, 2597 (1998). Pierre Werner Family archive. Note that in 1958 Collin also brought out the study *L'utilisation d'une monnaie de compte européenne dans les emprunts internationaux* (Geneva: Institut international d'études bancaires).
36. R. Leboutte (2008) *Histoire économique et sociale de la construction européenne* (Bruxelles: P.I.E. - Peter Lang), p. 215.
37. J. van Yperseele, J.-C. Koeune (1998) *Le système monétaire européen* (Luxembourg-Brussels: Perspectives européennes), p. 41.
38. P. Werner (1968a) 'Perspectives de la Politique Financière et Monétaire Européenne', in *Documentation Bulletin*, 2 (Luxembourg: Information and Press Service, Ministry of State), pp. 1–8 (p. 5). See also 'Lettre de Louis Camu, président de la Banque de Bruxelles à Pierre Werner (Bruxelles, 2 février 1968)'; 'Lettre de Karl Schiller, ministre allemand de l'Économie à Pierre Werner (Bonn, 23 février 1968)'. Pierre Werner Family archive.
39. The five main lines of the Action Plan were as follows: (1) Definition of the monetary operations which the partners could undertake only following consultation with their partners within the Council of Ministers or the Monetary Committee, or possibly in a special body consisting of the Finance Ministers and the Governors of the Central Banks; (2) Completion and approval of the definition of the European unit of account, after amalgamating the formulae used in the European Treaties and the various regulations. The use of this unit of account in relations between the Six would develop quite naturally, in line with the needs of Community action, internally and externally; (3) With or without reference to the accounting currency, the Six should set out their reciprocal undertakings for the maintenance of fixed relations between their currencies; (4) Monetary cooperation between the Six must be geared to that taking place on the world level of the IMF, in the interests of pursuing the objectives of security and freedom of trade advocated by the financial organisations set up at Bretton Woods. This is an indication of the great importance of consultation and the coordination of points of view in relations with these organisations. These will become particularly important as and when the plan for special new drawing rights on the Fund enters into force; (5) Looking ahead, steps should be taken to draw up the outlines of an intergovernmental agreement in which, as and when appropriate, the extent of each country's

obligations in relation to mutual assistance under Articles 108 and 109 of the Treaty would be set out. Assistance could be organised through a Community instrument. The European Monetary Cooperation Fund would be a channel for two types of operations: internally—forms of mutual assistance which would rectify imbalances in balances of payments, with the proviso that they were coordinated with drawings on the IMF; and externally—international credit operations deriving either from the common trade policy or from assistance provided in the international payments system.

40. After the end of the Second World War, the United States, and the UK undertook a vast programme of financial aid for the reconstruction of Western European countries. The monetary consequences of this policy soon became evident: thanks to this economic revival in Europe, the currency reserves of Germany, Italy, Belgium, France, and Luxembourg gradually increased. This initially affected central banks, and then commercial banks, since central banks authorised commercial banks to hold a large proportion of the dollars earned by the respective countries, which the commercial banks deposited in turn in American banks. But a regulation in force since the early twentieth century stated that US banks could not pay interest on overnight deposits. This meant that European banks, seeking a more profitable solution for their dollar deposits, turned to the exchange markets. Their opening between 1948 and 1953 therefore enabled European banks to work together to use their dollar deposits to fund trade with the United States in these countries, and gradually to fund international trade in general. See J. C. Nahoum (1969) 'Les Marchés monétaires internationaux', in *Politique étrangère*, 4, pp. 437–449.

41. P. Werner (1968b) *Perspectives de la politique financière et monétaire européenne* (Roma: Bancaria). Werner's article (1968) 'La réforme du système monétaire international' published in *Academia—Nouvelle Revue Luxembourgeoise*, 1 (1968), pp. 53–62, also aroused a great deal of interest in European financial and banking circles. See also G. Carli (1988) *Pensieri di un ex governatore* (Pordenone: Edizioni Studio Tesi); G. Carli (1993) *Cinquant'anni di vita italiana* (Roma-Bari: Laterza); M. G. Melchionni, R. Ducci (2007) *La genèse des Traités de Rome: entretiens inédits avec 18 acteurs et témoins de la négociation* (Lausanne: Centre de recherches européennes).

42. Letter from Karl Schiller to Pierre Werner (Bonn, 23 February 1968), BArch B 102, Bundesministerium für Wirtschaft (Federal Ministry of Economic Affairs)/93454. Pierre Werner Family archive.
43. P. Werner (1968c) 'Benelux et les perspectives de la politique financière européenne'. An address given in The Hague by Pierre Werner, Minister of State, President of the Government, and Minister for the Treasury, to the Benelux Committee in *Documentation Bulletin*, 6 (1968) (Luxembourg: Information and Press Service, Ministry of State), pp. 8–11. Pierre Werner Family archive.
44. 'Address given in Rotterdam by Pierre Werner, President of the Government, Minister for the Treasury, at the Meeting of the Council of Finance Ministers of the EEC, 10 September 1968', in *Documentation Bulletin*, 8 (1968) (Luxembourg: Information and Press Service, Ministry of State), pp. 5–11. In the Pierre Werner Family archive.
45. See J. Gillingham (2003) *European Integration, 1950–2003: Superstate or New Market Economy* (Cambridge: Cambridge University Press), pp. 59–60.
46. P. Werner (1960) 'Signification d'une intégration monétaire'. Address given by Pierre Werner in Strasbourg on 21 November 1960 in *Documentation Bulletin*, 15 (1960) (Luxembourg: Information and Press Service, Ministry of State), pp. 3–11. Pierre Werner Family archive.
47. K. Rücker (2004) 'L'adhesion de la Grande-Bretagne à la CEE et la question de la livre sterling', in M. Dumoulin (ed.), *Réseaux économiques et construction européenne* (Bruxelles: P.I.E. - Peter Lang).
48. The 'gold pool', set up in 1961 with the Kennedy plan, brought together the world's main central banks, which decided to coordinate their operations by intervening on the markets to maintain the gold parity at USD 35 an ounce, as required by the gold-standard system. The gold-standard system was set up by the Bretton Woods agreements. The value of the US dollar was pegged directly to gold (at USD 35 per ounce) while other currencies were pegged to the dollar. Central bank reserves then had to consist of currencies convertible into gold and no longer solely of gold. The US Administration guaranteed the value of the dollar but was not required to hold the equivalent in gold of the dollars issued. In May 1968 the 'gold pool' fell victim to excessive speculation and was dissolved. See B. Eichengreen (2007) 'Global

Imbalances and the Lessons of Bretton Woods', in *The Anatomy of the Gold Pool* (Cambridge: MIT Press), pp. 35–72; M. Bordo (1999) *The Gold Standard and Related Regimes: Collected Essays* (Cambridge: Cambridge University Press).

49. P. Werner (1992, II) *Itinéraires*, p. 121.
50. B. Eichengreen, H. James (1996) *International Monetary Cooperation Since Bretton Woods* (Oxford: Oxford University Press), p. 53. See also A. Bloomfield (1973) 'The Historical Setting', in B. L. Krause, W. Salan (eds.), *European Monetary Unification and Its Meaning for the US* (Washington: Brookings); I. Maes (2002) *Economic Thought and the Making of European Monetary Union* (Cheltenham: Edward Elgar).
51. R. Barre (1969) 'L'ordre monétaire européen' [A European Monetary Order], in *Aussenwirtschaft*, March, p. 7. See also P. Werner (1969a) 'Politique monétaire européenne' [European Monetary Policy], in *Bulletin de Documentation* (Luxembourg: Ministère d'État, Grand-Duché de Luxembourg), 6, pp. 3–11; P. Werner (1969b) 'Déclaration de Pierre Werner, ministre d'État et ministre des Finances du Luxembourg, à l'Assemblée annuelle du FMI (Washington, 2 octobre 1969)', in *Bulletin de Documentation* (Luxembourg: Ministère d'État, Grand-Duché de Luxembourg, 9. Pierre Werner Family archive.
52. 'Minutes of the 27th meeting of the Committee of Governors, Basel: 9 December 1968, 10.00 a.m.'. Archives of the European Central Bank, Frankfurt.
53. R. Barre (1968) 'Les problèmes monétaires internationaux et la politique monétaire de la Communauté', in *Bulletin of the European Communities* (Luxembourg: Office for Official Publications of the European Communities), I/1, p. 17; D. Howarth (2016) 'Raymond Barre: Modernizing France Through European Monetary Cooperation', in K. Dyson, I. Maes (eds.), *Architects of the Euro: Intellectuals in the Making of European Monetary Union* (London: Oxford University Press), pp. 75–92.
54. K. Dyson, L. Quaglia (2010) 'European Economic Governance and Policies', in *Commentary on Key Historical and Institutional Documents* (Oxford: Oxford University Press), p. 151.
55. 'Commission Memorandum to the Council on the coordination of economic policies and monetary cooperation within the Community, submitted on 12 February 1969', in *Bulletin of the EEC*, Supplement (Luxembourg: Office for Official Publications of the European

Communities), 3 (1969), p. 13. See also 'Avis du comité monétaire sur le mémorandum de la Commission au Conseil du 12 février 1969' Archives *historiques de l'Union européenne.* Fonds des institutions communautaires européennes, EC. Conseil des ministres CEE et Euratom, CM2. 1969. 406; 'Réaction du Royaume-Uni au mémorandum de la Commission au Conseil du 12 février 1969 (le plan Barre) (Novembre 1970)', in *Public Record Office* (Britain's negotiations to enter the EEC) (London: Foreign Office—9 November 1970), FCO 30/789.

56. 'Council Recommendation of 15 April 1964 to the Member States on the steps to be taken to re-establish the internal and external economic balance of the Community', in *Official Journal of the European Communities*, 64 (1964) (Luxembourg Office for Official Publications of the European Communities).
57. I. Maes (1998) 'Projets d'intégration monétaire à la Commission européenne', in É. Bussière, M. Dumoulin (eds.), *Milieux économiques et intégration européenne en Europe occidentale au XXe siècle* (Arras: Artois Presses Université), pp. 35–50, here p. 4.
58. 'Communication from the Commission to the Council on the development of a plan by stages for an economic and monetary union', in *Bulletin of of the European Communities*, Supplement, 3 (1970) (Luxembourg: Office for Official Publications of the European Communities).
59. G. Dell'Amore (1970) 'Pour un système monétaire européen', in *Europe* (Bruxelles: Agence Europe), 568, p. 1.
60. Point 8 of the final Communiqué from the conference. 'Final communiqué of the Hague Summit (2 December 1969)', in *Bulletin of the European Communities* (Luxembourg: Office for Official Publications of the European Communities), 1 (1970), pp. 12–17, here p. 15.
61. 'Aide-mémoire from the European Commission to the Conference of Heads of State or Government (19 November 1969)', in *Bulletin of the European Communities*, 1 (1970) (Luxembourg: Office for Official Publications of the European Communities), p. 17.
62. See L. Magnusson, B. Stråth (eds.) (2001) *From the Werner Plan to the EMU: In Search of a Political Economy for Europe* (Brussels: P.I.E. - Peter Lang).

63. Point 15 of the final Communiqué from the conference: '[The Heads of State or Government and the Foreign Ministers of the Member States of the European Communities] agreed to instruct the Ministers for Foreign Affairs to study the best way of achieving progress in the matter of political unification, within the context of enlargement. The Ministers would be expected to report before the end of July 1970'. 'Final communiqué of the Hague Summit (2 December 1969)', in *Bulletin of the European Communities* (Luxembourg: Office for Official Publications of the European Communities), 1 (1970), pp. 12–17, here p. 15. See also P. De Schoutheete (1980) *La coopération politique européenne* (Paris-Bruxelles: Éditions Lador).
64. 'Report by the Foreign Ministers of the Member States on the problems of political unification', 'Davignon Report (Luxembourg, 27 October 1970)', in *Bulletin of the European Communities*, 11 (1970) (Luxembourg: Office for Official Publications of the European Communities), pp. 9–14.
65. After the failure of the referendum of April 1969, General de Gaulle immediately resigned. Following the election of 15 June 1969, the former Prime Minister to General, Georges Pompidou, became President of the French Republic. After the federal elections of September 1969, Willy Brandt became, on 21 October, the fourth Federal Chancellor of the Federal Republic of Germany. He was previously (1966–1969) Foreign Minister and Vice-Chancellor in the Government of Kurt Georg Kiesinger.
66. The French attitude led to a number of critical situations which were instrumental in slowing down the process of European integration: the empty chair crisis at the EEC in 1965, France's monetary difficulties, the rejection of the UK's application to join the EEC, and the empty chair affair at Western European Union. See M.-T. Bitsch (2004) 'Le sommet de La Haye. L'initiative française, ses finalités et ses limites', in *Revue d'histoire de l'intégration européenne*, 9/2 (Baden-Baden: Nomos Verlag), pp. 83–99; J.-R. Bernard (1993) 'L'élargissement de la Communauté vu de Paris', in *Georges Pompidou et l'Europe* (Bruxelles: Éditions Complexes), pp. 237–252.

67. M. Dumoulin (ed.) (2007) *La Commission européenne, 1958–1972: Histoire et mémoires d'une institution* (Luxembourg: Office des Publications Officielles des Communautés européennes), pp. 138–139.
68. 'Letter from Chancellor Willy Brandt to President Georges Pompidou (27 November 1969)'. Depositum Egon Bahr. Box 441. Archiv der sozialen Demokratie der Friedrich-Ebert-Stiftung, Bonn.
69. I. Maes (2007) 'Projets d'intégration européenne à la Commission européenne au tournant des années 1970', in É. Bussière, M. Dumoulin, S. Schirmann (eds.), *Milieux économiques et intégration européenne en Europe occidentale au XXe siècle, La relance des années quatre-vingt (1979–1992)* (Brussels: P.I.E. - Peter Lang), pp. 35–50, here p. 38.
70. 'Draft note by Robert Triffin concerning German's government proposals to set up a European reserve fund (29 October 1969)' (handwritten and typed note). Triffin Archives Louvain-la-Neuve; 'Letter from Jean Monnet to Willy Brandt (31 October 1969)'. Wirtschaftskomitee Deutschland e.V. (WBA), Bundeskanzler, 14; 'Notes on the Meeting Monnet—Chancellor (7 November 1969)'. Bundesarchiv Koblenz (BAK) B136, 6410. See also A. Wilkens (2002) 'Une tentative prématurée. L'Allemagne, la France et les balbutiements de l'Europe monétaire', in É. Du Réau, R. Frank (eds.), *Dynamiques européennes. Nouvel espace, nouveaux acteurs: 1969–1981* (Paris: Publications de la Sorbonne), pp. 80–81; A. Wilkens (1999) '*L'Allemagne et le projet d'union économique et monétaire (1969–1972)*', in G. Bossuat, A. Wilkens (dirs.), *Jean Monnet, l'Europe et les chemins de la paix* (Paris: Publications de la Sorbonne), pp. 466–467.
71. R. Barre (2004) 'Entretien avec Raymond Barre', in M.-T. Bitsch, É. Bussière, G. Lavezzi, Histoire interne de la Commission européenne 1958–1973 (CONHIST.COM), 20 February (Louvain-la-Neuve: Université catholique de Louvain). http://archives.eui.eu (home page), accessed on 6 March 2018.
72. 'Statement by Willy Brandt (The Hague, 1 December 1969)', in *Bulletin of the European Communities*, 2 (1970) (Luxembourg: Office for Official Publications of the European Communities).
73. P. Werner (1969) 'Statement to the Conference of Heads of State or Government, The Hague (1 December 1969)', in *Documentation Bulletin*, 14 (Luxembourg: Information and Press Service, Ministry of State), pp. 3–7. Pierre Werner Family archive.

74. Ibid.
75. Ibid.
76. R. Barre (1970) 'Perspectives de la construction européenne après La Haye', in *Bulletin of the European Communities*, 2 (Luxembourg: Office for Official Publications of the European Communities), pp. 9–14, here p. 11.
77. 'Rapport de la 34e réunion des ministres des Finances des Communautés européennes à Paris, les 23 et 24 février', by Jan Willem Vredenberg van der Horst, Dutch Finance Minister. Archives of the Council of Ministers (2.02.05.02), No. 990. National Archives of the Netherlands (The Hague). Translation: Huygens ING, The Hague.
78. Originally published in 'Tagesnachrichten' [Latest News] of the Federal Ministry of Economic Affairs, No. 6122/27 February 1970, the German report was reproduced in H. Tietmeyer (1996) 'Währungsstabilität für Europa. Beiträge, Reden und Dokumente zur europäischen Währungsintegration aus vier Jahrzehnten' [Monetary Stability for Europe. Contributions, Speeches and Documents for four Centuries] (Baden-Baden: Nomos Verlag), pp. 88–94. See also 'Stufenplan zur Verwirklichung der Wirtschafts- und Währungsunion in der EWG' [Stage-by-Stage Plan for the Achievement of Economic and Monetary Union in the EEC] (Bonn, 22 January 1970).
79. 'Un plan de solidarité monétaire européenne en trois étapes 1971–1977' [A Three-Stage Plan for European Monetary Solidarity, 1971–1977], 27 January 1970 (Brussels: Ministry of Finance).
80. J.-C. Snoy et d'Oppuers (1989) *Rebâtir l'Europe: Mémoires, entretiens avec Jean-Claude Ricquier* [Rebuild Europe: Memories ans Conversations with Jean-Claude Ricquier] (Louvain-la-Neuve: Duculot). See also V. Dujardin, M. Dumoulin (eds.) (2010) *Jean-Charles Snoy. Homme dans la cité, artisan de l'Europe, 1907–1991* [Jean-Charles Snoy: Man in the City, Architect of Europe, 1907–1991] (Brussels: Le Cri Biographie).
81. P. Werner (1970) 'L'Europe en route vers l'Union Monétaire (28 février 1970)', in *Documentation Bulletin*, 1 (1970) (Luxembourg: Information and Press Service, Ministry of State), pp. 5–12. Pierre Werner Family archive.
82. Ibid., p. 11.

83. Ibid., p. 8.
84. 'Jeu de tableaux synoptiques concernant les quatre plans par étapes vers une union économique et monétaire: plan Werner, plan Schiller, plan belge et plan C.C.E' [Comparative tables concerning the four plans for the achievement by stages of an economic and monetary union: the Werner Plan, the Schiller Plan, the plan drawn up by Belgium, and the plan drawn up by the EEC], 18 March 1970 (Brussels: Commission of the European Communities, Directorate-General for Economic and Financial Affairs/Working Party on Economic and Monetary Union). Pierre Werner Family archive. Reproduced in Marc Dierikx (ed.) (2012) *Common Fate, Common Future: A Documentary History of Monetary and Financial Cooperation, 1947–1974* (The Hague: CVCE-Huygens ING), pp. 123–136.
85. Ibid.

4

Formation of the Werner Committee and an Overview of Its Work (March–October 1970)

On 4 March 1970, the Commission submitted proposals to the Council for the establishment by stages of an economic and monetary union, and the Council took its lead from these proposals in deciding on the composition of the ad hoc group.[1] There were three main reasons for the choice of members. First, responsibility for examining the issues raised by the Hague Summit had to be in the hands of officials in charge of economic and financial policy in the Member States. Second, the figures concerned had to have a special commitment and considerable experience in European integration. Lastly, any solution put forward had to have the widest possible support at government level.

On 6 March 1970, the Council of Ministers reached agreement on a decision on the procedure to be followed in respect of economic and monetary cooperation, and decided how the group of experts should be composed. The group was formed of the leaders of

E. Danescu (2012) 'Summary of the Werner Committee's Schedule and the Main Issues Addressed (6 March 1970–22 March 1971)', in *A Rereading of the Werner Report of 8 October 1970 in the Light of the Pierre Werner Family Archives* (Research corpus). https://www.cvce.eu/project/werner/ (home page), accessed on 6 March 2018.

E. Danescu, *Pierre Werner and Europe*,
Archival Insights into the Evolution of Economics,
https://doi.org/10.1007/978-3-319-96295-5_4

the various specialized committees of the EEC, who also held high national offices. They were the chairs of the EEC Monetary Committee (Bernard Clappier, Deputy Governor of the Banque de France); of the Committee of Governors of the Central Banks (Hubert Ansiaux, Governor of the National Bank of Belgium); of the Medium-Term Economic Policy Committee (Johann Schöllhorn, State Secretary in the German federal economics ministry); of the Anti-Cyclical Policy Committee (Gerard Brouwers, State Secretary in the Dutch economics ministry); and of the Budgetary Committee (Gaetano Stammati, Treasurer-general in the Italian ministry of the treasury). The Commission was represented by the director general for economic affairs (DG II), Ugo Mosca. It also ran the ad hoc group's secretariat, which was coordinated by Georges Morelli, a Commission official.

The experts were supposed to exercise their role on the committee in an individual capacity and in full independence. However, their behavior increasingly reflected the positions of their governments.

4.1 Pierre Werner's Appointment as Chairman—Three Different Accounts

This was how the idea of bringing together the chairmen of the Monetary Committee, the Committee of Governors of the Central Banks, the Medium-Term Economic Policy Committee, the Anti-Cyclical Policy Committee and the Budgetary Committee came about. They were all prominent figures who were listened to for their expertise, well-known for their wide experience and respected for their commitment to the European ideal. The composition of the group was such that Luxembourg was the only of the Six not be represented. It was at this point that Pierre Werner's name was put forward.

The decision-making process concerning the structure of the ad hoc committee and the choice of chairman was not straightforward, given the differing interests at play; it gave rise to complex diplomatic negotiations and confidential discussions. As to why he was chosen to chair the ad hoc group, our researches have turned up three different accounts.

The first version of what happened was given by Werner himself, in his memoirs, where he says that it was

> Baron Snoy, the Belgian Finance Minister, [who] telephoned on 25 February 1970 to see if I would agree to take on the chairmanship of the group on a proposal from himself and Valéry Giscard d'Estaing, the French Minister for Economic and Financial Affairs. The advantage they saw in this was that the political authority would thereby be represented in the group and they saw a parallel between this structure and that of the Spaak Committee which had drafted the Treaty of Rome. After thinking it over for a few days and having been given an assurance that the six governments would look favourably on such an appointment, I accepted. Pierre Harmel, the Belgian Foreign Minister, also encouraged me to do so. Emilio Colombo lost no time in siding with the, and Gaston Thorn had welcomed it and supported it. Mr. Schiller, the Minister from Germany, was also in favour. Only the Dutch Finance Minister, Mr. Witteveen, had had reservations to begin with.[2]

The verbatim transcript of the Council session on 6 March 1970 confirms that at this point it was Snoy who put forward Werner's name for the chairmanship of the group of experts. In his speech, the Dutch Prime Minister, Joseph Luns, welcomed the proposal, stressing that '[...] regarding the very interesting and detailed speech which the Belgian Finance Minister, Baron Snoy, has just made [...] I regard his proposal that the Prime Minister of Luxembourg be invited to assume the chairmanship of the ad hoc group as very timely, since, aside from his many other qualities, Mr. Werner has had a great deal of quite specific experience in this field; what is more, the importance of the office which he holds will make a definite contribution to the work of the group which Baron Snoy proposes we set up [...]'[3] On a proposal from Prime Minister Luns, the deadline for the completion of the group's report—May 1970 had been mentioned in the debates but was seen as being too short—was put back to the end of August of the same year.

A second account came from Bernhard Molitor, who revealed that

> [...] it was Mr Raymond Barre who put forward the name of Mr Pierre Werner — who was highly respected both for his political, economic and financial skills and for his commitment to Europe — for the chairmanship of the group [...]. Raymond Barre felt that it should be a minister from a Member State who made this proposal to the Conference of Finance Ministers in Paris which followed the Commission's adoption of the proposals. He talked about it to the Belgian Finance Minister, Snoy, who thought it was an excellent idea. But Baron Snoy did not put the proposal forward at the first exchange of views and it was the German Minister for Economic Affairs, Karl Schiller, who took on the task.[4]

According to this account, it was therefore Barre who was behind the proposal, most probably supported by Snoy, to whom he was very close—the latter had consulted Werner on his availability to chair the group of experts—but it was Karl Schiller who actually voiced the idea.

Gaston Thorn supplied a third explanation of events. In a filmed interview he gave in 1998, he said:

> Had Pierre Werner not made a start — and such a good start — I'm not sure, we might have had the euro one day all the same, but certainly not now! [...] When Pierre Werner produced his report, I was the one who put his name forward. I was Foreign Minister and it was at the Foreign Affairs Council where people were saying: 'What shall we do?' It was the old argument [...]: some people were saying you had to complete the economic union first and the currency would follow from that; others were saying 'you have to set up the currency and then the economy will follow'. Of course, what you had to do was both of those things! Which we did in the end, but it took a long time. And then when people were saying: 'Which working group shall we get to do this report and who is to chair it?', I was the one who proposed Pierre Werner, and certain people were surprised [...] A Foreign Affairs colleague, quite a high-placed one at that, came to see me and said: 'Gaston, withdraw this proposal! We've decided to do this report but some people are keener on it than others! The day might very well come when we will want to kill off this idea and it will be hard to do if the Prime Minister (Werner) is the head of the working group.' I said: 'Don't you see? That's exactly why I want him to be the head of it!' And that's how the Werner report was launched.[5]

Thorn's account seems apposite, because the Foreign Ministers of the Six met from 19 to 21 December 1969 and the agenda included discussions relating to the harmonisation of economic policies and monetary cooperation following on from the conclusions of the Hague Summit.[6] As the final communiqué from the summit only set out the Council's objective, which was, working in concert with the Commission, to draw up a plan by stages in 1970 looking ahead to economic and monetary union, it is conceivable that responsibility for the technical discussions on defining the framework and the practical means of achieving it was given to the Foreign Ministers of the Six. It is therefore quite possible that political negotiations concerning the name of the chairman took place there and that Snoy, with an agreement in principle from the specialist ministerial grouping already in place, then officially raised Werner's name.

The reality, though, was more complex, and sometimes quite different from the accounts that witnesses have left us. Documents recently identified in the German diplomatic archives throw a new and unexpected light on both the structure of the ad hoc committee and the choice of its chairman.[7]

We learn, for example, that at the meeting of Ministers for Economic Affairs and Finance on 24 February 1970, the question of the group of experts (consisting of the five chairmen of the specialist committees) being jointly chaired by a Luxembourg representative and a representative of the Commission arose. On that basis, emerged a French–German proposal to put forward the name of Clappier, Chairman of the Monetary Committee and Deputy Governor of the Banque de France.[8] On 3 March 1970, the Permanent Representation of Belgium to the Commission distributed, through confidential diplomatic channels, a proposal by J.-C. Snoy, whose country held the Presidency of the EC Council of Ministers in the first half of 1970. It was suggested that in the event that Prime Minister Werner became the Luxembourg representative, the chairmanship of the group should then be held by him alone. In his memoirs, Snoy confirms that Giscard d'Estaing was hoping to offer this position to Clappier. He himself recommended that the

Governor of the National Bank of Belgium, Ansiaux, become chairman and Clappier wanted to withdraw in favour of Ansiaux. 'After several private discussions, I proposed that Luxembourg be [represented] too, through its Minister of State, Pierre Werner himself'.[9]

The Belgian diplomatic communication stated that all the delegations had come out in favour of this proposal, except Germany which had not yet given its view. The German Permanent Representative received this news with concern, 'as the Luxembourg chairmanship might serve as a counterweight to the German position, which was in favour of harmonising the members' economic policies'.[10] A day later, the Belgian Ambassador to Bonn sent a personal letter to the Federal Minister for Economic Affairs officially reiterating Snoy's proposal and attaching a draft decision to be submitted to the Council of Finance Ministers for consideration at its meeting of 6 March 1970.[11] This document contained the final structure of the ad hoc committee (comprising the chairmen of the five specialist committees, a representative of the Luxembourg Government and a representative of the Commission), the timetable and the results expected from the committee's work (the drafting of a report to be submitted to the Council and the Commission in May) and the fact that the Commission would make its own proposals (which would be put before the Council for consideration at its meeting of 8 June 1970).

> Baron Snoy hopes that his colleagues will be able to accept the suggestion that Mr Werner be appointed chairman of the ad hoc committee. [...] Mr Werner, having received favourable opinions from Mr Colombo and Mr Giscard d'Estaing, declared that he was prepared to take on that task.[12]

Germany had to decide its position quickly, and it was not an easy matter. This was firstly because, in taking as its basis the principle of a joint chairmanship of the ad hoc committee and relying on the French–German proposal putting forward Bernard Clappier, it had made no provision for the about-turn executed by France (without informing Germany, what is more), nor had it given any other thought to the matter; and secondly because the prestige Pierre Werner enjoyed as the Prime Minister of a friendly country meant that extreme care had to be taken.

The Belgian proposal was of great interest to the Dutch, who wanted to react, but at the same time avoid a diplomatic blunder at all costs. Finance Minister Witteveen reportedly intended to oppose a single chairmanship, and Werner's name being put forward, citing as his official argument that Werner was of too high a rank compared to the group as a whole. The fact was that the Dutch considered that the Luxembourg Prime Minister's views on economic and monetary union differed too widely from its own and that it might have too strong an influence on the work of the group. The counterproposal from the Netherlands for the chairmanship of the ad hoc group (subject to acceptance by the person concerned) was State Secretary Schöllhorn, Chairman of the Medium-Term Economic Policy Committee. The Federal Ministry of Economic Affairs rejected any such invitation, on the pretext of the joint agreement reached with France to nominate Clappier, but the Germans were not in fact planning to oppose the choice of Werner under any circumstances.[13] Note, too, that on 5 March 1970 the *chef de cabinet* of Finance Minister Giscard d'Estaing asked the German Embassy in Paris if it was State Secretary Rohwedder who had put forward Werner's name! A few hours later, the French informed the embassy that they would not oppose the name of the Luxembourg Prime Minister being put forward, and the candidacy of Clappier was therefore dropped.

In the end, Germany's position was to back Werner's candidacy, which also had the support of the other delegations, including that of France, but to remain open to any other solutions which might emerge at the Council of Ministers' meeting.

Each of these versions of Werner's appointment as chairman of the committee of experts is true, but the reality seems to have been more complex. In the light of the archive documents and accounts explored and cited above, we have reached the following conclusion. It was the Commission's Vice-President Barre who proposed that Luxembourg should chair the committee on its own. Snoy on behalf of Belgium launched the official proposal, drafted and published the diplomatic document, and worked to secure the agreement of the three partners. But it was thanks to Karl Schiller, who managed to bypass the double-dealing by France and bring the Netherlands on board, that the initiative came to fruition.[14]

4.2 The Work of the Werner Committee—An Ambitious Task

Whatever the case may be, Pierre Werner's appointment as chairman was ratified by the Council on 6 March, and in that capacity he convened a preliminary meeting of the committee of experts in Luxembourg on 11 March 1970.

Of the fourteen official meetings of the Werner Group, nine were held in Luxembourg (consolidating its reputation as a permanent capital of the Communities), three in Brussels, one in Paris, one in Rome and one in Copenhagen, on the sidelines of the annual meeting of the IMF and the World Bank.[15]

4.2.1 Preliminary Meeting (Luxembourg, 11 March 1970)

The main purpose of the preliminary meeting of the Werner Committee was to approve the working method to be adopted and to set the deadline for reaching its conclusions.

It was established that the group would have a quorum for discussion if at least five of the seven members (the group's secretary did not have voting rights) were present and that decisions would be taken by simple majority. 'The group will do its best to present unanimous conclusions, but any member may ask for a minority opinion to be put forward'.

If required, experts could be called into elucidate specific points. Each member of the committee could appoint an assistant of his choice, and secretarial services for the group were provided by the secretariat of the Monetary Committee. The group's discussions were considered to be confidential and would only be minuted briefly. They decided to meet 'at intervals such as to allow for a preliminary report to be delivered to the Council by the end of May and for its discussions to be concluded, if possible, by the end of July'.

At the first meeting, Werner in the chair gave his colleagues a preliminary comparative overview of the discussions on monetary integration and the proposals put forward at the beginning of the year by the Belgian Government (the Snoy Plan), the German Government (the Schiller Plan), the Luxembourg Government (the first Werner Plan, also known as the five-point Luxembourg Plan) and the Commission. He set out what he felt should be the priority focus for their work, namely putting forward practical ideas and methods for achieving the short-, medium-, and long-term objectives. He emphasised the need to take all avenues and experiences that might prove useful at the various stages into account, even if their usefulness was not apparent at the outset. He also called on his colleagues to draw up notes describing the measures they planned to take to achieve the final objective and to put them forward for discussion.[16]

To underpin the reflection and documentation of its representative on the Werner Committee, the Commission set up an inter-directorate working party on economic and monetary union (based around DGII), which included the directors and secretary of the Monetary Committee. For reasons of efficacy, the private office of Commission Vice-President Barre was also involved in this working party and offered its support to the committee of experts, among other things for logistical and financial questions and matters of protocol.

The preliminary documentation mentioned above consisted of political and scientific papers, explanatory presentations about economic union and currency, 'stage-by-stage' plans which already existed and accounts of similar experiments in that area, articles, and press releases. As the work went ahead, further material was added, to elucidate points of interest which came up in the course of discussion. Two major issues command attention in the documentation: the accession of the UKto the EC and the establishment of a European Reserve Fund. On this latter point, the two main papers were drafted by Robert Triffin, including one which arose out of discussions in the Monnet Committee. Through the whole period of the committee's work, Werner and Triffin, who knew each other and were working together since early 1960, kept in close touch by way of dialogue and joint action, particularly thanks to the good offices of Monnet.

4.2.2 First Meeting (Luxembourg, 20 March 1970)

The chairman convened the inaugural meeting of the Werner Group on 20 March 1970 in Luxembourg City.

By way of preparation for this meeting, Barre notified the group 'that it is likely that over the next few months and at least until the end of July, the ad hoc group will be meeting at least three times a month', and requested that any governmental experts called into assist the group should be treated in the same manner as the members of the group 'in view of the very high level of those involved and the nature of the matters with which the group is dealing'.[17]

The comparative overview, the target dates and the content of the various stages as set out in these notes, and the fact that they came first (dating from the preliminary meeting of the Werner Group on 6 March 1970), suggest to us that they were the inspiration behind the Commission's paper (dated 18 March 1970), in which the comparative analysis adopts the same layout.

At the inaugural meeting, the members of the group introduced their deputies, whom they had each chosen and who took part in the work. They were Johnny Schmitz (from Luxembourg, assistant to the chairman), Jacques Mertens de Wilmars (from Belgium, assistant to Baron Hubert Ansiaux, Chairman of the Committee of Governors), Anthony Looijen (from the Netherlands, assistant to Gerard Brouwers, Chairman of the Anti-Cyclical Policy Committee), Jean-Michel Bloch-Lainé (from France, assistant to Bernard Clappier, Chairman of the Monetary Committee), Hans Tietmeyer (from Germany, assistant to Johann Baptist Schöllhorn, Chairman of the Medium-Term Economic Policy Committee), Simone Palumbo (from Italy, assistant to Gaetano Stammati, Chairman of the Budgetary Policy Committee) and Jean-Claude Morel (assistant to Ugo Mosca, Director-General for Economic and Financial Affairs at the EEC).

Then, there was a first exchange of views on the main problems associated with setting up a plan by stages. Werner made a detailed presentation and comparison of the various plans, measures and proposals for bringing about economic and monetary union ('where there is a variety of monetary plans, there has to be a synthesis'), laid down the priority areas for reflection (the final objective and the creation of the institutional structure), and set out the main target dates for the group's work, including the final result, which, in the form of a report to the Council, was to be achieved by the end of July at the latest.

The description of the starting point did not raise any major debates.

> [...] We weren't starting from a blank canvas. Economic integration was already under way. [...] The liberalisations that had already taken place were resulting in a degree of interdependence such that national imbalances were having an impact on the economic situations of the other partners. The final objective was economic and monetary union, in other words an area in which goods and services, people and capital could circulate freely and without distortion of competition. A union of this sort would involve the full and irreversible convertibility of national currencies and the elimination of exchange rate fluctuations.[18]

Although the main objective was clear and all parties were in agreement on this, determining its exact details gave rise to bitter clashes between the 'economists' and the 'monetarists': 'from the outset, the German representative J. B. Schöllhorn [...]assisted by H. Tietmeyer, supported the position of the German Minister for Economic Affairs, Schiller, that prior convergence of economic policies was imperative. [...] H. Ansiaux (from the National Bank of Belgium), advocated the monetarist stance with a fervour that surprised me at the time. B. Clappier [...] assisted by J. M. Bloch-Lainé, supported Ansiaux's position, as did G. Stammati [...]. Brouwers [...] was closer to Schöllhorn'.[19]

The discussions bring out the fundamental thinking of its members as regards the objective to be attained, the means of getting there and the recommended timetable. Priority issues were the pooling of the Six's reserves and the establishment of a Community central bank. Werner's promptings at the preliminary meeting therefore took the form of a decision. The Commission representative was given responsibility for drawing up a note 'describing the final stage of the process of economic and monetary integration, with a reference to the part to be played, at that stage, by common reserves and, possibly, a Community central bank'.[20]

The other members, each according to the area for which he is responsible in his capacity as chairman of one of the EC Committees, were to draft a note describing the steps each planned to take to achieve the final objective. The group agreed that the chairmen were not obliged to consult their respective committees on either the drafting of these notes or the subsequent work of the group.

4.2.3 Second Meeting (Brussels, 7 April 1970)

By the time of this meeting, the group's documentary collection was supplemented with a forward-study note dated 31 March 1970 entitled 'L'état de l'Union économique et monétaire en 1978 à l'issue du plan par étapes' ['The state of economic and monetary union in 1978 following completion of the plan by stages'], drawn up by the inter-directorate working party. It dealt with monetary solidarity (the irrevocable fixing of the parities between EC currencies, abolition of any possibility of exchange-rate fluctuation around the parity relationship between EC currencies, general use of a European unit of account, a European Reserve Fund), taxation (harmonisation of indirect taxation and limits on VAT-rate variation between countries to around 2–3%, substantial rapprochement in the area of excise duties, commentaries on the advisability of extending forms of direct taxation), capital markets, economic policy in general, specific economic policies and monetary, budgetary, structural, and salary policies.

In response to promptings by the chairman at the inaugural meeting, Brouwers, the Chairman of the Anti-Cyclical Policy Committee, drafted this confidential document 'La méthode de réalisation d'une union économique et monétaire, vue dans l'optique de la politique conjoncturelle' ['The method for the achievement of an economic and monetary union from the perspective of conjunctural policy'], which he submitted to the other members of the Werner Committee on 3 April.[21] This document did not aim to look at the question from every angle but to indicate the main priorities with regard to the establishment of a homogeneous common market for which short-term economic policy would serve as an instrument for optimum, balanced growth.[22] The main points of this note can be summarised as follows. If a Community of growth and stability were to be established, it was vital for the Community's objectives to be clearly defined. To this end, a prior consultation procedure was deemed to be appropriate. This should contain a 'system of indicators' that would be able to identify points of divergence, delays, and exceptions and would be accompanied by appropriate instruments for analysis, notably in the areas of statistics and forecasting. The countries would be able to agree on the creation of political instruments for direct action by means of specific legislation or practices directly linked to the economic climate as part of a comprehensive structural policy. (In this area, the package of legislation on stability implemented by Germany on 8 June 1967, known as the *Stabilitätgesetz* ('Gesetz zur Förderung der Stabilität und des Wachstums der Wirtschaft', or Law for the Promotion of Stability and Growth), was taken as a basis). This recommendation was based on the budgetary philosophy in the Netherlands, whereby action in the fields of both expenditure and taxation would serve either to moderate or to incentivise, according to changing economic circumstances, and would be part of a comprehensive structural policy.

All short-term economic policy instruments had to be harmonised, including budgetary policy instruments (the main matter at hand was the short-term economic impact of the volume of deficits and their financing) and monetary policy instruments. As progress continued to be achieved in policy harmonisation, the possibility that Community policy might be exercised by a central authority would take shape, and it was at this stage that national responsibilities in the area of short-term economic policy would be transferred to the Community, with considerable repercussions at institutional level. Brouwers noted that this did not necessarily mean that everything had to be centralised and applied in a uniform manner, but it had to be the case for the essential elements of budgetary policy, as well as for monetary and income policy. Once the process of harmonisation had been concluded, the economic union could be completed by a monetary union.[23]

The Chairman of the Medium-term Economic Policy Committee, Schöllhorn, submitted the document 'Wirtschaftsunion als Grundlage der Währungsunion' ['Economic union as a basis for monetary union'], the title of which—stressing the primacy of economic union—was in fact a summary of the German view of the question.[24]

The Commission representative, Mosca, then tabled a paper focusing on the first stage of a plan by stages and stressing the part to be played by capital markets.[25] The document provides for the establishment of a special group attached to the Monetary Committee responsible for conducting regular exchanges of information and consultations on trends in the capital markets and for launching action to coordinate Member States' policies in respect of them.

In line with the concerns on the imminent accession of the UK Werner asked the Commission representative to look into the questions arising from setting up economic and monetary union with Community enlargement in prospect. A study was drawn up and was distributed to the members of the group at the meeting of 7 April 1970.[26] This document dealt in particular with the implications of British accession for the coordination of economic policies, the capital market and taxation. The study looked in detail at the role of the pound sterling,[27] the strengthening of monetary solidarity and the consequences if the UK were to take part in the mechanisms of monetary cooperation, as well as the European Reserve Fund.[28]

As the intellectual disagreements between 'monetarists' and 'economists' in the Werner Group grew more and more acrimonious, and out of a concern to hammer out a common Benelux countries position, Werner marshalled the political forces around Belgians Snoy and Ansiaux. It was in this context that the Finance Ministers and the Governors of the Central Banks of the three countries met in Brussels on 2 April 1970, on the invitation of Belgium, which was holding the presidency of the EC Council of Ministers at that time. The discussions focused on how the final objective of economic and monetary union should be defined, and what resources should be put into getting there, especially as regards monetary and credit policy, budgetary and fiscal policy, the integration of the capital markets, and in terms of institutions.[29] Issues raised also included the strengthening of monetary solidarity, the consequences of possible participation by the UK in the mechanisms of monetary cooperation, and the impact of the pound sterling on the European Reserve Fund.

Despite the efforts of all involved, the desired aim was only partially achieved. The Belgians and Luxembourgers shared the monetarist view of France, while the Dutch sided clearly with the German economists. This meant that there could be no agreement. On the other hand, the meeting was an opportunity for the Belgians to assert their position as supporters of the idea of setting up a currency equalisation fund, to offset the floating rates which were increasingly applied.[30]

Even though the Dutch Minister Witteveen thought the priorities lay in other areas (he was concerned about the majority votes which would be taken in a monetary organisation and which would affect the Member States' credit policy), the Governor of the National Bank of the Netherlands, Zijlstra, shared the Belgian view, believing that a fund of that kind would be a way of making the currencies of the Six more independent from the dollar.

At the meeting on 7 April, the discussions between 'economists' and 'monetarists' were set off and stimulated largely by the tabling of the German paper with its calls for economic and budgetary harmonisation. Werner—who appreciated the Germans' views in principle but saw them as 'too severe and not measured enough'—moved the discussion in another direction by launching, as a counterproposal, the idea of the exchange stabilisation fund which was backed by Baron Ansiaux.[31] The discussions also focused on how the final objective of economic and monetary union should be defined, and what resources should be put into getting there, especially as regards monetary and credit policy, budgetary and fiscal policy, the integration of the capital markets, and in terms of institutions.[32]

In line with the proposal he had made at the preliminary meeting, and as a way of organising the committee's work in the future, Werner suggested that an open-ended summary be drawn up, summarising the ideas set out in the various documents or verbally in the group. This summary—drafted by the chair with the assistance of the secretariat—would be tabled at the next meeting, scheduled for 30 April in Rome.

4.2.4 Third Meeting (Rome, 30 April 1970)

Rome hosted the third meeting of the Werner Group, following approaches by the Italian member, Gaetano Stammati, Chairman of the Budgetary Policy Committee. His request to the European Commission sparked off a great deal of discussion in the Secretariat-General, which, as it was in charge of the logistics of the ad hoc group, had to put in a great deal of effort.[33] Considering what was on the agenda, the preparations for this meeting had been very lively.

As the ideas, aims, and strategies of Werner and Baron Ansiaux were in line with each other and they knew each other well thanks to regular political and personal contact, they worked together on the questions relating to the exchange stabilisation fund and the reserve fund. The Luxembourg monetary plan submitted in February 1970—based on the arguments Pierre Werner had published and developed since 1962—allowed for mutual assistance to be incorporated, from stage one, into the international monetary relations system by partly assigning to it special drawing rights (SDRs) from the various Member States and managing them on a Community basis. It would, he thought, be the first step towards the establishment of a reserve fund and this would give practical support for the medium-term monetary assistance which would shortly be decided upon.

Baron Ansiaux was gradually won over to the Luxembourg view and, at the meeting on 7 April 1970, came forward as the standard-bearer of an exchange stabilisation fund. On 22 April, he sent Pierre Werner, at the latter's request and on the letterhead of the National Bank of Belgium, a note on the 'legal and technical aspects of a pooling of special drawing rights', particularly since 'there had been a proposal in The Hague that the EC countries should pool a part of their SDRs to support the creation of a medium-term credit fund'.[34] The Belgian document refers to SDR transfer operations between the EC partners.

Two days later, Ansiaux responded to another request from Werner and sent him a confidential technical note 'setting out the functioning and the merits of a European exchange equalisation fund' and highlighting the difficulties associated with stabilising the exchange rates between Community currencies.[35] This document was debated at the Werner Group meeting on 14 May 1970 and amended as a result. The conclusions which emerged from it were included in the final report.

At the same time as his exchanges with Ansiaux, the chair and the secretariat of the ad hoc group set about drafting a route map for the plan by stages.[36] It identified the starting point and defined the final objective and the requisite and desirable steps—in terms of economic policy, monetary solidarity and institution-building—to be taken to get there. Alongside this summary, there was a list of the specific planned measures—especially for the first stage, which was regarded as having started—in accordance with medium-term Community regulations and directives. The document was sent to the members of the group on 22 April 1970 as preparation for the Rome meeting.[37]

The Werner Group continued with its work in select committee form and in a confidential atmosphere. The media, which had given wide coverage to the Hague Summit and the appointment of Pierre Werner to head the group, fell silent, particularly since the committee of experts was sparing in the information it disclosed to the outside world. However, the questions raised by the plan by stages aroused some degree of creative and participatory enthusiasm, which swelled when the final report was being written and continued after it had been published. Pride of place went to the *Deutscher Gewerkschaftsbund* [General German Trade Union Confederation] which, 'being prepared to shoulder its share of the responsibility by taking part in the democratic decisions which the establishment of an economic and monetary union involves [...] drew up a proposal for a plan by stages', which it submitted to the President of the European Commission, Jean Rey, on 20 March 1970, the very day that the Werner Group started holding its official meetings.[38] This viewpoint was a valuable addition to the compendium of documents supplied to the group of experts.

Academic and university circles in Europe and the United States were very interested in the Werner Group's work, especially since, as well as working out practical solutions, it produced theoretical definitions relating to economic and monetary union. When the Commission representative attended a seminar on the optimum monetary zone in Madrid at the beginning of February 1970, he was asked to give the university teachers there, especially those from the US, information about the various plans for building economic and monetary union by stages and to supply them with the relevant documents. There were more than a dozen requests, but in the end only those from Professors Triffin and Machlup were met. The other requests were met later through the good offices of the directorate of the Commission.[39]

Following the meeting on 30 April 1970, the group adopted, as its report to the Council, 'a model including a description of the present situation, the finishing line and the principles to be followed in carrying out the plan by stages', and decided—at least for the purposes of this report—to confine itself to a definition of the first stage, containing the steps which should be taken in various fields.

For the organisation of its work, the group decided 'to delegate the writing of a draft report to the assistants [...] who will meet on 6 and 8 May under the chairmanship of Jacques Mertens de Wilmars, an economist and professor at the Université Catholique de Louvain and economic adviser to the National Bank of Belgium'.[40]

4.2.5 Fourth and Fifth Meetings (Luxembourg, 14 May and 20 May 1970)

On the agenda for the fourth meeting was a further exchange of views on economic and monetary union. The deputies' group was expected to supply a draft report as a basis for reflection so that a final document could be drawn up by July to meet the deadline set at the outset.

The Werner Committee met for this purpose, as planned, in Brussels on 6 and 8 May, with support from the Commission's Directorate for Economic and Financial Affairs (DGII). The Pierre Werner Family archives mention a 'Draft Report to the Council and the Commission' in the form of a 'Plan by stages for the establishment of economic and monetary union', dated 11 May 1970, which was submitted by Jacques Mertens de Wilmars. In a covering letter sent with this confidential document, Mertens de Wilmars pointed out that

> the experts have not heard decisions being taken on certain issues of principle which remain open, even though the text of their draft includes proposals and solutions relating to those issues.

The sensitive subjects included the transfer of responsibility from the national to the Community level without engendering lasting tension, medium-term conjunctural policy, the necessity for the main decisions on monetary and credit policy to be taken in common, and real decision-making power being given to the Community bodies. The deputies' group concluded that the establishment of economic and monetary union must be embarked on in an evolving, gradual manner, building on the measures already adopted to enhance the coordination of economic policies and monetary cooperation.

It should be noted that, while aware of the need for economic and monetary policies to be developed centrally (even if the decision-making power remained in the hands of the existing structures), the Werner Committee stated straight away that it was not in a position to make proposals regarding political structures. The subsequent criticism of the final Werner Report for its failure to offer a detailed analysis of the architecture of the Community institutions was therefore unjustified, given that the Committee had removed this matter from the scope of its reflections from the outset.

The two plenary sittings of the Werner Group held in Luxembourg on 14 and 20 May were undoubtedly the occasion for hard-fought discussions and arguments. There are no minutes, even summary minutes, of them in the archives. In his memoirs, Werner tells us that

> after five working meetings studded with arguments, not to say incidents of various kinds, we are nevertheless managing to put forward a summary view of the questions raised, in the form of an interim report to the Governments.[41]

If we put all these elements together, one theory could be that when the interim report was being written, there were such confrontations going on within the group that it was impossible to reach any unanimous conclusions. This means that a fundamental principle of the group—and one adopted at the outset of its work—was breached. The reason why there were no minutes may, therefore, be not so much that there was negligence on the part of the secretariat but the profound differences of opinion among the members. Mediation by Werner from the chair would then have played a decisive part in putting the different factions back together. At the end of the fifth meeting, agreement was reached on the text of the interim report and it was sent to the Finance Ministers and the Presidents of the Council and the Commission on 22 May 1970.

The German version of the interim report caused yet more friction: Hans Tietmeyer, on behalf of State Secretary Schöllhorn, 'draws attention to the fact that the German text [...] is not in keeping with the decisions the Werner Group took in Luxembourg. On a proposed amendment put forward by Director-General Mosca, the group agreed on the following text:

> 'These transfers of responsibility represent a process of fundamental political importance, entailing the gradual development of political cooperation in the various fields.' The text given in the present document ('these transfers of responsibility entail the gradual development of political cooperation in the various fields') is a considerable weakening of the originally agreed wording. Mr. Schöllhorn is very concerned that the political character of economic and monetary union should be clearly and unequivocally stated.[42]

4.2.6 Further Work by the Werner Committee

On 29 May 1970, the Finance Ministers met in Venice, under the chairmanship of Giscard d'Estaing, to debate the aims of economic and monetary union. The governors of the central banks of the Six, the Chairman of the Monetary Committee, Clappier, and the Chairman of the Committee of Alternates of the 'Group of Ten', Rinaldo Ossola, were also invited to attend.[43]

The agenda for the first day of this session of the Council of Ministers included multi-year projections for the Community budgets (a study drafted by the Budgetary Policy Committee, chaired by Stammati), the use of budgetary policy as an instrument for short-term economic policy,[44] and the need for a push towards fiscal harmonisation.[45] A special section was devoted to the issues arising from the question of monetary integration in the Community and international monetary aspects.

On the second day, discussions focused on the interim report. Werner gave a summary account of the conclusions reached by the group of experts, identifying the points on which members agreed and disagreed and the questions which required further discussion.[46] The debates were lively and threw up contradictions but led to no decisions as to the priorities for economic and monetary union.[47]

Schiller noted the fundamental political importance of the planned process and emphasised the need for further reflection on the transfer of responsibilities to the Community bodies. With regard to institutional aspects, he suggested 'a body [that would be] given responsibility for short-term economic policy and a body tasked with the central preparation of decisions in the monetary field. The latter body should be federal in nature and should be given a large degree of autonomy from political authorities'.[48] Schiller was against setting up the exchange stabilisation fund during the first stage and against reducing the margins for fluctuation, seeing this as premature.

France, represented by Giscard d'Estaing, emphasised that the political architecture of economic and monetary union was a question of perspective, and that therefore a body with federal-type responsibilities was a matter for the final stage and it was not yet appropriate to go any further. It was important to concentrate on the first stage, in which he believed that 'economic convergence was not a prerequisite for monetary progress'. Belgian Minister Snoy took the same view. He also shared the French opinion on the implementation of an exchange stabilisation fund during the first stage.

In his address, the Dutch representative turned his attention to a question raised by the Werner Group's interim report. Should six currencies or one single currency be envisaged? He believed that retaining six national currencies involved a degree of risk. 'A currency always reflects the confidence we have in a government responsible for managing economic and monetary policy. [...]

For the final stage of economic and monetary union, a single currency should be planned. On the other hand, there could be several national banks within a "federal reserve" system, but this must be independent from the governments'.[49]

Exchange arrangements were the area which sparked off the most discussions. Werner gave his views on the economic implications of the various exchange systems, such as the impact of reducing the margins for fluctuation on interest rates. Giscard d'Estaing wanted the technical conditions which would have to be brought about if such a regime were to be implemented to be clearly defined. Minister Colombo and Governor Zijlstra both proposed that the group, working with the Governors, should consider whether the stabilisation fund could not be replaced, as a first step, by greater cooperation between the central banks as regards their intervening on the exchange markets. Snoy stressed that the report must set out the economic consequences of a special monetary regime for the Six and emphasised the need to consider both the advantages and drawbacks of an exchange stabilisation fund.

This idea took shape a few days later, in the form of a common strategy worked out by Werner and Snoy according to which the task of delivering technical opinions on the monetary problems under consideration would be delegated to the Committee of Governors (we will come back to this point later).

Lastly, Barre gave the Commission's view on what was expected of this new period of reflection. The Werner Group would have to make it clear that there were three levels which needed to be reached one after the other: concerted policy by the central banks in this field and in terms of their interventions on the foreign exchange markets, followed by the use of Community currencies in intra-Community settlements (and a preliminary cut in margins) and, lastly, the setting up of an exchange stabilisation fund.

Summarising the conclusions of the meeting, the Emilio Colombo firstly noted that general agreement had been reached on a large number of suggestions formulated by the Werner Committee. The ultimate aims of economic and monetary union as identified in the interim report were considered to have been accepted. In this gradual process, there would be specific objectives for each stage, the first of which—lasting three years—would involve specific, stringent goals in the areas of coordination of economic policy and monetary aspects. These processes had to be carried out in parallel. There were no longer any differences of opinion with regard to the fundamental options concerning the need for a coordinated budgetary policy, quantitative objectives for a medium-term economic policy, coordination of short-term economic policy and consultation with both sides of industry (the 'social partners') to determine an income policy. Concerning this matter, it was noted that the related consultation procedures would have to be made more precise and more stringent.

At the end of the Venice session, the Council of Ministers approved the interim report and reached the unanimous conclusion that the group should continue its work with a view to reaching the requisite agreement on the issues in dispute and making further progress on the questions on which there was consensus. The ministers asked the Werner Group to determine the obligations of the Member States in coordinating economic policies to reach convergence in economic development. The aims and instruments that would enable the integration programme to be achieved should be set out in as much detail as possible. It was important to analyse whether these instruments could be created on the basis of the existing treaty or whether it had to be amended. The results of this reflection were to be set out in a final report.

Emilio Colombo proposed that the structure of the final report should be better defined and the specific targets and instruments of the monetary integration programme be more clearly stated. Werner suggested a series of 'warning lights' to give the alert when sensitive situations arose in that area, and also that the report should include proposals for the harmonisation of monetary and credit policy. Regarding monetary and budgetary policy, the Governor of the National Bank of the Netherlands supported precise criteria for the adoption of a budgetary stance (structure, main areas, deficit, and financing). Zijlstra then proposed making a more thorough study of ways of harmonising monetary policy instruments.

Although the ministers were in agreement on many common conclusions, there were still differences of opinion, notably regarding the creation of an exchange equalisation fund prior to a common reserve fund. Nevertheless, it seemed essential to improve coordination of the policies of intervention by the central banks on the exchange market.

In preparation for this meeting, Pierre Werner had several conversations with Jean Monnet. The first was about the monetary individualisation of the ECy. Monnet was asked to use his good offices to consult the Director of the IMF, Pierre-Paul Schweitzer. The IMF had no objections to Europe adopting a common or even single currency. The two men then held lengthy discussions on the exchange stabilisation fund and the influences that needed to be harnessed for this to become a reality. On this topic, Monnet made a point of recommending Werner 'not to rush the decision on the exchange stabilisation fund too much, because there would not be unanimity on the question. His concern doubtless echoed that manifested by Willy Brandt, whom he advised me to contact when the time was ripe'.[50] Monnet's counsel of moderation was very probably prompted by the heated discussions that had taken place at the last two meetings of the Group, during which Werner and Clappier had been particularly voluble on the subject of the exchange stabilisation fund.

Discussion of economic and monetary union was the main item on the agenda for the Council of Ministers, which met in Luxembourg on 8 and 9 June and approved a continuation of the work on the basis of the interim report. 'The discussion as such did not lead to anything new, except that the Dutch minister, Mr. Witteveen, carried Mr. Schiller's position further by making further demands on the institutional front'.[51] A primary aim was the establishment of economic and monetary union within ten years (from 1 January 1971).

> With a view to getting its decisions implemented and in order to obtain a definition, as quickly as possible, of certain institutional and technical aspects of the agreements reached, the Council called on the ad hoc group chaired by Mr Werner to submit its final report to it at the beginning of September 1970. It made clear what its remit was by instructing it, in particular, to draw up, in specific terms, practical arrangements for the first stage.[52]

Werner set out the work involved in the plan by stages and the content of the interim report, and went on to stress the need for further discussion of the issues. In his handwritten notes for the speech, continuing along the lines already laid down in Venice, Werner said he believed there should be six priority subject areas for these further discussions. These were additional study of the institutional aspects, and the devising and setting up of effective instruments—obligations combined with sanctions—for the coordination of short- and medium-term economic policy. 'Limited, specific proposals as to budgetary policy' would have to be worked out, and further thought given to deficit financing and the effects of a policy of general liquidity on the economic system. Another area was the overall harmonisation of monetary policy and credit policy instruments. As far as exchange regulations were concerned, he specifically made provision for 'consulting the governors'. He also recommended 'examining all the existing funds' (in this connection the name of Triffin, and his definition, were noted). We do not know whether Pierre Werner stuck to the same order of subjects in his speech as in his notes, but all the proposals in them appeared in the Council's decision on continuing the work of the group. It also stipulated that the views of the Committee of Governors on specific monetary problems should be sought.

The Venice meeting probably led to further informal discussions between the members of the Werner Group, the Finance Ministers and the Vice-President of the Commission, Barre. In Werner's private archives we found a document with no letterhead, date or signature entitled 'Travaux supplémentaires du groupe ad hoc "plan par étapes" à la suite de la conférence des ministres des Finances de Venise' ['Further work of the ad hoc "plan by stages" group following the Venice conference of Finance Ministers')—with handwritten comments by Pierre Werner. These notes refer to proposals on the main lines of action (on which, in all probability, there was general agreement) and say who made them. Specific points of view are also highlighted.[53] It emerges from this that four main lines for further progress were worked out: the institutional field,[54] stepping up the coordination of economic policies,[55] budgetary and monetary policy and exchange arrangements.

This document was probably the outcome of direct collaboration between Pierre Werner and the secretary of the 'plan by stages' committee, Georges Morelli, who not only managed all the information and documentation but also took part in all the meetings relating to the work of the group (meetings of ministers, meetings of various committees of experts, the inter-directorate working party at the Commission, etc.). The proposals were expanded and, together with practical measures, appeared sometime later in the route map for further discussions in the Werner Group.

The contribution Werner made to defining how the work was to continue was a significant one. Because of his authority as group chairman and his know-how as consensus builder, the group's proposals were taken up by various decision-making bodies (Finance Ministers and the Council of Ministers) and translated into official decisions. A telling example is the special involvement of the central bankers in the Werner Committee's work.[56]

As it had been fairly obvious since 22 May that the work of the group will be pursued, Werner continued to explore ways to move forward and the arguments to be worked on and carried on a constant, often confidential dialogue with Baron Ansiaux. Their exchange of letters between 3 and 12 June shows that the two men, confident of the vital part the Committee of Governors could play in setting up the exchange stabilisation fund, put together a cunning strategy. Werner asked Ansiaux to draft a proposal for a letter which the chairman of the ad hoc group (Werner) would send to the Chairman of the Committee of Governors (Ansiaux) asking the committee to deliver opinions on several matters. The letter was about the exchange arrangements—in particular, a shrinking of the margins between the currencies of the Common Market countries; the advantages and disadvantages of an exchange stabilisation fund in the first stage; and consideration of what should be accomplished during the first stage in order to tighten up monetary policies.

As the Council Decision of 9 June 1970 recommended seeking the point of view of the central bankers, three days later Werner, in line with the strategy he had worked out with Ansiaux, sent a letter asking for this specialised opinion. The previous day, through diplomatic channels, Werner had received comments from Clappier, supplying him with further details regarding technical procedures and the consequences of reducing the margins for fluctuation, and on the questions surrounding the exchange stabilisation fund.[57]

On 16 June, Ansiaux sent Werner a reply undertaking to supply an opinion by 15 July, focusing 'on the advisability of harmonising monetary policy instruments and effectively tightening up the Member States' monetary policies'.[58] The detailed study on the measures to be adopted, on the other hand, was postponed until the last three months of the year (1970), to be carried out as and when the information available would make it possible to reach specific conclusions. This was a very cautious approach. Ansiaux at once set about convening the committee of experts, which held its inaugural meeting on 25 June 1970. After holding five other meetings (on 1–2 July, 9 July, 16 July, 23–24 July, and 30 July 1970) the committee delivered its opinion.

4.2.7 Sixth Meeting (Luxembourg, 24 June 1970)

With the backing of the mandate given to him by the Council Decision of 9 June, Werner convened the sixth meeting of the group, which was held in Luxembourg on 24 June 1970.

At the beginning of the sitting, he told his colleagues that they needed to continue with their work, to return to problems which had been left unresolved in the interim report and supply the additional information requested. In the ensuing discussion, the argument between economists and monetarists broke out again. Schöllhorn, sticking to his earlier position, repeated that the group must focus its efforts on economic policy coordination. Brouwers endorsed this view. On the monetarists' side, Clappier and Ansiaux played an active part while Stammati stayed more in the background. The debate was open and passionate, with Werner tending to side with the monetarists, although he abided by the chairman's obligation to remain balanced and by the need to push for a 'parallel movement' approach to economic and monetary progress. To give them an opportunity to explain and argue their shared point of view, the Dutch and German members, working together with the Commission representative and the group secretariat, were asked to draw up a note setting out 'the ideas which might be put forward with regard to tightening up the procedures for economic policy coordination'.[59] The Dutch member was also responsible for submitting a note on the kind of institutional problems that would appear at the final stage of economic and monetary union.

To put the finishing touches to the interim report, of which a first draft had been requested for the end of August, the group's working timetable made provision for the following four meetings: 7 July 1970 in Paris, 27 July and 11 September in Luxembourg and 25 September in Copenhagen, at the Annual Meeting of the Governors of the International Monetary Fund.

Werner carried on his informal dialogue with Baron Ansiaux, who was incidentally very close to Triffin, and tried to find a path to appeasement in a dispute which was becoming increasingly heated. The German position, which was supported by the Dutch, was becoming more entrenched and thereby jeopardising hopes of a consensus and final agreement. Ansiaux wrote to Triffin on 23 June 1970, with a copy to Werner. In his letter he asked Triffin to exercise his good offices. Ansiaux was sorry that '[his] initiatives are not meeting only with approval; our German and Dutch friends, in particular, are fiercely opposed to them. They say that nothing can be accomplished in the monetary area until complete convergence in economic policies has been achieved'.[60] He then went on to summarise the nub of his position, arguing for 'progress in parallel, which can be accomplished in both the monetary and the economic fields, and that parallel progress on the monetary question will support that which must be made in the economic field'. As regards the exchange stabilisation fund, Ansiaux asked Triffin to help him '[…] by getting the Germans to accept the idea; once the Dutch are isolated, they will surrender in the end, although they will be very difficult in the negotiations'. We also learn from the letter that Monnet had also been asked to give his backing for this position, but that he did not do so. 'Jean Monnet never brought out his paper and he said nothing to the Germans at all'.

Triffin sent his reflections on the interim report directly to Werner in a document entitled 'Vers l'union économique et monétaire de la Communauté' ['Towards economic and monetary union in the Community']. This document, in which the principle and the spirit of 'parallel movement' were fully shared, left its mark on the subsequent work of the Werner Committee, which made this principle the backbone of the final report.

4.2.8 Seventh Meeting (Paris, 7 July 1970)

On the sidelines of the Finance Ministers' meeting, the Werner Group met in Paris on 7 July.

On 3 July, the Chairman of the Budgetary Policy Committee, Stammati, at the chairman's request, drew up a note on stepping up the coordination of economic policy and proposed to submit it at the meeting. At the same time, the note drafted by the Germans and Dutch, in collaboration with the Commission member and the group secretariat, was produced. Focusing on increased coordination of economic policies, it pointed to the fundamental part which must be played by two Community bodies: the Council of Ministers for Economic Affairs and the Committee of Governors.

These two documents were the focus of discussion at the meeting of the Werner Committee. In his oral presentation, Stammati enlarged on some of the subjects covered in his written note, particularly taxation. So as to have available to it complete, detailed papers on the matter under discussion, the group asked for the original note to be expanded and for additional information to be supplied in relation to the coordination of budgetary policies, 'particularly as regards the degree of fiscal harmonisation which should be planned for at the various stages in the establishment of economic and monetary union and in drawing up the calendar for work on budgetary issues'.[61] The note by the Dutch representative on institutional aspects was not discussed, probably for lack of time. These three documents were therefore placed on the agenda for the group's next meeting, which was scheduled for 27 July 1970 in Luxembourg.

Werner took advantage of being in Paris to have private meetings with Monnet on two occasions, on 7 and 9 July, if we are to believe a note of telephone conversations and a handwritten slip of paper by Pierre Werner.[62] It is not known what was said, but it is highly likely that the two men discussed how to exert influence—especially on the Germans and the Dutch—to make sure that the work of the group produced an outcome.

4.2.9 Eighth Meeting (Luxembourg, 27 July 1970)

At the eighth meeting, held in Luxembourg on 27 July, the group continued with its exchange of views on various points to be covered in its final report.

Brouwers put forward for discussion a paper on the institutional aspects which also dealt with transfers of sovereignty from the second stage of the plan onwards.[63] Monetary union, as defined in the interim report inevitably implied the transfer of powers in some areas from national bodies to Community bodies, one of whose main responsibilities was the efficient management of short-term economic policy. As a result, and with regard to the requirements of the final stage, a high degree of harmonisation of short-term economic policy instruments in the Member States had to be established from the first stage. Two bodies seemed essential for the effective management of short-term economic policy.

The first was a central policy body that could have a decisive influence on the deflationary and inflationary effects of national budgets and would govern the access of national authorities to the Community's capital market.[64] A common central bank was then to be created and would be given responsibility, in the Community, for issuing banknotes, for, for managing official currency reserves and for maintaining the external value of the currency. The central bank was to be an autonomous and financially independent institution whose status and powers would be laid down in Community law. Its relations with the central body for economic policy coordination would be regulated in that the latter entity could give the bank certain specific directives, while respecting its guaranteed' independence. Such a bank could be created by fully merging the current central banks, but it would seem more realistic to envisage a sort of federal reserve system. Its implementation would require significant changes being made to the Community institutional structure and new treaty provisions would be imminent.

Stammati, and the secretariat, presented their respective rewritten notes. The Werner Group debated in detail the practical arrangements for a harmonisation of short-term, budgetary and medium-term policies. A great deal more material was added to this chapter in the course of laborious discussions.

Having regard to the documents already drafted and the remarks made in the course of the discussions, the group considered that a preliminary draft report to the Council could be written.

> This report, which will retain the structure of the interim report, will nevertheless leave open those points which are to be the subject of the report by the Committee of Governors of the Central Banks and of the note drawn up by Mr Ansiaux and Mr Clappier.[65]

The group secretariat was instructed to draw up the preliminary draft and submit it at the next meeting, which was scheduled to be held in Luxembourg in two stages: 10 September, in the afternoon, and 11 September all day.

The secretariat of the 'plan by stages' group, urged on by G. Morelli, moved very fast and on the day after the eighth meeting, 28 July 1970, drew up a provisional version of the preliminary draft report.[66] This version was reworked in a select committee consisting of U. Mosca, H. Tietmeyer, A. Looijen and J-M. Bloch-Lainé. 'Leaving Part VI vague and drawing up [...] no conclusions was deliberate, the point being to leave room for manoeuvre in discussions on the monetary mechanisms'.[67] The document was immediately forwarded to Werner and then submitted to the group by official dispatch on 27 August, so that the substance of it could be debated at the meeting on 10 September.

On 4 August, Werner received another document. Ansiaux sent him a personal letter containing the report which the experts from the central banks had drawn up. Ansiaux stressed that 'it [the Committee of

Governors] will adopt the opinion you have asked it for at the meeting on 12 September next, so that you can have it before you before the meeting your committee is holding in Copenhagen'.[68] The reason for the very confidential nature of this letter—this time the addressee was Werner as Minister for Finance and not as Prime Minister (the holder of that post was subject to additional administrative constraints as regards the processing of mail)—was that it was an internal working document of the Governors which had to remain confidential until it was published or officially forwarded. This document was dated 1 August 1970.[69]

4.2.10 Ninth Meeting (Luxembourg, 10 and 11 September 1970)

The Werner Group held its ninth session on 10 and 11 September in Luxembourg.

The agenda included consideration of the main lines of the preliminary report drawn up by the secretariat. Ansiaux, with Clappier, drafted a note containing proposals regarding the points to be included in the final report on domestic monetary policy. The note stressed the need for setting quantitative and operational criteria in each of the Member States, taking account of the differences between their economic and banking structures, for the desired short- and medium-term development of the liquidity supply. It also covered the setting up, during the first stage, of a practical programme of measures that it would be desirable to take to harmonise monetary policy instruments applying to banks and credit institutions, in order to cut down on the problems caused by the opportunities available to banks to sidestep the constraints of monetary policy. It also stipulated that central banks should be able to use the instrument of regulating the net position of banks (setting limits on asset/liability positions, etc.).

Following discussion of these subjects and, in particular, the points made in the Ansiaux–Clappier document, it was agreed that the secretariat should draw up a new draft report incorporating them. It was to be discussed in Copenhagen on 23 and 24 September 1970.

4.2.11 Tenth Meeting (Copenhagen, 23 and 24 September 1970)

The annual meeting of the International Monetary Fund and the World Bank in Copenhagen (19–26 September) provided a setting for the tenth meeting of the Werner Group, which was held in two parts, as the previous one had been. Two archive documents, however, show that at least one extra meeting was held on 25 September 1970.[70] The fact that the technical preparation was taken on and the entire cost borne by the Federal Ministry of Economic Affairs and the German Embassy in Copenhagen suggests to us that the meeting in question had been requested by Germany and that, after the debates and discussions which took place, and after confidential mediation on various occasions, a way was found to reach a compromise with the Germans and very probably with the Dutch too, so that the group was able to adopt a common position.[71] No minutes of this meeting seem to have been produced, and given our theory on the way in which the Werner Committee reported on its tense meetings, we can draw the conclusion that it was probably marked by disagreements and dissensions.

Priority in the debates in plenary session was given to the report from the Committee of Governors and to defining the content of the final chapters of the report, which had still to be written. The Governors supplied a technical report which was valuable later, but for the moment it remained very cautious as regards political initiatives.

The IMF meeting and the many associated protocol occasions gave the members of the Werner Committee and the Finance Ministers of the Six opportunities for informal conversations with their American colleagues and other international officials and experts, and thus for sounding out their views and eliciting their comments on various aspects of the plan by stages. Pierre Werner's private diaries mention two meetings with the Chairman of the IMF, whom he had already consulted on Europe's monetary identity through Jean Monnet, and talks with the Chairman of the US Federal Reserve Board, Arthur Burns. Werner, though, was regularly in contact with the federal and political authorities in the United States. His good relations with financial circles across the Atlantic and with Luxembourg bankers who were especially active in America, and his cordial relations with the US Ambassadors in Luxembourg, all gave him opportunities for compiling the information he was interested in for the international dimension which the plan by stages entailed.[72]

The group agreed to meet in Luxembourg on 7 October 1970, on which date the secretariat was to draw up a final draft report.

4.2.12 Eleventh Meeting (Luxembourg, 7 October 1970)

At the end of the meeting on 11 September, the group secretariat, led by Georges Morelli, set to work on writing the draft report, incorporating the structure and the subject matter decided on during the discussions.

A first rough outline was dated 14 September and a second 18 September 1970, but these documents changed over time.[73] This happened firstly with the contribution by Tietmeyer, Loijen and Bloch-Lainé, who had also intervened during the drafting of the interim report and who this time met in select committee on 17 September 1970.[74] The alternate members of the group also met on two occasions on 29 September 1970, in Brussels, under Mertens de Wilmars.[75] Werner was sent the working versions of the draft final report as they came out, and made suggestions and amendments on them which the group secretariat gradually incorporated.

On 7 October, the day before the Council of Ministers was to meet, the group met in Luxembourg to put the finishing touches to the report and approve it. It was not an easy task, and the fact that there are no minutes or other documents reporting what happened at the sitting proves that the discussions were heated, as they had been at the rowdy fourth and fifth sittings. Clearly, the focus of the arguments was the establishment of an exchange stabilisation fund. The rigid attitude to this displayed by the Germans, and possibly by other members, was not encouraging when it came to finding a compromise solution. In his memoirs, Pierre Werner tells us that

> [...] Schöllhorn insisted that we propose the establishment of the stabilisation fund only during the second stage, before which in any case the matter had to be given detailed consideration. At the risk of jeopardising the unanimity of the group, I felt that I had to take a tougher stand. I was certain that a plan which made no provision for any innovation on the monetary front in the first three years, and involved nothing but pushing forward procedures for harmonising economic and budgetary policies without any monetary incentives to support it, would very probably become bogged down in interminable discussions at the Community level. [...] What is more, Raymond Barre's proposals called for a new financial facility. The plan, to which the members of the group proposed to attach my name, could not simply disregard my earlier initiatives in that area. I therefore very firmly called for the fund to be created in the first stage. My point of view was supported by Ansiaux and Clappier. There was still fierce opposition, nevertheless. In the end, after heated debates, everyone did their bit to avoid a failure, and I secured a compromise which was accepted unanimously.[76]

So, after seven months of work, discussions, arguments, horse-trading, and reversals, the final report was approved. On 8 October 1970, as chairman of the group, Pierre Werner officially presented the plan for the achievement by stages of economic and monetary union in the Community to the Council of Ministers' meeting in Luxembourg.

> I had managed to avoid a report that was fragmented by differences of opinion on important points. The price of this unanimity was a rigour in our thinking that we might have feared would hinder the implementation of the plan. [...] Soon the Community would be exposed to monetary upheavals that would have an impact on the priorities as we had envisaged them.[77]

In its first edition, officially submitted to the Council of Ministers and to the EC Commission on 15 October 1970, this document bore the subheading 'Werner Report', which the members of the committee of experts had unanimously decided to give it as a tribute to their chairman.

Some days later, when the official report was sent to the European Parliament this heading was 'omitted', and was subsequently systematically forgotten. We do not know why this happened, but we might imagine that the Commission—which, through its DGII, was in charge of the technical secretariat of the Werner Committee—had something to do with it. The words spoken a few weeks later by Commission Vice-President Barre are particularly enlightening:

> I would like to restate [...] that it is not reports, plans or statements of intent that count, but decisions. [...] And that is the responsibility of the Commission and the Council.[78]

On 26 October 1970, the Council of Foreign Affairs Ministers met in Luxembourg to take official delivery of the report on the achievement of economic and monetary union in the Community. Pierre Werner, chairman of the committee of experts but also host of the meeting in his capacity as Prime Minister of Luxembourg, launched discussions with a brief, tightly worded statement. Looking back over the way the process of reflection in the ad hoc group had evolved, Pierre Werner highlighted the legitimacy of the conclusions in the interim report, which had been approved by the EC Council of Ministers at its session of 8 and 9 June 1970, as well as the efforts the experts had put into going more thoroughly into certain specific questions. The closing words of Pierre Werner's statement provide, perhaps, the best key to a reading of the aim in view:

> I am happy to note that on all these aspects we forged a unanimous collective view. Of course these joint replies do not reflect all the individual preferences of the members of the group. But we do think that having looked at the question from all sides, at long sessions where we compared a range of ideas, we have succeeded in giving shape to the wish for proceeding in parallel on the measures to be taken in the economic and financial fields. What we aspired to do was, once and for all, to break the vicious circle consisting of setting prior economic and political conditions. We have tried to draw a line midway between the view that monetary union is the crowning glory of European integration and

the view that would turn it into the virtually all-powerful engine driving integration. I think the proposals are in line with the existing treaties, and that they do, precisely, ensure that the objectives of the treaties will be achieved in full. Thus for stage one we can go a great deal of the way without amending the treaties. However, there must be a strong political will backing up this process all the time that it is being put into effect.[79]

Notes

1. 'Communication from the Commission to the Council on the development of a plan by stages for an economic and monetary union', in *Bulletin of of the European Communities*, Supplement, 3 (1970) (Luxembourg: Office for Official Publications of the European Communities).
2. P. Werner (1992, II) *Itinéraires*, p. 116. See also Interview with Baron Bernard Snoy et d'Oppuers (Ophain, 23 October 2015). https://www.cvce.eu/project/werner/ (home page) and http://www.cvce.eu/en/oral-history (main page), accessed on 6 March 2018.
3. 'Proceedings of the 105th session of the Council of 6 March 1970' reel No. 2385/Direction I, in *Official Journal of the European Communities*, 8 and 12 (1970) (Luxembourg: Office for Official Publications of the European Communities). Pierre Werner Family archives.
4. B. Molitor (2002, II) 'Les origines du plan Werner', in *Comité pour l'histoire économique et financière de la France* (ed.), *Le rôle des ministères des Finances et de l'Économie dans la construction européenne (1957–1978)*, 2 volumes (Paris: Comité pour l'histoire économique et financière de la France), pp. 109–111.
5. 'Address by Gaston Thorn (1998) (time code 0:20:29–0:23:59)' in the film *Les pères de l'Europe*: *Pierre Werner* (produced by CLT-UFA, length 1:06:24), Luxembourg. Pierre Werner Family archives. https://www.cvce.eu/project/werner/ (home page), accessed on 6 March 2018.
6. 'European Yearbook 1969', in *European Yearbook*, XLVII (1999) (Dordrecht: Kluwer Law International).
7. See, in particular, 'Wirtschafts-und Währungsunion in der EWG. Einsetzung des 5-Präsidentenausschusses' [Economic and monetary union in the EEC. Establishment of the committee composed of the

five chairmen]. Telegram No. 4160 from the Director, Department E, Federal Ministry of Economic Affairs, to State Secretary Rohwedder, with copies for information to State Secretaries Arndt and Schöllhorn, Bonn, 3 March 1970. Copy from the Federal Archives, Koblenz. BArch B 102 (Federal Ministry of Economic Affairs)/93469, and 'Wirtschafts- und Währungpolitik in der EWG. Bestellung des Präsidenten des ad hoc-Ausschusses' [Economic and monetary union in the EEC. Appointment of the chairman of the ad hoc committee]. Telegram from the Director, Department E, Federal Ministry of Economic Affairs, to State Secretary Rohwedder, with copies for information to State Secretaries Arndt and Schöllhorn, Bonn, 5 March 1970. Copy from the Federal Archives, Koblenz. BArch B 102 (Federal Ministry of Economic Affairs)/93457.

8. This was the conclusion reached at the talks between Detlev Rohwedder, State Secretary in the Federal Ministry of Economic Affairs, and Valéry Giscard d'Estaing, French Finance Minister, in Paris at the end of February 1970. Ibid. *Wirtschafts-und Währungpolitik in der EWG. Bestellung des Präsidenten des ad hoc-Ausschusses*, Bonn, 5 March 1970, Copy from the Federal Archives, Koblenz. BArch B 102 (Federal Ministry of Economic Affairs)/93469.
9. J.-C. Snoy et d'Oppuers (1989) *Rebâtir l'Europe: Mémoires, entretiens avec Jean-Claude Ricquier* [Rebuild Europe: Memories Ans Conversations with Jean-Claude Ricquier] (Louvain-la-Neuve: Éditions Duculot), p. 174.
10. Ibid., *Wirtschafts-und Währungpolitik in der EWG. Bestellung des Präsidenten des ad hoc-Ausschusses*, Bonn, 5 March 1970, Koblenz. BArch B 102 (Federal Ministry of Economic Affairs)/93469.
11. 'Letter from Constant Schuurmans, Ambassador of Belgium, to Prof. Dr. Karl Schiller, Federal Minister for Economic Affairs', No. D. 41, Bonn, 4 March 1970. Copy from the Federal Archives, Koblenz. BArch B 102 (Federal Ministry of Economic Affairs)/93457.
12. Ibid., p. 3
13. This took place in a telephone call on 4 March 1970 to the Federal Minister for Economic Affairs in Bonn from a representative of the Dutch Finance Ministry, informing him of Mr. Witteveen's intentions and sounding out the German reaction. See '*Wirtschafts-und Währungpolitik in der EWG. Bestellung des Präsidenten des ad hoc- Ausschusses*', Bonn, 5 March 1970, Copy from the Federal Archives, Koblenz, BArch B 102 (Federal Ministry of Economic Affairs)/93469, p. 3.

14. E. Danescu (2012) *A Rereading of the Werner Report of 8 October 1970 in the Light of the Pierre Werner Family Archives* (A research corpus). https://www.cvce.eu/project/werner/ (home page), accessed on 6 March 2018.
15. Brussels was an obvious setting for the meetings, as it was a permanent capital of the Community institutions and Belgium held the Presidency of the Council of the EEC in the first half of 1970. Concerning Rome, at the express request of the Italian Finance Minister, who wished 'to demonstrate clearly Italy's commitment to the path of economic and monetary union' and to reassert Rome's place among the active players in moves towards European integration. Documents in the archives show that satisfying this political request put the Commission under a great deal of stress from a logistical viewpoint. See 'Request for authorisation to hold a meeting outside Brussels', European Commission, pursuant to Note No. S/01875/64 of 26 June 1964 from the Executive Secretariat, 13 April 1970, 3083. Pierre Werner Family archives.
16. These are the 'Handwritten notes Pierre Werner' made when preparing for the opening of the Werner Group's discussions. The document contains various remarks on the Snoy Plan, the Schiller Plan and the first Barre Plan (submitted respectively by Belgium, Germany and the EC Commission at the meeting of Finance Ministers on 24 February 1970), which therefore influenced Werner's own stance. This note, which can be dated to between 25 February and 10 March 1970, was also the basis for his speech inaugurating the Werner Committee's work. Pierre Werner Family archives. https://www.cvce.eu/project/werner/ (home page), accessed on 6 March 2018.
17. Letter from Raymond Barre to the Members of the Commission dated 13 March 1970. Source: Ref. II-DG/AM.1f/13.III.1970, p. 29, Historical Archives of the Commission, Brussels. In this request, Raymond Barre refers both to aspects of protocol and also remuneration of the experts, for whom a derogation to the Commission regulation was applied.
18. P. Werner (1992, II) *Itinéraires*, p. 126. See also Interview with Étienne Davignon (Brussels, 10 January 2013). https://www.cvce.eu/project/werner/ (home page) and http://www.cvce.eu/en/oral-history (main page), accessed on 6 March 2018.
19. Ibid.

20. 'Draft minutes of the first meeting of the ad hoc 'plan by stages' group, 20 March 1970', European Communities, Secretariat of the 'plan by stages' group, Brussels, 31 March 1970, ORII/22/70-F. Pierre Werner Family archives.
21. G. Brouwers (1970) 'La méthode de réalisation d'une union économique et monétaire, vue dans l'optique de la politique conjoncturelle' [The Method for the Achievement of an Economic and Monetary Union from the Perspective of Conjunctural Policy], 6.477/II/70-F, Brussels: 3 April 1970. Pierre Werner Family archives.
22. The common aims in the area of growth and development were specifically mentioned in the Proposals from the Commission to the Council concerning the third programme for medium-term economic policy, Commission of the European Communities, COM 189/70.
23. Monetary union would involve a further transfer to Community level of responsibilities in the area of short-term economic policy. Should the monetary aspect be implemented more quickly, 'or even imposed as a matter of course', the transfer of some monetary responsibilities to the Community could occur more rapidly. Measures to be considered in this field were a narrowing of the current exchange margins, the adoption of fixed exchange rates and/or the creation of a Community reserve fund. Given the fact that the narrowing of exchange margins would not improve the possibility of harmonising short-term economic policies, the early adoption of completely fixed exchange rates would be reasonable. See G. Brouwers (1970).
24. J.-B. Schöllhorn (1970) 'Contribution à la discussion sur le thème de l'union économique comme fondement de l'union monétaire (Bonn, 2 April 1970)', 6.515/II/70-F, Bruxelles: 6 April 1970. Pierre Werner Family archives.
25. U. Mosca (1970) 'Suggestions concernant la première étape du plan par étapes, en matière de Marchés des capitaux' [Suggestions Regarding the First Stage of the Plan by Stages, as Regards the Capital Markets], European Commission, Directorate-General for Economic and Financial Affairs, II-C-2/MS.gs/31.03.1970, Brussels: 1 April 1970. Pierre Werner Family archives.
26. Note on 'The establishment of Economic and Monetary Union with Community enlargement in prospect', European Commission, Interdepartmental Group, Brussels, 28 April 1970. Historical Archives of the European Commission, BAC 375/1999 578, Vol. 2, pp. 181–191.

27. In the monetary debates that focused on enlargement, the role of the pound sterling was a major concern. How would this currency—which was both a reserve currency and a national currency—develop during the period between the UK's accession to the Common Market and the introduction of a single European currency? The main danger came from the fact that sterling's nature as a reserve currency could have a negative impact on its role as a national currency and introduce exogenous, sometimes artificial, parameters for a common or single currency. The considerable balances in sterling held by central banks, companies and individuals in countries in the sterling area other than the UK, the exchange rate guarantee enjoyed by assets in this currency and the high interest rate applied in the London financial market (considered to be Europe's leading financial centre) had enabled the pound sterling to retain its role as a reserve currency despite its devaluation in 1967. By the end of 1970, cracks had reappeared in the British balance of payments, despite its strong recovery in 1969. This fluctuating short-term development hinted at the transitory nature of some factors that had led to its recovery. The shaky balance of payments, the policy of restraint, the lack of productive investments and slow growth in the face of increasing demand all conspired to create a vicious circle that had a negative impact on the balance of payments. It seemed increasingly clear that if Britain's position in terms of exports had not improved by the time it joined the Community, the Community's monetary assistance mechanisms would be incapable of fully absorbing the shocks generated by the existence of balances in sterling.
28. For the Six it was essential that British accession went hand in hand with a stabilisation of sterling's role as a reserve currency. This was because, with its future common currency, the Community (including the UK) was to contribute to the stability of the international monetary system. Such a consolidation process implied the gradual elimination of support measures for the pound sterling (mentioned previously) and the establishment of a more balanced relationship between the UK's monetary reserves and its short-term debt obligations. To meet the need for additional international reserves, it was envisaged that reserves be created independently of gold resources or reserve currencies. To this end, the creation of SDRs within the IMF seemed a sensible solution. Debates on the role and future of the pound sterling could not be separated from the question of the other reserve currency, the US dollar,

especially in the context of a Eurocurrency market under constant development, in which Eurodollars had a significant role to play.

29. 'Report of the Chief Treasurer of the Netherlands Ministry of Finance (Willem Drees Junior) on the Conversations with the Belgians and Luxembourgers on the Monetary Union on 7 April 1970', Archive of the Cabinet of the Prime Minister (02.03.01), inv. no. 8864. National Archives of the Netherlands (The Hague). Reproduced in Marc Dierikx (ed.) (2012), *Common Fate, Common Future: A Documentary History of Monetary and Financial Cooperation, 1947–1974* (The Hague: CVCE-Huygens ING), pp. 150–155.
30. An exploration of the Pierre Werner Family archives reveals that on 22 April 1970, Baron Hubert Ansiaux submitted a note to the committee of experts entitled 'Aspects juridiques et techniques d'une mise en commun des droits de tirage spéciaux' [Legal and technical aspects of a pooling of SDRs] in which he discussed SDR transfer operations between the EC partners. Two days later, he responded to another request from Pierre Werner and sent him a confidential technical note 'setting out the modus operandi and the merits of a European exchange equalisation fund'. These two documents were analysed at the meeting of 7 April 1970.
31. P. Werner (1992, II) *Itinéraires*, p. 126.
32. 'Verbatim of statements by Mr Ansiaux and Mr Clappier. Meeting of the ad hoc group on the plan by stages', 7 April 1970. Brussels, 10 April 1970, confidential, ref. ORII/28/70F. Pierre Werner Family archives.
33. 'Request for authorisation to hold a meeting outside Brussels, pursuant to the Executive Secretariat's Note No. S/01875/64 of 26 June 1964'. European Commission, Secretariat-General, 13 April 1970, No. 3083. Pierre Werner Family archives. The outcome of the debate was decided by Raymond Barre, who gave the authorisation, mindful of the wish of the Italian member that 'these meetings, attended by high-level personalities, should be held successively in each of the Community Member States'.
34. 'Letter of 22 April 1970 from the Governor of the National Bank of Belgium, Baron Hubert Ansiaux, to Pierre Werner, President of the Luxembourg Government, with an annex on the "Legal and technical aspects of a pooling of special drawing rights"'. Pierre Werner Family archives.

35. 'Letter of 24 April 1970 from the Governor of the National Bank of Belgium, Baron Hubert Ansiaux, to Pierre Werner, President of the Luxembourg Government, with a confidential annex on a "European exchange equalisation fund"'. Pierre Werner Family archives.
36. 'Working document (for members' eyes only)', Secretariat of the 'plan by stages' group, Brussels: 21 April 1970. Historical Archives of the European Commission, BAC 375/1999 578, Vol. 2, pp. 168–180.
37. Ibid., p. 166
38. 'Vorschlag für einen Stufenplan zur Errichtung einer Wirschafts- und Währungsunion in der Europäischen Wirtschaftsgemeinschaft' Deutscher Gewerkschaftsbund, Bundesvorstand ['Proposal for a Plan by Stages for Economic and Monetary Union in the European Economic Community', Confederation of German Trade Unions, Federal Bureau], Düsseldorf, 20 March 1970. Historical Archives of the European Commission BAC 375/1999 575, Vol. 1, pp. 0059–0067. The list annexed to the document shows that it was also sent to the Federal Chancellor, the Federal Ministries of Economic Affairs and Foreign Affairs, the German representative to the EEC, as well as to the European Confederation of Free Trade Unions and the national trade unions belonging to it. The trade union channel was a way of spreading an interest in questions relating to EMU in several European countries, among the widest possible range of trade union and professional circles. The European Confederation of Free Trade Unions, for example, also drew up a paper setting out its own views on EMU by stages and submitted it to the President of the Commission, Jean Rey, on 15 May 1970. Pierre Werner Family archives.
39. See Historical Archives of the Commission of the EEC, Brussels, and Pierre Werner Family archives.
40. 'Draft minutes of the first meeting of the ad hoc 'plan by stages' group'. European Communities, Secretariat of the 'plan by stages' group, Brussels, 30 April 1970, ref. ORII/22/70-F, 6 May 1970. Historical Archives of the European Commission, BAC 375/1999 578. Pierre Werner Family archives
41. P. Werner (1992, II) *Itinéraires*, p. 125.
42. 'Telex from Mr Tietmeyer to the Secretariat of the Werner Group', sent at 7 p.m. on 25 May 1970, concerning the interim report (doc. 9.504). Pierre Werner Family archives.

43. In the terms of a public communiqué issued on 2 October 1963, the ministers and governors of the central banks of the ten countries participating in the General Arrangements to Borrow within the IMF—namely: (1) the US., (2) the UK, (3) France, (4) Italy, (5) Japan, (6) Canada, (7) The Netherlands, (8) Belgium, (9) The Deutsche Bundesbank, and (10) The Sveriges Riksbank—while attached to the principles of stability of exchange rates and of the price of gold, deemed it useful to undertake a thorough examination of the prospects with regard to the workings of the international monetary system and its probable liquidity needs for the future. They tasked their alternates to carry out this analysis and asked them to submit any practical suggestions resulting from their research. On 1 August 1964, on this basis (the Roosa Report), the ministerial declaration of the Group of Ten was adopted. This recognised the need for multilateral monitoring of the ways and means used to fund balance of payment imbalances, and approved the establishment by the alternates of the ministers and governors of a study group to examine the various proposals for the creation of new reserve instruments, by the intermediary of the IMF or otherwise. This marked the official establishment of the Committee of Alternates of the Group of Ten.
44. This question, raised by the presentation by Mr. Möller from Germany, which focused on the instruments available to Germany to respond to changing economic conditions by means of budgetary policy, sparked lively debates. The contributions by the various ministers indicated that the instruments available to national administrations in this area differed from one country to the next and were often highly insufficient. In this context, particular focus was placed on the budgetary policy of Italy, which was facing a significant public sector deficit. The ministers stressed the need to respect the imperatives of a prudent budgetary policy. These discussions highlighted an interesting general trend: monetary instruments alone should not be used to monitor the development of economic conditions; on the contrary, budgetary and fiscal instruments should also be largely used for this purpose.
45. On this point, the European Commission, in an address by Hans von der Groeben, presented the broad outline of a three-stage action plan to eliminate fiscal disparities between Member States, which was imperative if a true economic union was to be established. The disparities that needed to be eliminated mainly concerned turnover taxation (the first

step had already been taken with the gradual adoption of VAT in the six Community countries), excise duties and corporate taxation. The aims for the year 1978 were the harmonisation of both structures and VAT rates, the establishment of a unified, non-discriminatory capital market and a high degree of harmonisation of corporate taxation.

46. As a preamble to the presentation of the conclusions of the interim report, Ministers Snoy (Belgium), Schiller (Germany), and Werner (Luxembourg) presented the plans on economic and monetary union that their respective countries had proposed before the ad hoc group began its work and Raymond Barre summarised the European Commission's view on the matter. See Cable from the Italian Foreign Ministry to the Italian Permanent Representation to the EC on the conclusions of the meeting of EC Finance Ministers to discuss the Werner Report (Rome, 2 June 1970). 'Telegramma in partenza', No 10210/02.06.1970, Vol. 30/1970–1971. (Telegramma ordinario. In partenza. Politica economica e monetaria.) Foreign Ministry, Italian Diplomatic Historical Archives.
47. 'Draft minutes of the 35th conference of the Finance Ministers of the Commission of the European Communities, held in Venice on 29 and 30 May 1970', confidential. Commission of the European Communities, Directorate-General for Economic and Financial Affairs, ref. ORII/57/70-F, Brussels, 5 June 1970. Historical Archives of the European Commission.
48. Ibid., p. 4
49. Ibid., p. 6
50. P. Werner (1992, II) *Itinéraires*, p. 125.
51. Ibid., p. 128
52. 'Communiqué drawn up by the Belgian Presidency at the end of the meeting of the Council of Ministers', Luxembourg, 8–9 June 1970. Pierre Werner Family archives.
53. Pierre Werner Family archives, ref. PW 047.
54. The shared view that more work should be done on the aspects relating to the institutions, summarised by Werner in the chair, was influenced by the Schiller Plan (published on 12 February 1970), which recommended describing the powers of the bodies responsible, at a point beyond the first stage, for short-term economic policy on the one hand and monetary policy on the other.

55. Werner was keen to involve J.-B. Schöllhorn and G. Brouwers, whose inflexible economist's views were known, in the reflection on practical methods for the effective coordination of economic policies. It should also be noted that Schiller wanted to establish and implement more efficient procedures for bringing about economic policy convergence.
56. Some years later, when the Delors Report was being drawn up, the Committee of Governors, which was called on to assume the essential role, concluded that 'before the Werner Report [...], the Member States had a view of an economic union—or at any rate a common market—that they deemed to be achievable via the coordination of their monetary policies alone. After the Werner Report, they admitted that economic union could not be achieved without the gradual establishment of monetary union.' See H. Ansiaux, M. Dessart (1975) *Dossier pour l'histoire de l'Europe monétaire 1958–1973* (Bruxelles: Vander).
57. 'Telex from Bernard Clappier, Banfra (Banque nationale de France)', Paris, 11 June 1970, 4.07 p.m./Ministry of Foreign Affairs, Luxembourg. Pierre Werner Family archives.
58. 'Letter from the Chairman of the Committee of Governors of the Central Banks, Hubert Ansiaux, to Pierre Werner, President of the Government', Minister for Finance, Brussels, 16 June 1970. Pierre Werner Family archives.
59. 'Draft minutes of the sixth meeting of the ad hoc "plan by stages" group, 24 June 1970', Brussels, 1 July 1970, OR II/63-70-F. Pierre Werner Family archives.
60. 'Letter from Baron Ansiaux, Governor of the National Bank of Belgium, to Professor Robert Triffin, Berkeley College, Yale University, New Haven, Connecticut; Brussels', 23 June 1970. Pierre Werner Family archives.
61. 'Draft minutes of the fifth meeting of the ad hoc "plan by stages" group, 7 July 1970', European Communities, Secretariat of the 'plan by stages' group, Brussels, 14 July 1970, OR II/67-70-F. Pierre Werner Family archives.
62. In Pierre Werner Family archives, ref. PW 047.
63. Note by Gerard Brouwers, 'Phase finale de l'union monétaire: transfert nécessaire de compétences nationales aux institutions communautaires' [Final stage of Monetary Union: The Necessary Transfer of National Powers and Responsibilities to the Community Institutions]. European Communities, Secretariat of the 'plan by stages' group, Brussels, 13351/II/70, 22 July 1970. Pierre Werner Family archives.

64. In accordance with the remarks in the note by Gerard Brouwers, the central policy body had to be able to pursue an effective policy and, to this end, to be able to take decisions independently of national bodies. This central body would have a collegiate structure, would be totally independent from national governments and would be subject to democratic scrutiny by the European Parliament. See Note by Gerard Brouwers, 'Phase finale de l'union monétaire: transfert nécessaire de compétences nationales aux institutions communautaires' [Final stage of monetary union: the necessary transfer of national powers and responsibilities to the Community institutions]. European Communities, Secretariat of the 'plan by stages' group, Brussels, 13351/II/70, 22 July 1970. Pierre Werner Family archives.
65. 'Draft minutes of the eighth meeting of the ad hoc "plan by stages" group, 27 July 1970', European Communities, Secretariat of the 'plan by stages' group, Brussels, 14 August 1970, OR II/74-70-F. Pierre Werner Family archives.
66. 'Preliminary draft report to the Council and the Commission on the establishment by stages of economic and monetary union in the Community', European Communities, Secretariat of the "plan by stages" group, Brussels, 28 July 1970, OI II/72/70-F. Pierre Werner Family archives.
67. Commission of the European Communities, Directorate-General for Economic and Financial Affairs, II-A-6.JCM.mw.13.VIII.70, Brussels. Pierre Werner Family archives.
68. 'Personal letter from Baron Ansiaux, Chairman of the Committee of Governors of the Central Banks, to Pierre Werner, Finance Minister', Brussels, 4 August 1970. Pierre Werner Family archives.
69. 'Report on the questions asked by the 'ad hoc' committee chaired by Werner, Prime Minister', 1 August 1970. Committee of Experts chaired by Baron Ansiaux. Committee of Governors of the Central Banks of the Member States of the European Economic Community. Pierre Werner Family archives.
70. 'Note to Mr A. Wegener, Directorate-General for Personnel and Administration, ref. II/GM.nj/14.08.1970, Brussels, 17 August 1970'. Historical Archives of the European Commission, BAC 375/1999,578, Vol. 2.
71. The second document is in another register: it consists of agreement by Raymond Barre, Vice-President of the Commission, to the holding of a meeting of the 'plan by stages' group outside Brussels, but also

to the fact that the cost of the meeting concerned (2120 DM), which was borne by the Ministry of Economic Affairs in Bonn, would not be charged to the budget of the group.

72. G. Grygowski (2009) *Les États-Unis et l'unification monétaire européenne* (Brussels: P.I.E. - Peter Lang), pp. 131–215. See also Chapter 5.
73. 'Commission of the European Communities. Secretariat of the "plan by stages" group, ref. OR II/72/2-70, Brussels, 18 September 1970'. Pierre Werner Family archives.
74. 'Note to Mr L. Lambert, Director-General for Personnel and Administration', Brussels, ref. II/GM.jt/17.09.1970. European Commission, Directorate for Economic and Financial Affairs. Historical Archives of the European Commission, BAC 375/1999,578, Vol. 2
75. 'Request to hold a meeting (p. 704248) and Request to hold an official reception (p. 704330)', European Commission, Directorate for Economic and Financial Affairs, Brussels, 28 September 1970. Historical Archives of the European Commission, BAC 375/1999,578, Vol. 2.
76. P. Werner (1992, II) *Itinéraires*, p. 130.
77. Ibid., p. 131
78. 'Address by Raymond Barre. Economic Committee of the European Parliament, meeting of 28–29.09.70 in Brussels', reel 218, transcription p. 8. Pierre Werner Family archives. See also Chapter 4, which attempts to shed light on the relationship between Pierre Werner and Raymond Barre.
79. 'Statement by Pierre Werner to the Council of Ministers, Luxembourg, 26 October 1970', in *Documentation Bulletin*, 6 (1970) (Luxembourg: Ministry of State). Pierre Werner Family archive.

Date	Title	Location	Subject	
06.03.1970	Decision of the Council of the European Communities on the procedure regarding economic and monetary cooperation. Definition of the composition of the ad hoc committee. Consensus surrounding the appointment of Pierre Werner as chairman of the group of experts	Brussels	**Composition of the Committee**: Chairman: Luxembourg Prime Minister, Mr Pierre Werner Chairman of the Monetary Committee: Mr Bernard Clappier	**Deputies**: Mr Johnny Schmitz Mr Jean-Michel Bloch-Lainé
			Chairman of the Committee of Governors of the Central Banks: Baron Hubert Ansiaux	Mr Jacques Mertens de Wilmars
			Chairman of the Medium-Term Economic Policy Committee: Mr Johann-Baptist Schöllhorn	Mr Hans Tietmeyer
			Chairman of the Conjunctural Policy Committee: Mr Gerard Brouwers	Mr Anthony Looijen
			Chairman of the Budgetary Policy Committee: Mr Gaetano Stammati	Mr Simone Palumbo

(continued)

(continued)

Date	Title	Location	Subject
			Representative of the Commission—Director-General for Economic and Financial Affairs of the EEC: Mr Ugo Mosca — Mr Jean-Claude Morel *Secretary: Mr Georges Morelli*
06.03.1970	Meeting of the Committee of Governors of the Central Banks (the 37th session of the EC Committee of Governors of the Central Banks)	Basel	Attended by: the Governor of the National Bank of Belgium and chairman of the committee, Baron Ansiaux, accompanied by Mr de Strycker; the Governor of the Deutsche Bundesbank, Mr Klasen, accompanied by Mr Emminger; the Governor of the Banque de France, Mr Wormser, accompanied by Mr Clappier; the Governor of the Banca d'Italia, Mr Carli, accompanied by Mr Baffi; the Governor of the Nederlandsche Bank, Mr Zijlstra, accompanied by Baron Mackay. They are assisted by the Vice-President of the Commission of the European Communities, Mr Barre, accompanied by Mr Mosca; the chairman of the committee of alternates of the Group of Ten, Mr Ossola, as well as Mr Mertens de Wilmars, chairman of the group of experts on the Community system for short-term monetary support. The secretary-general of the committee, Mr d'Aroma, his deputy, Mr Bascoul, and Mr Rainoni are also present The Committee of Governors has a first exchange of views regarding a note from the Council on the creation of an ad hoc committee chaired by Pierre Werner that is to be tasked with analysing various suggestions and identifying the fundamental options for an economic and monetary union in the Community. The committee discusses a working document for the creation of a European Reserve Fund, based on a report by Professor Robert Triffin from December 1969. Questions relating to the short-term European monetary system are also addressed

(continued)

(continued)

Date	Title	Location	Subject
11.03.1970	Preliminary meeting of the Werner Committee	Luxembourg	Adoption of the committee's working methods. Fixing of deadlines—May for preliminary conclusions and end of July for the conclusion of the meetings. The chairman invites committee members—in accordance with their respective responsibilities—to draft memorandums describing the measures they envisage to attain the final objective. The chairman, Mr Werner, gives his colleagues a first comparative overview of the debates regarding monetary integration and the proposals put forward by various governments (Germany, Belgium, Luxembourg), as well as by the Commission
20.03.1970	First meeting of the Werner Committee	Luxembourg	Exchange of views on the documents submitted by certain members. Discussions on the definition that should be given to the final objective of economic and monetary union, particularly in the fields of monetary and credit policy, of budgetary and fiscal policy, of integration of capital markets, as well as in the institutional domain. Mr Werner proposes that a synthesis report be drawn up summarising the ideas and positions presented. The Commission sets up an inter-directorate working party on economic and monetary union to be responsible for carrying out the necessary work to supply the Commission's representative in the Werner Group with points for consideration and documentation. The directors and secretary of the Monetary Committee are part of this working party. The group takes office on 18 March 1970. The full members of the ad hoc group present the deputies they have chosen to take part in the work

(continued)

(continued)

Date	Title	Location	Subject
07.04.1970	Second meeting of the Werner Committee	Brussels	Submission of a document drawn up by Johann-Baptist Schöllhorn. Discussions on the drafting of a diagram portraying the present situation, the point of departure, the point of arrival and the principles of the plan by stages. The group decides to limit itself to defining the first stage, at least for the current report. Another decision of the group is to entrust the writing of the draft report to the deputies. The latter are to meet on 6 and 8 May 1970 under the chairmanship of Mr Mertens de Wilmars. The inter-directorate working party draws up a planning memorandum entitled 'The state of economic and monetary union in 1978 following completion of the plan by stages'

(continued)

(continued)

Date	Title	Location	Subject
13.04.1970	Meeting of the Committee of Governors of the Central Banks (the 38th session of the EC Committee of Governors of the Central Banks)	Basel	Attended by: the Governor of the National Bank of Belgium and chairman of the committee, Baron Ansiaux, accompanied by Mr de Strycker; the Governor of the Deutsche Bundesbank, Mr Klasen, accompanied by Mr Emminger; the Governor of the Banque de France, Mr Wormser, accompanied by Mr Clappier; the Governor of the Banca d'Italia, Mr Carli, accompanied by Mr Baffi; the Governor of the Nederlandsche Bank, Mr Zijlstra, accompanied by Baron Mackay. They are assisted by the Vice-President of the Commission of the European Communities, Mr Barre, accompanied by Mr Mosca; the chairman of the committee of alternates of the Group of Ten, Mr Ossola, as well as Mr Mertens de Wilmars, chairman of the group of experts on the Community system for short-term monetary support. The secretary-general of the committee, Mr d'Aroma, his deputy, Mr Bascoul, and Mr Rainoni are also present Baron Ansiaux reports on the first two meetings of the Werner Committee. The first meeting demonstrated 'the importance of making progress in parallel on economic and monetary issues', as well as 'the importance of achieving a balance between the measures that need to be taken in various fields—monetary, budgetary, fiscal and economic—in order to achieve an economic and monetary union. The definition and length of the stages could be determined at a later date.' The second meeting saw discussions on the final objective, namely 'full economic and monetary union […] with three lines of action: voluntary coordination between the EEC countries, harmonisation (common guidelines), and decisions taken by Community bodies. For the third meeting, to be held in Rome, Mr Werner will present a document on the progressive development that might be envisaged.' Questions on the unification of banking legislation and the flexibility of exchange rates are also discussed

(continued)

(continued)

Date	Title	Location	Subject
21.04.1970	Confidential meeeting between the chairman and the secretariat of the Werner Committee	Luxembourg	Creation of the 'roadmap' for the plan by stages, identifying the point of departure and describing the final objective and the necessary and desirable actions to take—in the fields of economic policy, monetary solidarity and institution-building—in order to attain this. This summary is accompanied by an inventory of the practical measures cited—particularly for the first stage. Strengthening monetary solidarity, the implications of possible participation by the UK in the monetary cooperation mechanisms, as well as the European Reserve Fund and the pound sterling are examined in detail. The document is sent out on 22 April to the members of the group in preparation for the Rome meeting
30.04.1970	Third meeting of the Werner Committee	Rome	At the start of the group's work, Gaetano Stammati demands that 'meetings, attended by high-level personalities, should be held successively in each of the Community Member States'. Thus the third meeting of the group is held in Rome. Continued exchange of views on the issue of economic and monetary union
06.05.1970 08.05.1970	Meetings of the deputies' group	Brussels	Meetings of the group of deputies chaired by Mr Mertens de Wilmars, with the support of the Commission Directorate for Economic and Financial Affairs responsible for drawing up the draft interim report. Systematisation of the issues to be dealt with in the report. On 11 May 1970, an 'Interim report to the Council and the Commission. Plan by stages for the establishment of economic and monetary union' is submitted by J. Mertens de Wilmars to the secretariat of the Werner Committee

(continued)

(continued)

Date	Title	Location	Subject
11.05.1970	Meeting of the Committee of Governors of the Central Banks (the 39th session of the EC Committee of Governors of the Central Banks)	Basel	Attended by: the Governor of the National Bank of Belgium and chairman of the committee, Baron Ansiaux, accompanied by Mr de Strycker; the Governor of the Deutsche Bundesbank, Mr Klasen, accompanied by Mr Emminger; the Governor of the Banque de France, Mr Wormser, accompanied by Mr Clappier; the Governor of the Banca d'Italia, Mr Carli, accompanied by Mr Baffi; the Governor of the Nederlandsche Bank, Mr Zijlstra, accompanied by Baron Mackay. They are assisted by the Vice-President of the Commission of the European Communities, Mr Barre, accompanied by Mr Mosca; the chairman of the committee of alternates of the Group of Ten, Mr Ossola, as well as Mr Mertens de Wilmars, chairman of the group of experts on the Community system for short-term monetary support. The secretary-general of the committee, Mr d'Aroma, his deputy, Mr Bascoul, and Mr Rainoni are also present Baron Ansiaux informs the committee about the meeting of the Werner Committee that took place in Rome and notes that on 14 May there is to be a further meeting at which a draft report drawn up by a group of deputies will be discussed. 'The following meeting, in theory the last, is scheduled for 20 May, such that the final document should be ready for 23 or 24 May and examined at the quarterly meeting of the Finance Ministers and Governors on 29 May in Venice.' Raymond Barre explains that the Commission has asked the Foreign Ministers to accompany the Finance Ministers to this meeting. Baron Ansiaux then sets out the broad lines of the preliminary draft of the Werner Report, emphasising the principle of parallelism and synchronisation between various measures, but 'the Council would take the decisions that it saw fit to take'
14.05.1970	Fourth meeting of the Werner Committee	Luxembourg	Continuing exchange of views on the issue of economic and monetary union; submission of the preliminary draft report drawn up by the 'Mertens de Wilmars group'

(continued)

(continued)

Date	Title	Location	Subject
20.05.1970	Fifth meeting of the Werner Committee	Luxembourg	Discussions on the draft report; amendment; adoption of its final structure for presentation to the Council of Ministers
25.05.1970	Meeting of the group of experts of the Committee of Governors of the Central Banks	Brussels	Pierre Werner, chairman of the committee, and the group of experts of the Committee of Governors of the Central Banks meet to put the final touches to the draft report
29.05.1970	Meeting of the Committee of Governors of the Central Banks (the 40th session of the EC Committee of Governors of the Central Banks)	Venice	The Committee of Governors of the Central Banks meets on the margins of the meeting of the Finance Ministers Attended by: the Governor of the National Bank of Belgium and chairman of the committee, Baron Ansiaux, accompanied by Mr de Strycker; the Governor of the Deutsche Bundesbank, Mr Klasen, accompanied by Mr Emminger; the Governor of the Banque de France, Mr Wormser, accompanied by Mr Clappier; the Governor of the Banca d'Italia, Mr Carli, accompanied by Mr Baffi; the Governor of the Nederlandsche Bank, Mr Zijlstra, accompanied by Baron Mackay. They are assisted by the Vice-President of the Commission of the European Communities, Mr Barre, accompanied by Mr Mosca; the chairman of the committee of alternates of the Group of Ten, Mr Ossola, as well as Mr Mertens de Wilmars, chairman of the group of experts on the Community system for short-term monetary support. The secretary-general of the committee, Mr d'Aroma, and his deputy, Mr Bascoul, are also present The governors discuss the interim report drafted by the Werner Committee. The Governor of the Bundesbank emphasises that the fact that the authorities in one country set out their stance on the subjects covered in the report should not hinder the freedom of thought of the members of the Werner Committee, who are fully independent in their role. The governors deem this report to be 'excellent' but feel that it needs to be taken further in various areas; this would be possible if the mandate of the Werner Committee were to be extended. They note the consensus of the experts regarding the document

(continued)

(continued)

Date	Title	Location	Subject
29.05.1970	Meeting of the Finance Ministers of the European Communities	Venice	Meeting called to discuss the interim report. Pierre Werner delivers a summary of the interim report, underlining the points of agreement and disagreement and issues requiring further study. Adoption of the interim report. The unanimous conclusion of these exchanges is that the work carried out by the group must continue in order to be able to reach agreement on the controversial issues and to consider further those on which there is consensus
09.06.1970	Meeting of the Committee of Governors of the Central Banks (the 41st session of the EC Committee of Governors of the Central Banks)	Basel	Attended by: the Governor of the National Bank of Belgium and chairman of the committee, Baron Ansiaux, accompanied by Mr de Strycker; the Governor of the Deutsche Bundesbank, Mr Klasen, accompanied by Mr Tüngeler; the Governor of the Banque de France, Mr Wormser, accompanied by Mr Clappier; the Governor of the Banca d'Italia, Mr Baffi, accompanied by Mr Masera; the Governor of the Nederlandsche Bank, Mr Zijlstra, accompanied by Mr van den Bosch. They are assisted by the Director-General for Economic and Financial Affairs of the EC Commission, Mr Mosca, as well as Mr Mertens de Wilmars. The secretary-general of the committee, Mr d'Aroma, and his deputy, Mr Bascoul, are also present The Committee of Governors continues its examination of the report by the Werner Committee and holds an exchange of views on the studies to be conducted by the Committee of Governors in connection with the work of the Werner Committee. Given the holidays and the need for a permanent contact with the Werner Committee, Baron Ansiaux proposes that a liaison group within the Committee of Governors be created, which he himself will chair, with Mr Clappier as alternate. Mr Zijlstra proposes that two experts be included in this group from the Committee of Governors and puts forward the name of Baron Mackay. An initial examination of the questions at issue could take place on 6 July, at the next meeting of the Committee of Governors

(continued)

(continued)

Date	Title	Location	Subject
09.06.1970	Meeting of the Council of Ministers of the European Communities	Brussels	Given the need for a further examination of certain aspects of the plan for the establishment by stages of an economic and monetary union, the Council of Ministers asks the Werner Committee to continue its work. The Council Decision recommends that the Committee of Governors of the Central Banks be consulted regarding specific monetary aspects
24.06.1970	Sixth meeting of the Werner Committee	Luxembourg	In accordance with the Council mandate, the Werner Committee resumes its examination of the issues that remain open in its interim report for the purpose of adding further information. Pierre Werner, chairman of the committee, invites the Dutch and German members, together with the member from the Commission, to draft a memorandum on those ideas that might be proposed in order to strengthen procedures to coordinate economic policies. The Dutch representative is invited to submit a memorandum on the institutional issues as they will appear in the final stage of economic and monetary union

(continued)

(continued)

Date	Title	Location	Subject
06.07.1970	Meeting of the Committee of Governors of the Central Banks (the 42nd session of the EC Committee of Governors of the Central Banks)	Basel	Attended by: the Governor of the National Bank of Belgium and chairman of the committee, Baron Ansiaux, accompanied by Mr de Strycker; the Deputy Governor of the Deutsche Bundesbank, Mr Emminger; the Deputy Governor of the Banque de France, Mr Clappier, accompanied by Mr Théron; the Governor of the Banca d'Italia, Mr Baffi, accompanied by Mr Masera; the Governor of the Nederlandsche Bank, Mr Zijlstra, accompanied by Baron Mackay. They are assisted by the Vice-President of the Commission of the European Communities, Mr Barre, accompanied by Mr Mosca; the chairman of the committee of alternates of the Group of Ten, Mr Ossola, as well as Mr Mertens de Wilmars. The secretary-general of the committee, Mr d'Aroma, his deputy, Mr Bascoul, and Mr Rainoni are also present Baron Ansiaux, chairman, informs the meeting of the letter dated 12 June 1970 that he received from Mr Werner, in which the Committee of Governors is invited to give its views on three series of questions. On 24 June, the Werner Committee completed this document, providing details on the first two series of questions associated with the reduction in the fluctuation margins for the currencies of the Community countries, on the one hand, and the exchange equalisation fund, on the other. The committee of experts of the Committee of Governors met concerning this matter on 25 June and 2 July Mr Barre sets out the orientations of the Commission on these questions

(continued)

(continued)

Date	Title	Location	Subject
07.07.1970	Seventh meeting of the Werner Committee	Paris	Exchange of views on the issues remaining open in the progress report; exchange of views on the memorandums submitted by the Dutch and German representatives, in agreement with the member of the Commission, as well as that by Gaetano Stammati. A supplementary memorandum dealing with budgetary policies (in particular the degree of fiscal harmonisation involved in the various stages of economic and monetary union and the timetable for the budgetary studies) is requested of Gaetano Stammati. The memorandum of the Dutch representative regarding the institutional aspects is also examined
27.07.1970	Eighth meeting of the Werner Committee	Luxembourg	Debates on the institutional aspects (memorandum by Gerard Brouwers), the fiscal aspects (Gaetano Stammati) and on coordination of economic policies. The chairman asks for a summary of all the documents cited and of the observations submitted during earlier discussions in order that a preliminary draft report be submitted to the Council. This report is to maintain its interim structure and to leave open those points that are the subject of the report by the Committee of Governors of the Central Banks (Messrs Ansiaux and Clappier)
28.07.1970	Closed meeting of the experts of the Werner Committee	Brussels	The Werner Committee secretariat, together with U. Mosca, H. Tietmeyer, A. Looijen and J.-M. Bloch-Lainé, submits a provisional version of the preliminary draft report to the chairman, Pierre Werner. 'Leaving Part VI vague and drawing up [...] no conclusions was deliberate, the point being to leave room for manoeuvre in discussions on the monetary mechanisms.' The document is delivered to the group by official courrier on 27 August so that a debate on the substance may take place at the 10 September meeting

(continued)

(continued)

Date	Title	Location	Subject
10.09.1970 11.09.1970	Ninth meeting of the Werner Committee	Luxembourg	Analysis of the memorandums prepared by Hubert Ansiaux and Bernard Clappier. Analysis of the main thrust of the preliminary draft report to the Council and observations on the substance. A new report, amended with elements concerning internal monetary policy (memorandum of Messrs Ansiaux and Clappier) is to be submitted for the next meeting
12.09.1970 13.09.1970	Meeting of the Committee of Governors of the Central Banks (the 43nd session of the EC Committee of Governors of the Central Banks)	Basel	Attended by: the Governor of the National Bank of Belgium and chairman of the committee, Baron Ansiaux, accompanied by Mr de Strycker; the Governor of the Deutsche Bundesbank, Mr Klasen, accompanied by Mr Emminger; the Governor of the Banque de France, Mr Wormser, accompanied by Mr Clappier; the Governor of the Banca d'Italia, Mr Carli, accompanied by Mr Baffi; the Governor of the Nederlandsche Bank, Mr Zijlstra, accompanied by Baron Mackay. They are assisted by the Vice-President of the Commission of the European Communities, Mr Barre, accompanied by Mr Mosca; the chairman of the committee of alternates of the Group of Ten, Mr Ossola, as well as Mr Mertens de Wilmars. The secretary-general of the committee, Mr d'Aroma, his deputy, Mr Bascoul, and Mr Rainoni are also present. The Committee of Governors discusses the opinion to be submitted to the Werner Committee following the letter from Pierre Werner and the explanatory questionnaire detailing some of the points in this letter. The experts in the committee will complete specific studies on: the direct communications network between the central banks; the harmonisation of monetary policy instruments; the conditions for the establishment of a 'Fund'. The committee also considers the timetable for the gradual progress envisaged and discusses the strengthening of coordination in the area of monetary policy during the first stage

(continued)

(continued)

Date	Title	Location	Subject
25.09.1970	Tenth meeting of the Werner Committee	Copenhagen	Held on the fringes of the annual meeting of the IMF. The Werner Committee debates the conclusions of the report by the Committee of Governors of the Central Banks and decides on the content of the last chapters of its report, which is still to be drawn up
07.10.1970	Eleventh meeting of the Werner Committee	Luxembourg	Discussions on and adoption of the final form of the report on the establishment of an economic and monetary union
08.10.1970	Twelfth meeting of the Werner Committee	Luxembourg	Final meeting of the Werner Committee. Unanimous adoption of the final report. Submission by Mr Pierre Werner of the report on the establishment of economic and monetary union
15.10.1970	Werner Committee	Brussels	Referral to the Council and the Commission of the report to the Council and the Commission concerning the establishment by stages of economic and monetary union in the Community (the 'Werner Report')
26.10.1970	Council of Foreign Ministers of the European Communities	Luxembourg	The Werner Report is officially submitted to the Council of Foreign Ministers
29.10.1970	Commission of the European Communities	Brussels	Communication and proposals from the Commission to the Council on the establishment by stages of economic and monetary union. COM(70)1250. The proposals are based on and inspired by the Werner Report. This communication contains a draft resolution, a proposal for a decision on strengthening the coordination of the short-term economic policies of the Member States and a proposal for a decision on strengthening cooperation between the central banks

(continued)

(continued)

Date	Title	Location	Subject
08.11.1970	Meeting of the Committee of Governors of the Central Banks (the 44th session of the EC Committee of Governors of the Central Banks)	Basel	Attended by: the Governor of the National Bank of Belgium and chairman of the committee, Baron Ansiaux, accompanied by Mr de Strycker; the Governor of the Deutsche Bundesbank, Mr Klasen, accompanied by Mr Emminger; the Deputy Governor of the Banque de France, Mr Clappier, accompanied by Mr Théron; the Governor of the Banca d'Italia, Mr Baffi, accompanied by Mr Masera; the Governor of the Nederlandsche Bank, Mr Zijlstra, accompanied by Count van den Bosch. They are assisted by the Director-General for Economic and Financial Affairs of the EC Commission, Mr Mosca, and the chairman of the committee of alternates of the Group of Ten, Mr Ossola. The secretary-general of the committee, Mr d'Aroma, his deputy, Mr Bascoul, and Mr Rainoni are also present. Exchange of views on the Werner Report. Baron Ansiaux, chairman, emphasises the parallelism between the monetary measures and the economic policy measures advocated by the report. The Commission representative, Mr Mosca, presents the document that the Commission has drawn up on the basis of the Werner Plan and which differs from the source in several places
18.11.1970	European Parliament	Strasbourg	Exchange of views between the European Parliament, the Council and the Commission on economic union and the prospect of a monetary union within the Community. Establishment by stages of economic and monetary union in the Community
23.11.1970	Council of Ministers of the European Communities	Brussels	First debates on the proposals from the Commission to the Council on the establishment by stages of economic and monetary union

(continued)

(continued)

Date	Title	Location	Subject
03.12.1970	European Parliament	Strasbourg	Exchange of views between the European Parliament, the Council and the Commission on economic union and the prospect of a monetary union within the Community. Establishment by stages of economic and monetary union in the Community. European Parliament resolution in support of economic and monetary union within the Community
12.12.1970	Meeting of the Committee of Governors of the Central Banks (the 45th session of the EC Committee of Governors of the Central Banks)	Basel	Attended by: the Governor of the National Bank of Belgium and chairman of the committee, Baron Ansiaux, accompanied by Mr de Strycker; the Governor of the Deutsche Bundesbank, Mr Klasen, accompanied by Mr Emminger; the Governor of the Banque de France, Mr Wormser, accompanied by Mr Clappier; the Governor of the Banca d'Italia, Mr Carli, accompanied by Mr Baffi; the Governor of the Nederlandsche Bank, Mr Zijlstra, accompanied by Mr van den Bosch. They are assisted by the Director-General for Economic and Financial Affairs of the EC Commission, Mr Mosca, and the chairman of the committee of alternates of the Group of Ten, Mr Ossola, as well as Mr Mertens de Wilmars. The secretary-general of the committee, Mr d'Aroma, his deputy, Mr Bascoul, and Mr Rainoni are also present Continuation of the exchange of views on the Werner Report of 8 October 1970 and on the proposals from the Commission of the European Communities of 29 October 1970 on the establishment by stages of economic and monetary union

(continued)

(continued)

Date	Title	Location	Subject
14.12.1970	Council of Ministers of the European Communities	Brussels	Debate on the launch of the first stage of economic and monetary union. Discussions focus on the nature and powers of Community decision-making bodies at an advanced stage or at the final stage of economic and monetary union. Links with the negotiations on British accession are constantly raised. France expresses its disagreement. Given that the idea of symbolically stopping the clock at midnight on 31 December 1970 is rejected, this meeting ends in failure and the Council of Ministers does not adopt a decision before the end of the year 1970
09.01.1971	Meeting of the Committee of Governors of the Central Banks (the 46th session of the EC Committee of Governors of the Central Banks)	Basel	Attended by: the Governor of the National Bank of Belgium and chairman of the committee, Baron Ansiaux, accompanied by Mr de Strycker; the Governor of the Deutsche Bundesbank, Mr Klasen, accompanied by Mr Emminger; the Director General of Foreign Services at the Banque de France, Mr Théron; the Governor of the Banca d'Italia, Mr Baffi, accompanied by Mr Masera; the Governor of the Nederlandsche Bank, Mr Zijlstra, accompanied by Baron Mackay. They are assisted by the Director-General for Economic and Financial Affairs of the EC Commission, Mr Mosca, and the chairman of the committee of alternates of the Group of Ten, Mr Ossola. The secretary-general of the committee, Mr d'Aroma, his deputy, Mr Bascoul, and Mr Rainoni are also present. Continuation of discussions on the establishment by stages of economic and monetary union. Committee chairman Ansiaux explains that the session of the Council of the European Communities of 14 December 1970 did not culminate in a decision on the matter 'because the debates focused on political aspects and not on technical aspects'

(continued)

(continued)

Date	Title	Location	Subject
08.02.1971 09.02.1971	Council of Ministers of the European Communities	Brussels	Adoption of the resolution on the achievement by stages of economic and monetary union in the Community Adoption of the decision on strengthening the coordination of short-term economic policies in the Member States, the decision on strengthening cooperation between the central banks and the decision on the implementation of a medium-term financial assistance mechanism Adoption by the Council and the Member State Governments of the third medium-term economic policy programme
06.03.1971	Meeting of the Committee of Governors of the Central Banks (the 47th session of the EC Committee of Governors of the Central Banks)	Basel	Attended by: the Governor of the National Bank of Belgium and chairman of the committee, Baron Ansiaux, accompanied by Mr de Strycker; the Governor of the Deutsche Bundesbank, Mr Klasen, accompanied by Mr Emminger; the Governor of the Banque de France, Mr Wormser, accompanied by Mr Clappier; Mr Ercolani of the Banca d'Italia; the Governor of the Nederlandsche Bank, Mr Zijlstra, accompanied by Mr van den Bosch. They are assisted by the Vice-President of the Commission of the European Communities, Mr Barre, accompanied by Mr Mosca. The secretary-general of the committee, Mr d'Aroma, his deputy, Mr Bascoul, and Mr Rainoni are also present Debate: economic and monetary union—follow-up to be given to the decisions and resolutions adopted by the Council of the European Communities on 8 and 9 February 1971
22.03.1971	Meeting of the Council of Ministers of the European Communities	Brussels	Adoption of the report to the Council and the Commission concerning the establishment by stages of economic and monetary union in the Community

(continued)

(continued)

Date	Title	Location	Subject
19.04.1971	Meeting of the Committee of Governors of the Central Banks (the 48th session of the EC Committee of Governors of the Central Banks)	Basel	Attended by: the Governor of the National Bank of Belgium, Mr Vandeputte, accompanied by Mr Janson; the Governor of the Deutsche Bundesbank, Mr Klasen, accompanied by Mr Emminger; the Governor of the Banque de France, Mr Wormser, accompanied by Mr Clappier; the Governor of the Banca d'Italia, Mr Carli, accompanied by Mr Baffi; the Governor of the Nederlandsche Bank, Mr Zijlstra, accompanied by Baron Mackay. They are assisted by the Vice-President of the Commission of the European Communities, Mr Barre, accompanied by Mr Mosca, and the chairman of the committee of alternates of the Group of Ten, Mr Ossola. The secretary-general of the committee, Mr d'Aroma, his deputy, Mr Bascoul, and Mr Rainoni are also present Mr Carli is unanimously elected as new chairman of the Committee of Governors Debate: economic and monetary union—follow-up to be given to the decisions and resolutions adopted by the Council of the European Communities on 8 and 9 February 1971. Matters given particular consideration are the coordination of the policy of the (five) central banks in monetary and credit matters and the reduction of fluctuation margins between the Community currencies. To this end, regulations are adopted concerning the policy of intervention in the event of a reduction in the fluctuation margins within the EEC

E. Danescu (2012) 'Summary of the Werner Committee's Schedule and the Main Issues Addressed (6 March 1970–22 March 1971)', in *A Rereading of the Werner Report of 8 October 1970 in the Light of the Pierre Werner Family Archives* (Research corpus).

5

The Werner Report

The discussions and exchanges which took place at the preliminary meeting in Luxembourg on 11 May 1970 and the first two working meetings (on 20 March in Luxembourg and 7 April in Brussels) helped the Werner Group define the main points of its future common position and set up the framework for the report in its successive forms and stages.

The various monetary integration plans put forward by three Member States (Belgium, Germany, and Luxembourg) and the EC Commission were merely rough outlines, drafts, statements of intent, while the measures suggested for the period covered by the stages were set out in the form of extremely general indications—although there was no ambiguity about them. Taking these factors into account, and out of a desire to hammer out some practical solutions, as they had been instructed to, the members of the group decided to make as coherent a summary as they could of the various features of these plans and then try to make them specific or fill in the detail.

E. Danescu, *Pierre Werner and Europe*,
Archival Insights into the Evolution of Economics,
https://doi.org/10.1007/978-3-319-96295-5_5

The Main Concepts

To give them a clearer view of the outlines of economic and monetary union in the plan by stages, the members of the Werner Group agreed that they should define a number of basic objectives and then try to identify and clarify the conditions to be met so that they could be achieved.

The essential objective of the plan by stages was to 'bring into being an area within which goods, services, people, and capital would move freely while monetary transactions carried out by businesses would not be hindered in any way or exposed to exchange-rate risks'.[1]

Joint action in the field of economic policies—simple coordination, more sustained harmonisation, common policies—stands out as another very fundamental objective, designed to help hold the whole construction together more tightly and enable it to achieved sustained growth against a background of stability. The concept of common policies entailed the idea of shared risks and therefore the need for common solidarity. 'In the event of a serious imbalance in one of the Member States, due, in particular, to a grave, unforeseeable mishap, the end result could be that the Member State concerned might be forced to take all requisite corrective steps and it might be necessary for Community solidarity to come into full play'.[2]

Economic and monetary union implied a common currency, 'though it would hold together just as well, to begin with, if there were a system guaranteeing that the exchange rates between the Member States' currencies were fixed irrevocably. It also involved setting up a capital market at the European level and a sufficient degree of tax harmonisation'.[3] If the exchange rates between Community currencies were irrevocably fixed, it would be impossible to devalue or revalue any one of the currencies on its own; but their exchange rate as a bloc could always be changed. Irrevocably fixed exchange rates and solidarity between Community currencies would be backed up by the Community's foreign exchange reserves, which would have to be available to meet all settlement requirements involving external parties, according to practical arrangements to be decided on jointly. The easiest way of achieving this aim would be through a European reserve fund.

It was also agreed that in international monetary relations the Community would speak and act as an entity in its own right.

Another common conclusion from the Werner Group was that there needed to be some transfer of decision-making powers on economic policy from the national to the Community level, particularly as regards budgetary matters, and centralisation in the field of monetary policy.

An aspect which was only lightly touched on in these early discussions, but which was to be dealt with in detail as the group pressed ahead with its work, was the question of the part the two sides of industry were to play in establishing economic and monetary union. It was stipulated that 'a Community body consisting of representatives of both sides of industry and of those responsible for economic policy in the Community' would be set up.[4]

This body, whose purpose would be to closely involve the two sides of industry in the shaping of the Community's economic policy, would be especially vital when it came to ensuring that incomes and assets developed satisfactorily, which was necessary both from the social point of view and from the point of view of compatibility with the Community's economic objectives.

5.1 The Interim Report[5]

The interim report, the product of the first five meetings of the Werner Group (from 11 March to 20 May 1970)—and the outcome of a great many clashes, frequent arbitration, 'not to mention the odd incident from time to time'—was submitted to the Finance Ministers' meeting in Venice on 29 May 1970 for discussion.[6]

On the basis of an analysis of the suggestions from the governments, the Commission's Communication to the Council and the ideas and proposals from the group of experts, the interim report sought to work out the basic options for the establishment of economic and monetary union by stages. As the introduction put it, '[the report does not reflect] the separate and individual preferences of the members of the Working Party: [it] tries to provide a joint reply despite the fact that on certain points opinions still differ. The ideas in it are put forward solely on the individual responsibility of the members of the Working Party'.[7]

From the outset, the experts had agreed to start by examining the initial situation, so that the 'point of departure' could be accurately defined. Without seeking to devise an ideal system which would, more than likely, be doomed to remain purely theoretical, the group also identified the 'ultimate goal', whose main merit was that it was attainable and would thus bring together the features essential to the existence of full economic and monetary union. Alternative routes for linking the two points together were looked at, with special attention being given to the basic principles and certain specific positions so that, during the first stage, the process which was to lead the Member States to economic and monetary union could be embarked upon.

This working method, based on point of departure, final goal and alternative routes, a very basic feature of the plan by stages, came from Pierre Werner, who—probably inspired by the method used for the establishment of the Common Market—had suggested it at the preliminary meeting of the group held on 6 March 1970 in Luxembourg. It was, in fact, the approach underlying the drafting of the 'Luxembourg plan for European monetary integration', submitted to the meeting of Finance Ministers held on 24 February 1970 in Paris.

5.1.1 The Start Point of EMU

In the minds of the group of experts, the European Community's major achievements in the field of economic integration were the completion of the customs union and the defining of a common agricultural policy. There were also certain negative aspects to the progress made on integration, such that the general economic imbalances in the Member States had direct—and sometimes swift—repercussions on the overall growth of the Community and could do damage to the progress made in establishing the free movement of goods, services, and capital. The common market in agricultural products was the most sensitive area in this respect.

The main aim on which the Six agreed unanimously was the achievement of growth and stability, and real economic policy harmonisation would protect those countries against the disparities which the special features of the domestic situation in each one could cause.

The increasing interpenetration of their economies had compromised each country's freedom of action in short-term domestic economic policy, and it had become especially difficult to keep control over economic policy in that the loss of independence at the national level had not been made up for by the establishment of Community policies. The shortcomings and the imbalance in the process of establishing the Common Market were therefore plain to see.

Given the framework of the Treaty of Rome, the efforts made and the partial progress achieved as a result had not in practice led to any coordination or actual harmonisation of economic policies in the Community.

It was noted that the Community '[lacked] sufficiently harmonized quantitative objectives, although without these effective co-ordination is impossible', and analysis of the short-term economic situation in the Community had often led only to 'recommendations worded in very general terms, even when it was in the Community interest that more specific views be expressed'. Consultation procedures had not produced the expected results, either because they were purely formal in character or because the Member States had bypassed them by invoking exemption clauses.

There were several areas in which progress was still inadequate.

Firstly, the freeing up of the movement of capital had not been sufficiently extended and the right of establishment for banking and financial undertakings had not been introduced. This delay was caused mainly by the absence of proper coordination at the economic and monetary policy level and by unilateral action de jure or de facto. Free movement for persons had still not been completely satisfactorily achieved, and real progress had not been made on harmonising social policies.

Neither had the Community satisfactorily managed to assert its personality by the adoption of common positions in international relations—and especially in international monetary relations—owing to differences in policies or thinking.

Against this background, it proved difficult for the Six to keep control over economic developments, particularly since the increasingly close interdependence of the industrialised economies made the question of the Community's uniqueness stand out in ever sharper relief.

Setting its sights on the building of economic and monetary union, 'which must be completed as soon as possible', the Werner Group defined the aims to be achieved. Note that in the Commission memorandum of 12 February 1969, which stressed the need for progress on economic policy and monetary solidarity, these elements were seen as potentially 'giving a fresh impetus to efforts to coordinate and harmonise economic and monetary policies', thereby serving as a starting point for the building of a new Community.[8]

5.1.2 The Final Goal

This was seen as complete economic and monetary union, which could well take a different form under the pressure of circumstances and of policy desiderata. A zone would be set up in which goods, services, persons, and capital would be able to move freely and without distorting competition, yet without causing any structural or regional imbalances. Implementing such a union should heighten well-being in the Community on a durable basis and enhance its contribution to the global economic and monetary equilibrium. For this to happen, the various interests active in the economy and society would have to do their bit to help, so that through the combined effect of market forces and policies devised and deliberately implemented by the authorities responsible, satisfactory growth, high levels of employment, stability, a lessening of regional and social disparities and environmental protection would be achieved.

A feature of economic and monetary union would be a separate monetary zone, with internally convertible currencies, irrevocable fixed exchange rates, the elimination of margins for exchange-rate fluctuation and the complete deregulation of capital movements. Alongside this monetary union, national currencies could be retained or there could be a single Community currency, '[which would make it] very difficult to revert to the old system'.

To ensure that the economic and monetary union would hold together, 'certain responsibilities [would have to be] shifted from the countries to the Community authorities. Such transfers of power would be kept down to the limits necessary to ensure the effectiveness of Community action; they are mainly those concerning the group of policies involved in the maintainance [sic] of general equilibrium. In addition, economic policy instruments would have to be harmonized in the various appropriate areas'.

To make up for the weaknesses in the way the 'point of departure' was defined, the experts emphasised the paths to be followed in various fields. Regarding the need to establish medium-term quantitative objectives compatible with each other and with the end-purposes of the Common Market, the paper stipulated that they should be set for growth, employment, prices, and external equilibrium. These objectives would be updated annually by means of sliding projections.

Short-term economic policy would have to be decided in broad outline at the Community level. As a means of gauging the conditions for regulating global demand—especially through monetary and budgetary policy—normative, compatible economic budgets would have to be drawn up annually and their implementation monitored.

As regards monetary policy (liquidity, interest rates, intervention on the exchanges and management of the reserves), decisions would have to be taken centrally and the Community would have to be equipped with the full range of instruments needed for the task, though they could be used differently in different countries. In monetary and financial relations with non-Community countries and international economic organisations, there would have to be a common policy and shared representation.

Great importance was attached to budgetary policy as a means of steering overall economic development, in which harmonised budgeting would be an essential element in keeping the union together. The paper envisaged an annual budget and planning over several years, with ceilings on major government revenue and expenditure (the size of the balance and the arrangements for financing the deficit or using any surpluses). Allowance would be made for the short-term economic situation and structural peculiarities of each country, with provision for setting up instruments which could be managed according to common guidelines, care being taken not to succumb to any form of over-centralisation. Transfers of power to Community bodies would have to be made where needed for the smooth running of the union and there would have to be a variable budgetary structure operating at several levels—the Community level, the national level, etc.

To prevent any distortion of competition, taxation arrangements would have to be harmonised to a certain extent (particularly as regards value-added tax and taxes likely to influence movements of capital and certain excise duties). This harmonisation would mean that tax frontiers could be abolished, but it should also remain flexible enough to allow fiscal policy to perform its functions at the various levels. Another way of eliminating distortions of competition would be cooperation on structural policy. Structural and regional policies could not be solely a matter for national budgets and financial offsetting measures would have to be devised to rectify disparities in that area.

If economic and monetary union were to hold together, it was vital that incomes in the various Member States should develop on lines that did not diverge too widely. Income development at the Community level should therefore be monitored and discussed with the involvement of both sides of industry, which, in a more general sense, it would be politic to involve closely in the drawing up and implementation of Community policy.

As regards institutional reforms, economic and monetary union called for the establishment and/or adaptation of a number of Community bodies, to which powers previously exercised by the national authorities should be transferred. This process was of fundamental political importance, involving as it did the gradual development of political cooperation in the various fields. In the interim report, the group of experts

> [preferred] not to submit detailed proposals at the present time as to the form the various Community agencies should take', while emphasising that it was 'important that these agencies should be able to work effectively in compliance with democratic rules, and that they should have clearly defined responsibilities and an effective power of decision.[9]

The establishment of economic and monetary union was seen as an objective which could be attained in the course of the decade from 1970 to 1980, as soon as there was confirmation of the political will of the Member States as solemnly expressed at the Hague Conference.[10]

5.1.3 An Irreversible Process by Stages

The final objective set clearly and specifically by the Werner Group—the establishment of an economic and monetary union—was an irreversible process.

Between the point of departure and the end goal, a whole host of operations on a range of fronts would have to be accomplished successfully: the setting of overall economic guidelines, the coordination of short-term economic policies by means of currency and credit , budgeting and taxation and incomes policy, and the adoption of Community policies on structures. If they were to be implemented propitiously, these operations would first entail more effective coordination of national policies, then the harmonisation of these through the adoption of common directives, and, lastly, the transfer of responsibilities from the national to the Community authorities. As these advances were made, steps would have to be taken to ensure that Community instruments were set up to take over from national instruments or supplement their effects.

In all these fields, the steps to be taken would be interdependent and mutually reinforcing; in particular, movement towards monetary unification would have to be dependent on adequate progress being made in regard to the coordination and then the unification of economic policies. In pushing ahead with its economic and monetary unification, the Community would have to state what its own economic and international policy objectives were. It was important that in adapting its internal structures, the Community should continue, through its Member States or on its own account, to be involved in measures, decided on a global scale, to liberalise trade, promote economic and monetary cooperation and aid the developing countries. If that were done, economic and monetary union would have served to strengthen the international division of labour and not to set up a new, self-sufficient bloc within the world economy.

The guiding principle for the experts was that establishing economic and monetary union would require a transitional period—especially when it came to increased coordination of economic policies and monetary cooperation—during which these features would be introduced, developed and consolidated progressively, building on the measures already adopted.

In these circumstances, and having regard to the fundamental principles which it had laid down, the Werner Group considered it would be wise

> [to attempt] to clarify the main measures to be contemplated during the first stage with a view to strengthening the habits of working together adopted by the national authorities and to setting up the necessary machinery. These measures [would] constitute […] a manifestation of the political determination of the Member States to commit themselves, with no going back, along the road to economic and monetary union.[11]

The preparatory work designed to adapt and supplement the Treaty would be completed during the first stage, so that at a later stage increasingly binding commitments could be taken on and Community institutions and instruments could be set working.

5.1.4 The First Stage

At the technical level, the experts considered that a deadline must be set if the enterprise is to win credibility and to progress smoothly a period of three years is the right length of time. It would require a major effort from the Member States and the Community.

Consultation procedures would be given greater force by increasing the number of cases requiring consultation before any decision is taken, and by making full use of the powers conferred on the Community bodies. The areas covered by such consultations were medium-term economic policy, short-term economic policy, budgetary policy, monetary policy and the use of other economic policy instruments; they should lead to the shaping of national decisions in keeping with the points of view agreed on in common. The practical methods and instruments whereby the effectiveness of such consultations would be ensured would be defined later.

Action to harmonise and coordinate national budgetary procedures was regarded as a prerequisite for the implementation of Community decisions in that area.

Taxation and internal currency and credit policy must be dealt with in a harmonised manner and on the basis of a common definition of the overall guidelines for general policy (especially as regards currency and credit, with particular reference to liquidity, credits for the public and private sector and interest rate levels).

As regards external monetary policy, the Werner Group recommended that the Member States genuinely display solidarity in determining their exchange-rate parities, after strengthening consultation procedures in that area. European solidarity could also be shown in the gradual setting up of a unit to represent the Community to the IMF and other international financial bodies.

As the liberalisation of capital movements within the Common Market had been subject to delay as compared with other production factors, the group proposed that, to begin with, a ceiling be set on liberalisation with respect to issues of securities by residents of Member States. Forms of technical harmonisation were also recommended. With a view to this, the Six were urged to hold regular consultations on capital movements within the Community and between it and the outside world, and to take concerted action on the relevant national policies.

5.1.5 An Exchange Stabilisation Fund in the First Stage?

To bind the European partners closer together in the conduct of their monetary relations, an exchange stabilisation fund should be created. It could also make it easier to move through the various stages of monetary unification in a harmonious balance between monetary progress and economic progress. The idea of an exchange stabilisation fund was agreed to by all the members of the Werner Group.

Opinions differed, however, as to when it should be set up. Some members of the group (Pierre Werner, Hubert Ansiaux and, to some extent, Gaetano Stammati) thought the fund should be set up in the first stage. Others (in particular, Johann-Baptist Schöllhorn, with support from Gerard Brouwers) felt that neither an institutional narrowing of the margins for fluctuation nor the establishment of an exchange stabilisation fund were desirable in the first phase. The interim report expressly recorded both these viewpoints which had emerged during the debates in the Werner Group.

Supporters of the fund's being set up during the first stage believed that it would be 'a powerful adjunct to co-operation between central banks'. It would help to harmonise their policies on managing reserves and make it possible to reduce the over-dependence of the Member States on the dollar by facilitating the settlement in Community currencies of payment imbalances within the Community and encouraging the adoption of common stances in monetary relations with the United States. There would also be clear political and psychological advantages to setting up the fund, and bringing it into effect would supply the Community with 'an effective weapon in the drive to ensure balanced development of the economic and monetary union'.[12]

To narrow the margins between European currencies, a 'European exchange rate' would be established as a result of close cooperation between the stabilisation fund and the central banks. An agreement of this kind would symbolise the determination of the Member States to introduce their own currency unit in due course. The experts in the Werner Group who supported the establishment of the fund during the first stage considered that this structure would create, through the operation of a credit mechanism similar to that of the former EPU, a sense of shared interest which might work in favour of economic harmonisation, and would help those involved prepare for the possibility of a widening of the fluctuation margins in the international monetary system.

The other members of the group took the opposite view, believing that it would not be advisable to set up an exchange stabilisation fund or institutionally narrow the margins of fluctuation during the first stage. They felt that major Community monetary policy measures could only be considered when, as a result of effective progress in the harmonisation of economic policy, certain conditions which would guarantee the equilibrium of the economy as a whole throughout the Community had been created.

This other school of thought within the Werner Group wanted swift movement towards the abolition of the margins and guaranteed, fixed exchange rates. The arguments they put forward emphasised that 'guaranteed exchange rates, without bands, are an important objective of the economic and monetary union', but they believed that this aim could be achieved on a lasting basis only if there were a genuine policy of equilibrium throughout the Community. A strengthening of economic policy harmonisation was the key to Community cohesion during the first stage. Such a convergence of economic policies would of itself bring about a narrowing of the variations in exchange rates between European currencies.

The opinion of these members was that 'the establishment of an exchange stabilization fund during the first stage [...] would [not] be the best way of achieving the ultimate objective of a European central bank'. There was no doubt that in the final stage the Community would have to be given an independent central body similar to the US Federal Reserve Board. To make the establishment of such an institution possible, it would be necessary to prepare, during the first stage, for a revision of the Community treaties.

5.1.6 Conclusions

Moving beyond certain opposing points of view and the different slants given to the points at issue, the Werner Group adopted a set of unanimous conclusions. These would be added to the 'road map' for further discussions and would form the backbone of the final report.

The group affirmed that economic and monetary union meant that the main decisions on economic policy would be taken at the Community level. For this purpose, the presumption was that the requisite powers would be transferred from the national to the Community level.

> The ultimate goal could be the adoption of a single currency, which would ensure that there was no going back on the decisions taken.[13]

Most of the steps needed between the point of departure and the final goal would have to be accomplished in parallel and progressively on several fronts. Substantial progress are possible within the framework of the existing Treaty, but amendments would be required and would therefore have to be adopted in the first stage.

The first stage should begin on 1 January 1971 and be carried out within a predetermined time frame, which the group put at three years. During that period the Community instruments would be made more and more operational and the Community would begin to assert its individuality within the international monetary system. In no sense would the first stage be equivalent to a complete process of economic and monetary integration, but it would be a vital stage on the path to the final objective.

With regard to the initial stage, the group was unanimous in recommending a strengthening of consultation procedures (according to methods which were still to be determined). It was also emphasised that the Member States should conduct their budgetary policies in line with Community objectives, that there should be some degree of harmonisation in the fiscal field, that currency and credit policy should be tightly coordinated and that the integration of the financial markets should be stepped up.

In international monetary relations with other countries and with financial organisations operating at the international level, the Community should gradually adopt common positions.

Particular attention was placed on exchange relations between the Member States. To safeguard their stability, the Community should not avail itself of any provisions allowing for a slackening of the international exchange system. As for the advisability of equipping the Community with a special exchange arrangement, and the means of doing so, during the first stage, the options remained open. Some members of the group argued for a reduction, even a limited one, in fluctuations of the exchange rates between Community currencies.

The setting up of an exchange stabilisation fund and coordinated intervention by central banks on the foreign-exchange markets could make it possible to achieve that aim. The establishment of the fund would be of value in itself, even if there were no narrowing of the margins. Other members, in contrast, considered that monetary solidarity must come after the harmonisation of economic policies and situations and 'not be derived from specific monetary measures, which they feel would be both premature and too risky in the first stage'.

5.2 The Final Report

The interim report was given the backing of the meeting of Finance Ministers in Venice and then became the main item for discussion on the agenda for the Council of Ministers' meeting in Luxembourg on 8 and 9 June, which gave approval for the Werner Group to continue its work.[14]

In his capacity as chairman of the group of experts, Pierre Werner explained the thinking behind the plan by stages, presented the interim report and ended by stressing that further work needed to be done, focusing on certain priority areas.[15]

On the basis of the interim report and the themes mentioned above, the experts set to work drafting the final report, holding six meetings between 24 June and 8 October 1970. The discussions were animated, with frequent lively clashes; but the interests at stake fostered a concern to hammer out a consensus on a common position, and doctrinaire and political pride was set aside. This spirit would not last long, however, as France was already beginning to severely criticise the report.

5.2.1 Final Objective and Institutional Aspects of EMU

While keeping the same structure and the strong points singled out in the interim report (the starting point and final objective for the plan by stages), the final report, which contained more material and went into greater detail, did nevertheless clarify additional points, offer new solutions and set forth new methods of achieving them in practice. The final objective—and therefore what economic and monetary union at the first stage involved—was defined in greater detail, as was the transitional period leading to the final objective.

With an eye to the introduction of a common currency and to monetary solidarity in the international arena, and to back up the measures to be put into effect during the first stage, the Committee of Governors of the Central Banks—urged on by Werner and following the strategy devised with Ansiaux—issued a technical opinion on particular monetary topics. This opinion was an integral part of the final report, while still continuing to be a separate paper.

Although the assessment of the starting point was very similar to what was said in the interim report, the final objective—economic and monetary union—was defined in summary form as having seven features.

It had initially been planned that the Community currencies should be completely and irreversibly mutually convertible, without any exchange rate fluctuation and at permanently fixed rates of parity. It was deemed preferable for these currencies to be replaced by a single common currency.

The creation of liquidity throughout the zone and monetary and credit policy should be conducted in a centralised fashion. Monetary policy vis-à-vis the outside world would be a Community responsibility. The same would apply to the basic data in all official budgets and, in particular, to variations in their volume, the size of balances and the methods of financing or using these. The Member States' policies on capital markets would be unified. Regional and structural policies would no longer be exclusively a matter for the Member States. Lastly, there would be routine, ongoing consultation of both sides of industry at the Community level.

Establishing economic and monetary union would require institutional reforms, i.e. the creation or conversion of certain Community bodies to which powers exercised by the national authorities would have to be transferred. It was noted that

> These transfers of responsibility represent a process of fundamental political significance which implies the progressive development of political cooperation. Economic and monetary union thus appears as a leaven for the development of political union, which in the long run it cannot do without.[16]

Detailed proposals regarding institution building were not made, but the Werner Group did say it was imperative that two supranational bodies seen as vital to mastering economic and monetary policy within the union should be set up: a centre of decision for economic policy and a Community system of central banks.

The centre of decision for economic policy would act in the Community's interests and, operating independently, would exercise a crucial influence over the Community's overall economic policy. It should, therefore, be able to influence budgets, since the part which the Community budget could play as an instrument of short-term economic policy would not be sufficient. The decision-making centre was seen as having a particularly important part to play with regard to the level and purpose of the balances and the methods of financing deficits or using up surpluses.

Changes in the parity of the single currency or all the national currencies would also be a matter for the decision-making centre. To ensure that there was the requisite link to overall economic policy, its responsibilities would extend to other fields of economic and social policy which would have been transferred to the Community level.

As the Werner Group saw it, the transfer to the Community level of powers hitherto exercised by national bodies would go hand in hand with the transfer of corresponding parliamentary accountability from the national level to that of the Community. The centre of decision for economic policy would be politically answerable to a European Parliament, which would have to be given a status commensurate with the expansion of the Community's business, not only as regards the extent of its powers but also as regards the election of its members.

The second Community body seen as essential would be a Community system of central banks. In setting it up, a structure such as that of the US Federal Reserve System could be taken as a model. In line with the demands of the economic situation, this Community institution would be empowered to take decisions on internal monetary policy. Its areas of competence would relate to liquidity, interest rates and the granting of loans to the public and private sectors. In the field of external monetary policy matters, it would have authority to intervene on the exchange markets and to manage the Community's monetary reserves.

As regards the transfers of national powers to the Community level, the Werner Group drew attention to a number of political problems associated with the relationship between the centre of decision for economic policy and the Community system of central banks, and between the Community bodies and the national authorities.

> While safeguarding the responsibilities proper to each it will be necessary to guarantee that the Community organ competent for economic policy and that dealing with monetary problems are aiming at the same objectives.[17]

5.2.2 Key Features of the First Stage

Stage one was to start on 1 January 1971 and would last three years.

One of the main operations to be undertaken was to step up the coordination of economic policies, backed up by the development of a swift, effective system for the exchange of information between Member States so that the basic guidelines for economic and monetary policy could be worked out jointly. The Werner Group pointed out that economic policy coordination would be bound to mean some constraint, but that such coordination would only be implemented and developed gradually. The systems and measures to be established would have to be dictated by the view of economic and monetary union ultimately taken. During stage one, the requisite mechanisms and institutions would be set up and would operate under existing treaty provisions.

The coordination of economic policies was seen as involving at least three detailed annual surveys of the economic situation in the Community, such as to allow the common definition of economic policy guidelines.[18] Consultations would cover medium-term economic policy, short-term economic policy, budgetary policy and monetary policy, and should lead to the shaping of national decisions in keeping with the points of view arrived at in common. Consultation procedures would be reinforced by being made an obligatory prior condition.

The key Community bodies responsible for coordinating economic policies would be the Council, the EC Commission and the Committee of Governors of the Central Banks. The Council would be the central decision-making body for overall economic policy; the Commission would have to take on major responsibilities and make all appropriate proposals to the Council; the Committee of Governors would have an increasingly important part to play with regard to both internal and external monetary policy questions.

As an expression of economic policy coordination the production of a more official document is envisaged at least once a year—the 'Annual report on the economic situation of the Community', which would be sent to the European Parliament, the Economic and Social Committee and the governments of the Member States. The latter would pass it on to their national parliaments so that they could take account of it when discussing draft budgets. A similar procedure would be followed for the medium-term quantitative objectives set at the Community level.

Joint consultations with the two sides of industry and their involvement in preparing the Community's economic policy was seen as one of the main factors for success in the establishment of economic and monetary union. '[…] Major guidelines on economic policy should not be adopted until they have been consulted' and, from the first stage, procedures for regular joint consultation between the Commission and the two sides of industry would have to be established.

In the spirit of the Werner Group, there should be special emphasis on the efforts to be made to coordinate and harmonise budgetary policies. Quantitative guidelines would be given for the main components of official budgets, particularly overall revenue and expenditure, the dividing of these between investment and consumption, and the purpose and size of the balance, with special attention being paid to ways of financing deficits or using surpluses. Efforts would be made to devise and develop comparable instruments in each country (such as 'fiscal regulators' on the revenue side, and 'cyclical budgets' on the expenditure side).

As regards fiscal policy, indirect taxes are a matter of the highest priority. The value-added tax system would become general practice and a programme of action to bring taxation rates closer together would be adopted. Some types of direct taxes which could precisely influence capital movements inside the Community would have to be harmonised (as is the case of the system for taxing interest on fixed-interest securities and dividends, and, in some respects, the taxes on corporations).

As the liberalisation of capital movements inside the Common Market had always been beyond the scope of the objectives laid down in the treaty, the Werner Group believed swift action needed to be launched on two fronts: the elimination of obstacles in the way of capital movements and, in particular, the remaining exchange control provisions, and coordination of the policies regarding money markets. Allowing securities from other Member States to be traded on stock exchanges would be free of any form of discrimination. As regards the coordination of policies relating to financial markets, a distinction would be made between current aspects[19] and structural aspects.[20]

The general thrust of monetary and credit policies would be defined in common and, in that context, the instruments of monetary policy and credit policy available to the Member States should be gradually harmonise (under the responsibility of the Committee of Governors).

From stage one, the process of embarking on the establishment of economic and monetary union would require greater cooperation on external monetary policy. Solidarity between Member States in determining their exchange rates should be given practical expression in a strengthening of the consultation procedures in that area. Thus is envisaged a unit representing the Community to the IMF and other international financial bodies. The Community would have to progressively adopt common positions in its monetary relations with non-Community countries and international organisations. In exchange-rate relations between the Six, the Community must not in any circumstances rely on provisions which would make the international exchange system more flexible.

In this connection, the Werner Group made proposals for special, detailed measures. It was proving to be essential to carry out a thorough study of the conditions for the establishment and operation of the 'European fund for monetary cooperation' whose purpose was to ensure the requisite switch to the Community system of central banks planned for the final stage, and to define its rules of procedure.[21]

The preparatory work towards amending and supplementing the treaty should be brought to a successful conclusion so that an intergovernmental conference to discuss any proposals drawn up on the question could be convened before the end of stage. This would set in motion the procedures for laying down the legal bases needed for transition to the establishment of full economic and monetary union and the implementation of the vital institutional reforms which that would involve. The Council would then be able to draw up a new programme.

5.2.3 Transition to the Final Objective

Stage one would be followed by a later stage for which the Werner Group laid down the main lines. There should be still more vigorous coordination of national policies, after which they would be harmonised by means of common directives or decisions, leading eventually to the transfer of responsibilities from the national authorities to the Community authorities. As this progress was achieved, Community instruments would be set up to take over or supplement the work of national instruments.

The coordination of economic and monetary policies should be bolstered by taking the common interest into account to an increasingly forceful degree. This should apply first to short-term economic policy. The points at which national policies clashed or converged should be identified so that strategies could be worked out with an eye to achieving the optimum solution for the Community (which would not necessarily involve merely combining the optimum solutions at the national level). At the same time, the definition and general thrust of economic policy should be made progressively more binding and there should be a proper harmonisation of monetary and budgetary policies.

Medium-term economic policy programmes should be focused more and more towards achieving Community objectives. As regards budgetary policy, comparable instruments developed during stage one would gradually be applied in common. By sweeping away miscellaneous obstacles and harmonising financial structures, it should be possible to attain a real common market in capital through the gradual interpenetration of national markets.

In parallel with the measures to achieve overall balance, thought should be given to measures addressing certain structural aspects closely associated with the implementation of this process (especially regional policy and employment policy). Action should also be taken to work out, progressively, a Community line on industrial policy and policies on transport, energy, housing and regional development.

With regard to monetary issues, the Werner Group advocated a strengthening of intra-Community ties so as to make the transition towards economic and monetary union easier. Balance between the Member States' economies would be ensured by the free movement of production factors and by financial transfers in the public and private sectors. During stage two, with the progress already achieved in the area of economic and monetary policy convergence, the Six should no longer need to resort independently to changing the parity rate as an instrument of policy. At the final stage, independent changes in parity rates would be ruled out completely.

For the preparation of the final stage, a 'European monetary cooperation fund' (EMCF), under the authority of the central bank governors, should be set up as soon as possible. If the techniques for intervening on the exchange markets scheduled for stage one worked as planned, and if an adequate degree of economic policy convergence were achieved, the fund could perhaps be set up in stage one and should absorb the mechanisms for short-term monetary support and medium-term financial assistance. The fund would gradually become a Community-level reserve management body, until it was incorporated, at the final stage, into the Community system of central banks which would be set up at that time.

5.3 Input from the Committee of Governors of the Central Banks

The establishment of a EMCF was a principle very dear to the heart of Pierre Werner. He raised the idea as early as 1962, and in a more sustained manner from May 1967, in European political and economic circles by sketching out the idea of such an institution and giving it the name it was later to bear. In January 1968, and subsequently in the 'Luxembourg plan for monetary integration', he described the structure, role, functions, and powers of the fund and set out how they would gradually be put in place as from the first stage of the implementation of economic and monetary union.[22]

Pierre Werner and Hubert Ansiaux, chairman of the Committee of Governors of the Central Banks, took the same view of the main points at issue in relation to the exchange stabilisation fund and the reserve fund, and their thinking was on the same lines when it came to their ideas, their objectives and the strategies they thought should be adopted; this, indeed, was what was behind the emergence of this committee as a budding monetary authority for the Community and of the EMCF, as the work on the drafting of the Werner Report showed. In the group, their collaboration had already borne fruit in guiding the debates; in April 1970, at Werner's request, Ansiaux had already submitted his thoughts on the functioning of an exchange stabilisation fund as well as on the SDRs.

As the group pressed ahead with its work, Werner kept up an ongoing and often confidential dialogue with Ansiaux. Following an exchange of letters between them from 3 to 12 June 1970, Werner asked Ansiaux to get the Committee of Governors—which was seen as having a vital part to play in the establishment of the exchange stabilisation fund—to give its views on several subjects. The first of these was the exchange system and, in particular, a narrowing of the margins between the currencies of the Common Market countries.

With the Council Decision of 9 June 1970 endorsing the opinion of the Governors, Werner sent a letter three days later to the Chairman of the Committee, in line with a strategy the two men had devised, asking him to give his point of view on setting up of an exchange system specially for the Community. On 16 June, Ansiaux replied to Werner's letter with an undertaking to deliver an opinion by 15 July focusing 'on the advisability of harmonising monetary policy instruments and effectively bringing the Member States' monetary policies closer together'.[23] Detailed study of the measures to be adopted, on the other hand, was postponed until the last quarter of the year, as and when the information received would make it possible to draw specific conclusions.

The approach was a prudent one, not only in the sense of the natural reluctance of the central bankers to pronounce on the subjects on which they were being asked for their views, but especially because their approaches and positions were at variance—as Pierre Werner's private archives make plain. Baron Ansiaux quickly convened the panel of experts, whose inaugural meeting took place on 25 June 1970.[24] After five further gatherings, the committee gave its opinion on 1 August 1970. This document was annexed to the Werner Report.[25]

The experts mandated by the central bankers concluded that it would be technically possible to plan for a gradual process, which presupposed 'that sufficient progress would at the same time be made in the harmonization of economic policies'. The first step the central banks should take towards establishing a special exchange system for the Community would be to act together to limit the fluctuations between their currencies 'de facto'. This objective would be achieved by concerted action on the dollar. As a second stage, a narrowing of the margins would be announced, followed by concerted action on the dollar, possibly supplemented by intervention in Community currencies at the limits of the margins. The addition of intervention in Community currencies at the limits and within the margins to the concerted action on the dollar could be considered at a later stage.

The taking of these steps could be facilitated by using an 'agent', which could be the Bank for International Settlements (BIS). The task of this agent would be to record the balances on transactions on the Member States' markets, to total them and to notify each central bank of them daily, with suggestions for transfers which could be made in Community currencies and in dollars. If the central banks agreed to allow each other bilateral credits, clearing operations in dollars could then be carried out within the same framework.

If there were more effective coordination of economic policies, the technical operations referred to above should function smoothly and without a hitch, and the transition to a new stage, involving the establishment of a fund, would thus be possible. 'The experts think that the study in depth of the conditions of creation and operation of this Fund is worth undertaking, in conjunction with other studies, notably those aimed at the harmonization of monetary policies'.

Although it was approved and submitted to the Werner Group on 1 August 1970—the date also assigned to it in the Final Report—the technical opinion from the Governors was put on the agenda for the meeting of central bankers on 12 and 13 September 1970, with a view to 'finalising the opinion which the committee [had] been asked to deliver to Mr. Werner, chairman of the group'.[26]

This last gathering of the central bankers before the Werner Report was drawn up in its final form was attended by Vice-President of the Commission Barre, assisted by Director-General Mosca, and turned out to be extremely cautious in its approach. While proposing that participants should give a final statement of their overall view regarding the experts' report, Ansiaux suggested focusing discussion on two points: the gradual process set out in the plan by stages, and the provisions to be included when the further detailed studies which the experts wished to see done were carried out.

The governors' alternates on the committee debated and unanimously approved the technical opinion at the meeting held in Brussels on 2 September 1970.

As spokesman for the alternates, Cecil de Strycker (Vice-Governor and deputy to Ansiaux at the National Bank of Belgium) emphasised the fact that, given the disagreement on the subject, in the opinion they had approved, the alternates had not commented either on the calendar or on the measures to be proposed for various stages of the gradual phases referred to in the report. 'Differences came to light on these two essential points and the alternates felt that they should not be passed on to Mr. Werner, the chairman, especially since the conclusions in the report are specific enough to supply the Werner Committee and the Council of the European Communities with practical elements'. They declared, however, that it was vitally important that further work be done on the technical aspects before any genuinely committed concerted action could be taken by the central banks (as soon as the Council had taken a decision on such action). The study relating to the harmonisation of monetary policy instruments, which was among the priorities mentioned in Werner's letter, should be embarked upon without delay.

Members then went on to discuss the types of measures to be included as regards margin differentiation. Alongside these measures, there should be an evaluation of the credits that might be needed for them and—by a faster process than that proposed in the Werner Report—a Community body should be set up to look into the questions raised by the margins. Discussions focused only on the first point and differences of approach prevented the reaching of any agreement on the technical aspects, particularly the narrowing of margins and the setting of variable margins against the dollar. The conclusion was somewhat enigmatic: 'The governors acknowledge, on the whole, the usefulness of stating which solution they prefer in the covering letter forwarded with the report to Mr. Werner, but that solution is not the same for all'.[27]

There were two main camps. The Germans (represented at the meeting by the Chairman of the Bundesbank, Karl Klasen, and the Vice-Chairman, Otmar Emminger), with whom the French (Olivier Wormser, Governor of the Banque de France, and Clappier) and the Belgians (Ansiaux and de Strycker) sided, advocated a de facto reduction of the margins of fluctuation between Community currencies, followed by an official narrowing (the French saw the operations as occurring in the reverse order, but with the same results in the end). To test the application of these measures, the Deutsche Bundesbank said it was 'prepared to embark on the experimental stage as soon as the relevant decisions have been taken, for instance on 1 January 1971'. The Dutch, on the other hand (Jelle Zijlstra, Chairman of the Nederlandsche Bank, and Paul Mackay), partly supported by the Italians (Guido Carli, Governor of the Banca d'Italia, and Paolo Baffi), thought that more flexible margins would be preferable from a pragmatic point of view, since they would leave the same latitude for manoeuvre, which would make it easier to secure an official narrowing of the margins for exchanges within the Community. They were, however, prepared to agree to start with a de facto reduction in the intra-Community margins. Raymond Barre expressed his views, namely that the central question, the fixing of 'a Community level for the dollar', was somewhat occluded in the conclusions of the report and that the Council should basically ask the central banks whether they thought they would be able to change their current system of exchange rate relations.

Against this background of disagreement and doubt, Ansiaux and Clappier, as members of the Werner Group, drew attention to the risks of delivering an opinion which does not contain a specific choice for the first measures to be adopted and which will probably be done in less favourable conditions by the Werner Group. In any case, the choice had to be made after the Council had decided to launch the first stage of economic and monetary union. Carli therefore proposed that the decision on this be left to the Finance Ministers and the matter was considered closed as far as that meeting was concerned.

As regards further work on the aspects to be studied by the experts, Ansiaux mentioned three main lines of research: a network for direct communication between central banks, the harmonisation of monetary policy instruments, and the terms for the establishment and operation of a 'fund'. A new group of experts from the Committee of Governors would be set up to work with the Monetary Committee on harmonising monetary policy instruments and then give its attention to the 'fund'. As for the system for communication between central banks, it was unanimously agreed to launch the requisite technical and organisational procedures.

The same restraint was to be seen when it came to the calendar for any gradual process that might be proposed. C. de Strycker reminded the meeting that the deputies had considered the question and had not wished to propose that the governors give the Werner Group any specific dates. It was clear to the experts that the first stage—consultation between the central banks—should begin as soon as the Council so decided and that it was important that the requisite technical studies should have been carried out by that time.

Ansiaux and Clappier then put before the meeting a paper for which they both bore responsibility not having had an opportunity to discuss it with their associates. This was a document dated 4 September 1970 on stepping up the coordination of monetary and credit policy during the first stage, which will not be incorporated into the Werner Report but supplies ideas which can be taken up. Thus, there were proposals for developing and widening the consultations already taking place between the Committee of Governors and the Monetary Committee (procedure, bodies, topics discussed). In fact, as Mosca was to say during the discussions, the paper was a response to a request Werner, the chairman, had previously sent on refining the definition of the functions of the Committee of Governors during the first stage, and for this reason Ansiaux urged his peers to give thought to specific, practical means and methods. As the Monetary Committee was not an 'action body'—unlike the Committee of Governors—the central bankers proposed that a special body be set up to prepare the ground for the work to be done in common and the Monetary Committee agreed to steer its work in the direction of the action taken by Governors. As Vice-Chairman of the Monetary Committee, Emminger opposed this view, believing that his committee was the best placed to set up within itself a group to prepare the central bankers' work, since their delegates sat on the Monetary Committee.

The group consisting of these representatives could to some extent be institutionalised, its sittings could be held before those of the Committee of Governors, and it would serve as a guarantor of effective coordination between the Committee of Governors and the Monetary Committee. Clappier, who took a different view, put a stop to this new discussion and the meeting, which was supposed to have cleared up certain points and made them more specific before the Werner Report was finalised, ended in disagreement. This 'sensitive' issue was diplomatically postponed.

On 8 October 1970, Pierre Werner publicly presented the final report from his group, on which he had secured consensus from all those present. The document gave an outline of a comprehensive plan for the establishment of economic and monetary union in three stages, on the principle of 'parallel movement in practice'.[28] This principle applied in three areas: parallel movement in progress towards economic policy convergence and the imposition of additional monetary constraints; parallel movement in the imposition of monetary constraints and the transfer of powers over economic policy (monetary and credit policy) to the Community; parallel movement in the development of Community powers and the corresponding development of effective European institutions (strengthening the role of the European Parliament, the Commission and the system of central banks).

During the first stage, then, an effort was to be made to 'coordinate' and 'harmonise' budgetary policies and, as an experiment, limits were to be placed on the fluctuations in exchange rates between Community currencies. We should remember that, institutionally speaking, the Werner Report advocated, for the final stage, setting up a 'centre of decision for economic policy', which would be politically answerable to the European Parliament, and a 'Community system of central banks'. Economic and monetary union seemed to the Plan's authors to be an 'objective realizable in the course of the present decade', and the culmination of the process was supposed to be the 'irrevocable fixing of parity ratios' or, better still, a 'single currency' by 1980.

> Until the time of this report, which is inextricably associated with the Hague Conference, the Member States had always looked forward to an economic union, or at any rate a common market, which they thought could be achieved, as far as the monetary aspects were concerned, merely by coordinating their policies; from the Hague Conference and the Werner Report onwards, they realised that economic union could not be brought about unless they gradually established monetary union.[29]

5.4 Economists vs. Monetarists: Towards a Balanced Approach to EMU[30]

The work of the Werner Committee, the discussions, debates, and negotiations in the group of experts, and the ensuing agreements and arguments about the points at issue gave rise to clashes over the idea of currency as the principal vector for the integration process.

There were generally two opposing points of view, two contrasting ways of thinking.

On one side, there were the 'monetarists' (whose standard-bearers were the countries with), who argued for 'institutions'. To their way of thinking, the priority should be to set up institutions and lay down requirements to be met. After that, there would be a coordinating of economic policies, driven forward by concerted action on the single currency which would already exist. The 'monetarists' thought that the only way to give any credibility to the prospect of monetary union and influence the behaviour of players in the economy was to set a timetable and lay down some rules of conduct. On the other side were the 'economists' (the countries with strong currencies). According to them, a convergence of economic policies—monetary and budgetary policies—was vital and must come before the setting up of institutions. A single currency would come only at the end of the process, as the 'finishing touch' to a harmonisation which would already have been carried out.

In the Werner Group, economist positions were supported by the Germans—in particular, Finance Minister Karl Schiller, who tabled several documents on behalf of his government, including a 'German plan for monetary integration' published on 12 February 1970—and the Dutch. They were joined by the Italians, whose position on economic and monetary union, influenced by both economist and monetarist views,[31] evolved over time.[32] They thought that the fact that the word *economic* comes before the word *monetary* in the expression *economic and monetary union* proved that monetary union should come after economic union. The French and the Belgians (Baron Ansiaux) sided with the monetarists in considering that the economy is led by deliberate monetary decisions. For them, therefore, the priority was quick decisions on the margins for fluctuation between European currencies, concerted monetary action and the establishment of a reserve fund. Through his earlier public speeches and writings, Pierre Werner had tended to side with the monetarists. In discharging his duties as chairman of the group of experts, however, Werner chose to remain neutral, advocating a parallel approach to economic cooperation and monetary coordination as the underlying principle for the group's reflections.

These different views on the method of achieving economic convergence and thus promoting integration actually hid the divergences between France and Germany. The approach of the 'French monetarists' was the exact opposite of that of the 'German economists' as regards the political objectives to adopt. The perception supported by France was that of an economic and monetary union which, at the monetary level, guaranteed a fixed-rate Community system while allowing countries to hold onto national sovereignty over economic and financial policy.

In such a system, 'the formal maintenance of national autonomy means little since, because of the mechanism acting at the short-term, monetary level, what happens is [...] a forced alignment at the average level dictated by the economic climate at the time'.[33] This kind of forced harmonisation was against the interests of countries moving towards stability, such as Germany, which was convinced that monetary union without economic harmonisation was doomed to fail or to fall by the wayside. Germany also believed that countries going through balance of payments problems, like France, acted in favour of monetary union 'so that they would be able to solve their problems without reforming their economic policies and by relying on European reserves which would basically be German reserves'.[34]

Another sensitive point which was argued over was the existence of a supranational decision-making body for economic and monetary policy. During discussions in the Werner Committee, the German Minister for Economic Affairs and Finance, Karl Schiller, advocated strong coordination of domestic budgetary policies at the European level, which meant a political authority alongside the future Central Bank. France was fiercely opposed to this, as it wished to avoid national sovereignty being too severely truncated in this area.

The clashes between economists and monetarists among the Six had started to emerge long before the Werner Group started its work, as the debates around the first Barre Plan and the attitudes to it clearly show.[35] Following the recommendations in the Barre Plan for greater integration of the economies and the need for convergence, the Community countries reached agreement with the Council of Ministers' decision of 17 July 1969. The Germans advocated ongoing, parallel development and medium-term policy coordination. The Belgians, the Dutch, the Italians, and the Germans agreed on non-automatic short-term support. The Luxembourgers took a balanced, middle course. The Benelux countries also adopted a common position, calling for the veto on British accession to be lifted before any negotiations on further European integration. The representatives of the central banks had serious reservations about monetary cooperation, though they were finally won over to the view of the Monetary Committee and suggested monetary solidarity through the establishment of medium-term support and flexible exchange rates.

During the course of 1969, the debate was fanned on one side by the monetary difficulties caused by the floating of the franc and the West German mark, and on the other by the almost simultaneous change of leadership in France and Germany. The accession to power of Georges Pompidou (following the presidential elections of 15 June 1969) gave fresh impetus to France's action on behalf of Europe. The French view on economic integration was that 'the argument now is not only between economic coordination and monetary cooperation but between accepting a little flexibility and monetary cooperation. The option now is a minimum scenario leaving countries a wide margin for manoeuvre'.[36]

The new German Chancellor, Willy Brandt (elected on 21 October 1969), wanted to embark on a course of active diplomacy, and model cooperation with France was a vital part of his foreign policy, especially since Pompidou's accession to the French Presidency seemed to favour that prospect. The Chancellor—who was in regular touch with Jean Monnet—was convinced that setting up a real monetary dimension was a way of deepening the process of Community integration. The German Minister for Economic Affairs and Finance, Karl Schiller, took a different view of the matter and did not share the Chancellor's enthusiasm.

What is more, Brandt regarded the deepening of the EEC—especially in economic and monetary terms—as being less important than its enlargement.[37] This lack of domestic consensus caused the German Government to adopt a sceptical attitude to the feasibility of European economic and monetary projects. It was against this backdrop that Pompidou's proposal for a meeting of the Heads of State of the Europe of Six to discuss the 'completion, deepening and enlargement' triptych was made and the resulting summit meeting at The Hague was held on 1 and 2 December 1969. That meeting tasked the Council, working closely with the Commission, with looking into ways of making progress towards economic and monetary union by stages. A group of experts—the Werner Committee—subsequently came into being.

Going beyond their opposing views and differences over doctrine and political action, 'at the beginning of the 1970s, the Franco-German duo therefore thought that Europeanising the common market through expansion should be the priority and that economic and monetary Europeanisation should be a secondary issue'.[38] The main challenge was to pave the way for an area of consensus, an understanding between two diametrically opposed ways of seeing economic and monetary affairs.

This concerted tactical behaviour was permeated with a concern for the respective national interests of the two countries, but also influenced by the fact that minds at the time were focusing on the enlargement negotiations between the European Economic Community and four candidate countries—the UK, Ireland, Denmark, and Norway.[39] The Werner Report as written bears the imprint of this superficial Franco-German agreement on a monetary deepening of European integration. National stances heavily pervaded the attitudes of the Werner Group members, who, 'although [...] appointed because of the posts they held in the Community, put forward arguments which increasingly reflected the concerns of their governments'.[40]

After seven months of work, discussions, arguments, horse-trading, and reversals, a consensus was hammered out in the group of experts and the Werner Report was approved. On 8 October 1970, Mr. Werner, the group chairman, presented it publicly in Luxembourg. The compromise which made approval of the Werner Report possible was very probably a precarious compromise, obtained by opting for the lowest common denominator. The guiding principle behind the devising of the plan by stages—an evolving plan in three stages over a ten-year period—leading to the establishment of an economic and monetary union, was 'real parallel movement' on economic policy and monetary policy.

In Germany, the Werner Report was seen as serious and well-balanced and, all in all, reactions to it were positive. Speaking in the Bundestag in 1970, Chancellor Brandt described the plan for economic and monetary union by stages as 'the European Community's new Magna Carta'.[41] In a letter to the German Finance Minister, Karl Schiller, a few days after the public presentation of the plan by stages, the Chancellor made clear that he was aware of how important it was to the cause of European integration and said he believed that its final adoption by the Council—if possible, by the end of the year—would 'very probably [be] the most important decision since the signing of the Rome Treaties'.[42] Karl Schiller was on the same wavelength: a staunch supporter of the plan by stages, he regarded it as the 'leaven in the mix which would lead to political union'.[43] Schiller also stressed the need to remain true to the objective of stability as 'the indispensable condition for the transition from the first to the second stage' of the Werner Report.[44]

The Bundesbank, although it was in favour of a movement towards economic and monetary union by stages, was primarily concerned with safeguarding monetary stability during this process. The discussions of this issue in the Bundesbank's *Zentralbankrat* centred on two demands in relation to the system proposed by the Werner Report. Firstly, margins for fluctuation should not be reduced until after there had been genuine harmonisation of economic and financial policies. Secondly, the future council of the chairmen of the central banks should, from the outset, be responsible for laying down monetary policy guidelines, independently of the Council of Ministers, though they should nevertheless take the Council's guidelines for economic policy into account. The Bundesbank's leaders firmly believed that future monetary policy should be the responsibility of Europe's central bankers collectively.[45] What made the German Central Bank's view especially important was that the Bundesbank was expected to serve as the model for the future European Central Bank.[46] Both the minister and the Bundesbank were critical of statements by the Commission, which seemed to want to favour the monetary cooperation aspects at the expense of economic harmonisation and to be attacking the autonomy of the national central banks right from the first stage of the establishment of economic and monetary union.[47]

In France, discussions on the Werner Report focused on different issues. President Pompidou did not think that transferring vital powers over monetary matters to the Community institutions, as planned for the second stage, was either realistic or desirable. To him, only economic and financial cooperation as part of the first stage seemed realistic.

As to how this integration would develop in the future, Paris wanted to give as few undertakings as possible, thereby calling the single currency—the very essence of monetary integration—into question. This disavowal of the Werner Report is even more surprising when we consider that it had been drawn up with input from the French representatives, just like the interim report, which had been agreed to by the ministers responsible. We know that President Pompidou expressly gave orders for the negotiations not to be brought to a conclusion, as had been planned, at the Brussels Council of Ministers on 14 December 1970, as a sign of his disagreement with the 'European jokers' whom he believed he had identified, especially among the politicians from the Benelux countries. This is why the French delegation at the Council meetings of 23 November and 14 December 1970 was extremely reluctant to agree to successive transfers of powers to the Community institutions while at the same time rejecting the idea that there should be automatic transition from the first stage to the second. Germany, meanwhile, expressed reservations about the financing clauses as long as there were no tangible achievements to show in relation to policy coordination.

Although the objective of the plan for economic and monetary union was medium-term integration, actual agreement between the European partners went no further than the first three-year stage. With hindsight, the idea of setting up economic and monetary union in a decade looks somewhat out of step with the difficult situation in Europe at the time: the approach was probably over-optimistic. Even so, the original plan had the advantage of giving a focus to discussions and marking out a forward-looking vision.

The Council of Ministers of the Community officially ratified the plan for economic and monetary union on 22 March 1971. However, developments in the international monetary system, which went into full-blown crisis mode after the US decision on 15 August 1971 to devalue the dollar, would thwart the shared ambition set out in the Werner Report, already weakened as it was by the absence of any real political will.

Notes

1. 'Draft minutes of the first meeting of the ad hoc 'plan by stages' group, 20 March 1970', European Communities, secretariat of the 'plan by stages' group, Brussels, 31 March 1970, ORII/22/70-F. In the Pierre Werner Family archives.
2. 'Verbatim account of speeches. Meeting of the ad hoc 'plan by stages' group on 7 April 1970', Brussels, 10 April 1970, confidential, ref. ORII/28/70E. In the Pierre Werner Family archives.
3. 'Verbatim of statements by Mr. Ansiaux and Mr. Clappier. Meeting of the ad hoc group on the plan by stages', 7 April 1970. Brussels, 10 April 1970, confidential, ref. ORII/28/70F. In the Pierre Werner Family archives.
4. 'Note regarding progress with economic and monetary union at the end of the plan by stages', European Commission, secretariat of the 'plan by stages' group, OR II/24/70, Brussels, 3 April 1970. In the Pierre Werner Family archives.
5. The French title of the summary the Werner Group submitted for discussion at the meeting of Finance Ministers in Venice on 29 May 1970 was *Rapport intermédiaire* [intermediate report] *sur l'établissement par étapes d'une Union économique et monétaire*, published in *Bulletin of the European Communities*, Supplement, 7 (1970), OJC 94 (23 July 1970) (Luxembourg: Office for Official Publications of the European Communities). In the group's work, in the minutes of its meetings, in the press reports at the time and then in the specialist literature the term *rapport intérimaire* [interim report] was widely used. Both forms of words entered common parlance, with the same meaning. In English, however, there was not this distinction; the published report was headed *Interim report on the establishment by stages of economic and monetary union*.
6. P. Werner (1992, II) *Itinéraires*, p. 125. For an overview and further details about how the Werner Report was drawn up. See Chapter 4.
7. 'Interim report on the establishment by stages of economic and monetary union', Document 9.504/II/70-D (20 May 1970), in the Pierre Werner Family archives. Published in *Bulletin of the European Communities*, Supplement, 7 (1970), OJC 94 (23 July 1970) (Luxembourg: Office for Official Publications of the European Communities), p. 5.

8. 'Commission Memorandum to the Council on the coordination of economic policies and monetary cooperation within the Community, submitted on 12 February 1969', in *Bulletin of the European Communities*, Supplement 3 (1969) (Luxembourg: Office for Official Publications of the European Communities).
9. Interim report, p. 9.
10. 'Final communiqué of the Hague Summit (2 December 1969)', in *Bulletin of the European Communities*, 1 (1970) (Luxembourg: Office for Official Publications of the European Communities), pp. 12–17.
11. Interim report, p. 11.
12. Interim report, p. 14.
13. Ibid.
14. Communiqué drawn up by the Belgian Presidency following the Council of Ministers, Luxembourg, 8–9 June 1970. Pierre Werner Family archives.
15. See Chapter 4.
16. 'Report to the Council and the Commission on the realisation by stages of economic and monetary union in the Community (Werner Report) (definitive text)', Luxembourg, 8 October 1970, in *Bulletin of the European Communities*, Supplement 11/1970 (Luxembourg: Office for Official Publications of the European Communities), p. 8. See Interview with Philippe Maystadt (Nivelles, 11 November 2015). https://www.cvce.eu/project/werner/ (home page) and http://www.cvce.eu/en/oral-history (main page), accessed on 6 March 2018.
17. Ibid., p. 13.
18. Even though it was intended to cover a three-year period, this timetable remained relatively flexible. The Werner Group believed that the surveys would take place on fixed dates. These dates would be chosen at the outset to make for the closest possible match with the deadlines in force at that time in the Member States for the drawing up and adoption of their budgets. These deadlines would later be synchronised to make the coordination of policies more effective. To make sure that quantitative guidelines for the main components of all official budgets for the following year were defined, and to enable governments to be notified of Community reactions before they drew up their final ordinary and extraordinary draft budgets, there would be a second survey shortly before the middle of the year to identify the preliminary guidelines for the policy to be launched for the ensuing year and review to

the policy to be followed in the current year. This analysis would be carried out as part of the economic accounts and would enable preliminary economic budgets to be drawn up. A third survey, in the autumn, would make it possible to lay down in greater detail the guidelines identified during the summer. Economic budgets compatible with each other would then be drawn up. They would contain the same components as regards budgetary policy as in the preceding survey, plus additional data not previously available. The guidelines in the economic budgets would serve as reference points for the authorities responsible for the framing of monetary and credit policy. When this survey was carried out, the Council, on a proposal from the Commission, would adopt an 'annual report on the economic situation of the Community', setting out, among other things, the short-term economic policy guidelines for the following year. Specific, detailed recommendations for the economic policy guidelines to be followed would be sent to each Member State. The group also suggested the introduction of a general agreement whereby, in the event that certain recommendations gave rise to a vote, the country concerned would abstain.

19. As regards the current aspects, the Member States would hold regular consultations on the policy of balancing the markets and the problems caused inside and outside the Community by capital movements, and would start to take concerted action on national policies in those fields.
20. The structural aspects would target measures to harmonise certain types of investment, the legal instruments for 'technical' transactions in a number of fields such as regulations governing the activity of credit institutions and institutional investors, the provision of information and protection for holders of securities, and encouragement for saving.
21. From the start of stage one, the central banks, acting in concert, would place de facto limits on exchange-rate fluctuations between their currencies, confining them within tighter margins than those that would result from the application of the margins in force in respect of the dollar (at the time when the system was set up). After this experimental period, the limitations on margins could be officially announced. In addition to the concerted action, there could be intervention in Community currencies, initially at the limits and then within the margins. The first of the measures mentioned was to take place at the beginning of the first stage, when the Council had adopted the plan for achieving economic and monetary union; the group felt it was preferable not to

suggest a rigid timetable for subsequent measures. The group proposed that the Committee of Governors should report to the Council and the Commission twice a year on how the measures under way were proceeding. On that basis, and depending on progress made in bringing economic policies closer into line, the Council, or the Member States meeting in the Council, would take the appropriate decisions.

22. P. Werner (1970) 'L'Europe en route vers l'Union Monétaire (28 février 1970)', in *Documentation Bulletin*, 1 (Luxembourg: Information and Press Service, Ministry of State), pp. 5–12. Pierre Werner Family archive.
23. 'Letter from the Chairman of the Committee of Governors of the Central Banks, Hubert Ansiaux, to Pierre Werner, President of the Government', Minister for Finance, Brussels, 16 June 1970. Pierre Werner Family archives.
24. The panel of experts consisted of Baron H. Ansiaux in the chair, E. Blumenthal, and G. Jennemann of the Deutsche Bundesbank; J. Mertens de Wilmars and F. Heyvaert of the National Bank of Belgium; M. Théron and R. Floc'h of the Banque de France; F. Masera and F. Frasca of the Banca d'Italia; P. C. Timmerman, A. Szasz, and J. A. Sillem of the Nederlandsche Bank; F. Boyer de la Giroday, H. Wortmann, and A. Louw of the Commission of the European Communities; G. Morelli and G. Lermen of the Secretariat of the Werner Committee; A. Bascoul and R. Gros of the Secretariat of the Committee of Governors.
25. 'Annex 5: Report transmitted by the Committee of Governors of the central banks of the EEC on questions put by the ad hoc Committee presided over by Mr. Werner, and annexes', in 'Report to the Council and the Commission on the realisation by stages of economic and monetary union in the Community (Werner Report) (definitive text)', Luxembourg, 8 October 1970, in *Bulletin of the European Communities*, Supplement 11/1970 (Luxembourg: Office for Official Publications of the European Communities), pp. 39–68.
26. Summary report of the 43rd sitting of the Committee of Governors of Central Banks of the Member States of the European Economic Community, held in Basel on Saturday, 12 September at 2.30 p.m. and Sunday, 13 September at 10.00 a.m. Confidential, text revised and approved on 8 November 1970. European Commission, Committee of Governors of the Central Banks. Pierre Werner Family archives.

27. Ibid.
28. H. Tietmeyer (1971) 'L'union économique et monétaire au centre du débat politique', in *Hefte*, 1/1971 (Cologne: Institut für Wirtschaftspolitik). See Interview with Hans Tietmeyer (Königstein im Taunus, 11 February 2011). https://www.cvce.eu/project/werner/ (home page) and http://www.cvce.eu/en/oral-history (main page), accessed on 6 March 2018.
29. H. Ansiaux, M. Dessart (eds.) (1975) *Dossier pour l'histoire de l'Europe monétaire 1958–1973* (Brussels), p. 1.
30. In the theoretical discussions on European integration, the positions advanced by the 'economists' and the 'monetarists' had different connotations from those put forward by Milton Friedman, and are related to the approaches of the Member States regarding how to built EMU.

    To Friedman (1912–2006), founder of the 'Chicago monetarist school', 'monetarism', which originated in the ideas of the seventeenth and eighteenth century, was a term designating a school of thought which became established at the end of the 1960s and which saw government action in the monetary sphere as pointless, not to say pernicious. Friedman became the leading light of this movement in seeking to rehabilitate the quantitative theory of currency as opposed to the dominant paradigm of the age, Keynesianism (a school of thought founded by the British economist John Maynard Keynes [1883–1946]). According to monetarist theory, the currency supply is exogenous (determined by the central bank); the demand for currency is stable; inflation is 'everywhere and always a monetary phenomenon', due to an over-rapid increase in the money supply (the means of payment in circulation); people make anticipatory adjustments which, in the long term, diminish the effects of short-term policies; there is a natural rate of unemployment below which the economy cannot fall sustainably. Keynesians thought that the markets, left to themselves, do not necessarily lead to the optimum economic result. In the economic field, the State must intervene, particularly as part of a policy to stimulate the economy.
31. L. Tsoukalis (1977) *The Politics and Economics of European Monetary Integration* (London: Allen & Unwin). The author sees Italy as one of the 'economist' countries, alongside Germany and the Netherlands; one particular example mentioned is its opposition to the EMCF. But the Italian representative on the Werner Committee (Gaetano Strammati,

Chairman of the Budgetary Policy Committee) was seen as siding with the 'monetarists'. See P. Werner (1992, II) *Itinéraires*, p. 124.

32. I. Maes, L. Quaglia (2004) 'France and Italy's Policies on European Monetary Integration: A Comparison of "Strong" and "Weak" States', in *Comparative European Politics*, 2/1 (April 2004) (London: Palgrave Macmillan), pp. 51–72. According to the authors, when the Werner Committee began its work, Italy adopted a nuanced, central stance, positioning itself between Belgium, Luxembourg and France on the one hand (seen as being 'fervent optimists'), and Germany and the Netherlands on the other (seen as 'positively cautious').
33. H. Tietmeyer (1971) 'L'union économique et monétaire au centre du débat politique', in *Hefte*, 1/1971 (Cologne: Institut für Wirtschaftspolitik), p. 22.
34. S. Lefèvre (2002, I) 'Les ministères de l'Économie et des Finances allemand et français dans la mise en place de la CEE: politiques et compétences', in *Le rôle des ministres des Finances et de l'Économie dans la construction européenne (1957–1978)* (Paris: Comité pour l'Histoire économique et financière de la France), pp. 73–84.
35. This type of discussion had actually taken place at the economic and monetary conference held in London in 1933 and the Congress of Europe in The Hague in 1948. See F. Clavert (2009) 'Expérience économique de l'entre-deux-guerres et projets européistes', in J.-M. Guieu, C. Le Dréau (eds.), *Le Congrès de l'Europe à La Haye (1948–2008)*, 49 (Brussels: P.I.E.-Peter Lang), pp. 1–10.
36. G. Bossuat (1995) 'Le président Georges Pompidou et les tentatives d'Union économique et monétaire', in *Georges Pompidou et l'Europe. Colloque 25 et 26 novembre 1993* (Brussels: Complexe), p. 409.
37. A. Wilkens (1999) 'L'Allemagne et le projet d'union économique et monétaire (1969–1972)', in G. Bossuat, A. Wilkens (eds.), *Jean Monnet, L'Europe et les chemins de la paix* (Paris: Publications de la Sorbonne), p. 468.
38. R. Frank (1995) 'Pompidou, le franc et l'Europe 1969–1974', in *Georges Pompidou et l'Europe. Colloque 25 et 26 novembre 1993* (Brussels: Complexe), p. 349.
39. The negotiations for the accession of the United Kingdom, Ireland, Denmark, and Norway began in June 1970 and culminated in the first enlargement of the European Economic Community in January 1973. This first Common Market enlargement involved the UK,

a great European nation and medium-sized power, a winner of the Second World War, a member of the UN Security Council, head of the Commonwealth, a leading financial centre and a key member of the European Free Trade Association. In the 1960s, two applications for membership from the UK had come to nothing, paralysing a fair amount of intra-Community business.

40. P. Werner (1992, II) *Itinéraires*, p. 124.
41. W. Brandt (1971) 'Declaration on European Policy, 6 November 1970', in *Reden und Interviews* (Hamburg: Hoffmann und Campe), p. 238.
42. Letter from Willy Brandt to Karl Schiller, 21 October 1970. Historical Archives of the Bundesbank, No. 2, Vol. 156. Quoted by A. Wilkens (2002) 'Une tentative prématurée? L'Allemagne, la France et les balbutiements de l'Europe monétaire (1969–1974)', in É. du Réau, R. Frank (eds.), *Dynamiques européennes. Nouvel espace, Nouveaux acteurs, 1969–1981* (Paris: Publications de la Sorbonne), pp. 77–103, here p. 87.
43. K. Schiller 'Speech Before the Bundestag, 6 November 1970', in *Deutscher Bundestag. Stenographische Berichte*, Deutscher Bundestag, 6th legislature, pp. 4294–4297.
44. Ibid.
45. A. Wilkens (2002) 'Une tentative prématurée? L'Allemagne, la France et les balbutiements de l'Europe monétaire (1969–1974)', in É. du Réau, R. Frank (eds.), *Dynamiques européennes. Nouvel espace, Nouveaux acteurs, 1969–1981* (Paris: Publications de la Sorbonne), pp. 77–103.
46. The Minister for Economic Affairs, Karl Schiller, had undertaken before the *Zentralbankrat* of the Bundesbank 'to recommend the independent central bank as a model for the future European Central Bank'.
47. See F. Clavert, O. Feiertag (eds.), 'Les banquiers centraux dans la construction européenne', in *Histoire, économie et société*, 4/2011 (Paris: Armand Colin).

6
Reactions to the Werner Report

The work of the Werner Committee prompted a far-reaching wave of interest and creative enthusiasm, which gathered momentum after the final report was published.

The European Community institutions (the Parliament, Commission, and Council) and the political authorities in the Member States gradually responded, first to the interim report and then to the final report. Business associations and trade unions, as well as ordinary citizens, joined activists campaigning for European integration to voice their views.

Deeply concerned by economic and monetary union (EMU), with the sense of being both players in and witnesses to its construction, the various organisations and individuals fuelled the debate with their views and public statements, addressing in different ways the various aspects of the Werner Report and the Commission's proposals.

The resources collected and the issues covered in this chapter do not claim to be exhaustive. We have chosen to focus on the Pierre Werner Family archives and on other relevant sources from our exploration of institutional archives.

E. Danescu, *Pierre Werner and Europe*,
Archival Insights into the Evolution of Economics,
https://doi.org/10.1007/978-3-319-96295-5_6

The media reported on these diverse responses and views, doing their best to inform their readers and to explain the key concepts and significance of the plan by stages. Academics in European and American universities also devoted their attention to the work of the Werner Group.

To clarify one persistent terminological quibble relating to the term 'Werner Report', there were in fact two separate documents, from different sources (the report by the ad hoc committee and the Commission document), and also two separate forms of the plan by stages (the interim version and the final version). All these documents bore the same name.

The real Werner Report, published on 8 October 1970, was drawn up by the ad hoc group set up following the Hague Summit and led by the Prime Minister of Luxembourg, from whom it took its name. Its brief was to debate the ways and means of achieving EMU. The other report was the document which the Commission of the EC set before Council three weeks later, on 29 October, but which substantially toned down—and sometimes even contradicted—the ideas on which it was based. The genuine Werner Report was favourably received in the most diverse quarters. Its name became a media buzzword, gaining universal currency. This positive perception was naturally transferred to the Commission document, and the Commission used and took advantage of this misconception, which it helped maintain. Debates in the European Parliament (EP) and discussions by the Council attest to this confusion. Two other circumstances added depth to this misleading situation. The first was that during debates in the EP, both the interim and the final report were referred to as the Werner Report or Werner Plan. Secondly, the Commission document hinged on the interim report, which had been through the full Community vetting process. But its conclusions, which were relatively superficial or even different from those in the final report (given that the group's work was still under way), were certainly closer to a consensus view and less politically daring than those set forth in the final version.

6.1 The European Parliament

The work of the Werner Group and the issue of EMU prompted lively interest on the part of the EP. Several special committees and plenary sittings debated the interim and final versions of the report.

6.1.1 Debate by the Special Committees of the EP

The Economic Affairs Committee (EAC), the Political Affairs Committee (PAC) and the Committee for Finance and Budgets (CFB) of the EP debated on several occasions the broad lines of the plan to establish EMU by stages. They drafted internal reports which they amended as the work of the Werner Group progressed. Joint positions and opinions followed. The Parliamentary Studies department and the Information and Documentation departments made specific contributions. The Werner Report was also discussed at two plenary sittings of the Parliament (on 18 November and 3 December 1970), during which views were exchanged with the Commission and the Council, leading to a resolution being adopted.[1]

The EAC, which was most concerned by the handling of this matter, met ten times to discuss the plan by stages and the monetary outlook for the Community.[2] Most of the meetings were held after the Council decided on 9 June 1970 to further the work of the Werner Group. The Vice-President of the Commission, Raymond Barre, often assisted by Albert Borschette, the Luxembourg member of the European Commission (who attended seven out of nine of these meetings), was invited to attend all the debates. On 15 May 1970, the President of the EP asked the CFB for a specialist opinion, which was submitted two months later.[3] The secretariats of the political groups in Parliament were also involved, issuing various statements.

The EP produced a document which compared the outlines of the plans drawn up by Luxembourg, Belgium (the Snoy Plan), Germany (the Schiller Plan), and the second Barre Plan, and was based on the various stages planned for the decade from 1970 to 1980.[4]

Its conclusions drew primarily on two sources: the second Barre Plan and its Luxembourg counterpart. The EP thought that these two documents offered the clearest picture of the objectives and the means to achieve them. The second Barre Plan provided an overall sense of a plan by stages, in so far as it indicated a certain 'parallelism' for harmonisation of economic and monetary policy, fiscal harmonisation and free movement of capital. The Luxembourg Plan clearly defined the broad lines and practical measures for setting up a short-term monetary support system.

While the Werner Committee was busy debating and negotiating prior to approval of the final report, the EAC met on 28 and 29 September 1970. The Vice-President of the Commission of the EC was invited to state his position on progress by the ad hoc group. R. Barre started with a reminder of the work under way to achieve EMU, in the context of the medium-term outlook for the Community (1971–1975). Keen to see the adoption of these general guidelines (at the last meeting of the Council scheduled for 22–23 December 1970), which could result in a more effective framework for economic policy, he criticised certain trends apparent in some Member States to avoid approving a Community decision in favour of medium-term support, making do with merely an intergovernmental agreement. The Commission was determined to prevent this trend and would make it perfectly clear that Community mechanisms would prevail over their intergovernmental equivalent. Opposition between Community and intergovernmental methods had been a key feature of the work of the Werner Committee, but the plan by stages had established the primacy of the Community method.

According to the Vice-President Barre, convergence between Community countries hinged on several main factors. The first point concerned agreement on protecting the system of intra-Community monetary relations from any relaxation of exchange rate controls. The second one was related to the need for the Six to adopt the same line in dealings with the rest of the world—'[…] even if ministers do not yet see eye to eye on what needs to done […], even if they do not yet agree on the techniques'—and all the more so in the new context of reform of the international monetary system.[5]

On 15 October 1970 the EAC published its draft interim report, for which the MEP J. E. Bousch acted as rapporteur. On 19 November he returned with a supplementary report, which formed the basis of the resolution on the Werner Report which the EP subsequently adopted at a plenary sitting on 3 December 1970.

There followed the response by the EAC and the Committee for Finance and Budgets.[6] In turn the PAC adopted its position on the Werner Report.[7] Chronologically first in the sequence, the opinion of the PAC hinged on the creation or the transformation of a certain number of Community organs to which powers until then exercised by the national authorities will have to be transferred. These transfers of responsibility represent a process of fundamental political significance which implies the progressive development of political cooperation.

At the stage described as the 'final objective', the Werner Report recommended that EMU should have three consequences: firstly the transfer to the Community authorities of monetary policy with regard to the outside world; secondly the harmonisation of the policies of Member States with respect to the capital market and the adoption, at Community level, of decisions on the size of current account balances and the arrangements for funding public budgets. Lastly the plan provided for partial transfer of regional and structural policies to the Community. Transferring these powers, previously the preserve of states, to the Community would entail correlative institutional reforms to prevent a vacuum in terms of liability and management. Admittedly the Werner Committee did not make detailed proposals on the institutional architecture of the various Community bodies, but it did clearly stipulate the need to set up, at the same time, a Community system of central banks and a decision-making centre for economic policy. This centre, which would be independent and would be guided by Community interests, was to exert a decisive influence on the overall economic policy of the Community. It was to be politically answerable to a EP, which will have to be furnished with a status corresponding to the extension of the Community missions, not only from the point of view of the extent of its powers, but also having regard to the method of election of its members. This design implied a shift towards European-wide general elections and fitted into the larger framework of a transfer to the Community of powers and responsibilities previously exercised by national bodies. But the PAC expressed concern that the transfer of powers should not jeopardise Community institutions. Achieving EMU in the decade from 1970 to 1980 should lay solid foundations for the subsequent consolidation of Parliament's powers, providing that by this time its members were elected by direct universal suffrage.

The PAC highlighted the important role that the EP was called to play in the building of EMU. 'It will be forced to do so, if only because this transformation, which will affect it directly, will entail substantial changes to the way its members are elected and will give it new prerogatives and responsibilities'.[8] This profound institutional change '[…] cannot, and should not, be achieved unless the social substratum of the Community is able, by means of the parliamentary body which is its most vibrant — if not exclusive — expression at the Community level, to provide valuable suggestions and exercise the necessary controls for its implementation, upholding the spirit and principles underpinning the Rome Treaties'. In fact the PAC took up the whole of one of the conclusions of the Werner Report: 'EMU thus appears as a leaven for the development of political union which in the long run it cannot do without'.

When it met on 27 November 1970 the CFB unanimously approved its opinion on the Werner Report, organised around its six main conclusions. The first one concerned the need to harmonise budgetary policy, which must form the basis for measures promoting the progressive alignment of the economies of the Member States and therefore consolidate the monetary integration. The second conclusion focused on the need to transfer powers from the national to the Community level, a move which was seen as not only essential but as guaranteeing the democratic control of the Community. Attention was drawn to the need for the EP to be consulted on any fundamental or periodic decisions concerning the development of EMU. Another conclusion provided for a study, which the Council asked the Commission to carry out, to harmonise the units of account used in the Member States. Lastly, Parliament called for a debate to be held on the annual report which the Committee of Governors of the Central Banks was to draw up for the Council and the Commission of the EC.

Parliament's position was marked by the profoundly political significance of EMU. This conviction was demonstrated many times over, starting with the Hague Summit during which Jean Rey—then President of the Commission of the EC—presented a memorandum expressly demanding that 'the Conference of Heads of State and Government affirm the determination of the Member States of the Community to progress towards EMU'.[9] Parliament was thus in agreement with the Commission, which while the Werner Committee was still at work, often expressed the same belief. In his speech to the EP, when he took office on 8 July 1970, the new President of the Commission Franco Maria Malfatti highlighted the political import of the plans for EMU.

> [...] No one can deny the eminently political nature of a work of such large scope. No one can imagine that such an important political problem can be resolved simply by resorting to more or less sophisticated techniques and by mobilising the forces assembled together in the national and Community governments.[10]

The two bodies were also in full agreement as to the capacity of EMU to consolidate Europe as a centre of balance and stability in international relations.

The debate in the EAC shows that the EP was in full agreement with the ways and means identified by the Werner Report. The MEPs demanded that the governments of the Six demonstrate the necessary political determination and commitment so that monetary union could be achieved during the decade from 1970 to 1980. To this end, and given that major economic policy decisions were to be taken at Community level, the national governments must start by giving up certain powers. The first three-year stage (starting on 1 January 1971) would, thanks to more intensive economic and monetary talks, enable common ground to be established. The same applied to external monetary relations, and it was essential that the Community should display genuine monetary solidarity in this area. There was still disagreement on setting up a specific exchange regime for the Community during the first stage. Even if the current provisions of the treaty left room for some progress, the EAC agreed that it would ultimately have to be altered.

In its interim report, the EP's EAC disagreed with the Commission. Parliament hailed the flexibility advocated by the Werner Report, and the idea of setting key stages for achieving EMU without time constraints.

> It was not wise to establish a strict timeframe, which would subsequently turn out not to be feasible, or on the contrary not sufficiently ambitious. Currently unpredictable events might arise, forcing the Six to slow down harmonisation of their economic and monetary policies, or on the contrary enabling them to speed up progress towards EMU.[11]

The report by the EAC gave pride of place to interaction between and harmonisation of economic and monetary policies. The committee welcomed the need to consult both sides of industry, and for democratic control, as proposed by the Werner Report. It then addressed centralisation of budgetary and fiscal policy, and possible changes to the treaty. The document concluded with a section on enlargement, the imminent accession of the United Kingdom (UK), and the role of the pound sterling in the EMU. The Werner Group had taken an interest in this issue, returning to it several times in the course of its work and accumulating from the outset a large body of documentation on the subject.

With regard to harmonising monetary policy, a dilemma arose: should priority be given to monetary or economic unification? The controversy between 'monetarists' and 'economists' which emerged once again was set aside as a 'non-issue', since the two categories of measures would inevitably interact. 'It was not possible to harmonise monetary policy without harmonising economic policy; at the same time, measures to harmonise monetary policy would entail Community discipline on economic policy'.[12] But monetary harmonisation on its own was not sufficient to bring about economic unification. Even if monetary phenomena were the expression of economic reality, simply fixing parity relations or reducing the margin of exchange rate fluctuations would not bring the Community any closer to integration. Such measures must be based on increasing convergence between the economies of the Six, a process which would stimulate monetary solidarity in the

Community. The harmonisation of economic policies must go hand in hand with a reduction in fluctuation margins, which in turn would prompt Member States to adopt a particular stance in the international monetary system. 'Reducing margins would in fact be equivalent to agreeing to Community discipline on economic policy'.[13] In the event of such discipline breaking down, it would only be possible to maintain the stability of exchange rates through a monetary assistance procedure. This is why the debates suggested that it would make sense to start by proving that the proposed procedure for closer coordination of economic policy would work in practice and then, but only then, reduce the fluctuation margins.

The EAC took its analysis one step further, defining the 'parallelism' between economic and monetary harmonisation, based on two fundamental points: firstly that coordination of economic policy within the Community was still in its early stages, having barely started; and secondly that in Member States the authorities in charge of economic policy only enjoyed limited control over economic trends. Under these circumstances, the notion of 'parallelism' was not set in stone; it would have to evolve in step with the processes it was required to explain. Regarding the effectiveness of efforts to coordinate economic policy, the committee noted some progress, such as the discussions on short-term economic policy which the Council held every six months. Such progress was fairly general, and it was not backed up by the quantification of objectives or results. Efforts had been made to set up a medium-term financial support mechanism, as well as medium-term economic policy coordination. This gave governments a basis to commit themselves fully to convergence of their policies in the medium term coupled with close coordination of their short-term economic policies.

But the committee pointed out an essential difference—in both rationale and practical details—between measures to harmonise economic policy and equivalent monetary measures. To quantify progress towards convergence by their economies and to offer a uniform basis for comparison, Member States should set firm targets. Four significant indicators were necessary: growth, in terms of volume, of gross national product; unemployment; the balance of payments; and inflation. Using specific mechanisms, states could intervene in certain areas, to some extent, to correct and channel economic trends. Wage increases, speculative movements of capital, and the market for Eurocurrencies or Euroissues were factors, outside the control of governments, which could influence economic policy. On the other hand, the authorities had complete control over external monetary policy measures, such as reducing fluctuation margins or (short or medium-term) financial assistance. In view of this essential difference, the decision to harmonise economic policy was not sufficient in itself, and only the practical result of such a decision could be seen as a step towards the harmonisation of economic policy.

The harmonisation of economic policy would go hand in hand with specific support measures. The most significant included structural and regional policy (which sought to favour economic convergence inside the Community), as well as the consultation of both sides of industry on medium-term economic policy goals, the gradual transfer of certain powers to the Community level and improved procedures for parliamentary control. In keeping with the Werner Report, the Members of the EP recommended closely involving both sides of industry in the framing of goals for a common medium-term economic policy. This [policy] would be doomed to failure if both sides of industry do not agree on the share-out of the benefits of economic growth expressed in terms of percentage points and targets. A programme of this sort would not offer serious guarantees for the convergent development of the economies of the Member States. There was agreement with the Werner Report on the need for a gradual transfer of national powers to the Community—without genuine centralisation of economic policy, there seemed little chance of bringing about the convergence of six diverse and asymmetric economies. The first step towards a common policy was to set up a joint decision-making process, in both the economic (including budgetary and fiscal matters) and monetary arena.[14]

The EAC also considered the existing treaty provisions in this area. Member States are still responsible for their economic policy, but in defining such policy they must make allowance for the superior interests of the Community. At no point is there any reference to a common policy, but the provisions of the treaty do not prevent close coordination of policies. The treaty set no limits on Community action, on account of national legislation in some countries.[15] Legislation on indirect taxation would need to be harmonised. On the other hand the treaty made no reference to direct taxes, so there was no scope for harmonisation in this area. Deregulation of capital movements was seen to be lagging behind the timeframe provided for by the treaty.

On 5 November 1970, following further analysis of the plan by stages for an EMU in the Community, the EAC drafted a supplementary report, with a motion for a resolution to be tabled at the plenary sitting of the EP. This resolution confirmed Parliament's full support for the strategic thrust of the Werner Report. The ideal of a European currency was welcomed as an essential component in international trade in goods and capital. It was also a factor that would enable the Community to assert its own economic and monetary policy objectives with respect to the outside world. Since greater monetary integration was based on increased convergence between the economies of the Member States, a harmonised budgetary policy, with parallelism between harmonisation of both monetary and economic policy, must play a pivotal role. The resolution also stipulated that countries having applied to join the Community should be treated as active participants and allowance must be made for their interests. They should be fully informed on measures to implement EMU. With regard to the specific case of the UK, the EP stressed the need for the Community to resolve the problems posed by sterling as a reserve currency. During the initial stage of EMU, the Monetary Committee and the Committee of Governors were asked to consider in greater detail the organisation and functions of a European Monetary Cooperation Fund (EMCF). To enable systematic assessment of the progress made, the central bankers were encouraged to draw up an annual report—submitted to the Council and the Commission—which should also be presented to the EP.

The resolution reaffirmed the importance of dialogue with the Social Partners throughout the process of establishing EMU. It was up to the European Commission 'to organise, in close cooperation with the EP, regular talks with the representatives of both sides of industry in order to achieve a more Community-based approach to short-term economic policy, which would be more consistent with demands for a fair distribution of the benefits of economic growth, in order to obtain the broadest possible measure of agreement'.[16]

The In order to assert the central role of the EP in establishing EMU, the resolution took up two other key points in the Werner Report: firstly the need for Parliament to exercise democratic control in the event of additional powers being transferred to Community bodies; and secondly the need to consult Parliament on all decisions relating to the development of EMU.

6.1.2 Enlargement of the Community and the Outlook for EMU: What Role Should the Pound Sterling Play?

Much as the Werner Group, which debated at length the prospect of British membership of the Community and how the pound sterling would fit into the workings of EMU, the EP was also concerned about this issue.

Since the discussions on EMU coincided with the start of negotiations with Denmark, Ireland, Norway, and the UK on their accession to the Common Market, a one-to-one relationship was being established between the Community and the prospective members. For the applicant states it was very important to know whether they are negotiating with a Community which will stop halfway between a customs union and economic union, or with a Community which will continue to evolve until it achieves EMU. For this relationship to be balanced, the EP thought that priority should be given to assessing the implications of enlargement on EMU. During the negotiation phase itself, without anticipating its outcome, it would be highly opportune to involve the potential new members in theoretical and political debate on the matter.[17]

Considerable attention focused on the role of the pound sterling during the debates on monetary matters in the context of enlargement. How would this currency evolve, as both a reserve currency and a national currency, during the period between British accession to the Common Market and the introduction of a single European currency? The main danger came from the fact that its role as a reserve currency could have a negative impact on its role as a national currency, thus introducing external, possibly artificial factors, into a common, perhaps single, currency.

The substantial sterling reserves held by central banks, companies and private individuals in the sterling area other than the UK, the exchange guarantee enjoyed by the funds held in this currency, the high rate of interest on the London money market (recognised as the largest financial centre in Europe) had enabled sterling to retain its status as a reserve currency despite devaluation in 1967.

At the end of 1970, Britain's balance of payments was again in difficulty, in contrast with its speedy recovery in 1969. These short-term fluctuations suggested that some of the factors behind its recovery were only temporary. The fragile balance of payments, the policy of spending cuts, the lack of industrial investment and feeble growth in the face of increasingly strong demand set in motion a vicious circle which had an impact on the balance of payments. It seemed clear that if Britain's exports had not improved by the time it joined, the Community's monetary assistance mechanisms would be unable to absorb the full force of the shocks caused by the existence of sterling balances.

British membership must go hand in hand with a stabilisation of sterling's role as a reserve currency. By virtue of its projected common currency, the Community (including the UK) would be required to contribute to the stability of the international monetary system. This consolidation process would involve phasing out support measures for sterling (discussed above) and establishing a more balanced relationship between the UK's monetary reserves and its short-term obligations. To cope with demand for additional international liquidity, it was therefore suggested that liquidity should be constituted separately from the availability of gold or reserve currencies. To this end, the International Monetary Fund's introduction of special drawing rights (SDRs) seemed a wise move.

Discussion of the role and future of sterling could not be separated from the problem posed by the other reserve currency, the US dollar, particularly in the context of a fast developing Eurocurrency market, in which Eurodollars carried considerable weight.[18] Raymond Barre addressed the EP's EAC on this topic three times (on 29 September, 22 October, and 23 October 1970) while it was reviewing the work of the Werner Report. The subject was a particular cause for concern since the central banks of European countries had accumulated large dollar reserves.In the past the Eurodollar market had been beneficial for European countries. For example, in 1963–1964 Italy had used this market to finance its external deficit, thus staving off the loss of official reserves. The Eurodollar market had imposed its own restrictions on Italian borrowers once an impression of excessive debt made itself felt. In 1968–1969 Germany had used the Eurodollar market to recycle surplus liquidity. It had thus succeeded in preventing an unwanted increase in its official reserves and the erosion of its restrictive credit policy. In the 1970s this beneficial effect vanished and following various forms of speculative pressure it even had the contrary effect.

In his address on 29 September 1970, Barre drew attention to the fact that 'the Eurodollar market compromises the autonomy of European monetary authorities due to a two-sided phenomenon: […] the disparity between the size of the Eurodollar market (45 billion), on the one hand, and, on the other, the monetary mass in European countries (60–70 billion, sensu lato, in the largest countries)'.[19] This twofold condition consisted of a 'normal' deficit, in other words the balance of payments deficit of the United States US, which resulted in an influx of dollars to all the central banks in the Community, particularly Germany and The Netherlands. At the same time there was an influx of floating assets to Germany and the Netherlands, and to some extent Switzerland. 'Our central banks must adopt a concerted policy on speculative capital movements, but this policy should not necessarily assume that there will be variations in exchange rates and, above all, it should not assume that there will be revaluation'.

Individual monetary authorities in Europe had only limited means of defence for coping with US monetary impulses transmitted by the Eurodollar market. Concerted action at Community level was therefore required especially in the areas of policies on interest rates and credit, as well as policies on the balance of payments and reserves. Their influence would be more significant in two situations: if European countries applied a policy of monetary easing whereas the United States. adopted a contrary course; and if speculative flows were stimulated by funding from the Eurodollar market. The practical answer to these problems, taken in conjunction, was far from simple. It would be difficult to apply a restrictive monetary policy without prompting an unwanted increase in reserves, but it would be just as complicated to resort to monetary easing without an excessive loss of reserves.

On this point, the Werner Report was categorical: in the move to EMU, currency flexibility must be banned at all costs. But adjustments to exchange rates would be inevitable due to the differences in productivity and competitiveness between countries. What was needed was a gradual reduction in fluctuation margins. The Six were steadily increasing pressure alongside efforts of harmonisation. It was not a question of saying that the structural conditions of Member States had to be identical, but the problem was determining whether the differences were tolerable or not. Under these circumstances, and to ensure that an EMU with fixed exchange rates would ultimately be achieved, the Commission sketched out a roadmap indicating the actions to be taken by the Community.

6.1.3 Debates During the Plenary Sittings of the EP

The EP held two plenary debates on the Werner Report, on 18 November and 3 December 1970, chaired by President Mario Scelba.

The first sitting gave rise to a detailed exchange of views between the Parliament, the Council and the Commission on the prospects for EMU. The speeches were tightly packed and carried particular significance. A succession of speakers addressed the assembly: Karl Schiller, President-in-Office of the Council of the European Communities; Raymond Barre, Vice-President of the Commission in charge of Economic and Financial Affairs, and Franco Maria Malfatti, President of the Commission. The Chairman of the EP's EAC followed, assisted by the Chairman of the CFB, who substantiated the views of their respective committees. The leaders of each political group also spoke. At the end of the sitting a motion for a resolution was debated and some amendments to it were adopted.

Emphasising the relevance of increasingly systematic consultation between the Council and Parliament, Schiller expressed two reservations. The first—the Council had not officially adopted a position on the Werner Report. The second—the report only reflected the personal views of members of the Werner Group (as pointed out in its preamble). He noted that 'Werner, as chairman, and all those who took part in or contributed to the work of the group […] have produced a report which represents a compromise between views which were initially very divergent'.[20]

Given that the Council had already endorsed the conclusions of the interim report (debated at the sitting on 8 and 9 June 1970), Schiller stressed the importance of governments making a real political commitment. 'EMU today […] is no longer a problem to be solved in the distant future but […] a realistic prospect which the final report cites when it states that EMU "thus appears as a leaven for the development of political union, which in the long run it cannot do without"'.[21] In his view, the need for real political cooperation went hand in hand with another essential point in the Werner Report which certainly held political implications: both sides of industry will have an important part to play in bringing about this union.

The President-in-Office of the Council hailed the approach and the practical measures proposed by the Werner Report, which clearly did not set out to offer an exhaustive exploration of every issue related to EMU. The practical milestones for the first stage were abundantly clear, but the path leading to the final goal of EMU was less certain, which explains the existence of several alternatives for travelling from start to finish. Should the content and the various stages in this process have been specified precisely from the outset? The final Werner Report opted for a more flexible approach, only defining in detail the content of the first stage in the process, considered to run from 1 January 1971 to 31 December 1973. Schiller endorsed this approach. Regardless of the usefulness of a set timetable for all the stages, the sheer scale of the process was such that a certain amount of flexibility was essential, as was the accumulation of experience as the project progressed. In adopting this stance, even if it reflected the caution imposed by the lack of an official opinion by the Council, its President wholeheartedly endorsed the Werner Report.

Raymond Barre was far from sharing this point of view. The Vice-President of the Commission started by recalling the various measures which the European Commission had taken to promote EMU and outlined the parallelism principle of its building. 'Thanks to the authority and wisdom [of Emilio Colombo], an agreement was reached [at the meeting in Venice in May 1970] on the concept of "guaranteed parallelism"—the expression used by Mr. Colombo himself—in economic and monetary progress. [...] That is how the vain quarrel between "monetarists" and "economists" was finally settled'.[22]

Barre then reminded that, concerned by the economic aspects of European integration, the Commission had been responsible for instigating the considerable debate and practical action set in motion by the Hague Summit. Turning to the Werner Report itself, the speaker drew attention to the convergence of positions between the Commission and the central bankers concerning the Community's specific exchange rate regime. 'On this point the Commission is bound to be pleased to see the Committee of Governors recognising a principle which [the Commission] had supported for some time, namely the principle of reducing the margins for fluctuation between the currencies of the Community. For a long time this principle was held to be unrealistic and unacceptable; now the governors of the central banks in person are saying that setting up a system of this sort is neither impossible, nor improbable'.[23]

Since the stage-by-stage plan reflected the personal views of the members of the Werner Committee, Barre emphasised that the document was binding on neither the Member States nor the Commission, which had in fact been represented in the group. His message was perfectly clear. Despite the enthusiasm and almost unanimous support for principles, mechanisms, and means of action proposed by the Werner Report, it was up to the Commission to decide. This body would select and implement the most appropriate processes for achieving EMU, 'taking into account the Werner Report or not'.

Nevertheless, Barre emphatically paid tribute to Pierre Werner and his group. 'Werner, chairman of the committee, has for many years constantly expressed his support for establishing a monetary Europe. For my part, I cannot overlook the fact that, since 1968, the Commission has always enjoyed his full support at a time when it was trying to bring about economic and monetary progress in the Community, at a time when EMU was not fashionable and could not boast such enthusiastic and zealous supporters as those who have emerged in recent months. We cannot forget the support provided by Mr. Werner. As for the members of the group, the Commission is aware of their abilities and their loyalty to the Community cause, as they chair the [advisory] committees which regularly give the Commission and the Council the benefit of their discussions and opinions'.[24]

Barre concluded by presenting the Commission's position on EMU and submitted a draft resolution in three parts: a definition of the final objective; a programme of action for the first stage; and a commitment for the end of the first stage.[25]

Thus, three principles underpinned the definition of EMU. The first involved establishing a single economic space, with free circulation of goods, services, persons, and capital (without upsetting the social or regional order inside the Community). The second point was to set up a custom-built European monetary bloc—managed by a Community system of central banks—as part of the international monetary system. Lastly the Community would need to acquire the necessary economic and monetary skills in order to provide efficient management of the union. The necessary bodies would be defined once the transfer of powers to the Community had been decided. The Commission had set aside the 1970–1980 decade to achieve the final objective, in which the political commitment of Member States were essential.

The description of the final objective was accompanied by an action programme for the three-year period of the first stage. The programme would focus on more effective coordination of economic and monetary policy, and on greater fiscal harmonisation. There were also plans for the gradual establishment of a European capital market and the introduction of measures in favour of a specific exchange rate regime inside the Community, as suggested by the Werner Report. Although the treaty offered a suitable framework for the introduction of EMU in the near future, amendments would certainly be necessary. Analysis during the first stage would identify milestones for such changes, and the Commission would subsequently propose the necessary reforms to be deployed during the second stage.

Barre noted that the EP would need to play an active part for an improved coordination of economic policy between the Member States, which should be coupled with closer collaboration between the central banks. By referring to the annual report on the economic situation in the Community—another of the Werner Report's proposals—Barre suggested that this document could be adopted by the Council on the basis of a proposal by the Commission after consulting Parliament. In this way the EP would be directly involved in the definition of short-term economic and monetary policy. It also sought to make the exchange of views between the Commission and Parliament both systematic and consistent, prior to the Commission presenting its finalised initiatives to the Council.

Barre mentioned various the main priorities to be carried out by the end of 1970. The first one was for the Council to take decisions, within two months, on EMU. Such haste was justified by the expectations of public opinion following the enthusiastic response to the Hague Summit, and to the growing awareness of the difficulties facing the Community confronted with the monetary crises affecting the Common Market. Another action concerned the real political commitment of the Member States, because 'the economy and currency depended largely on politics'.

Since the Werner Report was simply a summary of its authors' personal views, it was in no way binding on the Commission. Vice-President Barre reiterated this several times, but its key points underpinned the proposals and subsequent action set forth by the Commission.

The EAC had not had time to draft a report on the final version of the Werner Report, published on 8 October. Plenary discussions had consequently not yet been held—but a debate of this kind was necessary. The Chairman of the EAC and the representatives of the political groups gave their views according to which the Werner Report was 'a realistic proposal for establishing EMU [and even] our great opportunity and our great hope'.[26]

Some of the speakers highlighted the fact that the gradual achievement of EMU should go hand in hand with vigorous action on the social front, with close involvement of Social Partners in framing common policy for the medium term.[27] Regular consultation of both sides of industry would be essential, but allowance must also be made for the fact that the unfettered action of social forces was subject to considerable corrective influence from the central authorities. This necessarily meant that the economy could only exert limited influence.

Concern also focused on the importance of democratic control.[28] EMU would involve transferring two important forms of control from the hands of national bodies to the Community level. Firstly this concerned national budgets, which would have to become instruments for the Community's economic policy and be adapted accordingly. The criteria would be decided at Community level, and although national institutions and parliaments would retain a certain margin for manoeuvre, they would have to reproduce them as they were. Another national power which would disappear in time was medium-term planning. Until now each Member State had enjoyed a fair degree of independence when framing its own plans and programmes in this respect, but with the first stage of EMU, their became mandatory. As the interface with national parliaments, the EP would have to fulfil new functions and its dialogue with the Commission would take on a new regulatory form. A third group of views stressed the fact that EMU must fit into political union a parallel process set in motion by the joint will of the Six and the Council.

The second plenary sitting that the EP devoted to EMU opened with a statement by the rapporteur of the EAC. Turning to the confidential aspects, he emphasised that, over and above the unanimous conclusions, '[these discussions] had shown that the projected EMU had prompted deeply divergent opinions, differences of views and even deep-seated emotions'.[29] The main bone of contention was whether priority should be given to the first stage or the final stage. Some believed that the only part of the Werner Report that was liable to be adopted immediately concerned the specific measures for the first stage. Others, on the contrary, maintained that the final stage was the most important, and that it was therefore vital to settle the institutional aspects of EMU promptly and to decide on the transfer to the Community of certain sovereign rights invested in the Member States. Ultimately these positions converged to achieve a balanced common position. On the one hand, the first three-year stage provided for in the Werner Report must be lived through, with experience being gathered in this way. On the other hand it was important to see the final outcome of negotiations on enlargement of the Community and to understand the positions of new members on monetary union. These changes involved sustained information and communication efforts. It was clear that without solid support from public opinion EMU would never really be achieved.

Even if the right to mint money remained an attribute of sovereignty (a 'regalian prerogative') it nevertheless seemed impossible to establish a single currency if the governments retained all their present monetary powers. It was quite unrealistic to attempt to define then and there the transfers of powers or the time frame for their completion. It seemed clear that the Treaty of Rome would soon have to be adapted, but it was impossible to define the issues or timetable of the changes immediately. Consequently, in keeping with the Werner Report, the EAC only focused on what should be done during the first three-year stage and recommended preliminary studies on the changes to be made to the treaty.

After lively discussions, the members of the EAC had reached a unanimous position, substantiated by a motion for a resolution. This document was a compromise between very different opinions, some of the key points being cited below. Of particular note was the social chapter. '[…] Paragraph 8 of the resolution introduces two very important items for social affairs: not only does it call — much as the Werner Group and the Commission — for consultations with both sides of industry, but it also asserts the principle of a fair distribution of the benefits of economic growth and the need to obtain the broadest possible measure of agreement'.[30] Provision should therefore be made for real parallelism between progress towards a social Europe and progress on the economic and monetary side. Monetary solidarity was another concern. In paragraph 6, the resolution simply opted not to rule out the possibility of reducing the margins of fluctuation in exchange rates between the currencies of the Member States.

The opinion of the CFB centred on a limited demand in terms of monetary integration, requiring that the relevant targets and measures should be founded on convergence of the economies of the Six and, in particular, on harmonised economic policy. A transfer of powers from the national to the Community level seemed indispensable, and democratic control at the Community level must be guaranteed by an increase in the powers of the EP. The looming controversy between national sovereign rights and Community rights was dismissed as superfluous. Many national rights had already been transferred to the Community without any real changes at an institutional level (e.g. by the EP itself, its organisation being considered as out of step with reality). A further demand from the CFB was that Parliament must be consulted on all fundamental or periodic decisions concerning the development of EMU. As the dialogue with the Commission was seen as inadequate, regular consultations with the Council appear to be indispensable.

The opinion submitted by the PAC concentrated on the eminently political nature of the decisions taken at the Hague Summit. Establishing EMU reflected the political will of the Member States, and this process must consequently go hand in hand with progress towards political unification. In setting up EMU the EP would be a key player and therefore budgetary and supervisory powers must be strengthened during the first stage, to make sure it could make an immediate, tangible contribution. Active involvement of the EP would be essential 'with regard to the transfer of powers which would occur during the second stage, when the EMU moved from the phase of simple coordination to the phase of genuine union, to which all the states must subscribe as part of their common efforts to achieve this fundamental aspect of political union'.[31]

Many of the reactions prompted by the presentation of these resolutions displayed not only a genuine interest in the issues raised by Europe's political and economic future, but also a sort of 'game' opposing individuals and political groups, illustrated by the frequent correction of specific terms and wordings, and amendments, which once set forth were immediately contradicted and cancelled by other amendments.

Raymond Barre, who had taken part in all the debates within the EAC as well as the first plenary sitting of the EP on the Werner Report, rounded off the proceedings. He defended the Commission's position, thereby responding to the flurry of criticism from MEPs. Many of these reactions pointed out that the Commission's proposals fell short of those set forth in the Werner Report, which was more ambitious and embraced broader horizons. 'On the one hand we have a report which we described in our draft memorandum to the Council as an essential contribution to establishing EMU. On the other hand we have proposals. The proposals are of a different nature than the report. Proposals must have a firm basis, a clear form and define a specific timetable for carrying out actions. Such is the reasoning behind the motion for a resolution and the proposals forwarded to the Council, for the very good reason that it is the Commission's responsibility to submit proposals to the Council. [...] of necessity the Community must be based on growth and development, at the same time as being based on stability'.[32] After a long voting procedure, punctuated by additional comments, the EP adopted the resolution on the establishment by stages of EMU in the Community.[33]

6.2 The European Commission and the Werner Report—Agreement and Discord

'The relationship between the Commission and the Werner Group was complex, but it was an integral part of the workings of the Werner Group'.[34] This was a clear, organised relationship between two fairly self-sufficient bodies, and at the same time links between individuals, whose affinity and understanding, pride and enmity transcended the official side. The Werner Group, which ultimately brought together representatives of the six countries making up the Community, was made up of the chairmen of the Commission's various specialist committees. The Commission also took charge of the technical coordination of work, so it kept track, both officially and unofficially, of what was happening in the Werner Committee.

Raymond Barre was on good terms with his compatriot Bernard Clappier as well as Baron Ansiaux. In his capacity as Vice-President of the Commission he systematically took part in the work of the committees they respectively chaired. He knew Pierre Werner too, having met him regularly at meetings of Community Finance Ministers since 1967.

They shared a strong commitment to European integration and their exchanges on monetary matters at the start of the 1970s strengthened their agreement. It was Barre who proposed the Luxembourg Prime Minister to chair the group of experts, leaving it up to the others to take action. For his part, in view of the length and breadth of his political responsibilities at a national level, Werner had long been on good terms with his partners—in particular in Belgium (Baron Snoy and Baron Ansiaux) and France (Giscard d'Estaing, Clappier), but also in Germany (Karl Schiller, Johann Baptist Schöllhorn)—who interacted with the ad hoc committee. Indeed, when Werner was eventually appointed as chair of the committee, it was by a unanimous vote.

So synergy between the Werner Group and the Commission was effective and mainly peaceful, though punctuated by occasional discord and tension. The members of the group were at liberty to debate for seven months, quite independently but in a personal capacity, on the broad lines leading to EMU. The Commission, meanwhile, had the difficult task of proposing and gaining approval for means of action which satisfied both the sensibilities of the Six and Community procedures, 'whether taking into account the Werner Report or not'. Barre made this position abundantly clear in his various statements to the EP. When the MEPs stood up for the Werner Report, defending the objectives and priorities of EMU as set forth in the report, the Vice-President of the Commission replied severely: 'I would like to repeat to the EP what I have been saying for many months — indeed, for many years to the Parliament [...] — what counts is not reports, plans, statements of good intention, what counts is decisions. And the goal for which the Commission is aiming is to obtain a certain number of decisions [...] Irreversible decisions'.[35] And it is the responsibility of the Commission and the Council to determine which are the best methods for reaching the necessary decisions on the plan by stages.

Reading between the lines of this statement, one senses the antagonism between the long-term thinking (spanning a whole decade) in the Werner Report, which, due to the large number of unknowns, could only provide for specific measures for the first stage, and the 'immediacy' of the existence and thinking of the Community's executive, for which the long term was often synonymous with its term of office.

Furthermore the Werner Report kept to a minimum the elements which were essential to the definition of a full EMU. The Commission's proposals, which were less ambitious than those of the ad hoc group, and lagged behind them, were in effect the legal formalisation (in the form of a resolution and two draft decisions to be adopted by the Council) of certain suggestions from the report. The intransigence apparent in Barre's statements is also linked to another factor, namely the Commission's aspiration to give its action fresh impetus and consolidate its position both in the implementation of the major projects launched by the Hague Summit and in striking a new balance in inter-institutional relations. It is worth recalling that the summit had been seen by its initiator, President Pompidou, as exclusively intergovernmental, without the Community institutions making any contribution. The Commission, which had misgivings at first, became more and more convinced that such a conference could generate issues of major importance for European integration. It went into action, mustered support from the other Member States and succeeded in becoming actively involved.[36] The decisions taken at The Hague gave the Commission the prospect of exerting influence on the projects adopted. This was particularly true in the case of economic and monetary cooperation, for which the Commission served as a laboratory. It was not, therefore, content merely to manage the day-to-day technical business or to be reduced to a sort of Secretariat-General. The same applied to institutional affairs, where the Commission, the guardian of the treaties, refused to let itself be marginalised and intended to bring all its Community powers to bear in the decision-making triangle which it formed with the Council and Parliament.

Another aspect may offer a further clue as to why the reaction from the Vice-President of the Commission was so severe. This was the personal relations between Barre and Werner. They had known each other for a long time, often met in European circles and had a great deal of respect for each other. However, and notwithstanding the personal ties which they kept up until the end of their lives (including on the euro front), at the time of the Werner Report they were not communicating with each other on the basic questions at issue in that matter. There is nothing to that effect in the Pierre Werner family archives. Barre also used to show his irritation whenever the merits of the committee of experts and Werner were vaunted. It was contradictory and paradoxical. The following theory might serve to explain it. Barre had a high regard for Werner's qualities as a man and politician, for his intelligence, his character, and his caution, an attribute which they shared. But where EMU was concerned, their views sprang from two different backgrounds. Because of his personality, and a career of nearly three decades at the highest levels of political life in a country enjoying great stability, Werner quite naturally gravitated towards taking the long-term view. Having broad horizons of this kind prompted him to think questions over and devise plans for the future which inevitably became reality years later. The long-term vision on EMU relegated immediate pragmatism to second place. Barre was on the side of those who, in the way they saw things, gave priority to the short and medium terms and put the emphasis on the pressing need to move forward. As a result, small but practical steps were the way to proceed. The result was greater caution and a special concern for procedures, and ambition was reined in when it came to the objectives pursued and steps taken.

After officially acquainting itself with the Werner Report, the Commission submitted to the Council, on 29 October 1970, its own proposals and two motions for resolutions on the establishment by stages of EMU.[37]

The Commission considered that the Report had highlighted the fundamental options for an EMU (thus contributing to progress in Community affairs), but, on the other hand, it reasserted that the ideas set forth by the experts were in no way binding. The Commission endorsed the key points in the plan by stages, which included the need for progress on political unification. Completing economic union and bringing about its monetary counterpart should go hand in hand with the transfer to the Community of certain powers hitherto invested in national authorities. But this transfer should be limited to what was necessary for cohesive unity and efficient Community action. Policies decided at a Community level would be subject to the democratic control exercised by the EP and to regular consultations with both sides of industry. Two supranational bodies were envisaged—a decision centre for economic policy and a Community system of central banks. These were seen as essential to the successful control of economic and monetary policy inside the union.

The Commission was unstinting in its criticism of the Werner Report, which, in its view, only offered general guidelines. Detailed studies would consequently be required. The first one was the Community system of central banks in charge of managing the Union's monetary affairs, by focusing on the nature and specific responsibilities of the system, and its institutional architecture. 'There is no question of anticipating the distribution of powers between Community institutions, on the one hand, and between these institutions and the authorities of the Member States, on the other. However this distribution must ensure that the Community institutions are genuinely effective, with a valid democratic basis'.[38]

The Werner Report recommended a certain amount of flexibility in implementing these measures. It consequently did not set a specific timetable with the exception of the first stage. At the same time, the path to the final objective was only sketched out with general guidelines. This outlook was neither superficial nor lacking in imagination and pragmatism, but it was the result of a working method inspired by the approach which Werner proposed to his group at their preliminary meeting in Luxembourg on 11 March 1970. The aim was to concentrate on priority issues, to provide ideas and practical solutions for achieving short-term goals, while taking into consideration possible avenues which might prove useful in the medium and longer term, even if this was not immediately clear. From the outset, Werner encouraged his fellow committee members to keep notes describing the stages and measures they were considering to achieve the final objective.[39] It was thus possible to identify the points on which they agreed and the divergences between various opinions, and ultimately to reach a political consensus. In the light of this principle, the group set forth in the text itself its determination 'to maintain a measure of flexibility to permit any adaptations that the experience acquired during the first stage may suggest'.[40]

The Commission did not share this view, believing a more precise definition of what followed the first stage to be necessary. It understood to some extent the approach adopted by the Werner Committee: since it had only a limited period available for its work (March–October 1970), this ruled out detailed examination of all the issues at hand. But it was less indulgent on another point: the committee of experts 'had not seen fit to address the suggestions for subsequent stages set forth in the documents submitted by the governments or in the Commission communication of 5 March 1970'.

On the matter of the first three-year stage, the Commission was on the same wavelength as the report. The key concern was the methods for coordinating short-term economic policies and gradually reducing the margins for fluctuation between the currencies of the Six. It was less happy about the terse account of the transition to the final objective. As for the European fund for monetary cooperation (ECMF), which was so important to the group as part of the first of EMU, the topic was dismissed by a faultless diplomatic pirouette: 'This very important question deserves more extensive examination, which should be continued without delay on the basis of the report by the Committee of Governors of the Central Banks'. The Commission's misgivings were not only due to the sketchy nature of the Werner Committee's comments, but above all to a difference in approach. At the instigation of Barre the Commission concluded that reducing the fluctuation margins should have been the focus of debate and a central plank of the strategy of the plan by stages, whereas an exchange rate stabilisation fund would only be required later, once the appropriate mechanisms had been set up. Moreover, Barre drew attention to the fact that '[…] the first Werner Report made the mistake of highlighting a secondary issue, namely the Stabilisation Fund, setting aside the key item which is to reduce the margins. It is certain that a number of Member States would not agree to set up an exchange rate stabilisation fund simply for its own sake. For my part, I deplore this, because I think that a stabilisation fund could lead to a more assured approach to monetary matters. But the Member States must be taken as they come and we must make allowance for the opinions of all parties'.[41]

This was not the first time he had made this point. He had stated his position on many occasions, in particular at the Venice meeting of Finance Ministers on 29 May 1970 and during the debates by the EAC of the EP (as mentioned above), but never in such incisive terms.

On the other hand, the Commission fully agreed with the report on the inevitability of changes being made to the Treaty of Rome to accommodate the establishment of EMU. As the necessary adjustments would be decided according to the areas in which progress was required, the Commission undertook to present the requisite draft amendments before the end of the first stage.

In view of the fact that 'the [Werner] Report makes an essential contribution to the work carried out by the Community institutions to finalise the plan by stages decided by the Heads of State or Government in The Hague', the Commission underlined that '[…] the way forward is sufficiently clear for the Community to launch, at the beginning of 1971, the process for the gradual establishment of EMU'.[42] It therefore recommended that the Council should adopt, before the end of 1970, a resolution on the establishment by stages of EMU until 1980. According to the Commission, two other decisions were essential to engage the Community politically: one targeted greater coordination of short-term economic policies, and the other concerned more intense collaboration between the Community's central banks. With these decisions the Council would mark the start of the action programme for the first stage of EMU (1971–1973).

Reflecting the spirit of the first Commission's resolution, the Council would devote three sittings a year to examining the economic situation in the Community, with a view to pinpointing common guidelines for the short-term policy. This analysis would be completed by an annual report on the economic situation in the Community, whose conclusions would determine broader guidelines for the following year. Governments would submit the annual report to their national parliaments for debate and as a basis for framing the budget for the following year. A mechanism of this sort would set in motion real coordination of budgetary policy in the Member States.

The second resolution dealt with another key item in the first stage—a closer collaboration between the central banks. To boost concerted action, they be required to follow convergent guidelines on monetary and credit policy, defined by the Committee of Governors. As for the ECMF, the Commission issued a mandate to the Monetary Committee to draft, in partnership with the central bankers, a report on its functions and organisation for submission to the Commission and the Council by 30 June 1972 at the latest. This resolution contained another of the Werner Report's recommendations relating to European monetary solidarity: the Community would gradually adopt common positions on monetary relations with third countries and in international organisations.

All the actions for the first three-year stage were due to start from 1 January 1971. The Commission would submit a communication to the Council before 1 May 1973 detailing the measures to be adopted beyond the first stage, including the changes to the treaty as stipulated in Article 236.

The central bankers were the first to voice their discontent on discovering how much the Commission had toned down the Werner Report. In the first meeting of the Committee of Governors which followed the publication of the Commission's proposals, the discussions highlighted their disagreement. The President of the Bundesbank, Karl Klasen, explained that whereas he fully accepted the report by the Werner Group, it was impossible for him to respond in the same way to the Commission's proposals. Although it affirmed similar goals, the Commission did not put forward the same views. The Italian members (Paolo Baffi, representative of Governor Guido Carli from the Banca d'Italia, and Rinaldo Ossola) deemed that the Commission's proposals lacked clarity and only had symbolic value. They held that it was important to achieve convergence between the economic and monetary development of the partners in order to make real progress towards EMU.[43]

Reacting to these concerns, Ugo Mosca, member of the ad hoc group as Commission's representative, claimed that any distinction between the two documents was purely formal. The difference was mainly a matter of presentation due to the fact that the Werner Group comprised highly qualified public figures who always thought in functional terms, whereas the Commission had expressed itself in terms corresponding to the legal and political necessities.

A brief comparison of the Werner Report and the Commission's proposals shows that their respective views were similar on a large number of key issues, but the emphasis varied. For a start both documents offered exactly the same definition of the final objective—a 'community of stability and growth'—with the affirmation of the irreversible nature of EMU, and of the principle of parallelism between tighter coordination of both economic and monetary policy. The Werner Group emphasised monetary policy, including its social repercussions, whereas the Commission, convinced that less progress would be needed in the first stage, paid less attention to this field. The need to adapt the Treaty of Rome was clear, as was the transfer of powers from the national to the Community level. Unlike the Werner Report, which put the emphasis on expanding the institutional fabric with new Community bodies, the Commission thought that such transfers were entirely possible within the framework of existing institutions. It would simply be necessary to redistribute powers and re-organise the links between institutions, on the one hand, and between Community bodies and national authorities, on the other.

'In all these fields we shall resume the work in hand with regard to relations between the Commission and the Council, in other words urge the Council to take specific decisions in various fields, for [...] what counts is not reports, plans, statements of good intention, what counts is decisions [...]. The goal for which the Commission is aiming, in the coming months and above all before the Council meeting at the end of December, is to obtain a certain number of decisions which will show very clearly that we are moving irreversibly towards better economic, monetary and financial organisation of the Community'.[44]

In keeping with the timetable set by the Heads of State or Government, the deadline for the decisions to be taken was 31 December 1970.

6.3 The Council[45]

A week after it was officially presented, the Werner Report was sent to the Commission, which took cognisance of it on 16 October 1970. A day before it was released in Brussels, Werner sent the paper to the other Finance Ministers of the Member States, as a gesture of political courtesy. The plan by stages still had pride of place in political discussions at the time and Werner, as chairman of the ad hoc committee, tirelessly defended the outcome of its work. He raised it, for example, on 15 October with the President of the Commission, Franco Maria Malfatti, who was on a working visit to Luxembourg, and expounded it in Paris 24 h later at a dinner-debate organised by the Cercle de l'Opinion.[46] To an audience of politicians and journalists, Werner set out the approach adopted in the report, highlighting that his group had opted for 'a middle way which was already indicated by the concept of moving forward by stages, gradually, and was confirmed by the parallel approach to economic development and monetary cooperation, with which political cooperation would align itself at a more advanced stage'.[47] In his view, 'the merit of the report, [it seems to me], is that it has broken the vicious circle of laying down political and economic preconditions and shows that there is a cautious, gradual way of evolving towards a state of affairs which will enormously ease the task of achieving, in full, the aims of the existing treaties. As regards putting together an economic system like the common market, we cannot in the long run afford to lose sight of the crucial part played by currency and credit. It would be a mistake not to draw the proper lessons, from the financial point of view, from a form of economic integration which is what now makes our national economies strong and will certainly show its face in international financial relations as well'. Robert Marjolin and Raymond Barre, both Members of the Commission (the first from 1958 to 1967; the second from 1967 to 1973), also attended this debate. In his speech, Barre was very circumspect on the pretext that the Commission had to let the Council of Ministers give its views on the report first. He said he hoped that '[The practical decisions taken in the next few months] must demonstrate the determination of our governments to gradually put together a multinational grouping which is effectively organised at the economic, monetary and financial levels and very much takes its own line towards the outside world. It is possible to achieve such an outcome within the present decade, provided we take heed of the prevailing economic, political and psychological conditions in the Community'.[48]

On 29 October 1970, the Commission submitted its own proposals, based on the Werner Report, to the Council, together with two draft resolutions. The reactions were many, starting with the positions adopted by the national governments on the various objectives, the ways of proceeding and the staging posts set out in the Werner Report.[49] Then came reactions, both from governments and from the various specialised committees, relating to the marked differences between the consensus-based plan hammered out by the ad hoc committee and the proposals from the Commission. The EP made its views known through its specialised committees, at political group meetings and in plenary sessions.

On 26 and 27 October, the Council met in a joint Ecofin-Foreign Affairs configuration because of the combined economic and political dimension of the subject. The Foreign Affairs Council started by looking at the plan by stages, then the Finance Ministers tried to focus more on the document in the context of an informal meeting scheduled for 9 November 1970. Werner prepared for this meeting cautiously, with a special eye to the French Government's reactions. '[...] [The meeting], which my colleagues Snoy, Schiller and Möller had been especially keen to have, was first postponed and then cancelled when Giscard d'Estaing, who had been very helpful to me in my work, informed me that he could not be present in person. Meanwhile the Commission had decided to examine the question. It was considered that from then on the follow-up to the reports would come in the form of official reports between the Commission and the Council'.[50]

On 13 November, the French Government confirmed that it still subscribed to the final communiqué from the Hague Summit, but refused to set specific deadlines or address the basic institutional problems of the Community. That set the tone for the political negotiations. The Council meeting on 23 November 1970 set 14 December as the date for the last meeting of the year. With that in view, it instructed the Permanent Representatives' Committee (Coreper),[51] taking the Commission's proposals as the basis for its work, to draw up the texts of the draft decisions of the Council on EMU.[52] So Coreper met on 2 and 10 December, with support from the technical working party on economic and financial questions.

After several arbitration sessions, all of which the French delegation attended (so as to oppose the others), the permanent representatives succeeded in bringing views together on a great many issues.[53] While the Commission's proposals were unanimously accepted as a working basis, the delegations agreed to tighten them up in certain areas by incorporating specific features from the Werner Report. The definition of the first three-year stage had to be precise, and based on the principle that EMU was irreversible. Five of the delegations stated categorically that stage one could not be dissociated from the full process of economic and monetary integration, the future development of EMU must be defined from the outset in a binding and irreversible manner. The French delegation fought to have the objectives defined only in broad outline and thought it was too early at that stage to set a precise date for the final result. On the question of the date, the French and German positions were in line with each other, though paradoxically for opposite reasons. The French looked to there being as few constraints as possible, whereas the Germans advocated a strict approach with flexibility where necessary (the twofold criterion *Stringenz und Flexibilität*).[54]

With regard to drawing up a calendar for the stages of EMU, two opposite approaches emerged. Five of the partners were in agreement that EMU should be set up by stages over a ten-year period, with stage one beginning on 1 January 1971. The French delegation preferred a wording stating that EMU would be established by 1 January 1980. There was also discussion over the procedure for the transition from stage one. All delegations (except France) considered, as did the Commission, that an assessment of what had been achieved should be carried out before the end of stage one, and, on that basis, the most appropriate measures for the gradual, full achievement of EMU should be adopted.[55] The idea that monetary union and economic union should progress in parallel was supported by all the delegations, and Italy insisted that the expression 'guaranteed parallel development' should appear in the draft.

All the delegations agreed that managing EMU would inevitably involve a transfer of decision-making powers from national to Community bodies. Five delegations thought that 'a decision-making centre at the Community level' was actually essential. The French announced that they could not approve any move whatsoever to decide the shape of the future institutional mechanisms because no details had yet been established on how powers over economic and monetary matters should be divided between the Community and national levels. Finally, the partners stipulated that 'the powers which should in any event be vested in the Community at the final stage of EMU and to emphasise the need for the Community institutions to develop correspondingly during the various stages'.[56]

Five delegations considered that a revision of the treaty appears inevitable, and the calling of an intergovernmental conference would be appropriate at the end of stage one. The French were fiercely opposed, even if might prove essential to amend the treaty in the future, and called expressly 'for this issue to be removed from the discussion'.

Another sticking point was the further extension of the EP powers so as to strengthen it as the organ of democratic control of EMU. Five delegations raised the question of transferring powers from the national parliaments to the EP and of having the EP elected by direct universal suffrage. The French, once again, came out against the idea, fearing that such a transfer of powers would lead to an imbalance in the Communities. They mentioned that in France decisions on monetary matters were outside the Parliament's sphere of competence. Nevertheless, even if that might be true of the limited monetary field, it certainly did not apply to the adoption of the economic plan, the major aspects of economic policy, the budget, etc., inasmuch as such measures were of short-term economic importance.

The German delegation emphasised the leading role of the central banks system in the building of EMU. The best source of inspiration was the Federal Reserve Board, a structure which, like the Bundesbank, had the necessary autonomy and had to pursue the same aims as the Community bodies with regard to EMU. The fact that the draft resolution proposed by the Commission put too much stress on fiscal harmonisation was not to the French taste. The Commission did not envisage full harmonisation of direct and indirect taxes but a harmonisation confined to what was needed for the smooth functioning of the future EMU. The Germans were also unhappy, but on the grounds that the fiscal proposals were too lax; they insisted that the wording of the Werner Report should be followed to the letter.

Two noteworthy comments came up as regards sectoral policy. The first was by the Italians, who, in order to eliminate structural and regional disparities, pressed for concerted action on sectoral policies of the Member States with knock-on effects on the Community's economic policy. The second was from the Germans, calling for a specific reference to 'a convergence of sectoral policies', to be added in the resolution.

On 14 and 15 December, the Foreign Ministers and the Ministers for Economic Affairs and Finance of the Six, assisted by the chairmen of the specialised committees of the Commission, met in the Council, with German Foreign Minister Walter Scheel in the chair on the first day and the Federal Minister for Economic Affairs, Karl Schiller, the next. In the second half of 1970, it was Germany which held the Presidency of the Council. The Council's wish for the December session was to reach the political decision implementing stage one of EMU. As the discussions progressed, the contradictions relating to the nature and powers of the decision-making bodies at an advanced or final stage of EMU stood out in ever sharper relief. France rejected any idea of a supranational institutional structure. The Netherlands tried to establish a link with the negotiations on UK accession. Germany then expressed reservations on the grounds that the financing clauses were drawn up before there had been any tangible achievements in relation to policy coordination. In the last part of the meeting, which lasted more than 12 hours, it became quite clear that no political agreement could be reached. To save the day, a select high-level group chaired by Karl Schiller (and including Raymond Barre) was mandated to draft the chapter on one of the most sensitive issues put before the ministers: the transfer of powers from the Member States to the Community.

Faced with the prospect of unavoidable deadlock that would continue beyond the end of the year, the meeting came up with a proposal to stop the clock symbolically at midnight on 31 December as a way of demonstrating the Council's determination to make headway. Germany was asked to carry on chairing the negotiations beyond this date, but Scheel rejected that possibility. He said that it was technically impossible to extend the German Presidency, but in practice it looked as though no one wanted to meet again before the end of the year. On 1 January 1971, France took the reins of the six-month Presidency: in that capacity, it was up to it to set the agenda for the ensuing Council meetings, in line with its priorities. EMU, however, was not one of Paris's pressing concerns. The attitude of the Germans raised a great many questions, particularly since the sudden caution they were displaying was in contrast to their early personal commitment to the plan by stages. The German Presidency's intention in making this highly political gesture was to show that it was now up to those who had brought the negotiations to a standstill to shoulder their responsibilities. Speaking to the press, Schiller said that the great majority of the Member States wanted to see the rapid adoption of the plan by stages, 'but others take a different view, start from different criteria and put forward prior conditions. […] The spirit of The Hague has not always been abided by'.[57] Finalising the discussions on EMU had to wait, and Coreper was instructed to carry on with its work.

At the December sitting of the Council, Werner deliberately kept his interventions to a minimum. Even so, the Werner Report, particularly in its final version of 8 October 1970, triggered a great deal of discussion. Since the Commission's proposals and hence the whole documents on which the Council was to decide were based on the interim report, what was to be done with the final report? It is true that the interim plan of 9 June 1970 set out the broad principles of EMU, but the final report went much further, not just defining the content of stage one of the process, but defining the main points of an EMU taking shape within a decade. The design of institutions and the transfer of responsibilities to the Community, which had not been mentioned in the interim report, were among the essential requirements of the final report. At the same time, they were proving to be sensitive points for some of the partners, especially France. Faced with pressing calls for the final version of the Werner Report to be taken into consideration, the Council achieved a wording which took a long time to negotiate: 'having regard to the suggestions made by the group and sharing the views expressed in the final Werner Report concerning the features essential to the existence of an EMU and the economic policy consequences which such a union will entail …'.[58] However, the failure of the Council to come to the necessary political decisions before the end of the year was obvious.

Werner decided to act once more to break the impasse. On 29 December, as Prime Minister of the Grand Duchy of Luxembourg, he wrote to the five Heads of Government to express his concerns with regard to the launching of EMU and say he trusted that a rapid and unanimously acceptable solution could be found. Chancellor Willy Brandt gave his answer to Werner four weeks later in a long letter focusing on the prospects for the plan by stages as laid down following the 15th French–German summit at the end of January 1971.[59]

At the meeting of the Council on 20 January 1971, there were signs of a closing of the gap, with the ground prepared by the Finance Ministers' meeting held in Arnhem (the Netherlands) a few days before. Coreper met on 22 and 27 January and went on with its work towards establishing a shared position on the texts of the Council's resolution.[60] The basis for the negotiations was a paper tabled by the Belgian delegation—which had summarised the previous points of agreement—proposing the adoption of a decision (*Beschluss*), not a resolution.[61] The Germans, Italians, and Luxembourgers backed this proposal for a compromise. The Dutch, having started out with reservations (by defining their position in more specific terms), also joined them. Once a number of amendments had been made, the French delegation also gave its agreement. The main sticking points were over the definition of the criteria for the transition from stage one to the next (successive) stages, the duration of the transitional period and the distribution of powers in the Community and parliamentary control. The decisions which related to fiscal questions (and there were some fierce discussions about these) were put forward by the Luxembourgers, who, together with the Belgians, came up with the wording on assessing, by 1 May 1973, the progress made towards setting up EMU and the need for a timetable for this.

At the Coreper meeting on 4 February 1971, two specific proposals for decisions took shape.[62] The first was to do with strengthening the coordination of short-term economic policies. The second aimed for further cooperation between the central banks. This plan—for which consultation of the Committee of Governors of the Central Banks proved decisive—was drawn up to safeguard the political responsibilities borne by Member State governments and, at the same time, the independence enjoyed by some central banks.[63] The Germans particularly insisted that the independence of the central banks should be guaranteed. With exception of the Dutch, all delegations agreed to the full text of the document.

The Council held its 141st session on 8 and 9 February 1971, with Maurice Schumann, Foreign Minister of the French Republic, in the chair. At the close of the proceedings, a final communiqué and a joint press conference by the French Foreign Minister and the President of the Commission, Franco Maria Malfatti, were an opportunity for the making of a long-awaited announcement. 'The Council has today agreed on a resolution concerning the establishment by stages of EMU in the Community. [...] The Council has also agreed on two decisions concerning, firstly, the strengthening of cooperation between the central banks of the Member States and, secondly, enhanced coordination of the Member States' short-term economic policies'.[64]

Looking back on this meeting of the Council, Werner remembered that 'we were able to reach an agreement by turning the negative safeguard clause into a positive clause, giving the currency mechanisms a duration of five years and guaranteeing that they would be extended if the rest were agreed on. [...] Essentially the basis for the launching of the union was the proposals in the report, which it was not particularly easy to set up. For me at the time, what was vital was the measures to be taken to assert the specific monetary character of the Community in a monetary environment which was becoming increasingly turbulent. [...] The working party's task was completed. It was no longer convened and was not set up again later. For me personally it was the start of a new era in which I was constantly in demand to explain and propagate the idea of monetary union'.[65]

On 22 March 1971, the Council officially adopted the programme for the establishment of EMU by stages, backed up by three specific decisions. The first related to strengthening the coordination of short-term economic policies, including three annual reviews of the situation in the Member States. The second doomed to stepping up cooperation between the central banks, by coordinating policies on currency and credit. The third dealt with the setting up of medium-term financial assistance. It was stipulated that the measures should be taken in parallel. The central banks had, in fact, been urged, on an experimental, unofficial basis, to narrow the margins for exchange rate fluctuation from June onwards.

6.4 Political Reactions in the Member States

After the publication of the Werner Report on 16 October 1970, political reactions soon started to come in from the Member States. The first to react were the media, before even the governments had had a chance to state their positions officially. The only political figures to take a stand on that day were the Dutch Finance Minister, Johannes Witteveen, and the Vice-President of the Commission, Raymond Barre.

Germany

On 20 October 1970, the Federal Minister for Economic Affairs, Karl Schiller, gave a press conference to explain the content of the plan by stages. His comments were positive: the Werner Report had struck a compromise between the countries which wanted to achieve EMU by giving priority to monetary issues and those, such as Germany, which put the coordination of economic policies within the Community forward as a prior condition. In fact it was the principle of striking a balance between these two trends that the Werner Committee opted for, as well as deciding that the coordination and convergence of the Six's economic and monetary policies needed to proceed in parallel. In the political negotiations on the plan by stages, the government in Bonn had therefore managed to preserve the basic principles of its economic policy, enunciated in the Schiller Plan put forward at the start of the year.[66] The German minister hoped to see the report approved as it stood by the end of the year 1970. At a domestic level, Schiller had already done all the necessary steps. On 4 October, before the plan by stages had been officially dispatched to the governments of the Six, the minister sent an official communication to the Federal Chancellor pointing out that 'the Federal Cabinet will be receiving the Werner Report shortly [...] and will be asked to approve it [...] It is important that approval should be given while Germany still holds the Presidency [of the EEC Council of Ministers], so that stage one [of the plan], which is to last three years, can start on 1 January 1970'.[67] Schiller was careful to stress the contribution made by the German member to the committee of experts—Johann Baptist Schöllhorn—who had 'driven the proceedings forward by his own proposals and helped to secure the requisite compromise [...] for which, in the interests of European policy, we went to the acceptable limit from the economic point of view and in terms of political stability'.

The Bundesbank was basically in favour of the Werner Report, which it considered to be serious and well-balanced, though possibly on condition that its modus operandi were later adapted to confirm more closely to its ideas.[68] The proposals in Germany's official statement included one drawing its fundamental inspiration from the statutes of the Bundesbank, advocating an autonomous central bank as a model for the future European central bank. At the meeting of Finance Ministers held on 29 May 1970 in Venice and during the debates on the interim report, Karl Schiller emphasised the fundamental political importance of an EMU and stressed the question of the transfer of powers to the Community bodies and its institutional issues. He mentioned, firstly, 'a body given responsibility for short-term economic policy and [secondly], a body with responsibility for drafting decisions in the monetary field centrally. This body should be federal in character and enjoy a wide measure of independence from the political authorities'.[69] Furthermore, strengthening economic cooperation and stepping up collaboration between the governors of the central banks and the Council were among the priorities the Schiller Plan set for stage one of EMU. The President of the Bundesbank, Otto Pöhl, issued warnings that 'monetary integration could not go ahead faster than overall economic integration'.

Once the Werner Report had been published, the Bundesbank constantly put that requirement to the forefront, reiterating that responsibility for future monetary policy must basically lie with Europe's central bankers as a collegiate body, 'independently of the Council, though with due regard for the guidelines drawn up by the Council with respect to economic policy'.[70] For the Bundesbank, another key principle referred to a 'genuine harmonisation of the Member States' economic and financial policies as a precondition for a reduction in exchange rate fluctuations between European currencies'.[71]

Chancellor Brandt took the same positive view of the Werner Report. He mentioned it openly to Pierre Harmel, on 14 October when the Foreign Minister of Belgium was in Bonn, and expressed the need to adopt as soon as possible the practical measures to implement EMU.[72] Harmel considered that 'France will side [with those who approve the Werner Report]. Italy will not raise any difficulties. The Netherlands can be expected to have some reservations, but those will disappear if the Federal German Government approves the report'.[73] In a letter to Schiller of 21 October 1970, Brandt emphasised the importance of the report to European integration and noted that its final adoption by the Council of Ministers, if possible before the end of the year, 'will very probably be the most important decision since the signing of the Rome Treaties'.[74] In a statement on the foreign policy of the Federal Republic which he made to the Bundestag, Brandt described the Werner Report as the 'new Magna Carta of the European Community'.[75]

It is worth noting that the Chancellor and the Federal Minister for Economic Affairs did not always see eye to eye and there were sometimes disagreements over EMU. Brandt advocated intra-European monetary cooperation, while his minister was in favour of joint consultation on the external aspects of the Member States' monetary policies. The consequence was that the German Government was against any initiative which favoured one position to the expense of the other.

At the end of October 1970, when the Commission submitted its own proposals for an EMU by stages, the German Government severely criticised the reductive interpretation it placed on the Werner Report. The Commission seemed to want to favour monetary cooperation aspects at the expense of economic harmonisation right from the first stage, and, as regards powers, it appears to be attacking the independence of the central banks.[76] The German Government's assessment was categorical: 'The Commission's proposals for the establishment of an EMU by stages are too limited and do not go far enough'.[77]

At the EP plenary sitting dedicated to the Werner Report, Karl Schiller spoke as the President-in-Office of the Council of Ministers of the EEC. After summarising the essence of the plan by stages as proposed by the Werner Committee and, at the same time, set out the main points of the official German position.[78] '[…] In keeping with the principle of parallel progress to which the Werner Report attaches paramount importance […] it is essential, not to say unavoidable, that the requisite steps be taken to bring about a convergence between the various economic policies and gradually fuse the monetary policies together. […] Targets to be achieved and actions to be taken in the economic policy field must be set, alongside the measures designed to bring about the convergence of monetary policies. We must give up the present system. We have a common market and a customs union but, as we all know, we are still living in a system in which separate national policies govern the economy, finance and the short-term economic situation, a system which is bound to give rise to never-ending imbalances. […] An abstract European monetary mechanism would quickly fall apart in the event of an imbalance unless it went hand in hand with a convergence or a parallel harmonisation of economic policies. […] The proposals put forward in the Werner Committee do not constitute a plan consisting of a set number of stages. All that is provided for is stage one and the final stage. As I see it, stage one will, according to the Werner Report, be a convergence and confirmation stage, because national policies need to start being harmonised from the outset. […] Stage two, and I would even say the intermediate stages, will, to judge from everything that can be deduced from the report, comprise the transformation stages, i.e. the gradual ceding of national powers to the Community bodies.

As for the final stage, which in Paris once we designated by the expression the "Paradise of Europe", it will put the seal on the full transfer of national powers over economic and financial policy to the Community. The seal will be set on the transfer of powers in the monetary field to a European system of central banks by the creation of a single European currency whose symbolic value cannot be overstated. [...] We cannot achieve this progress unless we first drop the idea of setting up any automatic procedure [and] unless we also introduce political breathing spaces, in other words unless the transition from one stage to another goes hand in hand with a consideration of the political issues. [...] Secondly, we will only get through this succession of stages up to the final stage if we take account, simultaneously and, as far as possible, head-on, of all economic, political and social points of view—if, in other words, when moving on from one stage to the next, we give all the attention due to the interdependence between all the economic and political factors in play. There is a third precondition: monetary union, which is our ultimate goal, must itself be part of a world monetary system which is itself evolving [...], reforming [...]. Our monetary union should be grounded in two principles, stability within itself and flexibility towards the outside world'. Schiller stressed that Europe should not be governed solely by technocrats but that it was also built on parliamentary foundations, and, as the Werner Report clearly stated, there seemed to be no way of establishing EMU without genuine parliamentary control.

France

Discussions on the Werner Report in France took a different turn. The French authorities saw EMU as a question of high politics: therefore, any development in a supranational direction was to be suppressed in favour of an intergovernmental structure.

While the Werner Report was being written, President Pompidou described how he saw political cooperation in Europe: 'it can only be a matter of building [Europe] out of what is already there, a confederation of states determined to harmonise their policies and integrate their economies, and if we see it that way, we realise that the quarrel over supranationality is a false quarrel. If some day a European confederation does come into being, there will of course have to be a government whose decisions are binding on all the countries which belong to it.

The problem is what this government is made from, and by what method and in what form we bring it about. [...] But the government of Europe can only emerge from a coming-together of the national governments, working together to take decisions that are valid for all'.[79]

The Werner Report sharply divided political circles in France. In government, the fiercest opponent was the Minister for National Defence, Michel Debré, who regarded the document as 'too supranational'.[80] His opinion was widely shared by the Gaullist ministers.

In contrast, the Minister for Finance, Giscard d'Estaing, who was responsible for presenting the case in Cabinet, welcomed the Werner Report. He turned for support to the centrist ministers Jacques Duhamel and René Pleven as a means of getting the Cabinet to approve the plan by stages. This division of opinion prompted Giscard d'Estaing to proceed with caution. He suggested that the government start by giving the green light to stage one of the Werner Report and make the ensuing stages subject to later approval.[81] The government, including Giscard d'Estaing, thought that close coordination of short-term economic policy and growth prior to monetary integration was not welcome; the many imponderables which such a process would inject into the economic development of the Member States would mean that France would have 'its hands tied' in the years to come. There was unanimous support in Cabinet, on the other hand, for a rapid transition to a monetary union, which was seen as a way of preventing, and safeguarding against, a crisis involving the franc. The Quai d'Orsay felt that the Werner Report needed to be taken further, given the prospect of an enlargement of the E.C. This would provide an opportunity to take greater account of 'the weaknesses which the sterling pound could cause to the foundations' of a monetary union. Note that the main reason for General de Gaulle's hostility to UK accession was the monetary question.

On 18 November 1970, a select Cabinet meeting convened to discuss European affairs was in fact devoted to the plan by stages. President Pompidou and most members of the French Government were opposed, in particular, to the idea of transferring monetary powers to Community institutions, as the Werner Report proposed in stage two of the building of EMU. 'There are some unbelievable turns of phrase in the Werner Report, it's as if a red rag had been waved in front of us to see if we were calves or bulls'.[82] At the same Cabinet meeting, Pompidou expressed the idea of making headway by conceding 'let us nevertheless accept this vocabulary, which is part of Europe's hopes'. He was particularly angered by the concept of 'European monetary hub', which in his view had no legitimacy. 'Europe is an economic, financial, political problem, but it is not just a monetary problem, far from it. As we long as we have not found a solution to the problem of subordination to the dollar, which is a political problem, let there be no talk of a European hub. We will only be able to talk of a European hub on the day European countries can ask the U.S. to take their dollars back and send them gold'.

Opposition from France without a counterproposal would be likely to isolate it and reduce its influence in the discussion. Giscard d'Estaing therefore recommended giving backing to a form of enhanced monetary cooperation between the Member States' central banks which would reduce the scope of the transfers of sovereignty. As for future developments on the integration front, France refused to accept any inordinate constraints being placed on its economic and financial policy and consequently wished to make as few commitments as possible. That is what Werner also picked up in his memoirs, recalling that Pompidou, after reading a few forceful extracts from the report, became angry and demanded explanations from the French members of the Werner Group.

The prevailing opinion in ruling circles in France was best described in a remark by Maurice Schumann in the monthly review *Vision*: 'We must not jeopardise the EMU of the Six by rushing into an institutional hotchpotch'.[83] What makes this disavowal of the Werner Report all the more surprising is that it had been drawn up with the full involvement of the French representatives and the intermediate report had been agreed to by the ministers concerned, including the French minister.

The Werner Group included two Frenchmen: Bernard Clappier, Chairman of the Monetary Committee (and also Vice-Governor of the Banque de France), and his alternate, Jean-Michel Bloch-Lainé. The members of group were supposed to exercise their role on the committee in an individual capacity and in full independence, but their reactions increasingly reflected the positions of their governments. An exploration of the German Federal Archives reveals the frequent communication (analyses, detailed explanations, comments on positions adopted, etc., as well as requests for instructions) that the German experts (particularly Hans Tietmeyer, deputy to the Chairman of the Medium-Term Economic Policy Committee, Johann Baptist Schöllhorn) sent through diplomatic channels to the Federal Ministry of the Economy, as well as to the Foreign Ministry and the Bundesbank. They were not alone; for example, 'it so happened that Mr. Clappier had the courtesy of keeping [the French Government] informed of what was going on, but of course it had no powers in this area'.[84] But Clappier, who was known for his European convictions, 'was able to calm the distrust and irritation that France, by its position and what it wants, often arouses; and he was able to do so without ever making any considerable concessions. One of the main difficulties of his role was being the committee member who insisted the most [...] on progress being made on monetary aspects, an area in which any headway naturally touches on the most sensitive aspects of national sovereignty. Mr. Clappier was strictly bound not to accept any institutional developments in this area'.[85]

In the National Assembly during the debate on 21 October, the nucleus of the Gaullist group became very active. By means of various interventions, it called on the French Government not just to explain its position on the Werner Report but also to take 'the right decision' for the country and take responsibility for it vis-à-vis the other European partners. 'Does the government intend to give consideration to the Werner programme, which proposes progressively abandoning national sovereignty to a Community authority that resembles a federal super-government? [...] If not, [...] does it intend to tell our Common Market partners that it finds this programme unacceptable?'[86]

Two weeks later, at Oral Questions on 5 November 1970, attended by the Foreign Minister, Maurice Schumann, the plan by stages once again sparked off lively debate. Some members explicitly stated their disagreement with the boldness displayed in the Werner Report and pointed to the more realistic approach adopted by the Commission in its own proposals. 'The Werner Report, which is an experts' report, seems to have approached the issues from the wrong end and to want to start building from the roof downwards, whereas we want […] to start with the foundations, and even there move forward step by step in the direction set by the Hague communiqué, in other words towards the establishment of EMU by stages. We are not against setting it up, but we do ask people to abide by the stages and not embark once again, in a different field, on the mistakes made in 1961 and 1962 in the field of political union, because asking for too much at a preliminary stage could well mean getting nothing. […] The wisdom the European Commission has shown in the face of a somewhat theoretical report from what were after all called wise men does tend to reassure us. […] We are not saying that we may not have to bring our economies closer and closer together […] or establish fixed exchange rates between [our] currencies, but there too, as with other areas, we think it is first and foremost up to the governments to act'.[87] Others spoke out strongly against the supranational elements in the Werner Report, and particularly against France's agreeing to them. This was the point made at the time by Roland Leroy, a member speaking on behalf of the PCF (French Communist Party) group, who stressed that 'it [the government] must explain its position. […] It must do it because the meeting of ministers from the smaller Europe to discuss this point is scheduled for 23 and 24 November. […] Is that the decisive step taken in 1970? It will be a decisive step, certainly, but a step towards the loss of all national independence'.[88]

There were also positive responses to the Werner Report from the House, both as regards making each stage of monetary integration dependent on a political decision and because of the prospects it opened up for giving Europe its own monetary individuality as against the dollar zone. 'On the economic level, the enhancing of monetary solidarity […] is a move which may turn out to be an effective one on the road to a united Europe. We do, in fact, know that however technical they may be, monetary measures between partners in Europe cannot remain purely neutral. On the contrary, their repercussions can only have major political implications, of which I will point out two aspects. Firstly, as currency is a sovereign prerogative, monetary union will obviously cause states to work together on problems which until now have now been dealt with at a strictly individual level, with the drawbacks and hazards that that attitude has entailed. The experts have taken the point well and propose that at each stage there should be a clear statement of political will before moving on to the next stage. […] Also, creating a new monetary hub calls the present international monetary system into question'.[89]

France's objections and the reservations put forward by Germany—openly sceptical about the financing clauses so long as there had been no tangible achievements in terms of policy coordination—prevented any agreement on the launching of the first stage of EMU. To defuse the situation, on 29 December 1970, in his capacity as chairman of the experts' committee, Werner wrote to the five heads of government to state his concern regarding the launching of EMU and express his confidence that a rapid and unanimously acceptable solution could be found.[90] Chancellor Brandt replied on 1 February 1971, focusing on the prospects for the plan by stages following the French–German summit held at the end of January 1971. Describing the Werner Report as a 'fundamental strategy document', Brandt reaffirmed the shared political determination to make progress on the matter, and reviewed the questions on which the two partners held diverging views, notably the 'escape clause', and their inability to hammer out a common position.[91]

The 15th French–German summit held in Paris (25–26 January 1971) gave a prominent place to the thorny European questions on the agenda, including EMU. Both countries shared the wish to see EMU set up relatively quickly. To do this, a suitable instrument needed to be created rapidly and the Council would have to take a decision on this matter, 'with or without amendments to the treaties'. The two governments agreed on the principle of parallel progress in developing economic union on the one hand and monetary union on the other. Yet this agreement disguised marked differences of opinion. While France was in favour of establishing EMU by the end of the 1970s, it refused to accept that aim as a legal obligation. Nor did Paris propose to set the duration of stage one in stone, despite the agreement on what it should involve, or consent to the setting up of a system of central banks with its own responsibility. France, in fact, called for the inclusion of an 'escape clause' for the duration of stage one. Germany was not opposed to this in principle, but it considered that such a provision was a matter for stage two. Faced with Pompidou, Brandt nevertheless tried to keep the overall prospect of the process open by hoping for an agreement on 'what will have to be done when stage one is over'.[92]

In a side-meeting during the summit, a German delegation met the Vice-President of the Commission, Raymond Barre, with, on the agenda, three questions linked to the plan by stages which were still open after the negative reactions from France. These were the definition of the final stage, the measures to be carried out in stage one and rules for the transition from one stage to another.[93] As regards the final stage, Barre thought that agreement would have to be reached on its principles, which must be formulated flexibly and cautiously, while at the same time refraining from attaching any constraints to them. The Commission would give thought to the drafting of satisfactory 'compromise wordings' on the subject of parliamentary control, the subsequent development of the institutions, the powers of the Community and the setting up of a system of central banks. The hardest task was proving to be that of laying down rules for the transition to stage two in the treaty framework. During stage one there were plans for certain monetary measures which would obviously not lead immediately to monetary union but would be such as to pave the way for future progress, by, among other things, preparing public opinion for the coming changes. The German Minister Schiller, was particularly concerned at the fact that in the absence of a consensus as to the measures to be adopted in stage two, 'stage one will go on forever'. If France could not be forced to move forward by the currently available legal means, the Council would have to impose on it the political duty of continuing along the path of EMU after stage one. It was obvious that failing a consensus, any progress towards EMU would be impossible.

At the end of the summit, France consented to allow certain powers to be transferred to the Community in the final stage. However, it rejected any idea of making structural adjustments to the decision-making process which was so dear to the Germans and the Dutch, as well any amendments to the Treaty of Rome and any encroachment on the predominant role of the Council of Ministers or the unanimity rule (in votes on important matters).[94] The parallelism principle underlying the Werner Report was substantially altered. Under German pressure, the French agreed to a future autonomous system of European central banks but remained hostile to a decision-making centre for economic policy. Germany considered it crucial that, alongside the future Central Bank, there should be a political authority responsible for firm European coordination of national budgetary policies. France was categorically opposed to this on the grounds that it would truncate national sovereignty in this field too drastically. As no agreement was reached, the decision was deferred, and the debate came to an end when this first plan for monetary unification was dropped following the collapse of the Bretton Woods system.[95]

Extending the Community method was, therefore, rejected in the field of economic union and it was up to the governments of the Member States to harmonise their economic policies through joint consultations. The Germans, in return, agreed to action being taken in stage one to reduce the margins for exchange rate fluctuation, set up a monetary support mechanism and create a EMCF. They also got their way on a principle defended in the Schiller Plan of 2 February 1970: the transition from stage one to stage two would not be automatic. The two partners agreed that if they did not manage to secure an agreement on the final stage, on its economic and institutional implications, the measures recommended for stage one, in particular the reduction in the margins for fluctuation, would be dropped.

In his memoirs, Pierre Werner recalled that 'President Pompidou and Chancellor Brandt reached agreement there on the method for establishing EMU. […] The price of this new understanding was a safeguard clause proposed by the Germans. It laid down that the monetary mechanisms would expire after four years if no agreement were reached on the content of stage two. There were objections to this clause, which virtually turned stage one into a test-run. Jean Monnet telephoned me to warn me against such a clause. Benelux was critical of the French–German side-agreement'.[96]

The Netherlands

Among the Benelux countries, the Netherlands broadly shared the German view and sided with the 'economists' from the outset. As soon as the Werner Committee was set up, Finance Minister Johannes Hendrikus Witteveen gave the first indications of his government's position in the negotiations by announcing that the development of monetary cooperation should be based on the harmonisation of economic policies.

It is worth noting that in European policy the Foreign Ministry took the lead, whereas the coordination of the Netherlands' monetary policy for Europe was a matter for the Finance Ministry.[97] Even if overall cooperation between these two institutions ran smoothly, generally speaking, this two-headed approach brought out certain diverging interests which created tension. For example, at a Cabinet meeting after the publication of the interim Werner Report, Witteveen reminded his ministerial colleagues that 'at the Hague summit, it was decided, under pressure from the Foreign Minister, that European monetary integration should be carried out without delay. This has always been a cause of concern to the undersigned'. In the end, the discussions which took place in the various Dutch bodies enabled a broad consensus to be reached and it was collegiality which used to win the day when it came to taking decisions.[98]

On 26 May 1970, when the Werner Committee's interim report had just been completed, Witteveen gave a speech to the Amsterdam Chamber of Commerce in which he came out in favour of a monetary union with a common currency, managed by a European central bank and a European Finance Ministry. A common currency—which amounted to the same thing as a single currency in that once it was introduced, the national currencies should cease to exist—was seen as vital in order to make European monetary unification irreversible. Pooling their reserves (the currencies) would make it possible for the participating countries to defend external monetary parity more effectively. According to the minister, the ground for the success of EMU would be prepared, in particular, by solid economic, budgetary and political integration of the Member States; in other words, by giving primacy to an economic union. The European Finance Ministry that he envisaged would be in charge not just of the Community budget but also of the national budgets, which he would supervise directly. In these circumstances, the autonomy of national Finance Ministers subordinate to this supranational body would be confined basically to executive tasks. Witteveen was thus prefiguring the functions of the decision-making centre for economic policy which was later included in the Werner Report.[99]

A few days before the final Werner Report was published, the Dutch Ministry of Finance produced an analysis of the document for the members of the Cabinet, evaluating it with regard to the position defended by the Netherlands during the negotiations, which was close to the 'German model'. The Werner Committee drew a number of conclusions from it with respect to the institutional reform of the Communities, broadly in keeping with the Dutch line of argument. This called for the establishment of a central administrative body, independent of the national governments, which would take on major powers in the economic sphere, as well as the setting up of a Community central bank system on the lines of the US Federal Reserve System. The transfer of powers from national governments to the central Community administrative body would have to go hand in hand with the transfer of the corresponding powers from national parliaments to an elected EP. The Dutch analysis emphasised that sustained efforts would have to be made in the coming years as regards the harmonisation of economic policies. If successful, it would be possible to set up a EMCF, which could be the beginnings of a federal bank.[100]

The Werner Report won backing from the Dutch Parliament and government, which considered it to be an 'acceptable compromise'.[101] On 29 October 1970 the European Commission published its own report, based on the interim Werner Report and therefore skating over the sensitive question introduced by the final report, namely, that economic policy be made a Community matter and a new institutional structure be created. In the eyes of the Dutch Government, which had stated its support for the key points of the Werner Report, the Commission's plan was inadmissible.[102]

It is worth recalling that from the very outset of the work of the committee of experts, when the first differences of approach between the members were becoming increasingly obvious, Pierre Werner, from the chair, attempted to hammer out a joint Benelux position.

Belgium

Belgium was prominent from the outset on the European integration front and in particular that of EMU. In the Werner Committee, it favoured the monetary approach, which was seen as the catalyst to economic convergence, but it was gradually won over to the arguments for a symmetrical EMU and to the underlying principle of the plan by stages, that progress on the economic and monetary fronts should take place in parallel.[103]

When the Werner Report was published, reaction in Belgium was positive. During the political consultations between Belgium and Germany on 14 October 1970, the Foreign Minister Pierre Harmel to put forward his government's official position, stressing 'the paramount importance that the Belgian Government attaches to carrying out the plan for EMU (the Werner Report). The Community must now find a method which makes it possible to give maximum political impact to the decisions it will have to take on this question'.[104] Keen to secure a consensus, he submitted to his German opposite number Walter Scheel a draft programme of action and joint consultations between the Six, for the aftermath of the official presentation of the report to the Council of Ministers (October 1970). 'We are faced with a fundamental choice here. Either we confine ourselves to confirming, and no more than that, the guidelines and objectives in the Werner Report, focusing exclusively on the first, experimental stage. Or, taking the Hague objective as our starting point, we are prepared to express our determination to reach the final objective by taking a long-term political decision to be put into effect in several stages. Just like the mechanisms set up for the Treaty of Rome, the transition from one stage to another would be obligatory, unless the Council decided otherwise'.[105] Supposing the Community were prepared to take a decision of that kind, it would have to adopt a very cautious line of conduct, avoiding too exclusive a focus on stage one by emphasising—'formally'—the political character of its decision and starting work on preparing the ground for the ensuing stages, including the appropriate legal instruments. Such a decision would make it possible for the UK and the other applicants for membership to associate themselves with the basic political option. At the same time, the new legal instruments should not enter into force until after the enlargement of the Community. Ministers Harmel and Scheel agreed that Belgium should consult its partners in the Benelux and Germany should consult the two other Member States (France and Italy), so that the strategy which had been sketched out could start to take shape.

Nothing came of this, as France quickly made clear that it disagreed with its other five partners. The unofficial joint consultation session between the Finance Ministers planned for 9 November was cancelled and four days later the French Government announced its refusal to set firm deadlines or to address the question of the Community's institutional structure. It nevertheless reaffirmed its attachment to the aspirations set out in the final communiqué from the Hague Conference regarding EMU.

Since the Council of Ministers' meeting on 24 and 25 November ended without any practical results, the Belgian Government decided to continue with its attempts at mediation. From then on, together with its natural ally Luxembourg, Belgium conducted a diplomatic offensive in the narrower, more technical setting of Coreper. In a situation where there was stalemate over the very principles behind EMU, the Belgian approach was to focus efforts on defining precisely and in detail the content of stage one, while there and then giving a firm commitment to carrying out the final objective until the end of a decade. 'By proceeding in this way, we draw our inspiration from our predecessors in 1957, since we would be giving those who will succeed us between now and 1980 the task of making decisive progress along the path of European unification, while at the same time allowing them to avail themselves of a commitment given in 1970 in order to overcome any obstacles which may arise'.[106]

The failure of the Council meeting of 14 and 15 December 1970 was a disappointment. The Belgians shared their feelings on this with the Luxembourgers, who also had long been committed to economic and monetary integration. Prime Minister Gaston Eyskens wrote to Pierre Werner of 'the remarkable work done under your chairmanship, during which you persevered with great skill in proposing solutions and reconciling different points of view and thereby succeeded in determining the options and methods for achieving EMU. [...] I understand and share the regrets to which the absence of a decision from the Council of the Minister of the EEC may give rise. [...] In analysing the differences of view, you yourself have pointed out the path towards a solution which could be acceptable to all, a solution which, as you say, would go some way towards singling out the vital and logical features of an EMU while allowing for the requisite sense of pragmatism which must dictate the first steps taken in this undertaking'.[107] It was also an opportunity to restate the unfailing commitment of the Belgian Government, 'which would continue to give these plans its full support'.[108]

Italy

Italy warmly welcomed the publication of the Werner Report, which prominent Italian figures had made a notable contribution to drafting. Gaetano Stammati, Chairman of the Budgetary Policy Committee, and his deputy Simone Palumbo, Guido Carli, Governor of the Banca d'Italia, Finance Minister Emilio Colombo, Rinaldo Ossola, chairman of the Group of Ten, were to help move the work of the experts' group forward by making substantial contributions to the discussions. The Secretary of the Werner Committee, who at the same time was the Director-General for Economic and Financial Affairs of the European Commission, Ugo Mosca, was also an Italian national.

The plan by stages took up ideas close to Italy's views, including, in particular, the principle of making progress in parallel on the coordination of economic policies and monetary unification, enhanced cooperation between the central banks, which were to act with full independence, as a preliminary stage in the establishment of an exchange rate stabilisation fund, the harmonisation of monetary cooperation instruments, the prospects for a common regional policy targeted on development or indeed the need to consult employers and labour in the major decisions on monetary cooperation.

The Italian Government had adopted a versatile and somewhat ambiguous position on the Werner Report. While the experts' committee was doing its work, the government insisted that the final objective should be clearly defined and stressed the need to take Italy's particular regional and structural aspects into consideration and to moderate some of the effects which the establishment of EMU might have accordingly. It advocated the notion of 'close parallel movement' on monetary cooperation and economic cooperation, emphasising one or other of the principles by turn, 'depending on the people it was speaking to rather than on its own concerns, which would have led it to press for monetary cooperation in the first instance', as certain documents from the French diplomatic archives stress.[109]

On the institutional question, Rome was gradually won over to the German position, which was to insist on the necessity for a transfer of powers to the Community level and for institutional changes, albeit without defining, any more than the Federal German Government did, the precise field where these adjustments should be made. The Italians highlighted the vital need for efficient management, and then placed increasing emphasis on the political implications of EMU, the crucible of a political Europe which would be federal in nature.[110]

The publication on 29 October 1970 of the Commission's proposals provoked a sense of dissatisfaction. The Italian members of the Committee of Governors considered that the Commission's plan lacked clarity and was only of symbolic value. To make concrete progress towards EMU, action should be taken to bring about genuine convergence in economic development and monetary cooperation between the partners.[111]

The government in Rome 'would have preferred the Werner Report to have been taken into account in full' by the Commission, but they had to be practical. Given the antagonisms among the Six, the Italians advocated the adoption of a political decision for the establishment of stage one of EMU from 1 January 1971, with a clear statement of the final objective and the deadline for reaching the final stage.[112]

At the Council meeting of 14 and 15 December 1970, the Italian Finance Minister, Mario Ferrari-Agradi, insisted on a specific political commitment which EMU demands. 'The Community must acquire its own decision-making powers and only with an eye to achieving a specific final objective can there be any point to the measures laid down for stage one.'[113] He also called for adjustments to the institutions and underlined the need for going beyond the unanimity principle and for 'introducing increasingly binding consultations'. Together with his German and Dutch colleagues, the Italian minister came out in favour of the Commission's proposal: by 1 May 1973 it should submit draft measures leading gradually to the full establishment of EMU, including draft amendments to be made to the Treaty. He also supported the idea of parliamentary control on the lines of that exercised by the national parliaments. As regards the deadline for setting up EMU, he subscribed to the French formula whereby the Community and the governments would do 'all in their power to establish EMU within the coming ten years'. Italy thus joined the Belgium–Luxembourg front and worked towards that objective within Coreper.[114]

A British Prospective

Looking ahead to UK accession, the Werner Committee examined the issues surrounding the pound sterling in the context of an EMU in the Community. It was therefore quite natural that the UK should take an interest in the Werner Report.

As the ad hoc committee produced its interim report (published on 20 May 1970), in London the Conservative victory in the elections of 18 June 1970 saw power pass into the hands of the government led by Edward Heath. The new Prime Minister publicly expressed his commitment to his country's membership of the European Community and stated what in his opinion were the sound reasons for EMU both for Western Europe and for the UK.[115] The whole of British Government action was based on this line. Consequently, both the Treasury and the Foreign Office, which had previously resisted the idea of a supranational Europe, now found themselves forced to support a policy of membership of which they feared the monetary consequences above anything else.

The final version of the Werner Report was carefully studied in London.[116] As the document focused on the three-year first stage and its implementation had few consequences for the UK (the strengthening of the consultation procedure would possibly involve British participation), the British Government's attitude was on balance positive. Pierre Werner involved himself heavily in the drafting of the English version of the report, of which he wrote some key passages himself. He made a hefty contribution to the work of disseminating it in the UK and explained the principles and concepts behind it in debates and lectures which he gave with his opposite number, and later friend, Edward Heath.[117]

In November 1970, the UK Foreign Office, which was negotiating the terms of UK accession to the E.C. at the time, reacted officially to the Werner Report and the second Barre Plan, and thus summarised the line the British were taking in the negotiations with the Six. With a view to accession in 1973, the Foreign Office spoke of the revolutionary and radical changes which the plan by stages presaged over the course of ten years. The political and economic implications for the UK were considerable, but once it had been agreed to put in the effort, it would have to be carried through to the end if it was to bear fruit.[118] The concepts of 'sovereignty', 'exchange rates', and 'monetary parity', as well as the timetable for implementing the binding measures in the Werner Report, sparked off lively debate and triggered arguments. The British were not against the idea of a single currency in the future, but they were against the prospect of taking part in a European monetary system before becoming a full member of the Community. They were also concerned about the status and management of the pound sterling—a national currency and at the same time an international reserve currency—in a Europe which was a monetary Community. The coordination of short- and medium-term economic policies and the other implications in terms of monetary cooperation as laid down in the second Barre Plan gave rise to further worries and were also matters to be dealt with in the accession negotiations. The UK side made a point of singling out the special characteristics which were to be safeguarded (with respect to currency and structural and regional policy) and the factors which made it different from or set it against the other Member States, while at the same time hoping that solutions acceptable to everyone could be found. What particularly concerned it was the institutional structure of the Community and the extent of the transfer of national powers to the Community level, both in stage one (which was regarded as experimental) and in stage two, where a monetary union built around a single currency would come into being. The UK decided to commit itself to the path of EMU, with the priority being given to the practical measures in stage one (in relation to the Barre Plan) and the establishment of coordination of economic and monetary policies. As for thinking about the next stage, that required 'experience and clarity' and was left for later.

6.5 Representative Economic, Social and Civic Organisations

There were several reactions to the official presentation of the Werner Committee's final report, not just from proponents of and activists for a united Europe but also from economic and business circles, professional associations and trade unions. The European and international media (particularly the press, radio, and television) reported the event and contributed to the explosion of interest. The type of discussion in those outlets differed, involving political reactions, technical opinions, or even specific proposals, as well as displays of commitment to the European cause on the part of ordinary citizens. The efforts by the press to inform the general public meant that they became increasingly aware of the active part they were destined to play in the building of a 'community of stability and growth', grounded in shared aspirations and freedoms and with a special identity vis-à-vis the outside world. A common, or indeed single, currency, shared social ideals and the prospect of direct involvement in the exercise of democratic control over this community all helped shape a growing feeling of belonging to a Europe with an emerging identity of its own.

6.5.1 The Economic and Social Committee

As prior consultation of the 'social partners' on 'the broad outlines of economic policy […] and quantitative guidelines for the principal elements […] of the public budgets' was among the recommendations in the Werner Report, the Council of the EC forwarded the report to the Economic and Social Committee (ESC) as early as 21 October 1971. In the sense used by the Werner Committee, the term 'social partners' was applied very widely, comprising all organisations representing economic and social life.[119] The ESC, which had already embarked on an analysis of the plan by stages, extended its debates to cover the Commission's proposals and decided to react by issuing an information report to which it devoted several discussion sessions on January and February

1971. Some months later, the programme for the establishment of EMU adopted by the Council consolidated the active part played by the ESC in this process, with its contribution being expressly mentioned as a channel for consulting the two sides of industry.[120]

The ESC's analysis stands out as focusing mainly on the Werner Report, which it saw as containing '[…] all the precepts needed to enable an EMU to be established in the course of the present decade'. The proposals from the Commission ('which wanted to provoke the Member States into taking a political decision') were then incorporated into the analysis, thereby giving rise to a series of observations and comments on certain major aspects which were deemed to have been consigned to the shadows, not to say overlooked in terms of practical action. The ESC line was that the progress made in building an integrated Europe needed to be continued by 'the establishment, without delay, of an EMU [without which] the benefits already secured in the area of the customs union and certain common policies could soon be called into question'.[121] EMU represented an intrinsic alteration in the exercise of building a united Europe and brought with it a need to evolve in the direction of a political union as well. The principle of achieving progress in parallel in different fields, which was what constituted the thrust of the proposals in the Werner Report, was a guarantee of movement in that direction. But, it depends basically on action and constant vigilance on the part of Member States to ensure that that balance is respected in the adoption and implementation of the specific measures.

Discussions within the ESC highlighted that the suggestions in the Werner Report, and still more those put forward by the Commission, took no account of the need for striking a balance between the various processes. There were even some who felt that this imbalance ran counter to the communiqué from the Hague Conference. If a balance were not achieved, the options open in terms of parallel development or the priorities to be given to this or that aspect of EMU would remain purely theoretical. Care should therefore be taken to ensure symmetry between the progress in the monetary and social fields, where the momentum would be slower, and progress on economic and institutional questions, especially the transfer of powers from national authorities to the Community bodies. The advancement towards the final stage would depend on the extent of the powers they were given and the practicalities of how they functioned, particularly in terms of voting procedures and democratic control. The Commission was as the 'central driving force behind the decisions which must be taken by majority vote'.

Satisfactory industrial relations proved to be a basic condition of success. The stakes in EMU were high, and it was obvious that without support from the general public and the representatives of organised civil society, including the two sides of industry, it could not take shape. The ESC therefore committed itself to urging management and labour to become involved in the building of EMU and to organising their participation. A preliminary set of guidelines recommended the holding of a wide-ranging consultation of economic and social interests on the planned changes. The framework and scope of such a procedure were still to be defined, in particular to make sure that the representatives of all shades of opinion were involved, in the most appropriate way, in a free-flowing process. Debates showed that implementing stage one of EMU inevitably accentuated the liberal trend in industrial policies because they gave a preponderant role to monetary aspects.[122] The economic policies pursued by the Community and the Member States were closely linked and, indeed, freed from democratic trade union pressure. The ESC considered, too, that it was imperative for it to be asked to give its opinion officially on the annual report on the economic situation in the Community.[123]

The ESC regarded the decade 1970–1980 as the maximum time limit for the setting up of an EMU. The process had to be run to a 'realisation timetable' with deadlines so that measures in different fields could be coordinated and forward plans drawn up by governments and the private sector could be harmonised. There was a warm welcome for the precise way in which the three-year first stage was charted, even though there was criticism of the way the monetary field to a certain extent took precedence over recommendations in the economic and institutional areas. As regards the economic aspects, the ESC pointed to the lack of progress planned for stage one in the areas of regional policy and structural policies (social policy, aid policy, energy policy, and transport policy); not until stage two, whose outlines had barely been traced, were there to be any common directives such as might produce parallel development in these various sectors.

The ESC hailed the aspirations to a monetary identity in the Community. Economic union required a common monetary arrangement and the monetary individualisation was seen as an ambitious but valid aim of the Werner Report. The specific measures involved shrinking the margins for fluctuation between the Six currencies and setting up a system of central banks in charge with overall guidelines for monetary and credit policy. At the same time, progress on coordinating economic, fiscal, and financial policies was essential. In addition to intra-Community monetary cooperation, emerged the idea of cooperation with the outside world, which had to go hand in hand with the rise of a common trade policy. According to the ESC, the EMCF would have a substantial role to play on this purpose. '[…] The existence of a common position on monetary questions will only be recognised by the outside world when a body acting as both a decision-making centre and a reserve fund for the Member States is set up. […] The cautious proposal on this question contained in the Werner Report is the only one which, in the present circumstances, has succeeded in bringing about unanimity'. The ESC recommended that the preparatory work be done swiftly and the fund implemented as soon as possible. The central banks were expected to tighten the links between them in preparing for the second stage of EMU, in which they would be required to act together to forge a common policy.

By conducting a comparative analysis of the Werner Report and the Commission's proposals, the ESC threw light on the inescapable differences between the two documents, owing to their dissimilar character. The first was the outcome of a process of reflection; the second was the legal formalisation of a number of suggestions arose from that reflection, in the form of a resolution and two draft decisions by the Council. However, 'the Commission's proposals lag behind those made by the Werner Group. […] It is regrettable that the Commission has not stuck more closely to the Werner Group's proposals, especially as regards the institutional aspects and the political objectives'.[124]

6.5.2 Professional, Trade Union and Civic Organisations

There was interest in the publication of the Werner Report and the Commission's proposals from professional associations, trade unions and, sometimes, private citizens. They were increasingly concerned by EMU, which they had a part to play in building as well as being onlookers, and they contributed to the debate through their various public statements, motions, comments, and ideas.

The European associations representing finance professionals were the first to react. Their remarks, addressed to the General Secretariat of the Council of the EC, were directed at specific aspects of their field and were very technical. The Savings Banks Group of the EEC in agreement with the European Banking Federation, reacted initially with a paper on the fiscal aspects of the plan by stages by making practical proposals for taxation on investments and share dividends, as well as taxation of investment interest, deposits and bonds.[125] It then proceeds to a comparative assessment of the final Werner Report and the Commission proposals.

After highlighting the joint work of the Werner Committee and of the Committee of Governors of the Central Banks in studying the issues, the association deplored the lack of ambition of the practical measures put forward by the Commission. '[…] Some fundamental problems [have] not been addressed in the [Commission's] resolution and the content of the decisions proposed sometimes departs from the thinking contained in the Werner Report. […] These departures cannot all be approved [without further debate]'.[126] The bankers expressed their disappointment at the absence of results from the Council meeting of 14 December 1970, though they considered that in the interests of EMU itself, 'rather than go for a hasty compromise [it is preferable to take] clear-cut, properly thought-out decisions later'.

Setting up EMU was a highly significant step politically. Consequently, transferring the requisite powers and democratic control over them to the Community called, before starting stage one, for a clear resolve on the part of the Member States to end up with a political union as a matter of necessity. On the substantive issue, institutional changes were seen as not being given suitable consideration. It was a matter, firstly, of setting up a decision-making centre for economic policy which would have to exert an influence on the drawing up of national budgets and make changes in the exchange rate of the single currency or of all the national currencies (the logical consequence of fixed exchange rates). Secondly, it involved setting up a Community system of central banks which would take decisions on internal monetary policy (liquidity, interest rates and credit) and external monetary policy (intervention in the money markets and reserve management). The mere proposal to establish two decision-making centres, without a detailed description of their structures and machinery or their links to existing bodies—the Council of Ministers and the European Commission—seemed inadequate. On the other hand, in recommending that the decision-making centre for economic policy, but not that for monetary policy, should be politically answerable to the EP, the Werner Report showed respect for central bank independence. The Commission took a different line. In its proposal for a decision on strengthening cooperation between central banks, the Commission left it up to governments to define the guidelines for liquidity, credit and interest-rate policy, 'having regard to the guidelines on general economic policy laid down by the Council'. But this called into question the independence of the central banks and their future common body, and the group openly criticised this approach.

As far as the economic objectives were concerned, the Werner Report proposed making the Community into a 'stability bloc', while the Commission seemed in its proposals to be shifting the stress here by mentioning stability only in third place, after growth and employment. The bankers thought it essential for the decisions on EMU to include a clearer obligation to fight for stability, particularly stability in monetary value. In the same vein, they supported the principle of working out a common attitude for the Six in international financial institutions. Efforts to make their currencies progressively more independent of the US dollar were recognised as equally important.

The Union of Industries of the European Community (UNICE) reacted on 2 December 1970. By reviewing the key points of the Werner Report, the industries welcomed especially the recommendations relating to consulting employers and labour before putting a Community policy into effect.[127] UNICE warned that looking for solutions to sensitive institutional problems could delay the rapid, energetic achievement of EMU. It also stressed the 'importance of working in parallel on harmonising economic policy and accomplishing closer monetary cooperation, as progress in either field could only boost progress in the other and vice versa'.

The various stages of EMU would have to be designed interdependently. In stage one, effective steps should focus to take control of the short-term economic realities while being aware of the repercussions the measures adopted by each Member State could have on economic developments in the other partner countries. The industrialists also thought that a formal commitment by mutual agreement on the economic policy objectives was even more important than joint consultation on the use of short-term economic policy instruments. Compatible development of the partners would be a way of avoiding differences in price levels, followed by external imbalances which would inevitably lead to protectionist measures or changes to exchange rates. Key guidelines with regard to liquidity, credit to the public and private sectors and the policy on interest rates must be defined jointly. The same would apply to set up a European monetary and financial market and to define budgetary and regional policies in the Community.

UNICE was in favour of setting up a EMCF as recommended by the Werner Report, and only regretted that the Commission was still not putting forward any specific proposals as to when the Fund should be set up. There was a vital role for such a mechanism. Firstly, the Fund could be 'the basis for an institution to carry out a Community monetary and financial policy towards non-member countries, as part of international monetary cooperation'. Secondly, the Fund was considered as the foundation of a mutual intervention policy in the Community. The industrialists proposed that once they had been defined, the short-term monetary support and medium-term financial assistance mechanisms should be brought into effect by the Fund. A common policy towards the outside world would be vitally important as it would attach figures to the Fund's opportunities for taking action. UNICE recommended, lastly, that any shrinking of the margins for the exchange rates between the Member States' currencies will go hand in hand with parallel progress in the harmonisation of economic policies.

Although they had been playing an active part in the debate on EMU from the outset, the trade unions reacted more strongly after the publication of the final Werner Report and the Commission proposals.[128] A few days before the Council of Ministers meeting which was to take a decision on launching stage one of EMU, the European Confederation of Free Trade Unions in the Community (ECFTU) expressed its concern.[129] '[We] note that the practical proposals for setting up an EMU do not provide adequate guarantees as regards the exercise of democratic control at the level at which decisions directly affecting the living and working conditions of the peoples of the six Community countries will be taken in future. In particular, it is likely that workers and their representatives will no longer enjoy, at the Community level, the rights and guarantees secured at the national level'.[130] The granting of powers in the economic, fiscal and budgetary fields to the Community institutions must be followed by a strengthening of democratic control: a widening of the EP's powers and its election by universal suffrage had become essential conditions. A social policy needed to be established and implemented simultaneously with the economic and monetary measures. The quest for stability would lead to the introduction of a deflationary policy which would ultimately result in wage and salary cuts. Such an 'incomes policy' would be unacceptable. According to the ECFTU, EMU should therefore be built around several major priorities: social progress through economic expansion, full employment against a background of harmonious regional development and a fair share-out of national income.

The European Organisation of the World Confederation of Labour (EOWCL) met in Brussels on 16 December 1970. The discussions centred on EMU and questions relating to employment.[131] The outcome was two motions which were at once forwarded to the President of the Council of Ministers.[132] The organisation did not propose to comment on the substance of the Commission's proposals, 'but was anxious to stress the advantages to the development of the Community of carrying out the ideas in the Werner Report'.[133] Without hiding its disappointment at the failure of the Council meeting of 14 December, the organisation warned against the risk of departing from the aims set out in the Hague Declaration and strongly urged the Council to come to an agreement quickly. The Community bodies must be given real powers, under the democratic control of the EP and in consultation with the European organisations representing workers and employers. The establishment of EMU raised, in an acute form, the question of political union, which would entail a revision of the current treaty at some point in the future. Public opinion expected EMU to bring rapid, practical results in the area of social policy. The Council was therefore invited to decide, as soon as possible and in specific detail, on the measures which had to be taken in stage one of such a union.

Militants for the European cause, whose active but discreet involvement backed up the work of the ad hoc group and helped create a consensus around the Werner Report, once again stated their support for EMU. For example, the European League for Economic Cooperation (ELEC) instructed its monetary panel to analyse the report and the Commission's proposals and adopted a motion on that basis.[134]

This document emphasised that the work of the Werner Group and its report are 'an important and, very probably, decisive contribution to the economic and monetary integration of the Community'. It stressed the importance of the measures to be adopted in various areas going forward in parallel and complementing each other, while urging the Member States to espouse the political determination to move ahead in order to carry this irreversible process through to completion. The establishment of the first stage of EMU from 1 January 1971 onwards was a clear demonstration of political will. Following on from that, the stages envisaged by the report had to be embarked on in succession in the ten-year period assigned for the task. ELEC called for an intergovernmental conference, before stage one, to decide on the institutional reforms required for the establishment of full EMU.

The issues surrounding EMU also sparked off reactions from ordinary members of the public, who seemed keen to give their views and spontaneously sent in their ideas, proposals, and suggestions on the subject. The Pierre Werner Family archives and, in particular, the Historical Archives of the Commission contain a number of letters and telegrams which citizens from the Member States, and also from Austria, Switzerland, and the USA., sent to the Werner Group, the Council and the Commission to give their ideas opinions on EMU. For example, in a letter of 18 November 1970 to the Council of Ministers

(No. 103791/18 November 1970), Ferdinand Lindebauer of Salzburg proposed making a start on EMU with the monetary aspect and, as soon as Europe had defined its own identity (through a common, or indeed single, currency for the partners), going on to tackle a monetary union between Europe and the United States.

Another example is the letter which Haller Belt, an American economist, sent on 31 January 1971 to Pierre-Paul Schweitzer, Executive Director of the IMF (a French citizen and therefore European) to explain how he saw the matter of bringing the inflationary tendency under control in Europe. He made the same points to the Commission of the EEC (letter of 11 February 1971), urging it, when setting up EMU, to make provision for 'the re-establishment of the international gold standard between the Member States by 1 January 1971'.

6.6 Reception by the International Media[135]

At its preliminary meeting held in Luxembourg on 11 March 1970, the Werner Group agreed to work as a select committee, subject to rules of confidentiality. The committee was so sparing in its release of information to the outside world that the media devoted little space to its work, despite having paid close attention to the Hague Summit and the appointment of Pierre Werner to chair the group.[136]

As chairman of the committee, Werner officially presented the final report at a press conference in Luxembourg on 8 October that was attended by a group of invited journalists and broadcast on the radio. A week later, the European Commission published the plan by stages, enabling it to be distributed more widely. The media were quick to respond. 'Before the governments even had time to issue an official response, commentaries in the press made it quite clear that the controversies which we defended in the committee would resurface in the judgement of public opinion and the governments'.[137]

The German press, while wondering, like many others, whether some views set forth in the report were not utopian, hailed the work done by the group of experts under Werner's leadership and stressed the need to keep to the schedule for achieving EMU set forth in the plan by stages.[138]

A few days later, German and foreign media reported comments made at a press conference on 20 October 1970 by Karl Schiller, the Federal Minister for Economic Affairs, in which he responded favourably to the report and expressed the hope for its ratification before the end of the year.[139] The German minister, whose country had endorsed the prerequisite of coordinating economic policies within the EEC, particularly welcomed the compromise enshrined in the plan by stages between 'economic' (primarily defended by Germany, the Netherlands and, in some respects, Italy) and 'monetarist' priorities (backed by France and Belgium), which had marked the discussions within the Werner Group, and 'the right balance' between the economic and monetary convergence which the Six would need to accomplish in parallel. Furthermore, '[EMU] will make it possible to ensure growth and stability within the Community and reinforce the contribution it can make to economic and monetary equilibrium in the world and make it a pillar of stability'. The Bonn Government had thus succeeded in asserting one of the key principles of its economic policy, as set forth in the proposals submitted to its partners at the beginning of the year.[140]

The French media started by reporting the statements made by Pierre Werner at the Cercle de l'Opinion, as well as Raymond Barre and Robert Marjolin on the topic of monetary union. The Werner Report was only mentioned in passing. Comment barely focused on the economic issues raised by monetary union—one of the major points decided at the Hague Summit—its usefulness not being in dispute. On the other hand, the sensitive political issues were highlighted, more specifically the transfer of sovereignty, prompting calls for action[141] or expressions of indignation.[142] Leading with the headline 'Les yeux ouverts' ['Eyes wide open'], the 18 October 1970 edition of *Le Figaro* cautioned readers with regard to the crucial decision which might call into question the notion of national independence on budgetary matters. 'This is a fundamental change of direction, which no one can decide apart from the President of the Republic. [...] We insist on no decision being taken on this issue without a clear debate involving public opinion. [...] Only with its eyes wide open may France decide what sacrifices it is prepared to take and what losses it must refuse'. *Le Monde* was the first to publish a long critical assessment of the Werner

Report.[143] The paper defended a different position from that adopted by *Le Figaro*, arguing that the problems were not of a political nature, in so far as, in practice, integration of the financial markets and coordination of monetary policy were constraints on national sovereignty. Europe should draw on the experience of the United States, which had operated for a century and a half without a central bank, but with a currency system which everyone used. 'This is what we currently lack, at a time when the sovereignty of the franc or the Deutschmark is an anachronism'.[144] The Werner Report should have explained how the European currency would be convertible into the other currencies and how the Six would harmonise prices. 'The price to be paid is not political: it is a question of accepting monetary discipline'. The journalist pointed out that the consultation procedure designed to bring economic policy into line with medium-term forecasts was every bit as open to question as the idea of adjusting the French economy to suit the uncertain predictions of the plan by stages. He deplored ultimately the report's failure to address the issue of British membership and concluded by emphasising the existence of two 'dangerous mirages'. The first was the risk of taking refuge in a more powerful economic and payments union, which would rule out convertibility with other currencies. The second danger resided in the setting up of a European reserve currency which would cause inflation in the same way as the US dollar.[145] However, the journalist did note that public feeling regarding monetary union in Europe was much more favourable than several months or years earlier.

The media in other European countries displayed just as much interest, particularly after publication of the Commission's proposals on achieving EMU by stages. In the Member States there were noteworthy public reactions on these topics in Italy,[146] Belgium (where Baron Ansiaux, a member of the Werner Committee, came to the plan's defence[147]) and the Netherlands (where Gerard Brouwers, another committee member, also spoke out[148]).

Of particular note was the keen interest in the report displayed by the British press, stirred by the prospect of the UK joining the Community. Two national dailies, *The Financial Times*[149] and *The Times*,[150] highlighted the Commission's lack of audacity compared with the Werner Committee on account of 'the doubts about the institutional aspects of EMU now being expressed in Paris'. On 16 November 1970, just a few days before the Council of Ministers of the EEC was due to meet, the British papers again looked at the proposals of the Werner Report, providing detailed analysis of the process to achieving EMU.[151] The British media deemed it a 'nebulous and esoteric' project, one which was little known to their readers, who were particularly concerned about the possible repercussions of the common agricultural policy on the nation's economy. The Werner Report, which was the result of a compromise between the 'economist' and the 'monetarist' approaches of EMU, seemed to be both a technical and a political document. It was technical in the sense that it set forth specific monetary measures to be taken, with greater detail on the first stage, in which the central banks of the Member States would be required to play a key role. It was political because to set in motion the construction of EMU it was imperative for the various undertakings announced at the Hague Summit to be backed by practical measures. British journalists believe in the green light for the implementation of the first stage of EMU—given at the Council of Ministers on November or December 1970—even if France would inevitably voice its reservations on certain supranational issues. The scheme to narrow exchange rate margins in the parity system between Community currencies and the dollar (the 'snake in the tunnel') was explained in detail, the assumption being that sterling might be concerned. British media maintained that a floating pound (though unthinkable at the time) might be justified either during the preliminary stage of accession or as one of a series of initial transitional provisions. In preparation for joining the Community, the UK had undertaken to gradually reduce the role played by sterling as an instrument of international monetary liquidity.

For the plan by stages to succeed, a common, even single, currency would be required, which necessarily implied 'a common budget, political union and some form of European government'.[152] The British press predicted that transferring responsibilities to the Community level and giving up certain aspects of national sovereignty would be difficult. In such a context the stand-off between 'national currencies' and a 'single currency' would very soon become an issue for policy-makers and the public opinion in the Member States.

The Swiss press was also interested in the plan by stages.[153] 'The Werner Committee goes further than the Swiss Constitution', announced the *Gazette de Lausanne* in an editorial on 22 October 1970, concluding that 'whatever the failings in the Werner Committee's outline which will inevitably come to light, and the sceptical response to a system whose application will require further, severe limitations on the prerogatives of national sovereignty, this ambitious monetary project must be taken seriously. Unless there is some major political upset, the Community is about to engage on a path which will lead to monetary unity and, in so doing, it is taking a step towards the European "super-state" of which it has been dreaming for a dozen or so years'.[154]

When the Commission's proposals were published, the comparison with the recommendations of the Werner Report became inevitable. The *Europe Daily Bulletin*, which had commented on the plan by stages from the outset, was the first to react.[155] 'The Commission certainly agrees with the Werner Report, [...] but the wording it uses is less incisive. [...] The only major difference concerns the "Community decision-making centre" for economic policy, which the report advocates but which is nowhere to be seen, as such, in the Commission's proposals. [...] Another difference is that the report recommends convening an intergovernmental conference before the first stage to set up new institutional instruments, whereas the Commission limits the problem to the Community framework. In other words, it rightly sees itself as being empowered to decide if and when reforms are necessary, reserving the right to table them accordingly'.[156] The German Government voiced its dissatisfaction regarding the interpretation which the Commission gave to the Werner Report. Bonn stated its case and the media subsequently passed it on: 'The Commission's proposals for setting up EMU by stages are too limited and do not go far enough'.[157]

The sessions of the Council of Ministers focused around the Commission's proposals and the decisions required to launch the first stage of EMU attracted media attention in the Member States. The German press devoted the most column space to the debates and provided a very critical analysis.[158] But newspapers in other countries also covered the story.[159] Of particular note in this respect were the comments by Pierre Mendès-France reported by the Luxembourg daily

Tageblatt regarding the decisions taken by the Council of Ministers of 8 February 1971 (on measures for setting up EMU). The former French Prime Minister particularly drew attention to the possible effects on Europe of a union along these lines.[160] Also noteworthy was the stance adopted by Archduke Otto von Habsburg, the Vice-President of the International Paneuropean Union, who hailed the agreement reached by the Six to set European monetary union in motion.[161]

Although the task of the committee chaired by Pierre Werner came to an end after the meeting of the EC Council of Ministers on 9 February 1971, he remains committed in defending the conclusions reached by his group, taking part in conferences, public debates and interviews. The media kept an eye on his efforts, with regular reports on progress.[162]

Notes

1. 'Résolution sur la réalisation par étapes de l'Union économique et monétaire de la Communauté' [Resolution on the establishment by stages of EMU in the Community], in Official Journal of the European Communities, 151/23 (29 December 1970). The European Parliament's Historical archives (EPHA).
2. 'Meetings on 6–7 May, 10 May, 6 July, 28–29 September, 22–23 October, 29–30 October, 9–10 November, 5–6 December 1970'. EPHA, PE/II/PV/70-13, PE/II/PV/70-14, and PE/II/PV/70-15.
3. 'Avis de la commission des Finances et du Budget sur la réalisation par étapes de l'Union économique et monétaire de la Communauté' [Opinion of the Committee for Finance and Budgets on the establishment by stages of EMU in the Community], drafted by Mr. Heinrich Aigner, PE 25908/def, EP, room documents 1970–1971. EPHA.
4. 'Communication aux membres: résumé des plans élaborés en vue de la création d'une union économique et monétaire' [Communication to members: summary of the plans drawn up for the establishment of an EMU], EAC, Directorate-General for Committees and Parliamentary Studies, Luxembourg, 5 June 1970, PE 24605. EPHA. Pierre Werner Family archives.
5. 'Meeting of the EAC on 28 and 29 September 1970', Brussels, tape 218, Transcription, p. 7. EP, EAC. Pierre Werner Family archives.

6. In a letter dated 13 May 1970, the President of the EP referred the problems posed by the establishment of an EMU to the Committee for Finance and Budgets for an opinion (the root issue fell within the competence of the EAC). On 17 July 1970 Mr. Aigner was appointed by the Committee for Finance and Budgets to draft this opinion. At the meeting on 22 October 1970 an interim opinion was reviewed and unanimously approved by the latter committee. On the basis of the final report to the Council and the Commission which Pierre Werner presented to the public on 8 October 1970, the Committee for Finance and Budgets once again examined the issue of EMU and unanimously approved the final opinion. Adoption of this opinion was dated 27 November 1970.
7. 'Note du secrétariat sur les aspects politiques et institutionnels du plan Werner concernant la réalisation par étapes de l'Union économique et monétaire de la Communauté' [Note by the secretariat on the political and institutional aspects of the Werner Report concerning the establishment by stages of an EMU in the Community], I. ob.di/tw, Brussels, 4 November 1970, document PE. 25715, EP, PAC. Pierre Werner Family archives.
8. Ibid., p. 4.
9. 'Memorandum by Jean Rey to the EP on 11 December 1969' reproduced in the final declaration of the Hague Summit: The Hague Summit (1–2 December 1969), Final Communiqué of the Conference and Memorandum from the Commission to the Conference, in *Bulletin of the European Communities*, 1 (1970), p. 15.
10. See Room documents 1970–1971, 16 July 1970. EPHA.
11. During its meeting on 22 October 1970, the EAC adopted an interim report on the establishment by stages of EMU in the Community. On 21 October 1970 the Council communicated to Parliament, for information purposes, the final report drawn up by the group of experts chaired by Pierre Werner. Subsequently, in a letter dated 18 November 1970, the President of the Council consulted the EP on the Commission's proposals to the Council regarding the establishment by stages of EMU.
12. 'Projet de rapport intérimaire sur la création d'une Union économique et monétaire' [Draft interim report on the establishment of an EMU], rapporteur Mr. J. E. Bousch, 25221/rev, p. 8. EPHA.
13. Ibid., p. 9.

14. In its interim report, the Werner Group specified that 'such transfers of power would be kept down to the limits necessary to ensure the effectiveness of Community action; they are mainly those concerning the group of policies involved in the maintainance [*sic*] of general equilibrium'. See 'Interim report on the establishment by stages of economic and monetary union', Document 9.504/II/70-D (20 May 1970). Published in *Bulletin of the European Communities*, Supplement, 7 (1970), OJC 94 (23 July 1970) (Luxembourg: Office for Official Publications of the European Communities), p. 20. Pierre Werner Family archives.
15. On 16 December 1965 the President of the EP asked the Economic and Financial Affairs Committee to draw up a report outlining the broad priorities for Community action in the field of monetary policy and with a view to achieving monetary union in the future. On 19 January 1966 the Economic and Financial Affairs Committee appointed the MEP Hans Dichgans as its rapporteur. The report was examined at the meetings of the Economic and Financial Affairs Committee on 21 July, 25 October, 9 and 21 November 1966, and was unanimously approved with a motion for a resolution at the last of the meetings cited above. The 'Rapport sur l'activité future de la Communauté dans le domaine de la politique monétaire et la création d'une union monétaire européenne' was published on 28 November 1966. EP, room documents 1965–1966. Document 138/28 November 1966. Pierre Werner Family archives.
16. 'Résolution sur la réalisation par étapes de l'Union économique et monétaire de la Communauté' [Resolution on the establishment by stages of EMU in the Community], EP. In Official Journal of the European Communities, C 151/23 of 29 December 1970, p. 4.
17. The MEPs on the EAC considered three possible approaches for examining the plans for EMU from this perspective: (a) To wait until the end of negotiations and their outcome. With this approach, precious, possibly decisive years would be lost and in the meantime disintegrating trends might emerge in the Community; (b)To consider that establishing EMU (as decided by the Hague Summit of 1–2 December 1969) was an official goal of the Community and, consequently, the Six should reach agreement amongst themselves, leaving prospective members on the sidelines of this process; and (c) To consider that the candidate countries must accept the decision

taken at the Hague Summit, setting EMU as the official goal of the Community, but that the Council, in its decisions bearing on the future, should make allowance for the interests of the candidate countries. The Six would continue their discussions on gradually establishing union, but on the understanding that the candidate countries should be consulted on the specific arrangements for establishing this union by stages. Such consultation should not slow the progress of negotiations on accession, unless Community Member States failed to agree among themselves. The members of the committee adopted the third approach as the appropriate line of conduct.

18. See, especially, G. Friot (1973) *Eurodollars et politique monétaire nationale: États-Unis, Allemagne, Grande-Bretagne, France* (Paris: Friot); D. Kane (1983) *The Eurodollar Market in the Years of Crisis* (Basingstoke: Palgrave Macmillan); and L. Allen (2009) *The Encyclopedia of Money* (Abingdon: Greenwood Publishing Group). Eurocurrency consisted of bank deposits denominated in a currency other than that of the country where the bank was registered. Eurodollars were defined as deposits in US dollars held in banks outside the U.S. This market, which was larger than the domestic American money market, result of several circumstances: US foreign trade imbalances; the decision by the Soviet authorities in the 1950s to deposit their dollar reserves in London (for fear of them being impounded if they entrusted them to US banks); and the US Regulation Q, which set an upper limit on interest rates for domestic bank deposits. With this rate lagging behind inflation in the early 1960s, a massive exodus of US capital started, moving in particular to London. In 1963 President J. F. Kennedy introduced the Interest Equalisation Tax (on interest paid on dollar bonds issued on behalf of European companies. The resulting change in financial flows led to the creation of an international Eurodollar market. Luxembourg, which did not have a central bank and enjoyed very flexible rules on banking and taxation, found itself in a favourable position, whereas traditional markets such as London, Zurich or Amsterdam were hampered by restrictive legislation. Luxembourg gradually established itself as one of the main centres for Euromarkets, marking the start of its role as an international financial marketplace. In July 1963 the Luxembourg stock market issued its first batch of 'Autostrade' Eurobonds. Rules in the United States were relaxed in 1974 with an

end to regulations and taxes (notably the Interest Equalisation Tax) and the United States started to emerge from the 'monetary isolation' which prevented banks from arbitrage between the domestic dollar market and Euromarkets.

19. 'Statement by Raymond Barre'. Follows on from tape 219. Transcription, p. 21. Meeting on 29 September 1970 in Brussels, EAC of the EP. Pierre Werner Family archives.
20. 'Réalisation par étapes de l'Union économique et monétaire de la Communauté' [Establishment by stages of EMU in the Community]. Minutes of parliamentary debate, sitting of 18 November 1970, in Official Journal of the European Communities, annex 151/23 of 29 December 1970, p. 99. The European Parliament's Historical archives (EPHA).
21. Ibid., 'Réalisation par étapes', EPHA, p. 100.
22. Ibid., 'Réalisation par étapes', EPHA, p. 103.
23. Ibid.
24. Ibid., p. 105.
25. 'Communication et propositions de la Commission au Conseil relatives à l'institution par étapes d'une union économique et monétaire de la Communauté' [Communication and proposals from the Commission to the Council on the establishment by stages of EMU].
26. 'Speech by MEP J. Löhr, of the Christian-Democratic group', in *Minutes of plenary sitting, Wednesday sitting, 18 November 1970*, pp. 109–110. EPHA.
27. 'Statements by the MEP J. E. Bousch, rapporteur of the EAC, and E. Boersma, leader of the Social Democratic group', in *Minutes of plenary sitting, Wednesday sitting, 18 November 1970*, pp. 110–113, 113–116. EPHA.
28. 'Intervention by the MEP Mr. Ad Oele, representative of the Socialist group', in *Minutes of plenary sitting, Wednesday sitting, 18 November 1970*, pp. 116–121. EPHA.
29. 'Réalisation par étapes de l'Union économique et monétaire de la Communauté' [Establishment by stages of EMU in the Community], in *Minutes of plenary sitting, Wednesday sitting, 18 November 1970*, Official Journal of the European Communities, annex 151/23 of 29 December 1970. EPHA.
30. Ibid., p. 3. According to the EAC, progress was unthinkable without a minimum amount of agreement on both sides of industry. To illustrate its point it cited the risk of widespread industrial action,

demands for large wage increases and a sudden acceleration of social transfers which could overturn economic and monetary decisions.

31. 'Minutes of the plenary sitting, Thursday sitting, 3 December 1970', p. 52. EPHA.
32. 'Speech by Raymond Barre, Vice-President of the Commission of the EEC', p. 51. EPHA.
33. 'Résolution sur la réalisation par étapes de l'Union économique et monétaire de la Communauté' [Resolution on the establishment by stages of EMU in the Community], in Official Journal of the European Communities, C 151/23 of 29 December 1970.
34. J.-C. Paye (1998, II) 'Le rôle de la Commission des Communautés, 1967–1973', in *Le rôle des ministères des Finances et de l'Économie dans la construction européenne (1957–1978)*, 2 volumes (Paris: Comité pour l'Histoire économique et financière de la France), p. 120.
35. 'Statement by Raymond Barre', tape 218. Transcription. EAC of the EP. Meeting on 28–29 September 1970 in Brussels, p. 11. Pierre Werner Family archives.
36. The Commission, which French reservations had relegated to a secondary, strictly technical role, went into action and secured the backing of the other Member States to allow it to take part in the summit. With this in view, it defined its own vision of the 'completion — deepening — enlargement' triptych and gave thought to the question of supplementing the customs union by setting up an EMU, with which Raymond Barre was very closely associated. See M. Dumoulin (ed.) (2007) *European Commission (1958–1972)—History and Memories of an Institution* (Luxembourg: Office for Official Publications of the European Communities). On 22 June 1970, just before President Malfatti took office, Secretary-General Emile Noël sent him a letter emphasising the risks of the Commission's being weakened and the need to redefine its relations with the Council and Coreper. 'Criticism of the Commission's actions and questioning of its role [...] have been easier to engage in and have become more and more open since 1967 in the Council, Parliament and the European and international press'. Document quoted by M.-T. Bitsch in 'Le développement de la Commission unique (1967–1972) in M. Dumoulin (ed.) (2007) *European Commission (1958–1972)—History and memories of an institution* (Luxembourg: Office for Official Publications of the European Communities), p. 148.

37. 'Communication et propositions de la Commission au Conseil relatives à l'institution par étapes d'une union économique et monétaire de la Communauté' [Communication and proposals from the Commission to the Council on the establishment by stages of EMU], document COM(70)1250, 29 October 1970, in Official Journal of the European Communities, C 140 (26 November), Supplement 11/1970 (Luxembourg: Office for Official Publications of the European Communities).
38. Ibid., p. 3.
39. This refers to handwritten notes by Pierre Werner in preparation for the start of proceedings by the Werner Group. The document contains various comments on the Snoy Plan, the Schiller Plan and the first Barre Plan (which Belgium, Germany, and the Commission had presented at the meeting of Finance Ministers on 24 February 1970), which affected Werner's own position (which took the form of the Luxembourg Plan, presented on the same occasion). These notes, which may have been drafted between 25 February and 10 March 1970, also served as the basis for his inaugural speech when the Werner Committee started work. Pierre Werner Family archives.
40. 'Report to the Council and the Commission on the realisation by stages of EMU in the Community (Werner Report)', Luxembourg, 8 October 1970, Supplement 11/1970 (Luxembourg: Office for Official Publications of the European Communities), p. 27.
41. EAC of the EP. Meeting on 28–29 September 1970 in Brussels. Statement by Raymond Barre, tape 218. Transcription, p. 10. Pierre Werner Family archives.
42. Ibid., p. 5.
43. The Italian representatives on the Committee of Governors who spoke on this matter were Paolo Baffi, representative of Governor Guido Carli from the Banca d'Italia, and Rinaldo Ossola. See 'Summary report of the 44th meeting of the Committee of Governors of the Central Banks, 8 November 1970'. Archives of the European Central Bank, Frankfurt.
44. Ibid., p. 11.
45. The treatment of this topic, in particular the task of relating this study to the various sources, has made it necessary to discuss the reactions to the Werner Report from the Council and from the Member States separately.

46. A foundation and club for political discussion set up in 1955 by the French intellectual Gabriel du Chastain (1934–1981). The Cercle de l'Opinion was firmly committed to the building of a united Europe and, in October 1970, held the series of debates 'A month for Europe', to which a large number of prominent figures were invited. The subjects on offer included 'A monetary Europe', 'A political Europe', 'The finances of Europe', and 'Europe and world trade'. In November 1970 du Chastain made a compilation of all the speakers' contributions and issued them in a special publication under the heading *L'Opinion en 24 heures*, for which he sought the support of Baron Ansiaux and the Committee of Governors of the Central Banks.
47. 'Statement by Pierre Werner to the "Cercle de l'Opinion" (Paris: 16 October 1970)'. Documentation bulletin 6(1970) (Luxembourg: Information and Press Service, Ministry of State), p. 3.
48. 'Address by Raymond Barre to the "Cercle de l'Opinion" (Paris: 16 October 1970)', at the dinner-debate on 'A monetary Europe', p. 3. In the Pierre Werner Family archives, ref. PW 048, case entitled 'Intégration monétaire de l'Europe. Le Plan Werner: 1970' [Monetary integration of Europe. The Werner Report: 1970].
49. See Chapter 6.
50. P. Werner (1992, II) *Itinéraires*, p. 131.
51. The Permanent Representatives' Committee (Coreper) is a body responsible for preparing the work of the Council. This across-the-board task is performed for whatever configuration the Council is meeting in, except for the Agriculture Council, which is traditionally prepared for, in the main, by the Special Committee on Agriculture. Coreper, which was created de facto as soon as the Communities were set up, was written into primary legislation by Article 5 of the Treaty of Brussels of 8 April 1965 merging the executives. Coreper consists of one delegate per Member State (most often a senior official of the Foreign Ministry, with ambassador rank). Individually, the permanent representatives are the intermediaries between the institutions of the Communities and their governments. Collectively, with their colleagues from the other Member States, they take part in the work of the Communities by contributing to the process of adoption of measures taken by the Council. Coreper discusses all the items due to appear on the agenda before they are considered by ministers.

If unanimous agreement is reached in Coreper, the ministers do not normally re-open the discussion but confine themselves to ratifying the result already arrived at. If no agreement has been reached, the ministers then discuss the matter. Since 1970, Coreper has been supported by specialist committees (the political committee, the monetary coordination group, etc.).

52. 'Attainment of EMU in the Community by stages', Docs. R/2247/70 (Fin 446) + Corr. 1 and R/2106/70 + Corr., Brussels, 23 November 1970. European Communities, the Council. Historical Archives of the Council of the EC.
53. 'Note to the Members of the Commission', Sec (70) 4408, Restricted, Item 7B, Agenda, 146, Brussels, 5 December 1970. Commission of the EEC, Secretariat-General. Historical Archives of the Council of the EC.
54. 'Minutes of the 579th meeting of the Permanent Representatives' Committee, Brussels, 2 December 1970. Commission of the EEC. Historical Archives of the Council of the EC.
55. 'Draft introductory note drawn up by the President'. Commission of the EEC, DG II 'Economic and Financial Affairs', Brussels, 10 December 1970, Historical Archives of the European Commission.
56. 'Questions concerning the attainment of EMU in the Community by stages'. Working Document T/37/71, Docs. R/2106/70 (Fin 427) + Corr. 1, R/2247/70 (Fin 446) + Corr. 1, and R/2687/70 (Fin 553). European Communities, the Council, Brussels, 25 January 1971. Historical Archives of the Council of the EC.
57. 'Statement by Karl Schiller. Communication to the press, Brussels, 15 December 1970' The statement presented by the Commission during the meeting (and annexed to the record of proceedings of the Council meeting) takes the same line: 'The Commission regrets, to begin with, the fact that the timetable set by the Hague communiqué has not been complied with and that a major political decision has not been turned into a practical reality as it could have been' (Bulletin of the EC, February 1971, 2-1971, p. 54). Pierre Werner Family archives.
58. See 'Attainment by stages of EMU in the Community', Docs. R/386 f/70 (Fin 73), Brussels, 15 December 1970, European Communities, The Council, Historical Archives of the Council of the EC. The identical words were used in the resolution of the Council and of the Heads of State or Government of the Member States of 22 March

1971. Reproduced in Monetary Committee, Compendium of Community monetary texts, 1974, p. 20
59. 'Letter from Willy Brandt to Pierre Werner, 1 February 1971'. Willy Brandt mentioned, among other things, the 'safeguard clause' proposed by Georges Pompidou. Pierre Werner Family archives.
60. 'Minutes of the 586th meeting of the Permanent Representatives' Committee'. European Communities, the Council, Brussels, 4 February 1971. Historical Archives of the Council of the EC.
61. 'Questions relating to the attainment by stages of EMU in the Community', Annex T/37/71 to Working Document T/37/71, and Docs. R/2106/70 (Fin 427) + Corr. 1, R/2247/70 (Fin 446) + Corr. 1, and R/2687/70 (Fin 553). European Communities, the Council, Brussels, 25 January 1971. Historical Archives of the Council of the EC.
62. 'Questions relating to the attainment by stages of EMU in the Community', Note R/230/71 (Fin 48), Docs. R/2106/70 (Fin 427), R/2247/70 (Fin 2242/70) (ASS 1386). European Communities, The Council, Brussels, 5 February 1971. Historical Archives of the Council of the EC.
63. 'Summary report of the 45th meeting of the Committee of Governors of the Central Banks of the EEC Member States', Basel, 12 December 1970, Section II.3, pp. 3–7. Pierre Werner Family archives.
64. Communication to the press. Council of the European Communities, General Secretariat, DG II Economic and Monetary Affairs, ref. 304/71, Brussels, 9 February 1971, pp. 0255–0271. Pierre Werner Family archives. The Council in fact agreed to four texts that day, in addition to the general resolution on EMU. These were the decision on strengthening the coordination of short-term economic policies, the decision on strengthening cooperation between the central banks and the decision on the implementation of a medium-term financial assistance mechanism. The fourth item was the medium-term economic policy programme of the Community (1971–1975) (Bull. EC, April 1970, 4-1970, pp. 26–27).
65. P. Werner (1992, II) *Itinéraires*, p. 136.
66. See Chapter 3, section 3.3.3.
67. 'Letter from Karl Schiller to the Chancellor of the Federal Republic of Germany, Mr. Willy Brandt. The Federal Minister for Economic Affairs', Bonn, 14 October 1970, Gesch.-Z:E1-IA1-03 00 00/10—(n.i.E). Copy from the Federal Archives, Koblenz. BArch B 102 (Bundesministerium für Wirtschaft)/93463.

68. For the official position of the President of the Bundesbank, see K. Klasen, *Die Verwirklichung der Wirtschafts- und Währungsunion in der EWG aus der Sicht der Deutschen Bundesbank*, Europa-Archiv, Collection of articles No. 13, Bonn, 1970, pp. 449–458.
69. 'Draft summary report of the 35th Conference of EEC Finance Ministers, Venice, 29 and 30 May 1970', Confidential, ref. ORII/57/70-F, Commission of the EEC, Directorate-General for Economic and Financial Affairs, Brussels, 5 June 1970, p. 4. Historical Archives of the European Commission.
70. '325th meeting of the Board of the Central Bank', Deutsche Bundesbank, 4 November 1970, minutes, p. 13. Historical Archives of the Bundesbank.
71. '315th meeting of the Board of the Central Bank, Deutsche Bundesbank', 3 June 1970, minutes, pp. 12–15. Historical Archives of the Bundesbank.
72. 'Conversation between Federal Chancellor Brandt and Belgian Foreign Minister Harmel'. 14 October 1970. Doc. 468. In *Akten zur Auswärtigen Politik der Bundesrepublik Deutschland. 1970. Band III (1.September bis 31.Dezember).* [*Documents on the Foreign Policy of the Federal Republic of Germany. 1970. Volume III (1 September–31 December).*] Published at the request of the Foreign Ministry by the Institut für Zeitgeschichte. R. Oldenburg Verlag, Munich, 2001, pp. 1752–1754.
73. 'Record of the conversation between the Federal Chancellor and Belgian Foreign Minister Harmel on 14 October 1970', 12.30 p.m. Office of the Federal Chancellor, Group II/1, Bonn, 16 October 1970. Copy from the Federal Archives, Koblenz, BArch B 102 (Bundesministerium für Wirtschaft)/93463.
74. 'Letter from Willy Brandt to Karl Schiller, 21 October 1970', Historical Archives of the Bundesbank, No. 2, Vol. 156.
75. 'Statement on European policy, 6 November 1970', in W. Brandt, *Reden und Interviews*, Vol. I, p. 238
76. See 'Plan by stages for the achievement of EMU, communication and proposals from the Commission to the Council on the establishment by stages of EMU' (DOK. COM(70)), 29 October 1970 (Subdivision E A, Bonn, 3 November 1970). Letter from the State Secretary at the Federal Ministry of Economic Affairs, Dr. Rohwedder, Bonn, 4 November 1970, to the Parliamentary State Secretary to the Head of

the Federal Chancellor's Office, Dr. Katharina Focke. Copy from the Federal Archives, Koblenz. See also 'Bonn kritisiert Interpretation des Werner-Plans durch Brüssel', in *Frankfurter Allgemeine Zeitung* of 5 November 1970.

77. 'Opinion on the Report to the Council and the Commission on the attainment by stages of EMU in the Community. Copy of a note by the President of the Bundesrat'. Bonn, 4 December 1970. Annex to the letter from the President of the Bundesrat on 4 December 1970 to the Federal Chancellor. Copy from the Federal Archives, Koblenz. BArch B 102 (Bundesministerium für Wirtschaft)/161037.
78. *Réalisation par étapes de l'Union économique et monétaire de la Communauté* ['Establishment of EMU by stages']. 'Minutes of proceedings, sitting of 18 November 1970', in Official Journal of the European Communities, 151 (23 of 29 December 1970), pp. 98–100. EPHA.
79. 'Press conference on European political cooperation given by Georges Pompidou, President of the French Republic'. Paris, 2 July 1970. In G. Pompidou (1975, II) *Entretiens et discours. 1968–1974* (Paris: Plon), pp. 79–80.
80. Michel Debré's objections to a common European currency were summarised in a letter he wrote to the Belgian-American economist Robert Triffin, who played an important part in the plans for EMU put forward by Jean Monnet and the Action Committee for a United States of Europe (ACUSE). Debré considered that the question of a common currency could not be raised as long as Europe had not decided to be independent of the United States. 'Letter from Michel Debré to Robert Triffin, 18 August 1970'. Triffin Archives, Université catholique de Louvain-la-Neuve. Reproduced in G. Bossuat (2005) *Faire l'Europe sans défaire la France. 60 ans de politique d'unité européenne des gouvernements et des présidents de la République française (1943–2003)* (Brussels: P.I.E. - Peter Lang), pp. 432–433.
81. On 10 November 1970, a secret German diplomatic dispatch gave a detailed report of the split in the ranks of the French Government, in particular, over the plan by stages. See Tgb. Nr. Room. i-7306/5848/70 Vs-Vertr. V.10.11.1970, Vs-Vertraulich, Official Secret, re French position on Werner Report. Federal Ministry of Economic Affairs, Secret, 10 November 1970. Copy from the Federal Archives, Koblenz. BArch B 102 (Bundesministerium für Wirtschaft)/93465.

82. 'Minutes of the select Cabinet meeting on European affairs of Wednesday 18 November at 3.20 p.m.', French Archives, 5 AG 2, Vol. 1043, point II. See also E. Bussiere, É.Willaert, *Un projet pour l'Europe: Georges Pompidou et la construction européenne* (Brussels: P.I.E. - Peter Lang, 2010), Collection Georges Pompidou—Archives no. 4.
83. P. Werner (1992, II) *Itinéraires*, p. 132.
84. J.-R. Bernard (2002, II) 'La position du gouvernement français face au plan Werner', in *Le rôle des ministères des Finances et de l'Économie dans la construction européenne (1957–1978)* (Paris: Comité pour l'histoire économique et financière de la France), pp. 127–132.
85. J.-M. Bloch-Lainé (2002, II) 'Le plan Werner: Quels enjeux? Quelle démarche?' in *Le rôle des ministères des Finances et de l'Économie dans la construction européenne (1957–1978)*, (Paris: Comité pour l'histoire économique et financière de la France), pp. 123–126.
86. This was an oral question which the UDR Member for the Pas-de-Calais, Jacques Vendroux, General de Gaulle's brother-in-law, put to the Foreign Minister. This speech—constituting the first part of the Telegram from Paris to the Federal Minister of Finance and the Bundesbank, No. 3071 of 22 October 1970, AZ.WI 3a2-84.01; 'French attitude to Werner Report', v.19.10 70, v.21.10.70. Signed Ruete. Copy from the Federal Archives, Koblenz—was carried by *Le Monde* in its 22 October 1970 edition. Pierre Werner Family archives.
87. 'Speech by RPF Member Michel-Habib Deloncle. Verbatim record of the 43rd sitting.' 3rd sitting of Thursday, 5 November 1970, National Assembly, Constitution of 4 October 1958, 4th legislature. First ordinary session 1970–1971, p. 5201. Pierre Werner Family archives.
88. Roland Leroy (member of the Communist Party) added 'Today [...] we are being told that the Commission of the EEC has, essentially, adopted the content of the Werner Report. Does that mean that when the next Budget comes round, in 1972, the supranational institutions would recommend, as the Werner Report says, "in a specific and detailed manner to each Member State", guidelines for the economic policy it will have to follow? That would be stage one, because the proposal after that is that *all* "the essential features of the whole of the public budgets" will be decided on at the Community level. To quote the Werner Report again: "The Community's centre of decision must be in a position to influence national budgets ... *its* responsibility will extend to other domains of economic and social policy which will

have been transferred to the Community level". And here the grand objective becomes clear: "The action will entail, first further coordination of national policies, then their harmonization by the adoption of directives or common decisions, and finally the transfer of responsibility from the national authorities to Community authorities". It is very clearly explained that "these transfers of responsibility represent a process of fundamental political significance which entails the progressive development of political cooperation. The EMU thus appears as a leaven for the development of political union which in the long run it will be unable to do without".' 'Speech by PCF Member Roland Leroy. Verbatim record of the 43rd sitting. 3rd sitting of Thursday', 5 November 1970, National Assembly, Constitution of 4 October 1958, 4th legislature. First ordinary session 1970–1971, p. 5206. Pierre Werner Family archives.

89. 'Speech by UDF Member Aymar Achille-Fould, Verbatim record of the 43rd sitting'. 3rd sitting of Thursday, 5 November 1970, National Assembly, Constitution of 4 October 1958, 4th legislature. First ordinary session 1970–1971, p. 5208. Pierre Werner Family archives.
90. 'Letter of 29 December 1970 from the Prime Minister of Luxembourg to the Federal Chancellor'. Federal Chancellor's Office, Group II/1, Bonn, 5 January 1971. Copy from the Federal Archives, Koblenz. BArch B 102 (Bundesministerium für Wirtschaft)/161037.
91. 'Letter from Willy Brandt to Pierre Werner, Bonn, 1 February 1971'. Pierre Werner Family archives. It was Karl Schiller who, during the negotiations on 14 and 15 December 1970, called for the insertion of an 'escape clause' which would allow the monetary integration measures to be suspended if the degree of convergence of the Member States' economies was deemed to be inadequate.
92. 'Results of the French-German consultations, Summary Report on the results of the French-German consultations on 25 and 26 January 1971', Subdivision E.A. Bonn, Dr. Hans Tietmeyer, Paris, 27 January 1971. Copy from the Federal Archives, Koblenz. BArch B 102 (Bundesministerium für Wirtschaft)/161038.
93. Confidential. Internal note on the talks between Vice-President Barre and Minister Schiller in Bonn on 22 January 1971 concerning the plan by stages for EMU. Subdivision E.A., Dr. Hans Tietmeyer, Bonn, 22 January 1971. Copy from the Federal Archives, Koblenz. BArch B 102 (Bundesministerium für Wirtschaft)/161038.

94. 'French-German talks at the Quai d'Orsay'—diplomatic report, 25 January 1971, Ministry of Foreign and European Affairs of the French Republic, EC Collection, Directorate for Economic and Financial Affairs, Economic Cooperation Department, series PM Vol. 973, 'Summit Meetings' section, file PM 19.6.1. French Diplomatic Archives, La Courneuve. See also 'Talks between Federal Chancellor Brandt and President Pompidou in Paris, 25 January 1971', Dok. 27. ZA 5-3.1/71. Secret. In *Akten zur Auswärtigen Politik der Bundesrepublik Deutschland. 1971. Band I (1.Januar bis 30 April).* Published at the request of the Foreign Ministry by the Institut für Zeitgeschichte (2002) (Munich: R. Oldenburg Verlag), pp. 115–123.
95. 'Talks between Federal Chancellor Brandt and President Pompidou in Paris', 25 January 1971 Dok. 27. ZA 5-3.1/71. Secret. In *Akten zur Auswärtigen Politik der Bundesrepublik Deutschland. 1971. Band I (1.Januar bis 30 April).* Published at the request of the Foreign Ministry by the Institut für Zeitgeschichte. R. Oldenburg Verlag, Munich, 2002, pp. 115–123. 'Foreign policy debate in the Bundestag: EMU', Incoming diplomatic telegram No. 601/09, Bonn, 30 January 1971, Ministry of Foreign and European Affairs of the French Republic, EC Collection, Directorate for Economic and Financial Affairs, Economic Cooperation Department, series PM Vol. 972, EMU/Bilateral Relations section, file PM 19.3. French Diplomatic Archives, La Courneuve. See also the interview with Jacques de Larosière: Reactions in France after the publication of the Werner Report (Paris: 22 May 2008). https://www.cvce.eu/project/werner/ (home page) and http://www.cvce.eu/en/oral-history (main page), accessed on 6 March 2018.
96. P. Werner (1992, II) *Itinéraires*, p. 136.
97. This problem was not peculiar to the Netherlands. The European dimension in economic policy was to move out of the domain of Foreign Ministers at the IGC of 1990–1991, where the Ministers for Economic Affairs and Finance took the lead in the negotiations and secured two declarations, annexed to the EC Treaty, recognising the power of the Ecofin Council over the General Affairs Council with regard to questions relating to EMU.
98. J. W. Brouwer, G. Anjo Harryvan (2002, I) 'Les Pays-Bas et la coopération monétaire européenne, 1968–1972', in *Le rôle des ministères des Finances et de l'Economie dans la construction européenne (1957–1978),*

Actes du colloque tenu à Bercy les 26, 27 et 28 mai 1999 (Paris: Comité pour l'histoire économique et financière de la France), p. 98.

99. See P. Catz (1970) *Politieke integratie nodig voor Europese monetaire unie. Witteveen vroeg zelf om spreekbeurt* (Elseviers Weekblad, 27 June 1970).
100. 'Analysis of the Werner Report by the Netherlands Finance Ministry'. Pierre Werner Family archives. Document dated 12–13 October 1970, probably the annex to a diplomatic cable addressed to Pierre Werner, Prime Minister, and Finance Minister of the Grand Duchy of Luxembourg. The analysis points out that, even though the Werner Committee had reached the conclusion that in an EMU the present currency units could possibly continue to exist, it was also adamant that the currencies in question must then be completely mutually convertible, without exchange rate fluctuations and at unchanging rates of parity. It would, however, be preferable to replace the currencies with a European currency unit. Furthermore, it would also be necessary for the creation of liquidity, monetary policy and credit policy to be centralised and for decisions on the main aspects of the Member States' budgets to be taken at the Community level.
101. See *Handelingen Tweede Kamer* [Proceedings of the Second Chamber] 1970–1971, 15 October 1970, pp. 371–373. *Eindrapport Groep-Werner inzake Economische en Monetarie Unie*' [Final report of the Werner Group on EMU], 21 October 1970, Foreign Ministry, IIIrd section 913.100, No. 5466, The Hague. See also the article '*Naar een econonomische en monetaire unie*' published on 28 October 1970 in the review *Economisch-Statistisch Berichten* by Gerard Brouwers, chairman of the Conjunctural Policy Committee and member of the Werner Committee.
102. Remarks of this kind also appear in the record of debates held on 21 December 1970 at which, during the adoption procedure for the national budget, the Standing Committee on Finance of the Dutch House of Representatives and the Minister for Finance consulted each other on the subject of the attainment by stages of an EMU in the Community. In 'Kamerstuk Tweede Kamer 1970–1971', Kamerstuknummer 10900 IX Bondernummer 10. http://www.staten-generaaldigitaal.nl, accessed on 6 March 2018.
103. The vision of a symmetrical EMU had already been put forward in '*Un plan de solidarité monétaire européenne en trois étapes (1971–1974)*' [A plan for European monetary solidarity in three stages (1971–1977)]

published on 27 January 1970]. This plan, better known as the Snoy Plan, or indeed the Belgian Plan, placed the emphasis on the establishment, during the final stage, of two institutions, a common monetary system and a *sui generis* economic government in charge of budgetary and income policy. See also J.-C. Snoy et d'Oppuers (1989) *Rebâtir l'Europe: Mémoires, Entretiens avec Jean-Claude Ricquier* (Louvain-la-Neuve: Duculot).

104. 'Political consultations with the Minister for Foreign Affairs of the Federal Republic of Germany and the Federal Chancellor in Bonn on 14 October 1970', No PN/rh, Ministry of Foreign Affairs and External Trade. Private Office of the Minister for Foreign Affairs, Brussels, 16 October 1970. Diplomatic Archives of the Ministry of Foreign Affairs of Belgium.
105. Ibid.
106. 'Belgian approach to EMU', 24 November 1970. Working document, Ministry of Foreign Affairs, Diplomatic Archives of the Ministry of Foreign Affairs of Belgium Brussels, p. 4.
107. 'Letter sent on 5 January 1970 by the Prime Minister of the Kingdom of Belgium, Gaston Eyskens, to the Prime Minister of Luxembourg, Pierre Werner'. Ref. CZ/B1/D9, Brussels, 5 January 1971. Pierre Werner Family archives. This is evidently a reply to the 'Letter sent by Pierre Werner on 29 December' to his five colleagues on the subject of the future of EMU.
108. I. Maes, A. Verdun (2005) 'Small States and the Creation of EMU: Belgium and the Netherlands, Pace-Setters and Gate-Keepers', *Journal of Common Market Studies*, 43/2, pp. 327–348.
109. 'Voyage à Paris de M. Colombo' [Visit to Paris by Mr. Colombo], Diplomatic Note of 25 January 1971, Ministry of Foreign and European Affairs of the French Republic, EC Collection, Directorate for Economic and Financial Affairs, Economic Cooperation Department, PM series, Vol. 973, EMU/Basic Documents section, file PM 19.3. French Diplomatic Archives, La Courneuve. See also Questions concerning the establishment by stages of EMU in the Community, Docs R/2106/70 (End 427), R/2247/70 (End 2242/70) (ASS 1386), European Communities, Council, Note R/230/71 (End 48), Brussels, 5 February 1971. Historical Archives of the Council of the EC.

110. See I. Maes, L. Quaglia (August 2003) 'The Process of European Monetary Integration: A Comparison of the Belgian and Italian Approaches'. In National Bank of Belgium, Working Papers—Research Series No. 40, Brussels.
111. See Chapter 5, section 5.3.
112. 'Note on Minister Schiller's conversation today with Italian Ambassador Luciolli', Bonn, 24 February 1971. Subdvision EA. Copy from the Federal Archives, Koblenz. BArch B 102 (Bundesministerium für Wirtschaft)/293320.
113. See 'Le résultat des délibérations de la nuit dernière' [The outcome of last night's talks], Agence Europe, Daily Bulletin No. 707 (new series). Brussels, 15 December 1970.
114. 'Questions concerning the establishment by stages of EMU in the Community', Docs R/2106/70 (End 427), R/2247/70 (End 2242/70) (ASS 1386). European Communities, Council, Note R/230/71 (End 48), Brussels, 05 February 1971. Historical Archives of the Council of the EC.
115. 'Speech by Edward Heath, Prime Minister of the UK, to the House of Commons on 21 July 1971'. In Parliamentary Debates. House of Commons. Official Report. First session of the Forty-Fifth Parliament of the United Kingdom of Great Britain and Northern Ireland. Twentieth year of the reign of her Majesty Queen Elizabeth II. Dir. of publ. Hansard. 1970–1971, No. 821; fifth series. London: Her Majesty's Stationery Office. 'United Kingdom and European Communities', pp. 1542–1460, 1465–1469.
116. The UK's contribution to progress on European monetary union was one of the main items on the agenda for the talks which Valéry Giscard d'Estaing (on 24 November 1970) and Karl Schiller (on 25 November 1970) had with the British Chancellor, Roy Jenkins, in London. Cf. German diplomatic cable from the FRG Embassy in London, No. 886747b bmwi d, Bonn No. 4239 of 27 November 1970. Copy from the Federal Archives, Koblenz.
117. See Interview with Henri Werner, son of Pierre Werner (Luxembourg, 1 June 2010), and the Pierre Werner Family archives. https://www.cvce.eu/project/werner/ (home page) and http://www.cvce.eu/en/oral-history (main page), accessed on 6 March 2018.
118. 'Statement by Mr. Heath on the trade and monetary policy of the EEC'. Note from the Ambassador of France in Great Britain to His

Excellency Mr. Maurice Schumann, Minister for Foreign Affairs, Ministry of Foreign and European Affairs of the French Republic, London, 30 March 1972. EC Collection, Directorate for Economic and Financial Affairs, Economic Cooperation Department, PM series, Vol. 972, EMU/Bilateral Relations Section/The UK, file PM 19.3. French Diplomatic Archives, La Courneuve.

119. The Economic and Social Committee was set up by the Treaty of Rome (1957) for the purpose of involving the representatives of economic and social life in the establishment of the Common Market. The point was to give organised forces in the economy and society the opportunity to make their views heard in the Community's decision-making process. Initially (Article 198) the Committee met only at the request of the Council or the Commission, and provision for it to be compulsory to consult it was made by the treaties only in a limited number of fields (agriculture, free circulation of persons and services, transport and social policy). Its members were appointed by the Council, voting by qualified majority on a proposal from the Member States, for a four-year term. They were divided into three groups, representing employers, employees and the various economic and social interests. The Paris Summit of 1972 decided to give the Committee the right of initiative. Thus, since its rules of procedure in 1974, the Committee has been able to deliver opinions on its own initiative. The Committee is not one of the Community institutions listed in the constituent treaties, but it does have autonomy in its organisation and workings. Its status and role give it a distinctive place among the many committees which assist the institutions.

120. 'Resolution of the Council and the representatives of the Governments of the Member States of 22 March 1971 on the achievement by stages of EMU in the Community', 22 March 1971. Official Journal of the European Communities (OJEC), 27 March 1971, C 28. The French delegation had made its agreement to the resolution subject to the explicit mention of the ESC as the sole framework for consultation of the two sides of industry.

121. 'Record of the proceedings of the Economic and Social Committee relating to the exchange of views on the information report on the achievement by stages of EMU in the Community', 92nd plenary session, Brussels, 27 and 28 January 1971, Doc. CES 80/71/mha, Brussels, 22 February 1971, p. 228. Historical Archives of the Commission of the EC.

122. 'It does not look as though the monetary problems which countries have to face—exchange-rate fluctuations and the speculation to which they lead—can be solved by measures which will ultimately be imposed by the major capitalist companies. [...] Economic and monetary policy favours the most powerful European monopolies and it is unlikely that it will be capable of acting as a counterweight to the hold that American companies have over Europe'. Ibid., p. 303.
123. There was provision for this consultation in the Council decision on the strengthening of the short-term economic policies of the Member States (adopted on 22 March 1971).
124. 'Information report by the specialist section for economic questions on the "Report to the Council and the Commission on the realisation by stages of EMU in the Community"', rapporteur Mr. Ameye, CES/70 fin/mha, Brussels, 2 December 1970, European Economic Community, p. 14. Historical Archives of the Commission of the EC.
125. 'Statement of views on the fiscal supplement to the plan by stages of the Commission of the EEC for the establishment of EMU', Doc.PAS/DB 42-4./27 November 1970, Savings Banks Group of the European Economic Community, Brussels, Historical Archives of the Council of the EC. This association, which was set up in Brussels on 23 April 1963, grouped together the savings banks of the six EEC Member States. At the end of 1969, these banks were managing approximately 100 million savings books, total capital of 72.7 billion UAs in deposits and securities portfolios worth 19.5 billion UAs. See also D. Blondel, T. Van Puyvelde (1966) 'La Communauté économique européenne et les caisses d'épargne', *Revue économique*, 17/4, p. 690.
126. 'Opinion on the Report by the Werner Group of 8 October 1970 (Doc. 16956/II/1970) and the European Commission Communication of 29 October 1970 (COM 70/1250) on the establishment by stages of EMU', Doc. F 87/70/2 February 1971, Savings Banks Group of the European Economic Community, Brussels, 2 February 1970, p. 2. Historical Archives of the Council of the EC.
127. 'Attainment by stages of EMU', Union of Industries of the European Community. Annex to the letter from Frédéric Berg, President of the Union of Industries of the European Community, to Walter Scheel, President of the Council of Ministers of the EC, Doc.FB/AG/14.C.1, Brussels, 2 December 1970. In the Pierre Werner Family archives.

128. The archive documents referred to are the statements of views of the European Confederation of Free Trade Unions in the Community and the European Organisation of the World Confederation of Labour (which brought together Christian-inspired trade union organisations and other democratic organisations). The World Confederation of Labour dissolved itself at its congress of 31 October 2006 to enable its members to be incorporated into the new International Trade Union Confederation.
129. The European Confederation of Free Trade Unions (ECFTU) was a grouping of most of the European trade union organisations, recognised as one of the main European industrial associations. In embryo it consisted of the miners' and steelworkers' trade unions which, in 1952, joined the International Confederation of Free Trade Unions (ICFTU); this set up a coordinating committee within the European Coal and Steel Community (ECSC) called the European Social Secretariat (ESS). After the signing of the Treaty of Rome (1957), a European Trade Union Secretariat was created, bringing together its members from the six EEC Member States. At the same time, the International Federation of Christian Trade Unions (IFCTU) initiated the European Organisation of Christian Trade Unions. In 1960, the ICFTU unions from the countries belonging to the European Free Trade Association (EFTA) joined together in a European secretariat. In 1969, the ESS became the European Confederation of Free Trade Unions and then, with the accession of the ICFTU unions from the EFTA countries in 1973, it became the European Trade Union Confederation, which was later joined by the European Organisation of Christian Trade Unions.
130. 'Letter from Theo Rasschaert, General Secretary of the Confederation of Free Trade Unions in the Community, to the President of the Council of Ministers of the European Communities', Brussels, 11 December 1970. The letter came with a 'Statement of views of the Executive Committee of the European Confederation of Free Trade Unions on the establishment of an EMU'. Historical Archives of the Council of the EC.
131. It was primarily a matter of setting up the European Communities' Standing Committee on Employment (SCE), established following the decision of the Council of Ministers for Social Affairs meeting on 26 November 1970 and as a result of the adoption of Council

Decision 70/532/EEC of 24 December 1970 [Official Journal L 273, 17.12.1970]. It was established at the wish of the representatives of employers' and workers' organisations at the conference on employment issues held in Luxembourg on 27 and 28 April 1970.

132. Letter from Jan Kulakowski, General Secretary of the European Organisation of the WCL, to the President-in-Office of the EC, Doc. DE/5-744/70-FS-VM IV.12, Brussels, 21 December 1970. Historical Archives of the Council of the EC and Pierre Werner Family archives.
133. 'EMU', Annex II to the letter from Jan Kulakowski, General Secretary of the European Organisation of the WCL, to the President-in-Office of the EC, Doc. DE/5-744/70-FS-VM IV.12, Brussels, 21 December 1970. Historical Archives of the Council of the EC and Pierre Werner Family archives.
134. 'Statement on EMU in the European Community by the European League for Economic Cooperation (ELEC)', Doc. 2204/11 December 1970, Brussels, 11 December 1970. This document was forwarded to the General Secretariat of the Council of Ministers of the EC, which distributed it to the Permanent Representatives of the Member States on 23 December 1970. Pierre Werner Family archives. The ELEC was an organisation founded in 1946 by Paul Van Zeeland (Belgium), Josef Retinger (Poland), and Pieter Kerstens (the Netherlands), who were soon joined by other prominent European figures including Edmond Giscard d'Estaing (France), Harold Butler (UK), Herman Abs (Germany). Although ELEC was among the founders of the European Movement at the Hague Congress in May 1948, it was not so much a mass movement as an 'intellectual pressure group' serving the cause of European integration and anxious to carry out its mission quite independently of private interests or official authorities. The mission, in the first instance, comprised educating its members in European affairs by providing them with information and holding debates on major European subjects. ELEC worked primarily through national committees.
135. This section is the fruit of detailed consultation of the Pierre Werner Family archives, which contain a remarkable diversity of articles, commentaries, analysis and such, published by newspapers and specialist journals (in Europe—Member States, but also the UK and Switzerland—and further afield, including the United States, Canada, the Soviet Union, and Japan) on economic and financial topics in

general, and focusing on the work of the Werner Committee (the framing of the Werner Report and what followed) in particular. The sources analysed belong to the archive sections bearing the following references: PW 048, 'Intégration monétaire de l'Europe. Le Plan Werner: 1970' [Monetary integration of Europe. The Werner Report: 1970]; PW 049, '1970–1971, UEM, Le Plan Werner, Réunion Ministres des Finances septembre 1970' [1970–1971, EMU, the Werner Report, Meeting of the Finance Ministers September 1970]; PW 051, '1962–1978, Union économique et monétaire: Rétrospective' [1962–1978, EMU: retrospective]; and PW 053, '1970–1972, Intégration monétaire de l'Europe. Études' [1970–1972, Monetary integration of Europe. Studies].

136. The only exception was the *Europe Daily Bulletin*, published by Agence Europe (founded in Brussels in 1953), which provided full, detailed, day-by-day coverage of European integration. Of the articles published in various publications on the work of the Werner Committee, the following are perhaps of note: 'Europäische Währung in Sicht. Staatsminister Pierre Werner legt Stufenplan vor', *Luxemburger Wort*, Luxembourg, 24 February 1970; 'L'Europe en route vers l'union monétaire. Esquisse d'un plan d'action en sept étapes présenté par M. Pierre Werner, président du gouvernement luxembourgeois, ministre des Finances', *La Quotidienne*, Brussels, 25 February 1970; and 'M. Werner présidera la préparation de l'Union économique et monétaire', *Le Monde*, 6 March 1970. On 4 June 1970, the French weekly *Problèmes économiques* reproduced an extract from an article published on 16 May 1970 in the British weekly *The Economist* on the British view of plans for European monetary union.
137. P. Werner (1992, II) *Itinéraires*, p. 132.
138. On 17 October 1970, under the title 'Bonn drängt auf Verabschiedung des Werner-Plans für die EWG' ['Bonn presses for adoption of Werner Report for EEC'], the German daily *Frankfurter Allgemeine Zeitung* published detailed comments on the need to meet the schedule for achieving European EMU as recommended in the conclusions of the Werner Report. The same day, the daily *Stuttgarter Zeitung* hailed the commitment of Pierre Werner, Minister of State, President of the Government and Finance Minister of Luxembourg, in favour of European EMU. On 24 October 1970, *Frankfurter Allgemeine Zeitung* published a long portrait of Pierre Werner.

139. See 'Le ministre Schiller commente favorablement le plan Werner' in the 21 October 1970 issue of the *Journal de Genève*.
140. This was the official German position on monetary integration—the Schiller Plan—which was published in a memorandum that the Federal Minister for Economic Affairs Karl Schiller presented on 12 February 1970. In *Tagesnachrichten des Bundesministeriums für Wirtschaft*, 27 February 1970, No. 6122. See also H. Tietmeyer (1996) *Währungsstabilität für Europa. Beiträge, Reden und Dokumente zur europäischen Währungsintegration aus vier Jahrzehnten* (Baden-Baden: Nomos), pp. 88–94.
141. In its edition dated 17–18 October 1970, *Le Figaro* analysed the Werner Report and concluded that it would involve imminent transfers of sovereignty and that 'its application would show that there is real political determination to achieve European integration'.
142. The articles on this topic published by the dailies *L'Humanité* and *La Nation*, respectively on 17 and 18 October 1970, emphasised the political implications for the Six of the plan by stages. They warned that 'the matter would certainly be disputed at a political level' and suggested that the French President should have the final word. On 19 October 1970 *L'Humanité* thought it inconceivable that the nation's budget could be decided in Brussels and deplored the idea that 'the Gaullist-Centrist government [...] was prepared to give up France's sovereign rights in exchange for monetary support for the present regime'.
143. 'Unification monétaire et souveraineté nationale' ['Monetary unification and national sovereignty'], by Paul Fabra, *Le Monde*, 20 October 1970.
144. In the previous issue (18–19 October 1970), *Le Monde* analysed the Werner Report without adding any comments, merely quoting the statement by Raymond Barre at the Cercle de l'Opinion lunch-debate, that 'progress could not be achieved by constraint nor injunction'.
145. The French media subsequently paid close attention to the various changes regarding approval of the Werner Report, keeping the general public well informed. (For example, 'Les discussions des Six sur l'union économique et monétaire' ['Talks between the Six on EMU'], *Le Monde*, 24 November 1970, reporting debate on the Werner Report at the Council of Foreign and Finance Ministers of the

Six with regard to the feasibility of EMU; and 'Le Rapport Werner engage l'avenir de l'Europe' ['The Werner Report commits the future of Europe'], *Le Monde diplomatique*, November 1970, with a favourable analysis of the Werner Report's proposals for achieving European EMU in stages.)

146. On 27 October 1970 the Italian daily *Corriere della Sera* published an article entitled 'Il "piano Werner" all'esame del Mec' ['The "Werner Report" under EEC scrutiny'], in which it voiced the hopes and criticism raised by the Werner Committee's proposals on the stage-by-stage achievement of EMU between the Six. (Document consulted on 10 October 2012.)
147. In 'Union économique et monétaire: premières propositions concrètes de la Commission européenne' ['EMU: the first specific proposals from the European Commission'], published on 5 November 1970, the daily *Le Soir* outlined the proposals made by the European Commission regarding the plan to achieve EMU as recommended by the Werner Report. Baron Hubert Ansiaux, President of the National Bank of Belgium, Chairman of the Committee of Governors of the Central Banks and, in this capacity, a member of the Werner Group, explained the report to Belgium's Société Royale d'Économie Politique at a conference on 6 November 1970. The next day, in the issue dated 7 November 1970, the daily *Le Soir* covered the talk by Baron Ansiaux in depth.
148. On 28 October 1970, Gerard Brouwers, Chairman of the Conjunctural Policy Committee and a member of the Werner Committee, published an analysis of the plan by stages in the magazine *Economisch-Statistische Berichten*, defending its visionary quality. See 'Naar een econonomische en monetaire unie' ['Towards an EMU'] from *Economisch Statistische Berichten.*
149. 'EEC tones down Werner Report to suit France', *The Financial Times*, 3 November 1970.
150. 'EEC Commission seeks political commitment to plan for economic union', *The Times*, 5 November 1970.
151. 'The politics of monetary union', *The Financial Times*, 16 November 1970.
152. *The Financial Times*, ibid.
153. 'Le rapport Werner' ['The Werner Report'], in the *Journal de Genève*, 23 October 1970; 'L'union monétaire, objectif de la prochaine décennie' ['Monetary union, an aim for the coming decade'], in *Journal de*

Genève, 24–25 October 1970; 'Un défi européen: l'union monétaire' ['A European challenge: monetary union'], in *Gazette de Lausanne*, 24–25 October 1970.

154. 'Le Comité Werner va plus loin que la Constitution suisse' ['The Werner Committee goes further than the Swiss Constitution'], by Paul Keller, in*Gazette de Lausanne*, 22 October 1970.
155. This publication took a keen interest in the Werner Report, its editor Emanuele Gazzo devoting editorials to the project on many occasions: 'Le Plan Werner — (1) Globalité et irréversibilité' ['The Werner Report — (1) Entirety and irreversibility'], in *Europe* (on 19 October 1970 the publication detailed the stakes for the monetary policy for the Six as examined in the Werner Report on EMU); 'Le Plan Werner — (2) Union économique et union politique: deux choses différentes' ['The Werner Report — (2) Economic union and political union: two different things'], in *Europe* (on 20 October 1970, the editor questioned the feasibility of applying the Werner Report's proposals on EMU and their impact on the process of European political union); 'Le Plan Werner — (3) Des transferts indispensables et ayant un but précis' ['The Werner Report — (3) Essential transfers with a precise objective'], in *Europe* (on 21 October 1970 he looked at the scope of reform of the Community's institutional framework advocated by the Werner Report); 'Le Plan Werner — (4) Le cercle vicieux des préalables a-t-il été rompu?' ['The Werner Report — (4) Has the vicious circle of preconditions been broken?'], in *Europe* (on 22 October 1970 he emphasised that to implement the Werner Report Europe would need to be politically strong).
156. In his editorial on 30 October 1970 Emanuele Gazzo compared the Werner Report with the Commission's proposals, highlighting the common ground and divergences between the two documents.
157. 'Bonn kritisiert Interpretation des Werner-Plans durch Brüssel' ['Bonn criticises Brussels' interpretation of the Werner Report'], in *Frankfurter Allgemeine Zeitung*, 5 November 1970.
158. The article 'Nicht nur Beifall für den Werner-Plan' ['Not just plaudits for the Werner Report'], published in the *Süddeutsche Zeitung* on 24 November 1970, commented on the first debates in the Council of Ministers on the Werner Report, of which certain conclusions were promptly disputed by the Federal Republic and France. The same day, in a comment piece entitled 'Frankreich bremst in Brüssel' ['France applies the brakes in Brussels'], the daily *Der Abend* reported on

discussion of the plan by stages by the Council of Foreign and Finance Ministers of the Six, drawing particular attention to the disagreement between France and its Community partners on this topic. On 14 December 1970, covering the negotiations on the Werner Report, the *Süddeutsche Zeitung* published an article entitled 'In Brüssel geht es um den Werner-Plan' ['Werner Report discussed in Brussels'], setting out France's stance on EMU. The *Frankfurter Allgemeine Zeitung* subsequently described the difficult talks between the Member States on setting up EMU, as recommended by the Werner Report, asking in particular how long France could withstand pressure ('Frankreichs letztes Wort?' ['France's last word?'], in *Frankfurter Allgemeine Zeitung*, 16 December 1970). On 21 December 1970 the German daily *Süddeutsche Zeitung* concluded that 'Frankreich will sich nicht zu früh binden' ['France does not want to commit itself too soon'], highlighting French hostility to any idea of revising the Rome Treaties with a view to setting up European EMU.

159. On 10 February 1971, the day after the Council of Ministers met in Brussels, the Dutch daily *Nieuwe Rotterdamse Courant* listed the various stages for achieving EMU set forth in the Werner Report (in its article 'Akkoord economische en muntunie en EEG' ['Agreement on EMU in the EEC']). On 11 February 1971, the Italian daily *Corriere della Sera* in turn presented 'Le decisioni di Bruxelles' ['The Brussels decisions'], stressing the possible effects of EMU for Italy. Also on 11 February 1971, in an article entitled 'La décision de créer une monnaie européenne' ['The decision to create a European currency'], the Belgian daily *Le Soir* detailed reactions to the decisions taken the previous day in Brussels by the EEC Council of Ministers on the establishment of EMU. *Le Figaro* did likewise, publishing 'Le programme de construction d'une Union économique et monétaire a pris le départ' ['The programme for the establishment of an EMU gets under way'] on 11 February 1971.
160. 'L'unité monétaire de l'Europe' ['Currency unit in Europe'], in *Tageblatt*, 26 February 1971.
161. Article entitled 'Vers une monnaie européenne' ['Towards a European currency'], *La Métropole* (Belgium: 23 February 1971).
162. 'Il n'y a pas d'alternative à l'unification monétaire' ['There is no alternative to monetary union'], in *La Tribune de Lausanne-Le Matin*, 23 February 1971. The Swiss daily reported on a talk given in Lausanne

the previous day by Pierre Werner on the need for and chances of European monetary union. The press in Luxembourg also reported on the talk: 'Staatsminister Pierre Werner sprach in Lausanne vor dem "Office Vaudois pour le développement du commerce et de l'industrie" über den Werner-Plan' ['Prime Minister Pierre Werner speaks on the Werner Report at the Vaud Office for the Development of Trade and Industry in Lausanne'], in *Luxemburger Wort*, 24 February 1971. In April 1971 the Swiss monthly *Wirtschafts Revue* published a long interview with Pierre Werner in which he analysed the outlook for European monetary policy. His views were published in a large number of business magazines and publications focusing on international affairs, such as *Problèmes économiques*, *Nieuwe Europa*, *Cahiers européens*, and the publications of the European Parliament.

7

The Implementation of the Werner Report

On 22 March 1971, in line with proposals from the Commission that had drawn their inspiration from the Werner Report, the Member States adopted a political resolution committing them to establishing EMU.[1] The resolution, albeit one with no legal force, made no mention of the concept of an 'economic policy centre', but it did state that economic and monetary union means that the main economic policy decisions will be taken at Community level, and therefore that the necessary powers will be transferred from the national to Community level. The culmination of EMU could be the adoption of a single currency which would guarantee that the operation was irreversible.

This process was to extend over a ten-year period, with progressive actions in parallel on the economic convergence and monetary cooperation fronts. Only stage one, planned to run from 1 January 1971 to 31 December 1973, was clearly defined, with an emphasis on the establishment of a medium-term financial assistance mechanism and the gradual shrinking of the margins of fluctuation between European currencies. The establishment of a European Monetary Cooperation Fund (EMCF) was foreseen by the end of 1973.[2] Stage one was also to see the gradual adoption of common standpoints in monetary relations with

E. Danescu, *Pierre Werner and Europe*,
Archival Insights into the Evolution of Economics,
https://doi.org/10.1007/978-3-319-96295-5_7

non-Community countries, particularly the United States, and within the international organisations, especially the International Monetary Fund.

As regards the substance, this resolution on EMU opted for a minimalist approach. It had far-reaching consequences, however, as it was the first time a resolution by the Council and the Representatives of the Member States had spoken openly about the wish to deepen monetary, financial, and fiscal integration. But the international monetary crisis which took off in 1971 was to upset the European countries' plans.

7.1 The First Stage Under Pressure

In the spring of 1971, given the overvaluation of the US dollar, the international monetary climate significantly deteriorated with a substantial impact on European countries.[3] The deepening dollar crisis triggered a massive influx of capital into Europe, upsetting the economies of countries with 'strong' currencies. This influx was such that on 5 May 1971, in line with the recommendations of its economic institutes, Germany suspended dollar operations. The Netherlands and Belgium did the same. This was almost tantamount to a decision to allow the mark to float, which was of course contrary to the recently established principle that a system of floating exchange rates inside the Common Market was not compatible with its objectives.

The Finance Ministers of the Six held an emergency meeting on 8–9 May. Faced with the massive stream of unwanted capital, which jeopardised the stability policy, Karl Schiller, the German Minister for the Economy, suggested two alternative solutions. The first was a joint revaluation of all the currencies in the Community. It was recommended that either the fixed exchange rate system be eliminated, or the exchange rates between EC currencies be changed and controls be introduced on foreign exchange transfers. The second option was to leave the German mark to float freely in order to 'allow the market itself to determine the appropriate parity relationship'.[4] The French Government could not accept this prospect, being very attached to the principle of fixed exchange rates and the introduction of controls on capital transfers.[5] Its Italian counterpart was concerned about the fragility of the Italian lira, whereas the Belgian Government was disappointed that the two-tier dollar market represented a step away from the instrument advocated by the EC Commission. In view of the close links between the Dutch and West German currencies, allowing the mark to float would have entailed doing the same for the guilder. In this context, Pierre Werner and Baron Snoy et d'Oppuers, his opposite number at the Belgian Finance Ministry, discussed the possibility of doing the same for the Belgian franc. But they both feared that if the parity between Benelux currencies was allowed to vary, it could undermine the smooth workings of this union, which was founded on a sound monetary basis. The Dutch, sharing these concerns, agreed to maintain, within Benelux, the system of restricted margins planned for the Six, with variation on either side of a par value limited to 1.5%.

The UK authorities made no official comment on the Community's monetary worries, but a long-term delay in efforts to achieve economic and monetary integration suited some British interests. The German decision to allow the mark to float was a serious blow to the common agricultural policy, to which the UK was fiercely opposed. It also delayed monetary union, to which the City was hostile. The British, who advocated greater exchange rate flexibility, hoped that France's relative isolation would soon enable such a solution to be adopted. As for the United States, it was only too happy to witness this quarrel within the Community, especially since this split in the European bloc gave it good reason to hope that it would be able to convince the IMF to adopt a flexible exchange rate system, thereby firmly establishing the pre-eminence of the dollar system.[6]

When the West German Government decided to suspend trading in the mark, it seemed to throw doubt on the process of EMU. On 9 February 1971, the Finance Ministers had adopted the third medium-term economic policy programme, of which one practical measure was to aim to reduce the fluctuation margins between the Member State currencies from 1.5 to 1.2% as from June 1971.[7] The German authorities still hoped to restore fixed exchange rates very shortly, but given the persistent uncertainty surrounding the dollar, it became clear that the process would take longer than planned.[8] On 10 May the German and Dutch Governments decided to stop defending the lower limit at which the dollar was pegged and allow their respective currencies to float. But this actually had the opposite of the intended effect; instead of a process of rapprochement, it led to a sort of fragmentation.[9]

In the midst of the international monetary crisis the Ecofin Council meeting on 12 May 1971 ended without decision having been reached on the continuation of EMU. On the same day, Valéry Giscard d'Estaing, the President-in-Office of the Council, explained to the French National Assembly the measures the government planned to take against the European monetary crisis, affirming that '[…] we must uphold the spirit and the letter of the Bretton Woods Agreements, in other words return to a system of fixed exchange rates and maintain progress towards economic and monetary union'.[10] The considerable increase in international liquidities and the uncontrolled movement of large volumes of Eurodollars boosted by speculation were seen as the prime causes of the monetary crisis.

In the early summer of 1971, the US balance of payments deficit reached a dramatic level. The price of gold soared on the open market. On 15 August, President Richard Nixon announced the US Administration's unilateral decision to suspend the convertibility of the dollar to gold. (This also meant suspending the convertibility to other reserve currencies based on gold, such as special drawing rights, or SDRs, created by the IMF in 1969 in response to the system's need for liquidity.) The vulnerability of a fixed exchange rate system to speculation, together with the systematic failure of the international authorities, such as the IMF, to coordinate and act upon national policies, meant that Bretton Woods was ultimately doomed. It therefore became imperative to frame a new international monetary order. Europe was caught off guard. Due to the delays in introducing a Community system, the Member States were technically ill equipped and badly prepared mentally to respond in good order.

It was in this context that the Ecofin Council met on 19 August. Karl Schiller advocated that European currencies should be allowed to float against dollar, but in a concerted manner. Their greater flexibility in relation to the dollar seems to be particularly suited to ward off speculative movements of capital. The circumstances ruled out, 'at least in the short term, a return to a system of fixed parities within narrow fluctuation margins'.[11] Italy and the Benelux countries shared this view. These three partners framed a plan—presented by Baron Snoy—which involved allowing all the European currencies to float against the dollar, while maintaining the system of limited margins within the Community.[12]

France defended a different position, supporting the two-tier foreign exchange market. For the purposes of trade, the official exchange rates should be maintained, whereas for financial dealings a joint floating system should be adopted. It also outlined plans to retain fixed parities thanks to foreign exchange controls. Concluding his statement, Giscard d'Estaing affirmed the French view that it would be 'illusory to consider [...] further European integration without fixed exchange rates between the currencies of Community Member States'.[13] So the Community partners were deeply divided on what monetary policy should be adopted. Unable to agree on a joint strategy, they preferred to act separately. That day the Community missed a fine opportunity to unify monetary policy and form a united front against the monetary disorder which had taken hold worldwide.

Between August and December 1971 the turmoil in international money markets continued unabated, but the positions of Member States gradually converged. Backed by the British, the Six exerted considerable pressure on the US Administration to consider devaluation of the dollar and the fixing of a new official price for gold. On 10 September, the EC Commission addressed a memorandum to the Council of Ministers detailing the measures planned by Europe to cope with the American decision to suspend the convertibility of the dollar to gold.[14] On this basis, the Six succeeded on 13 September in setting forth a joint position on the dollar, centring on demands for devaluation of the US currency and an end to the surtax on imports.[15]

Since the beginning of the monetary crisis, the differences between France and Germany had become more evident. In an effort to establish a common line of conduct, the two partners initiated parallel talks at several levels. The German and French diplomatic archives show that between June and the end of November 1971, five specific diplomatic consultations were focused on EMU issues. The two central banks were in regular contact to ensure that they were familiar with their reciprocal arrangements. Having prepared the ground, President Pompidou and Chancellor Brandt agreed, on 3–4 December, on an overall agreement based on a return to fixed exchange rates, which was nevertheless more flexible than the Bretton Woods system. Under this arrangement, the dollar would be devalued, the franc would stay at its existing level, and the mark would be revalued. It was also possible that the fluctuation margins between European currencies would be reduced.

The Community also maintained its diplomatic pressure on the United States through the Group of Ten. At the start of the talks (in London on 14 September 1971), the Americans demanded revaluation of the other currencies, a lowering of trade barriers and more even distribution of the international defence budget, whereas the ministers of the other countries suggested unilateral devaluation of the dollar by raising the price of gold. At the second meeting (in Washington on 26 September 1971), the parties still disagreed. The United States seemed prepared to allow the crisis to continue because speculation was resulting in revaluation of the other currencies, which was in fact its principal aim. The third meeting (in Rome on 30 November–1 December 1971) saw the beginnings of a compromise.[16] The US Secretary of the Treasury, John Connally, raised the idea of realigning the various currencies, including a possible 10% devaluation of the dollar.

On 13–14 December, Pompidou met Nixon to present the joint position adopted by the Community partners. The two leaders agreed on a swift realignment of the various currencies through devaluation of the US dollar and revaluation of the other currencies. On this basis, European, American, Canadian and Japanese representatives met on 17–18 December at the Smithsonian Institute to seal the Smithsonian Agreement. The signatories undertook to set new par values between their currencies and to provide for 2.25% fluctuation margins on either side of the official authorised rates. This, then, was the US 'monetary tunnel' through which the 'European monetary snake' would soon be passing. In view of the fact that European currencies were pegged against the US dollar (inconvertible to gold), the Community found itself once again tied to a currency and an economy over which it had no control.[17]

On the whole, the Smithsonian Agreement offered immediate temporary solutions to the monetary crisis, but it did nothing to solve the real, structural problems sapping the basis of the IMS. The dollar, which suffered its first devaluation since the end of the Second World War, remained inconvertible to gold. The agreement made little attempt to address the lack of symmetry in the adjustment, the political choice of an internal balance to the detriment of external equilibrium, problems of liquidities and the lack of confidence among international economic players. The end of the Bretton Woods system and the pressing need to erect a new IMS appeared imminent.

The lull which followed on the foreign exchange markets and the relative harmonisation of the position on the IMS reform enabled cooperation on monetary matters to resume within the Community. On 21 March 1972 the Council adopted a resolution to set in motion the first stage of the Werner Report.[18] The central banks concluded the Basel Agreement, which established a system for narrowing the fluctuation margins between the Community currencies, with intervention and short-term support mechanisms. This was the 'monetary snake'—the first European attempt to stabilise exchange rates. The currencies of the Six and those of the candidates for accession to the Community in January 1973 (the UK, Denmark and Ireland) joined this mechanism. The aim of the 'snake' was to limit exchange rate fluctuations by preventing the disparity at any one time between two EC currencies from exceeding 2.25%. This mechanism was associated with a 'tunnel', which set the limits for fluctuation against the dollar, which was highly unstable but remained the international reference currency. This threshold could be as much as 4.5% (twice the fluctuation limit between the European currencies). Beyond these limits (2.25 and 4.5%), the central bank of the country concerned had to intervene. The special rules for Benelux countries were maintained and came to be known as the 'worm in the snake'.[19] Subsequently, to shore up the 'monetary snake', the central banks created the very short-term financing facility, which would become a genuine arrangement for mutual credit between the central banks.

7.2 The Monetary Snake and the EMCF in Trouble

The monetary snake, the first manifestation of European solidarity on currency matters and of a resolve to be independent of the dollar, was to fall foul of instability.

In mid-1972, the German mark, the Dutch guilder, the Belgian franc, and the pound sterling fell prey to speculation that pushed them towards their ceilings. On 23 June, the British Government decided to cease application of the agreement on the narrowing of margins and allowed its currency to float on the exchange markets. This meant that the pound could no longer stay in the tunnel. In January 1973, Italy, which was in a similar situation to that of the UK, also left the tunnel and the snake, but obtained a derogation from the intervention arrangements provided for in the Basel Agreement. Firstly, it was to be allowed not to make reimbursements on the basis of the composition of monetary reserves for the credit it had already obtained by way of very short-term support (a procedure which would have required Italy to transfer gold at the official rate). Secondly, Banca d'Italia was to be authorised to intervene in dollars in the future, and not in Community currencies.

The economic situation in the United States continued to deteriorate, and, on 13 February 1973, a second devaluation of the dollar, by 10%, was necessary. That devaluation and the widespread floating of currencies that ensued heralded the irrevocable collapse of the Bretton Woods system in March 1973.

The fall of the dollar led to the closure of exchange markets in the Community. In the light of these difficulties, the Commission reaffirmed its position 'in favour of an IMS based on fixed but adjustable parities, convertibility of national currencies and including an efficient adjustment process'. It consequently proposed a system whereby European currencies floated jointly in relation to the dollar. The Council met three times (on 4 March, 8 March, and 11–12 March 1973) to debate monetary matters, and, it decided to retain the internal fluctuation margins ('the snake') but released the central banks from the obligation to intervene in order to ensure compliance with the initial 4.5% fluctuation bands for Member States' currencies vis-à-vis the dollar. The currency snake leaves the tunnel. Germany, France, Denmark and the Benelux countries decided to allow their currencies to float jointly within the 'snake'. The Italian lira, the British pound and the Irish pound were too weak to do so and therefore were authorised to float separately instead of entering the 'snake' until such time as their domestic circumstances recovered. As a result, an area of relative stability comprising Benelux, France, and Germany was established, and this encouraged Norway and Sweden to join the snake on 14 March. Austria was unilaterally a de facto participant in the snake and Switzerland considered the possibility of joining.

When the exchange markets reopened on 19 March 1973, the German mark was revalued by 3% in relation to the other five currencies. It was revalued again in June by 5.5%. The dollar continued to fall, causing the German mark to appreciate and creating new monetary tensions in Europe. Two groups of countries emerged: one whose currencies tended to appreciate, such as Germany, and one whose currencies depreciated, such as France. In September, the Government of the Netherlands unilaterally re-evaluated the guilder, demonstrating a lack of European resolve. As a result, there was a move away from a very rigid exchange rate system inherited from Bretton Woods towards the opposite extreme, namely, over-flexibility through widespread floating of currencies among themselves. The Yom Kippur War of October 1973 in the Middle East, the embargo on oil products and the energy crisis that ensued, quickly compounded by a financial crisis, accentuated the differences. France left the 'snake' in January 1974 but rejoined in July 1975, only to withdraw once more the following year, leaving behind a 'mini-snake' generally thought of as a 'German mark area'. The 'snake' had lost its Community nature. 'Sometimes referred to as the German mark area, the 'snake agreement' had the merit of introducing an area of stability into a disordered monetary landscape and of initiating the implementation of a policy of mutual support by the central banks'.[20]

The only genuine step forwards in 1973, a difficult year, was the establishment of the EMCF. In accordance with the resolution of the Council of Ministers on 22 March 1971, the EMCF was considered as a desirable, although not indispensable, stage in the Community organisation of the central banks. At its meeting of 21 March 1972, the Council asked the Monetary Committee and the Committee of Governors of the Central Banks to draw up a report by 30 June 1972 on the organisation, functions, and statutes of an EMCF.[21] The Council undertook to give a ruling before the end of the same year.

The two committees established a joint group, which drew up a draft report on the principal technical aspects of the issue. At its meetings of

11 July and 5 September, the experts aimed to identify the key options available.[22] The debates were lively, and opinion was divided even on whether it was appropriate to establish the fund, and on the fund's organisation and operation, the use of a European monetary unit of account and the pooling of reserves.

Broadly speaking, three approaches could be identified: the first was very guarded, the second was marginally positive, and the third was clearly in favour of establishing the fund. The most reticent countries were France and Germany, but for different reasons. The French authorities were, in principle, mistrustful of new Community institutions because they had a tendency to increase their autonomy and to extend their decision-making powers at the expense of the Council of Ministers and other pre-existing bodies. With regard to the future organisation of the fund, the French experts stated that 'although the technical issues fell within the scope of the issuing institutions, the monetary decisions fell within the purview of the government authorities'.[23]

German reluctance stemmed from fears that Germany's finances would be used by the fund to help to prop up less-developed members whose economic management was lax. Paris and Bonn would have been satisfied with a modest body for dialogue on monetary issues and statistical information. The Netherlands, Italy, the UK, and the three other candidate countries (Denmark, Ireland, and Norway) backed a less restrictive approach. They considered that the fund should conduct Community interventions using a multilateral technique for which a European unit of account would be used for accounting purposes. Italy went one step further and asked for 'the Ten to transfer a proportionate part of their dollar exchange, composite reserves and national currencies to the EMCF to a sum of 2.4 billion dollars'.[24] In agreement with the Commission proposal—that the EMCF must have its own resources and act to some extent as an airlock between national reserves and the world outside—Belgium, also representing Luxembourg, expressed a much more positive attitude and proposed providing for a multilateralisation mechanism as well. That mechanism would allow the very short-term credits (15 days) which were necessary for the Community interventions to become, quasi-automatically, the short-term support and medium-term intergovernmental assistance already furnished by the EC. In that respect, the EMCF was the beginnings of a European Central Bank. Belgians believed that the attainment of those objectives would have a particular psychological effect and would constitute genuine proof of monetary solidarity within the Community.

On 10 August, the two committees agreed on joint conclusions on the organisation and operation of the EMCF. Their report, which also acted as a draft opinion to the Council and the Commission, was based on two main conclusions.[25] The first was that, in addition to the initial arguments in favour of the fund—the contribution to the progressive building of EMU and to reinforce the European cooperation on monetary matters—there were other important rationales of a more practical nature. The fund could act as an instrument to reduce fluctuation margins in the Community (by conducting interventions at foreign exchange centres on behalf of the issuing institutions and settling the positions resulting from those interventions). Furthermore, depending on the degree of monetary solidarity sought, the fund could perform increasingly complex roles, including the pooling of a proportion of member countries' reserves. The experts on the Monetary Committee imagined a fund with fairly broad powers, but considered premature to entrust it with the task of managing the national reserves. A 'European unit of account' would also be defined and could be used in accountancy procedures for the fund's operations and as the basis for certain payments.

'The discussions [...] reveal the experts' concern about the fund's genuine scope and effectiveness, which will depend on the powers conferred upon it and the degree of discipline that will attend its rules of operation. [...] If the fund receives only minor powers [...] it would not provide any specific substance to Europe's monetary personality and would not invest Europe with the means to protect itself effectively from the dangers of speculative capital and national inflation'.[26] However, conferring significant competences upon the fund, such as interventions at foreign exchange centres, the multilateralisation of settlements, the use of a unit of account and the provision of short-term support, would not be enough to provide the Community with genuine autonomy in external financing. The report concludes by highlighting that 'the important factor [...] is the monetary policy that will be followed by those in charge in Europe, both internally and externally'. Therefore, the process of setting a fund of this nature in train had to be preceded by an agreement on the very principles of European monetary policy. It would firstly be indispensable to set a ceiling for interventions under the fund. Above this limit, governments would either have to revalue European foreign currencies or implement capital controls; in any event, changes to national and common economic policies appear to be unavoidable. A measure of restraint would also have to be introduced on internal payments to accelerate settlements and prevent persistence of sustained debit positions. A charter of this kind would fall foul of serious difficulties, first because it would have to take account of the individual circumstances of the economies concerned and secondly because it would have a bearing on the troubled matter of relations between the Community and the United States. There was a fear that 'if the fund was authorised to absorb all dollars presented to it, it would provide precious help to the US Treasury yet without safeguarding European interests'.[27]

Meeting in Rome on 10 and 11 September, the Ministers for Finance and Foreign Affairs of the enlarged Community (the Six plus the UK, Ireland, Denmark, and Norway) agreed on the need to establish a EMCF from the outset of the first stage of EMU. Their decision was based on the experts' most prudent proposal and made the fund a simple umbrella structure for cooperation between the central banks.[28]

On 19, 20, and 21 October, a summit meeting of the enlarged Community took place in Paris at the invitation of President Pompidou. In an official joint statement, the Heads of State or Government set out the objectives and policies to be pursued in order to achieve a 'European union'. 'When he opened the Summit, standing before nine delegations instead of six (Great Britain, Denmark, and Ireland had joined the founding countries), President Georges Pompidou had a stroke of linguistic inspiration that transcended playground quarrels in its disarming simplicity. He expressed the wish that the decade 1970–1980 should see the establishment of a 'European union' that was determined to fulfil its destiny. The decision was adopted, and it was decided once more to entrust one of our colleagues, this time Leo Tindemans, with the responsibility of drafting a report on implementing that project'.[29]

At the same time, they also formally reaffirmed the objective of economic and monetary union, to be completed no later than 31 December 1980, which would be a guarantee of stability and growth, the foundation of their solidarity and the indispensable basis for social progress. While emphasising the principle of fixed but adjustable parities between the Community currencies as 'an essential basis for the achievement of the union', the statement refers to the institution, before 1 April 1973, of the ECMF under the administration of the Committee of Governors.[30] By the end of the year, the competent bodies of the Community shall submit reports on the adjustment of short-term support and on the conditions for the progressive pooling of reserves. The need for close coordination of the Member States' economic policies was reiterated, as well as the 'parallelism principle'. The Nine also hoped to secure a common attitude to the international monetary system (international regulation of the supply of liquidity, reduction in the role of national currencies [meaning the pound sterling and the US dollar] as reserve instruments, equal rights and duties, and responsibilities towards underdeveloped countries).

The EMCF was established on 3 April 1973 and was the kernel of the future organisation of the central banks at Community level.[31] Its primary aim was to oversee the proper functioning of the progressive narrowing of the fluctuation margins between the Member States' currencies. It also had to monitor interventions in these currencies on the exchange markets. Finally, it was responsible for settlements between central banks leading to a concerted policy on reserves. The fund had legal personality and was administered by a board comprising the governors of the national central banks and one representative from the Commission (who was not a member of the board in the strict sense: he had the right of address, but not the right to vote).[32] Generally, it had to abide by the agreements between the central banks on the progressive narrowing of margins and short-term support. However, the fund did not have its own resources, and its powers were limited because the principle of pooling reserves was not adopted.[33] Following a diplomatic offensive strewn with problems, the Luxembourg Government highlighted its capital city's status as the 'provisional place of work of the Community financial bodies' and won its case, especially as it had been putting the logistics in place to ensure the fund's satisfactory operation: the provisional seat of the EMCF was established in Luxembourg.[34]

The responsibilities of the EMCF related to accountancy procedures for the operation of credit mechanisms and interventions within the framework of the exchange mechanism, as well as the administration of the various short- or medium-term support mechanisms. In reality, the fund was purely an accounting body (its meetings were entirely a matter of form, discussions between the central bankers being held within the Committee of Governors) and its transactions were conducted by the Bank for International Settlements (BIS). No controls on movements of capital, especially transactions in Eurodollars, were introduced.

7.3 The Report Is Shelved

In line with the resolution of 22 March 1971, the Council of Ministers was due to take a decision by the end of 1973 on whether to embark on stage two of economic and monetary union (to last three years), which was scheduled to begin on 1 January 1974.

In a communication dated 19 April, the EC Commission took stock of the progress made in stage one, reporting that the results had been meagre. There had been some advance in the field of overall economic policy coordination, through the setting up of procedures for regular joint consultation, even if the resulting convergence in economic and budgetary policy still fell short of the mark. In the monetary field, the Commission noted that there had been some setbacks.[35] The Commission communication referred, in particular, to the currencies which were still floating in isolation, the widening of the maximum fluctuation margins for the other currencies (which went up from 1.20% in March 1971 to 2.25% in April 1973) and the successive revaluations of some of them (the Deutschmark and the Dutch guilder). But the fact that the joint agreement to let six European currencies float against each other had held during a difficult period and that transactions in Community currencies had developed constituted a first positive achievement. The Commission also pointed to the difficulties caused by international monetary upheavals and by the insufficiently binding character of Community procedures. 'As regards the liberalisation of capital markets, [...] in some countries progress had even gone into reverse. [...] The Regional Fund had not yet been resourced'.[36]

Highlighting the experience which had already been gained and could be adapted in phase two, the Commission put forwards a complete action programme containing plans for measures in almost every area covered by EMU. These included the joint coordination of the Member States' short-term policies, the harmonisation of their budgetary and monetary policies and the establishment of a genuine European market in goods and capital, and the implementation of wide-ranging, efficient monetary cooperation mechanisms (the EMCF). But the programme proved not to be ambitious enough, since the planned rate of monetary convergence was relatively slow and priorities were not set in the areas regarded as vital.

At the Council meetings of 28 June and 9 November 1973 there was lively and conflicting discussion of the Commission's proposals. At the June meeting, the Council called for the drawing up of a report taking stock of stage one and analysing the points to be taken into consideration with a view to moving into stage two of economic and monetary union.

France thought that any given stage (stage one in this case) could not be regarded as completed once the closing date for it had been reached if the targets set for it had not been achieved. It emphasised the fact that there were glaring shortcomings in the monetary situation in the Community when measured against the targets for stage one. Ignoring the fact would be to court grave risks. Under those circumstances, it would be more sensible to work on improving the outcome of stage one than to focus efforts on launching stage two.[37] Some of the delegations, particularly the British, considered that giving thought to the progress made in stage one was a pointless exercise, but in reality the UK wanted to avoid having to give too clear a statement of their views on the monetary aspects of the results. Officially, they remained fully committed to the Community exchange system, but as far as they were concerned, putting it into effect would only create temporarily insuperable practical difficulties.

On this issue, the Germans saw eye to eye with the French. Emboldened by the part it had played in the practical implementation of operations in Community currencies in the 'snake', Germany pointed out that the sacrifices made could not be sustained without appreciable progress in the coordination of economic policies. As the results of stage one in this area were not very satisfactory, more work needed to be done on it. The meagre results meant that the 'escape clause' could not be regarded as having lapsed.[38]

The Germans, like the Dutch, shared the view that, even if the content of stage two had to be defined clearly, including the practical measures to go with it, automatic transition on 1 January 1974 was not desirable. Both of these Member States considered that there must be a consolidation stage during which efforts would be made to rectify the shortcomings noted in stage one. The special difficulties certain countries faced should not be a reason for toning down the shared objectives but only for modifying the practicalities of achieving them. Complex projects designed to supply a solid basis for decisions on the European Union in 1976 should be studied. The Netherlands regarded the institutional question as fundamental to any progress towards economic and monetary union.

There was no uniform point of view among the Member States which were in favour of an official transition to stage two either. The Belgians, the Luxembourgers, and the Danes focused on the need to abide by the commitments given at the Paris Summit of 19–21 October 1972,[39] but were concerned that the Community should catch up with what had not been accomplished during stage one. The link which the Paris Summit had made between the setting up and resourcing of the European Regional Development Fund and the transition to stage two of EMU led the Irish, the Italians, and the British to come out in favour of moving onto the new stage on the scheduled date.

Drawing conclusions from the profoundly differing views of the partners with regard to the transition to stage two, the Commission put before the Council a number of proposals (for the period 1974–1976) which aimed to establish the content of a second stage of economic and monetary union. The Council analysed these proposals at its meeting on 17 December 1973. The adoption of a directive on stability, growth and full employment in the Community should do more to promote a high degree of economic policy convergence. Budgetary coordination should be stepped up and the implementation of public budgets should be scrutinised regularly. There were also plans to merge the Conjunctural Policy Committee, the Budgetary Policy Committee and the Medium-Term Economic Policy Committee into a single entity. The role of the EMCF as a vector for the use of the European unit of account was to be reinforced by the gradual expansion of its functions and its resources. The Council was also called upon to decide on arrangements for providing short-term monetary support and on a gradual pooling of currency reserves. On this point, a Belgian–Luxembourgish proposal emerged calling for the Board of Governors of the EMCF to be tasked with formulating a Community policy on currency and credit. Nothing came of it. There was horse-trading over short-term support but it led nowhere. The British called for no limits to be placed on intervention, while other partners proposed setting ceilings at levels which were regarded as inadequate.[40]

The beginning of 1974 saw new monetary tensions. The dollar and the price of gold were climbing inexorably, and on 19 January the French Government temporarily halted its interventions to keep the franc within the 'snake'. This situation threatened to tear apart the arrangements already set up and to make the European crisis even more severe. It was primarily a matter of a 'crisis of confidence, of will and of clarity of purpose'.[41] These fresh difficulties accentuated the opposition, not to say the hostility, between the Member States as regards the transition to stage two of EMU and diluted European solidarity even further. There was no shared view which might have given grounds for hoping a common position could be arrived at, but '[t]here is nothing inevitable about European unity. Europe will not become united unless we make it so. […] The time has come to say clearly whether our nations wish to reinforce their solidarity or not, and whether they wish to react jointly or separately to the great internal and external challenges that each one of them faces. These are questions to which there is as yet no answer'.[42]

In these circumstances, the EC Council of Ministers met on 18 February 1974 to give its views on 'the transition from a stage which has not been carried out to a stage which has not been defined'.[43] The proceedings closed with the adoption of several measures of great importance for the economic aspects of the future economic and monetary union. The Member States agreed on a decision on the attainment of a high degree of convergence of economic policies (also known as the 'convergence decision'), the directive on stability, growth, and full employment in the Community and the decision setting up an Economic Policy Committee (a body assigned the functions previously performed by the Conjunctural Policy Committee, the Budgetary Policy Committee and the Medium-Term Economic Policy Committee).[44] But this lengthy resolution did not declare the formal transition to stage two of economic and monetary union.[45] The process of implementing the plan by stages was de facto suspended, as was any further advance by Europe along the path to EMU mapped out by the Werner Report.

History has subsequently shown that the Werner Report, which for the first time officially recommended the objective of a European monetary union, was ahead of its time—as largely proven by the Delors Report and the Maastricht Treaty. Looking back at how the 1970s represented a turning point in the major monetary debates of the twentieth century, Pierre Werner observed that:

> The most difficult or even desperate economic situations are likely to be reversed under the threefold influence of a desire for recovery, the interplay of economic forces and the time factor, in other words waiting patiently for the first two factors to work in conjunction with each other.[46]

What was needed, as it turned out, was time…

Notes

1. 'Resolution of the Council and of the Representatives of the Governments of the Member States of 22 March 1971 on the attainment by stages of economic and monetary union in the Community', in Official Journal of the European Communities, No. C 28, 27 March 1971.
2. 'Council Regulation (EEC) No. 907/73 of 3 April 1973 establishing a European Monetary Cooperation Fund', in Official Journal No. L 089 of 5 April 1973, pp. 2–5. The fund entered into force in June 1973.

3. In 1968 and 1969 the huge balance of payments deficit in the United States was funded by an unprecedented influx of short-term capital. Thanks to the Eurodollar market and extremely tight US monetary policy, the dollar credits brought into circulation by these deficits were held by private investors. They were consequently not presented for conversion on the foreign exchange markets. The two-tier gold system (established in March 1968 and maintaining dollar convertibility by force of law) had consequently not been put to the test. Central banks had no reason to ask the United States to convert dollars into gold. But the situation started to change in May 1970, when the US monetary authorities relaxed their grip on interest rates. American banks started considerably deleveraging on the Eurodollar market, where interest rates had fallen very low, below those in force in Europe itself. See G. Berger (1972) 'Le conflit entre l'Europe et les États-Unis', in *Revue française de science politique*, 2 (1972), pp. 348–356, particularly pp. 352–353. In contrast, West Germany had to cope with strong growth, forcing the Bundesbank to introduce high short-term interest rates. This attracted an influx of short-term capital, which in turn drove the value of the German mark up against the US dollar. To ensure that the mark remained within the fluctuation margins set by the Bretton Woods Agreements, the Bundesbank purchased $1 billion in the space of 40 minutes just before the markets closed on 5 May 1971! See also R. L. Hetzel (2002) 'German Monetary History in the Second Half of the Twentieth Century: From the Deutsche Mark to the Euro', in *Economic Quarterly—Federal Reserve Bank of Richmond*, 88/2, pp. 29–64, particularly p. 40.
4. *Betr.: Gegenwärtige wirtschaftspolitische Lage*. 6 May 1971. Internal Ministry of the Economy memorandum (Troll), W II 3, Az.75-11-02-01. Helmut Schmidt's papers. *Archiv der sozialen Demokratie der Friedrich-Ebert-Stiftung*, Bonn, Vol. 8635.
5. A diplomatic memo dated 27 July 1971, drafted by the Cooperation Directorate of the Foreign Ministry and entitled *La nécessité d'une initiative européenne*, notes that 'the German Government is trying to take advantage of the latest monetary crisis to control (imported and domestic) inflation using free-market methods. By allowing the mark to float upwards, without any guidelines or time limit, Bonn is thwarting speculation and holding back growth. [...] German economists have always maintained that economic and monetary union could only be founded on exchange rates which reflect the real economic forces at work. [...]

Bonn is afraid of having constantly to prop up the failing currencies of some of its partners.' Ministry of Foreign and European Affairs of the French Republic, EC Collection, Directorate for Economic and Financial Affairs, Economic Cooperation Department, PM series, Vol. 973 EMU, File PM 19.8. French Diplomatic Archives, La Courneuve.

6. Ibid., Reference to an open letter sent by a group of American economists to the *Wirtschaftsforschungsinstitute* (Economic Research Institute) congratulating it on having recommended that the mark should be allowed to float.
7. 'Third medium-term economic policy program', in Official Journal of the European Communities, Brussels, 1 March 1971, No. L 49/5.
8. See the letter from Brandt to Pompidou, dated 9 May 1971. Willy Brandt Archives, Bundeskanzler Collection, Vol. 51, quoted by A. Wilkens (2004) 'Willy Brandt und die europäische Einigung', in M. König, M. Schultz (eds.), *Die Bundesrepublik Deutschland und die europäische Einigung 1946–2000. Politische Akteure, gesellschaftliche Kräfte, internationale Erfahrungen* (Stuttgart: Franz Steiner Verlag).
9. Pierre Werner noted this date in his memoirs, but other sources mention 9 May as the moment of the decision by Germany, the Netherlands and Belgium to allow their currencies to float freely. See K. Kleps (1972) 'On the Way to the Next Monetary Crisis', in *Intereconomics*, 4, p. 107; see also M. Albert (1972) 'La désunion monétaire européenne', in *Revue française de science politique*, 2, pp. 382–390.
10. 'Declaration by Valéry Giscard d'Estaing to the National Assembly, 12 May 1971', in *La politique étrangère de la France.* Texts and documents, edited by the French Foreign Ministry (1 January 1971–31 December 1972 series). First semester (October 1971) (Paris: *La Documentation Française*), pp. 162–167.
11. 'Minutes of the restricted session of the European Council of Ministers', Brussels, 19 August 1971. Historical Archives of the Deutsche Bundesbank, R/1869 d/71, B 330, Vol. 10851.
12. 'Proposition des délégations de Benelux. Avant-projet d'arrangement monétaire entre les membres de la Communauté économique européenne' [Proposal by the Benelux delegations. Preliminary draft for a monetary arrangement between the members of the European Economic Community], August 1971. See 'Système de régime de change en vigueur dans les pays du Benelux depuis le 23 août 1971. Communication de la représentation permanente de la Belgique à la

Commission' [Exchange rate regime in force in the Benelux countries since 23 August 1971. Communication from the Belgian Permanent Representation to the Commission]. European Community, Secretariat of the Monetary Committee, Brussels, ref. OR II/506/71-F, 31 August 1971. In the Pierre Werner Family archives, ref. PW 042. Faced with their partners' refusal to endorse this proposal, the Benelux countries decided to allow their currencies to float against the dollar, while maintaining the rate between one another within the ±1.5% fluctuation margin. In fact this represented a miniature monetary snake *sui generis*. It should also be noted that the Belgian and Luxembourg francs were linked by a one-to-one exchange rate established as part of the monetary union between the two countries. The National Bank of Belgium acted as a central bank for the two countries. Belgian bank notes were legal tender in Luxembourg, in addition to a limited number of national bank notes which the Luxembourg authorities could issue.

13. 'Minutes of the restricted session of the European Council of Ministers', Brussels, 19 August 1971. Historical Archives of the Deutsche Bundesbank, R/1869 d/71, B 330, Vol. 10851. See also 'Communiqué Issued by Georges Pompidou on the International Monetary Situation' (Paris, 18 August 1971), in *Western European Union Assembly-General Affairs Committee*: A Retrospective View of the Political Year in *Europe 1971. November 1972* (Paris: Western European Union Assembly-General Affairs Committee).
14. 'Memorandum from the Commission to the Council on the Problems Raised by the Present Monetary Situation (10 September 1971)', in *Bulletin of the European Communities*, September–October 1971, No. 9/10, Office for Official Publications of the European Communities, Luxembourg.
15. 'Comments by Mr. Werner after the Council of Finance Ministers in Brussels'. Incoming diplomatic telegram, ref. No. 87, Luxembourg, 14 September 1971. Ministry of Foreign and European Affairs of the French Republic, EC Collection, Directorate for Economic and Financial Affairs, Economic Cooperation Department, PM series, Vol. 979 EMU consultations, File PM 19.11. French Diplomatic Archives, La Courneuve. For a broader presentation, see the press conference given by Georges Pompidou on 23 September 1971 in G. Pompidou (1975, II) *Entretiens et discours: 1968–1974* (Paris: Plon), pp. 38–47.
16. See C. Nappi (1978) 'La réforme du système monétaire international: une chronologie et interprétation des événements', in *L'Actualité économique*, 54/2, pp. 263–286.

17. 'Communiqué from the "Group of Ten", Washington, 18 December 1971', in *Bulletin of the European Communities*, January 1972, No. 1, Luxembourg. The full agreement addressed the following points: removal of the 10% surtax on a large share of US imports; increase in the price of gold from $35 to $38 an ounce, equivalent to an 8.57% devaluation of the dollar; inconvertibility of the dollar to gold was maintained. The realignment of the other currencies, including the effect of the 8.57% devaluation of the dollar, yielded the following gains in relation to the dollar: Swedish krone, 7.49%; German mark, 13.58%; Dutch guilder, 11.57%; Belgian franc, 11.57%; French franc, 8.57%; Italian lira, 7.48%; pound sterling, 8.57%; and Japanese yen, 16.88%. The IMF was tasked with establishing a new system by which member countries could allow their exchange rates to fluctuate within a margin of 2.25% on either side of the central exchange rate resulting from this new realignment. The Americans were very pleased with what became known as the Smithsonian Agreement, having obtained a significant realignment of their main competitors' currencies in exchange for a slight reduction in the value of the dollar through a rise in the price of gold. It should be pointed out that this 'concession' was in fact very slight: although central banks could theoretically exchange $38 for an ounce of gold, in practice this was impossible because the US dollar retained its inconvertibility to gold.
18. 'Resolution of the Council on the achievement by stages of economic and monetary union in the Community (21 March 1972)', in Official Journal of the European Communities, C 38, Luxembourg, 18 April 1972, pp. 43–46. At the same time the Ecofin Council approved several legislative measures designed to check inflationary pressures inside the Community and counter increasingly frequent foreign exchange crises.
19. The Council meeting on 6 March 1972 reached agreement on narrowing the margins. On 23 August 1971 the Benelux countries had introduced a system of tighter margins (1.5% instead of 2.25% in the subsequent Community-wide agreement). This system operated for some time alongside the snake, but with no close coordination of monetary policy between Belgium (also representing Luxembourg) and the Netherlands, it soon disappeared.
20. P. Werner (1992, II) *Itinéraires*, p. 140.
21. 'Resolution of the Council and of the Representatives of the Governments of the Member States of 21 March 1972 on the application of the Resolution of 22 March 1971 on the attainment by stages

of economic and monetary union in the Community', in Official Journal of the European Communities, C 38, 18 April 1972, English special edition: Series II, Volume IX, pp. 65–66.

22. 'Monetary policy in the countries of the European Economic Community, 1972'. Monetary Committee of the European Communities. Historical Archives of the Commission of the European Communities.
23. 'Note on the European Monetary Cooperation Fund', 26 July 1972, ref. GMC/GM, No 227/CE. Ministry of Foreign and European Affairs of the French Republic, EC Collection, Directorate for Economic and Financial Affairs, Economic Cooperation Department, PM series, Vol. 973 EMU, file PM 19.9. French Diplomatic Archives, La Courneuve.
24. B. Olivi, A. Giacone (2007) *L'Europe difficile. Histoire politique de la construction européenne* (Paris: Gallimard), pp. 186–194 and 459. Italy's proposal was interpreted as an attempt to take the quickest possible action to stave off dips in the lira. However, Rinaldo Ossola, Vice-President of the Banca d'Italia, stated that monetary gold should be held separately from the pool.
25. 'Mise au point définitive de l'avis du Comité des gouverneurs des banques centrales sur le rapport du groupe d'experts présidé par M. Mertens de Wilmars sur un Fonds européen de coopération monétaire (confidentiel)' [Finalisation of the opinion of the Committee of Governors of the Central Banks on the report by the group of experts chaired by Mertens de Wilmars on a European Monetary Cooperation Fund (confidential)]. August 1972. Committee of Governors of the Central Banks of the Member States of the European Economic Community. Archives of the European Central Bank, Frankfurt.
26. 'Minutes and documents relating to the 62nd meeting of the Committee of Governors of the Central Banks of the Member States of the European Economic Community (confidential)'. Basel: 11 September 1972, at 10 a.m. Archives of the European Central Bank, Frankfurt.
27. 'The European Monetary Cooperation Fund', note ref. GMC/RC, Paris: 8 September 1972, Ministry of Foreign and European Affairs of the French Republic, EC Collection, Directorate of Economic and Financial Affairs, Economic Cooperation Department, PM series, Vol. 975, EMCF file PM 19.9. French Diplomatic Archives, La Courneuve.
28. 'Note for the Chairman. Meeting of the Ministers for Foreign Affairs and the Ministers for Finance of the 10 countries of the enlarged Community in Rome (10–11 September 1972)', Paris: 14 September

1972, ref. 5AG2 7/PR/CT, Ministry of Foreign and European Affairs of the French Republic, EC Collection, Directorate of Economic and Financial Affairs, Economic Cooperation Department, PM series, Vol. 975, EMCF file PM 19.9. French Diplomatic Archives, La Courneuve.
29. P. Werner (1997) 'Les perplexités institutionnelles de l'Union européenne', in *La problématique de l'Union monétaire européenne*, Journals of the Institut Grand-Ducal, Political Sciences and Ethics Section, 12 (Luxembourg: The Institut Grand-Ducal), p. 28. See also 'Statement from the Paris Summit (19–21 October 1972)'. Bulletin of the European Communities. October 1972, No. 10. Office for Official Publications of the European Communities, Luxembourg.
30. In an initial phase the Fund will operate on the following basis: concerted action among the Central Banks for the purposes of narrowing the margins of fluctuation between their currencies; the multilateralisation of positions resulting from interventions in Community currencies and the multilateralisation of intra-Community settlements; the use for this purpose of a European monetary unit of account; the administration of short-term monetary support among the Central Banks; the very short-term financing of the agreement on the narrowing of margins and short-term monetary support will be grouped together in the Fund under a renovated mechanism; to this end, short-term support will be adjusted on the technical plane without modifying its essential characteristics and in particular without modifying the consultation procedures they involve. The competent bodies of the Community shall submit reports: not later than 30 September 1973, on the adjustment of short-term support; not later than 31 December 1973, on the conditions for the progressive pooling of reserves.
31. See 'Regulation (EEC) No. 907/73 of the Council of 3 April 1973 establishing a European Monetary Cooperation Fund', in Official Journal L 089, 5 April 1973, pp. 2–5. On 1 January 1994, the European Monetary Institute, the germ of the future European Central Bank, took over from the EMCF.
32. The specific situation of Luxembourg is worthy of note. Usually, it was represented by the National Bank of Belgium (BNB), in accordance with the Convention on Economic Union between the two countries. Luxembourg had one representative who was able to take part in decisions of the Board of Governors whenever the rights and obligations of the Grand Duchy of Luxembourg were not exercised by the BNB.

See Article 1, Statutes of the EMCF of 28 June 1973. Reproduced in *Monetary Committee, Compendium of Community Monetary Texts, 1958–1973*, OPOCE, Luxembourg, 1974, p. 85.

33. C.-D. Ehlermann (1973) 'Die Errichtung des Europäischen Fonds für Währungspolitische Zusammenarbeit', in *Europarecht*, 8 (H. 3) (Munich: Nomos), p. 193.
34. 'Decision of the Representatives of the Governments of the Member States of 24 July 1973 on the provisional location of the European Monetary Cooperation Fund (73/208/EEC)', in Official Journal L 207 of 28 July 1973, p. 46. Luxembourg and Paris were the candidates to be the seat of the EMCF, but Luxembourg ultimately won the day. See 'Mémorandum du gouvernement luxembourgeois concernant le siège du FECOM' [Memorandum of the Luxembourg Government on the seat of the EMCF], 18 December 1972, Embassy of Luxembourg in France. Pierre Werner Family archives. See also 'Adresse diplomatique à Paris: Conseil des 25 et 26 juin 1973: Lieu d'implantation du Fonds européen de coopération monétaire' [Diplomatic address in Paris, Council of 25 and 26 June 1973: Place of establishment of the EMCF]. Telegram from Brussels, No. 2133–2141 of 15 June 1973, Ministry of Foreign and European Affairs of the French Republic, EC Collection, Directorate of Economic and Financial Affairs, Economic Cooperation Department, PM, Vol. 975-1, EMCF file PM 19.9. French Diplomatic Archives, La Courneuve.
35. 'Communication from the Commission to the Council on the progress achieved in the first stage of economic and monetary union, on the allocation of powers and responsibilities among the Community institutions and the Member States essential to the proper functioning of economic and monetary union, and on the measures to be taken in the second stage of economic and monetary union' (submitted by the Commission to the Council on 30 April 1973). Doc. COM (73) 570 final, 19 April 1973, *Bulletin of the EEC*, Supplement 5/73.
36. P. Werner (1992, II) *Itinéraires*, p. 149.
37. French–German talks on Economic and Monetary Union. Note (confidential). Paris, 16 September 1973, Ministry of Foreign and European Affairs of the French Republic, EC Collection, Directorate for Economic and Financial Affairs, Economic Cooperation Department, PM series, Vol. 972 EMU–Bilateral relations, File PM 19.6.1, French Diplomatic Archives, La Courneuve.

38. In accordance with the 22 March 1971 resolution, this clause made any extension of the commitments given on monetary questions for longer than five years conditional on adequate progress being made on economic coordination. See also Sects. 2.2 and 4.3.
39. See Sect. 5.2.
40. P. Werner (1992, II) *Itinéraires*, p. 152.
41. 'Declaration on the State of the Community', in *Bulletin of the European Communities*, 1 (January 1974), pp. 5–8.
42. Ibid.
43. To quote the words used by Finance Minister Valéry Giscard d'Estaing in a speech to the Ecofin Council on 4 December 1973. See 'Preliminary Notes', 6 December 1974, Ministry of Foreign and European Affairs of the French Republic, EC Collection, Directorate for Economic and Financial Affairs, Economic Cooperation Department, PM series, Vol. 971 EMU, File PM 19.2.2. French Diplomatic Archives, La Courneuve.
44. See Official Journal, L 63, 5 March 1974, pp. 16–22.
45. 'Communiqué of the Council', in *Bulletin of the European Communities*, 2 (February 1973), p. 2.
46. P. Werner (1992, I) *Itinéraires*, p. 27.

8

The Werner Report: A Blueprint for EMU?

8.1 Plans and Studies Drawn up After the Werner Report

The setbacks suffered by the stage-by-stage plan initially disheartened the supporters of this major project. Despite the political impasse, reflection on economic and monetary union (EMU) continued at the initiative of the Commission and certain governments, in academic and university circles, and among private-sector organisations and economists.[1] This led to various reports, studies, and forecasts which helped to improve monetary cooperation and which played a part, through the problems discussed and the approaches proposed, in the revival of European monetary union in 1977.[2]

The purpose of the Marjolin Report of 8 March 1975—the outcome of a study conducted by experts appointed by the Commission under the chairmanship of its former Vice-President, Robert Marjolin—was to analyse the questions raised by the establishment of EMU given the major changes to be expected by 1980.[3] A review of overall developments in the period from 1969 to 1975 led to the observation that the Werner Report had not brought any results. 'If there has been any

E. Danescu, *Pierre Werner and Europe*,
Archival Insights into the Evolution of Economics,
https://doi.org/10.1007/978-3-319-96295-5_8

movement it has been backward. [...] The idea of a united Europe, while enjoying the passive sympathy of the majority of the population in most Community countries, is not one which carries force. The goodwill with which it is generally received is usually accompanied by scepticism, because of the lack of a clear political commitment by political leaders. [...] The centrifugal movement which characterises national policies has deeply affected Community achievements. [...] The monetary problems which have arisen since 1969, and the frequent refusal of governments to permit the price adjustments in national currencies, which would normally have resulted therefrom, have led to the creation of a system of compensatory payments of such complexity that it is incomprehensible to the uninitiated. The unity of agricultural prices in the Community is damaged and the single market split into several fragments which, given the attitudes of certain of them, it is hard to see being "stuck together again" in the foreseeable future'.

Besides the international environment and the priority accorded to national policies (French), resistance to supranational institutions was among the reasons why EMU reached stalemate, thereby highlighting the recommendations (never followed up) in the Werner Report. 'In an EMU, national governments put at the disposal of the common institutions the use of all the instruments of monetary policy and of economic policy whose action should be exercised for the Community as a whole. These institutions moreover must have a discretionary power similar to that which national governments possess now, in order to be able to meet unexpected events'.

The Marjolin Report considered it necessary to act quickly and in a spirit of solidarity in a Community facing an ever-growing balance of payments deficit, mounting inflation and rising unemployment. It also called for action from both sides of industry. In the monetary and financial sphere, it recommended going further than the intra-European exchange rate mechanism (the 'currency snake') and setting up a Community system of internal and external monetary policies (this would be the European Monetary System [EMS] of 1979). In this area, the report recommended creating a European exchange stabilisation fund and introducing a new European unit of account (based on a basket of Member States' currencies).[4]

However, the Marjolin Report noted that as soon it was set in motion, the Werner Report ran into a series of successive crises, culminating in its de facto suspension.[5]

After more than a decade of standstill, the European Council and the Hanover Summit (27 and 28 April 1988) decided to give a committee of experts chaired by Jacques Delors the task of studying and making proposals for the practical stages leading to EMU. It was Delors himself who suggested that this special committee responsible for looking into monetary union should consist of the governors of the central banks, who were more independent than the governments, rather than the finance ministers who already constituted the Council for Economic and Financial Affairs of the Community (Ecofin), and some of whom were manifestly hostile to the project. Following lively discussion, the President of the German Bundesbank gave the project his support, though with the proviso that the future European Central Bank (ECB) should be independent.[6]

The Delors Report, having been approved by the Commission, was presented on 12 April 1989 and adopted the definition of EMU already set out in the Werner Report in 1970. Three clauses were inserted: full and irreversible convertibility of currencies, complete liberalisation of capital movements and the setting of fixed exchange rates between the European currencies. For the achievement of EMU through the harmonisation of fiscal and budgetary policies, the Delors Report proposed a process in three stages. Stage one was the culmination of the single market through the sustained coordination of economic policies and monetary cooperation and the approval of all the currencies for inclusion in the exchange mechanism of the EMS). During this stage, an EMU treaty must be negotiated and ratified. The task for stage two would be to set up a European System of Central Banks (ESCB). The final stage would see the transfer of certain economic and monetary powers to the European Union institutions and the irrevocable switchover to fixed exchange rates and, if possible, a single currency to replace the national currencies. The Delors Plan therefore defined the steps to be taken to set up EMU and the transfers of sovereignty which it entailed. However, it set neither a timetable nor deadlines, which were to be determined as matters of policy by the Member States. The report from the Delors

Committee was submitted to the European Council held in Madrid on 26 and 27 June 1989 and the committee's work was unanimously approved by the 12 Member States.[7]

8.2 The Werner Report and the Delors Report

The Werner Report of 8 October 1970 offered a full definition of EMU, which was to be established in three stages over a period of ten years (1971–1980). The ultimate aim was to achieve irreversible convertibility between the currencies of the Member States, the complete liberalisation of capital movements, the irrevocable fixing of exchange rates, and even potentially the replacement of national currencies by a single currency as a natural and desirable further development of monetary union. Monetary policy vis-à-vis the outside world would be a matter for the Community. Only the first three-year stage, due to begin on 1 January 1971 and loosely based on the first Barre memorandum, was clearly defined. It should be noted that the characteristic feature of this memorandum is a particular association of traditional German and French concepts: 'a French-inspired medium-term analysis was applied to the German idea of economic convergence'.[8]

The report emphasised the pursuit of common policies by the Member States, the introduction of greater coordination of national budget policies (centralization of the size and balance of national budgets and how they should be funded), as well as the harmonisation of fiscal policies (VAT and excise duty rates) including taxation of capital, on which matter it called on the Committee of Central Bank Governors to define the appropriate guidelines. The report stressed the need to consult economic and social sectors before defining the guidelines of Community economic policy. Regular consultations with both sides of industry (the 'social partners') would be essentials.

From an institutional viewpoint, the report called for the creation of two new steering bodies: a 'centre of decision for economic policy', independent of governments and placed under the democratic control of the European Parliament, to be elected by universal suffrage; and a 'Community system for the central banks'. This system would be preceded by the establishment of a European Monetary Cooperation Fund (EMCF), based on Triffin's proposals but more limited in scope. EMU would serve as a 'leaven' for the development of a political union without which, ultimately, it would not be able to manage. This argument was prescient with respect to later criticisms of the architecture of the Maastricht Treaty, especially in the wake of the post-2008 euro area crisis.

The Werner Committee was most likely aware of the scope of their work, since the report emphasises that 'the Group has not sought to construct an ideal system in the abstract. It has set out rather to determine the elements that are indispensable to the existence of a complete EMU'. The union—as described in the report—represented the minimum that had to be done and was a stage in a dynamic evolution that would be shaped by the pressure of events and political will. Several main principles underpinned the drafting of the Werner Report:

- *The comprehensive approach*: no individual element (economic, monetary, social or political) could be removed from the plan without affecting the overall balance.
- *The Irreversibility*: once the process had been launched, it would not be possible to turn back.
- *The gradual realisation*, by means of a step-by-step approach which had been deemed to be the only viable approach to EMU.
- *A 'Parallel movement in pra*ctice'.[9] This principle applied in three areas: parallel movement in progress towards economic policy convergence and the imposition of additional monetary constraints; parallel movement in the imposition of monetary constraints and the transfer of powers over economic policy (monetary and credit policy) to the Community; parallel movement in the development of Community powers and the corresponding development of effective European institutions.
- *The European social model* as a vital dimension of economic integration.
- *Strong macroeconomic governance* introduced by the coordination of budgetary and monetary policies (even if the introduction of a single currency was not expressly stated). The report provided for full

financial integration involving *tax harmonisation*, including taxation of capital.
- EMU would serve as a 'leaven' for the development of *a political union* which, ultimately, it would not be able to manage without.

The Werner Report could have been the basis for a common response by the then Member States of the EEC to the dramatic change that occurred in the economic and monetary environment of the Western world in the first half of the 1970s, but the implementation of the plan by stages was de facto suspended, as noted by the Marjolin Report of 8 March 1975.[10]

The report did have some 'intrinsic weaknesses', including 'insufficient constraints on national policies, institutional ambiguities [from a monetary, economic, and fiscal viewpoint], inappropriate policy conception, [and] lack of internal momentum', which might explain its lack of success in the immediate term.[11] It was based on a regime of fixed (but adjustable) parities, despite the obvious weakness of the Bretton Woods system. Moreover, in its definition of the second and third stages of EMU, the report provided only general indications and did not lay down a timeframe. It was imprecise as to the definition of economic union and also relatively sketchy when it came to institutional matters. But could the Werner Group have acted any differently to reach unanimous conclusions? The compromise was finely balanced. It provided for a 'system of central banks' that would be responsible for monetary policy. However, it was not specified that this system would be 'independent', as the Germans wanted. At the same time, the 'European monetary identity' was not lacking in supranational aspects, as the Fre nch preferred. The plan also adopted a centralist approach, aiming to resolve the majority of doctrinal and constitutional problems associated with EMU despite the seeming lack of compatibility between national sovereignty and the Community interest. The Werner Report was at the vanguard, making it 'operationally, institutionally and politically incompatible with the constitutional realities of states and of the treaty'.[12]

Nevertheless, the Werner Report became a blueprint for EMU in the European Community, as the Delors Report and the Maastricht Treaty would confirm 20 years later.

The Delors Committee started its deliberations in September 1988 symbolically in Luxembourg with a thorough analysis of the Werner Report. It thus became the yardstick by which the feasibility and eventual success of the Delors Report would be measured.[13]

Werner and Delors both emphasised the principles of progressive realisation of EMU by stages and parallelism between economic convergence and transfer of powers to the supranational level. Moreover, their reports define monetary union in almost identical terms.

In a text he wrote in 1989, Pierre Werner cast a comparative eye over the two plans by stages.[14]

> Zwischen dem Delors- und dem Werner-Bericht gibt es keinen grundsätzlichen Unterschied hinsichtlich der Doktrin und der Methode... Der Delors-Bericht zitiert öfters den Werner-Bericht hinsichtlich der Voraussetzungen einer vollwertigen Union, nämlich die vollständige und unwidderrufliche Konvertibilität der Währungen, die Beseitigung der Bandbreiten der Wechselkurse, die unwidderrufliche Festsetzung der Paritätsverhältnisse und die völlige Liberalisierung des Kapitalverkehrs.
>
> ['There is no fundamental difference between the Delors and Werner Reports as regard doctrine and methods. The Delors Report more often quotes the Werner Report as regards the prerequisites for a complete union, that is to say the full and irreversible convertibility of the currencies, the abolition of the margins of fluctuation between currencies, the irrevocable fixing of exchange rates and the complete liberalisation of capital movements.'][15]

Jacques Delors, in a lecture he gave in 1992, then analysed the similarities and the differences between the two reports.[16]

> On peut dire que la philosophie d'ensemble de ce que nous avons proposé et même l'architecture du rapport Delors s'inspirent très fortement du rapport Werner... Le rapport du comité Delors s'inscrit dans le droit fil du rapport du comité Werner.
>
> ['It could be said that the overall philosophy behind what we proposed and even the structure of the Delors Report were very heavily influenced by the Werner Report ... The Delors Committee's report is a direct follow-on from the Werner Committee's report.'][17]

> Dans le rapport du comité Delors (…) nous nous sommes mis d'accord sur les trois phases, reprises du rapport Werner: première phase, consacrée au renforcement de la coordination, à partir du 1er juillet 1990; deuxième phase de transition vers la phase finale, préparant les institutions définitives de l'Union économique et monétaire; phase finale où seraient fixés irrévocablement les taux de change des monnaies entre elles et avec la monnaie unique.
>
> ['In the report by the Delors Committee (…) we agreed on the three stages taken over from the Werner Report: stage one, devoted to the enhancing coordination, from 1 July 1990, stage two, a transition stage on the way to the final stage, preparing the ground for what were ultimately to be the institutions for EMU, and the last stage, at which the exchange rates between the currencies themselves and between them and the single currency would be laid down irrevocably.'][18]

The main differences reside in the manner in which the two committees addressed two fundamental issues of EMU: namely, the design of the economic pillar of EMU and the development of this pillar into a political union.[19]

It should be mentioned that in some respects the Werner Report goes further and is more clear cut than the Delors Report. In its conclusions, the Werner Report clearly states that:

- EMU means that the principal decisions of economic policy will be taken at Community level and therefore that the necessary powers will be transferred from the national plane to the Community plane […]. Contrast this with the language of the new Article 3a inserted in the Rome Treaty by the Maastricht Treaty in February 1992, which vaguely refers to 'the adoption of an economic policy which is based on the close coordination of Member States' economic policies'.[20]
- On the institutional plane, in the final stage, two Community organs are indispensable: a centre of decision for economic policy and a Community system for the central banks […].[21]

Although its implementation in practice in the 1970s was not a success, the report marked a crucial phase in the process of European integration. In the history of Europe as a monetary entity, there is obviously a pre-Werner and a post-Werner period. 'Up until the time of the report, which is inextricably associated with the Hague Conference, the Member States still had a vision of an economic union, or at any rate a common market, which they thought could be achieved merely by resorting, where monetary affairs were concerned, to the coordination of their policies; from the time of the Hague Conference and the Werner Report onwards, they admitted that economic union could not be brought about unless monetary union were progressively established'.[22]

Notes

1. See D. Dinan (2004) *Europe Recast: A History of European Union* (London: Boulder), pp. 173–174; E. Mourlon-Druol (2011) 'Les banquiers centraux de l'échec du plan Werner à la création du SME, 1974–1979', in F. Clavert, O. Feiertag (eds.), *Histoire, économie et société. La revue d'histoire économique et sociale du XVIe au XXe siècle*, 30/4 (2011) (Paris: Armand Colin), pp. 39–46.
2. These documents included:

   - 'Concrete suggestions for the second stage of EMU'. EMU Group, chaired by Sir Lawrence Airey (Office of the UK Permanent Representative to the ECC) http://ec.europa.eu/ (home page), accessed on 6 March 2018.
   - 'European economic integration and monetary unification' (the Magnifico Report), October 1973. This report, drawn up under the aegis of the Commission's Directorate-General for Economic and Financial Affairs, examined all the potential implications of the establishment of an EMU, including issues relating to price stability policy, regional policy and employment policy.
   - On 16 September 1974, the French Finance Minister, Jean-Pierre Fourcade, sent a memorandum to the Member States (the Fourcade Memorandum) on new initiatives in the monetary field with a view to strengthening the institutional framework of the exchange rate mechanism. See E. Mourlon-Druol (2012) *A Europe Made of Money:*

The Emergence of the European Monetary System (Ithaca, NY: Cornell University Press), pp. 48–50.

- The 'All Saints' Day Manifesto' (1 November 1975). This was a report drawn up by nine economists from eight European countries focusing on the idea of a parallel European currency. The central banks were encouraged to issue a parallel currency called 'Europa' with constant purchasing power and the twofold objective of introducing a single European currency and eradicating inflation.
- 'Appeal for a realistic European monetary unification policy' (12 December 1975). The economist and professor Francis Woehrling, also an official in the Commission's Directorate-General for Economic and Financial Affairs, who had contributed to the drafting of the All Saints' Day Manifesto, drew up an individual discussion paper on the priorities of European unification which he submitted personally to the Commission of the European Communities. http://ec.europa.eu/ (home page), accessed on 6 March 2018.
- The Tindemans Report on European Union (29 December 1975). At the Paris Summit of 9 and 10 December 1974, Leo Tindemans, Prime Minister of Belgium, was asked to draw up a report defining what was meant by the term 'European union'. This marked the Nine's determination to breathe new life into the European integration process, which had been hampered by the economic crisis and the threats of disintegration of the Community. A deep-rooted federalist, Tindemans consulted the European institutions, which all submitted a report to him, as well as hundreds of eminent figures representing political, economic, trade union, voluntary sector and intellectual circles in the Community's nine Member States. The Report on European Union was released on 29 December 1975. On 2 April 1976 it was presented to the Luxembourg European Council, which held a preliminary exchange of views on it.
- The Optica Report (Optimum Currency Areas) (16 January 1976). The Commission of the European Communities assembled a group of experts to examine the notion of an optimum currency area in Europe.
- 'Some problems in connection with proposals for a European parallel currency' (19 March 1976). This was an internal note from the Directorate-General for Economic and Financial Affairs of the Commission of the European Communities. http://ec.europa.eu/ (home page), accessed on 6 March 2018.

- The Duisenberg Plan (27 July 1976). These proposals submitted by the Dutch Finance Minister, Wim Duisenberg, were intended to improve economic policy coordination and exchange rate management.
- 'Positions taken on EMU at summits and councils' (10 December 1976). The General Secretariat of the Council summarised the main positions taken at European Summits and Ecofin Councils, providing an overview of various political approaches.
- Report by the study group on the role of public finance in European integration (the MacDougall Report) (April 1977). This was a report drawn up by experts appointed by the EC Commission. See the MacDougall Report—Volume I (Brussels, April 1977) and the MacDougall Report—Volume II (Brussels, April 1977).
- The prospect of monetary union (16 September 1977). Note from the President of the EC Commission to the meeting of the EC Commission at which this issue was discussed (La Roche-en-Ardenne, 16–18 September 1977).
- Speech by Roy Jenkins, President of the European Commission, at the European University Institute (EUI) in Florence (27 October 1977). This speech advocated the introduction of a European monetary union. The time had come to put the question back onto the agenda. The proposal for a European monetary system was made in early 1978, and, once negotiations had been completed, the system—starting with the ECU as the embryo of a future European currency—came into force in 1979.
- Proposals for the reform of the Commission of the European Communities and its services (the Spierenburg Report) (4 September 1979). This was a report drawn up by experts appointed by the EC Commission.
- As part of the debate surrounding the revival of EMU, the CGCB instructed a group of 25 experts (the Heyvaert Group) to analyse the specifically monetary aspects of the unit of account on the basis of the Fourcade memorandum, and to explore avenues for a potential revision of the European monetary unit of account. See 'Propositions françaises concernant une action coordonnée sur les euro-marchés' [French proposals concerning coordinated action on the Euromarkets] (3 December 1974) and 'Propositions françaises relatives à l'unité de compte monétaire européenne' [French proposals on the European unit of account] (3 December 1974).

- 'Report on the problem of the European unit of account'. The Monetary Committee of the EC (4 December 1974).

3. 'Report of the study group 'Economic and Monetary Union 1980' (the Marjolin Report)'. EC Commission, Directorate-General for Economic and Financial Affairs.
4. In keeping with an idea of Robert Triffin's, the report also looked ahead to a parallel European currency. See P. Werner (1977) *L'Europe monétaire reconsidérée* (Lausanne: Centre d'études européennes), pp. 40–41.
5. This succession of crises included the monetary crisis in 1971 (non-convertibility of the US dollar), the first oil crisis in 1973, the iron and steel crisis in 1974, the economic crisis in 1975 and the second oil crisis in 1979. See Interview with Yves Mersch (Sanem, 24 August 2010). https://www.cvce.eu/project/werner/ (home page) and http://www.cvce.eu/en/oral-history (main page), accessed on 6 March 2018. See Chapter 6.
6. See Interview with Alexandre Lamfalussy (Brussels, 18 March 2010). https://www.cvce.eu/project/werner/ (home page) and http://www.cvce.eu/en/oral-history (main page), accessed on 6 March 2018.
7. J. Delors (1989) 'Economic and Monetary Union and Re-Launching the Construction of Europe', in *Committee for the Study of Economic and Monetary Union, Report on Economic and Monetary Union in the European Community* (Luxembourg: Office for the Official Publications of the European Community), pp. 63–67. See also D. Hodson (2016) 'Jacques Delors: Vision, Revision and the Design of EMU', in K. Dyson, I. Maes (eds.), *Architects of the Euro: Intellectuals in the Making of European Monetary Union* (Oxford: Oxford University Press), pp. 212–232.
8. I. Maes (1998) 'Projets d'intégration monétaire à la Commission européenne', in É. Bussière and M. Dumoulin (eds.), *Milieux économiques et intégration européenne en Europe occidentale au XXe siècle* (Arras: Artois Presses Université), pp. 35–50, here p. 4.
9. H. Tietmeyer (1971) 'L'union économique et monétaire au centre du débat politique', in *Hefte.* 1 (197) (Köln: Institut für Wirtschaftspolitik Press); H. Tietmeyer (2003) 'Der Bericht der Werner-Gruppe von 1970 und der Bericht der Delors-Gruppe von 1989—Ein Vergleich', in W. Hankel, K. Schachtschneider, J. Starbatty (eds.), *Der Ökonom als Politiker: Festschrift für Wilhelm Nölling* (Stuttgart: Lucius), pp. 345–359.

10. K. Seidel (2016) 'Robert Marjolin: Securing the Common Market Through Economic and Monetary Union', in K. Dyson, I. Maes (eds.), *Architects of the Euro: Intellectuals in the Making of European Monetary Union* (London: Oxford University Press), pp. 51–74.
11. G. Baer, T. Padoa-Schioppa (1989) *The Werner Report Revisited.* In *Committee for the Study of Economic and Monetary Union. Report on Economic and Monetary Union in the European Community*, April 1989 (Luxembourg: Office for the Official Publications of the European Community), pp. 53–60, here p. 57.
12. C. Ghymers (2015) 'Une relecture du plan Werner par rapport à ses antecedents et ses successeurs', in E. Danescu, S. Muñoz (eds.), *Pierre Werner and Europe: His Approach, Action and Legacy. Proceedings of the International Conference*, Luxembourg, 2013 (Brussels: PIE Peter Lang), pp. 183–201, here p. 135.
13. K. Dyson (2016) 'Hans Tietmeyer, Ethical Ordo-liberalism, and the Architecture of EMU: Getting the Fundamentals Right', in K. Dyson, I. Maes (eds.), *Architects of the Euro. Intellectuals in the Making of European Monetary Union* (London: Oxford University Press), pp. 138–169. Harold James' analysis reveals that the reality of EMU as it has taken shape is the result of a strange combination of doctrines. The existence of a currency without a state and an institutional framework designed to prevent monetary policy from funding government laxity recalls the theories of Friedrich Hayek. But intergovernmental cooperation on currency and the use of balance-of-payments adjustments reflect the theories of John Maynard Keynes and the ideals of the Bretton Woods Conference. See H. James (2012), *Making the Monetary Union* (Cambridge: Harvard University Press).
14. P. Werner (1989) *L'Union économique et monétaire d'un rapport à l'autre*, September 1989. Pierre Werner Family archives. See also Interview with Prof. Niels Thygesen (Copenhagen, 9 March 2016). https://www.cvce.eu/project/werner/ (home page) and http://www.cvce.eu/en/oral-history (main page), accessed on 6 March 2018.
15. P. Werner (1990) 'Der Werner-Bericht und der Delors-Bericht zur Europäischen Wirtschafts- und Währungsunion im Vergleich', in O. Franz (Hgr.), *Die Europäische Zentralbank* (Bonn: Europa Union Verlag), pp. 175–178.
16. J. Delors (1992) *Monetary Cooperation in the Building of Europe. The 1992 Jean Monnet Lecture* (London: The European Institute, London School of Economics). See Interview with Jacques Delors

(16 December 2009). https://www.cvce.eu/project/werner/ (home page) and http://www.cvce.eu/en/oral-history (main page), accessed on 6 March 2018.

17. J. Delors (1999) in *Pierre Werner—Testimonies at the Threshold of the 21st Century*. Documentary film, European Commission. Pierre Werner Family archives.
18. J. Delors (2004) *Mémoires* (Paris: Plon), p. 338.
19. H. Scheller (2015) 'The Werner Plan and the Delors Report: One or Two Approaches to EMU?' in E. Danescu, S. Muñoz (eds.), *Pierre Werner and Europe: His Approach, Action and Legacy. Proceedings of the International Conference*, Luxembourg, 2013 (Brussels: PIE Peter Lang), pp. 277–298.
20. J.-C. Koeune (2015) 'Challenges and Prospects of EMU', in E. Danescu, S. Muñoz (eds.), *Pierre Werner and Europe: His Approach, Action and Legacy. Proceedings of the International Conference*, Luxembourg, 2013 (Brussels: PIE Peter Lang), pp. 301–305, here p. 301.
21. 'Report to the Council and the Commission on the Realisation by Stages of Economic and Monetary Union in the Community (Werner Report'), Luxembourg, 8 October 1970 in *Bulletin of the European Communities* 11/1970, Supplement, 8 October 1970 (Luxembourg: Office for the Official Publications of the European Community), p. 28.
22. H. Ansiaux, M. Dessart (1975) *Dossier pour l'histoire de l'Europe monétaire 1958–1973* (Leuven: Vander), p. 1.

9

Pierre Werner and the Werner Report

Pierre Werner's private archives reveal that he made a major personal contribution to the method and substance of the Werner Report.

9.1 A Three-Point Method

On 11 March 1970, at the group's preliminary meeting, Werner proposed a three-point working method based on a starting point, a final goal and alternative routes between them—a very basic feature of the plan by stages. Inspired by the method used for the establishment of the Common Market, this was actually the vision of his five-point action program from 1968, which had been received with such enthusiasm. The Werner Committee sided with this approach and the Werner Report was developed on this basis.

E. Danescu, *Pierre Werner and Europe*,
Archival Insights into the Evolution of Economics,
https://doi.org/10.1007/978-3-319-96295-5_9

9.2 Deepening of the Werner Group's Work for the Final Report

At a meeting of the Finance Ministers of the Six on 29 May in Venice, Werner emphasised the need for further work in six priority areas, including institutional aspects, instruments for the coordination of short-term policy and economic policy in the medium term, and budgetary coordination instruments.

He based his view on the fact that economic union and monetary union had to work in tandem. Political union was a longer-term objective underlying the other two.

On the subject of exchange rules, Werner specifically stipulated that there should be 'consultation with the governors of the central banks. Although the ministers were in agreement on many conclusions, there were still differences of opinion, notably regarding the creation of an exchange equalisation fund prior to a common reserve fund. Nevertheless, it seemed essential to improve the coordination of the policies of intervention by the central banks on the exchange market.

All these proposals were to appear in the Council decision on furthering the work of the group and eventually in the final report. Note, too, that, deeply imbued as he was with Luxembourg's social market economy model, Werner was to propose 'consulting both sides of industry on any important monetary decision', recommending that they should be associated with the development of Community economic policy.

9.3 The Role of the Central Bankers in Shaping EMU

Werner was particularly in favour of giving the Committee of Governors of the Central Banks a leading role in monetary integration in the Community and advocated the essential role of the European Monetary Cooperation Fund (EMCF) as an area of gradual convergence between different domestic monetary policies.

Werner raised the idea of a European reserve fund as early as 1962, and in a more sustained manner from May 1967. In his 'five-point action plan' drafted in January 1968, he described the role and powers of such a fund, which would encourage financial solidarity and serve as an instrument to strengthen the coordination of economic policies in the Community. His approach was decidedly 'Triffinian'.

The strategy developed by Werner and Hubert Ansiaux with the support of Bernard Clappier initially resulted in the technical opinion from the Committee of Governors, which recommended taking action on three levels: firstly a concerted policy by the central banks with regard to intervention on the exchange markets; secondly, the use of Community currencies in intracommunity settlements (and a first reduction in margins); and finally, the establishment of the European Monetary Cooperation Fund. The EMCF was set up on 1 April 1973 but it was reduced to a mere accounting tool for cooperation between the central banks.

9.4 The External Dimension of EMU

Werner also worked to further the external dimension of EMU which the plan by stages entailed.

In 1969 and 1970 he was in regular contact with the US federal and political authorities and maintained close relations with American financial circles, particularly through the Luxembourg financial centre. The annual meetings of the IMF provided the opportunity to meet with international experts. Bernard Clappier and Rinaldo Ossola, members of the Committee of Governors, were also active in this area.

One idea that kept coming up was the consolidation of the future monetary identity and solidarity of Europe by ensuring that the Six spoke with one voice in international financial organisations, particularly in the IMF. Werner had several informal meetings with Pierre-Paul Schweitzer, Managing Director of the IMF, following the discussions that Jean Monnet had had with him, as well as with Arthur Burns, the Chairman of the US Federal Reserve Board. Washington had reservations as to the idea of a European monetary bloc, which would prevent the notion of increased flexibility in the IMS and seemed to be prompted by anti-American motives.

Werner was directly involved in the writing of the English version of the report and its dissemination in the English-speaking world, particularly in Britain, by means of the discussions he held with the Prime Minister Edward Heath.

9.5 Consensus Building Through Network Diplomacy

Werner took on the key task of mediating to bring the differing points of view in the committee closer together and secure an agreement on the interim report (20 May 1970) and the final report (7 October 1970).

Thorny issues included the transfer of responsibility from the national to the Community level without engendering lasting tension, medium-term conjunctural policy, the necessity for the main decisions on monetary and credit policy to be taken in common, and real decision-making power being given to the Community bodies. The differences of opinion between the 'economists' and the 'monetarists' were so marked that it was impossible to reach any unanimous conclusions—a fundamental principle for the group's work.

Werner therefore decided to draw upon a wide range of political influences. He negotiated a common position directly with Ministers Giscard d'Estaing and Schiller. He also called on Ansiaux, Clappier and some of the deputies, including Hans Tietmeyer, Jean-Michel Bloch-Lainé, Jacques Mertens de Wilmars and Cecil de Strycker, to mediate among the Member States. He consulted central bankers Jelle Zylstra, Guido Carli and Otmar Emminger, as well as Rinaldo Ossola, Chairman of the Group of Ten.

As the group carried out its work, Werner was in permanent contact with Robert Triffin and Jean Monnet. He consulted them a great deal on the influence which needed to be tapped, especially in Germany and the Netherlands, as those were the two countries most reluctant to agree to a common position in the Council concerning the final report. Werner and Monnet were close to Willy Brandt, using this relationship to good effect, and the approaches Belgian Prime Minister Gaston Eyskens and Baron Jean-Charles Snoy et d'Oppuers made to Dutch Finance Minister Johannes Hendrikus Witteveen also brought results.

The result of an astute compromise, the Werner Report can be considered as another 'Luxembourg Compromise' secured by Werner.[1]

9.6 A Parallel Approach to a Symmetrical EMU

In view of some of his writings prior to 1968, Werner was in favour of a monetary approach, which he also adopted in his political action, particularly to safeguard the interests of the Luxembourg international financial centre.

From 1968 onwards, he was one of the first to develop arguments for a symmetrical economic and monetary union and the principle of parallel progress in the economic and monetary fields.

In discharging his duties as chairman of the group of experts, Werner chose to remain neutral, advocating a parallel approach to economic cooperation and monetary coordination as the underlying principle for the group's reflections. He adopted a median position in the dispute between the various trends in monetary and economic thinking, between which it fell to him to arbitrate in order to bring the work of the Werner Committee to a successful conclusion.

Note

1. The Luxembourg Compromise (January 1966).

   The latent crisis between France and its partners in the European Economic Community reached boiling point in 1965. General de Gaulle was opposed to two major institutional reforms to the EEC. The first involved the arrangements for voting in the Council of Ministers, which were set to change from the principle of unanimity to qualified majority voting. (The Treaty of Rome provided for qualified majority voting from 1 January 1966. The qualified majority was set at 12 votes, with France, the FRG and Italy each holding 4 votes, Belgium and the Netherlands 2 votes and Luxembourg 1 vote.) The second was the strengthening of the budgetary powers of the European Parliament (known at the time as the Assembly) and the European Commission in connection with the funding of the common agricultural policy (CAP) during the completion phase of the Customs Union.

   France could not agree to these developments, which it regarded as an unacceptable renunciation of sovereignty. In addition, General de Gaulle criticised European Commission President Walter Hallstein for having prepared his budgetary proposal without prior consultation of the governments of the Member States. France was also afraid that a coalition of Member States might, on the basis of a majority decision, challenge the common agricultural policy, which France had persuaded its partners to accept only with great difficulty.

   France held the Council Presidency until 30 June 1965, and its stance only exacerbated the latent conflicts between the ideas of the Hallstein Commission and those of the Council of Ministers. By refusing any solution based on compromise, Maurice Couve de Murville, French Foreign Minister in the second Pompidou Government, brought down the negotiations on the financial regulation of the agricultural policy. On 1 July 1965, the French Government recalled to Paris its Permanent Representative to the EEC and announced France's intention not to take its seat in the Council of Ministers until it had its way. This was the beginning of the 'empty chair' crisis. It was the first time since the entry into force of the Treaty of Rome in 1958 that the EEC had been prevented from operating by the actions of a Member State.

   For six months, France stayed away from Brussels and boycotted the Community. Aware, however, of the risks of prolonged isolation and of its impact on the national economy, the country eventually agreed to resume negotiations. At the meetings held in Luxembourg on 17–18 and 28–29 January 1966, the Prime Minister of Luxembourg and President-in-Office of the Council, Pierre Werner—known for his consensus-seeking character and the good personal relations he maintained with all the parties present—made a decisive contribution to the working out of an agreement which freed the Community from deadlock.

In his memoirs, Pierre Werner says that the discussions which culminated in the 'Luxembourg Compromise' were based on an evolving document called the 'Luxembourg document', drafted by the Luxembourg delegation (Pierre Werner, Albert Borschette and Christian Calmes) and constantly adjusted according to the question under discussion and the wordings on which the Five had agreed unanimously, the adjustments being made by two successive pairs of delegates, Schroeder–Luns and Colombo–Spaak. As the chairman of the conference, Pierre Werner steered and led the debates from the outset along 'two main lines: majority voting and relations between the Council and the Commission', and 'the conference achieved what it mainly set out to achieve: France's return to the negotiating table, and [...] the legal integrity of the Treaty of Rome, [which] remained intact.

This was the 'Luxembourg Compromise', or 'Luxembourg reconciliation'. This arrangement, later referred to as an 'agreement to disagree', stipulates that if a Member State believes that its vital interests are at stake, negotiations have to continue until a universally acceptable compromise is reached. The agreement signed in Luxembourg on 29 January 1966, containing French concessions in the area of voting rights, was worded as follows:

> Where, in the case of decisions which may be taken by majority vote on a proposal of the Commission, very important interests of one or more partners are at stake, the Members of the Council will endeavour, within a reasonable time, to reach solutions which can be adopted by all the Members of the Council while respecting their mutual interests and those of the Community. [...] [T]he French delegation considers that where very important interests are at stake the discussion must be continued until unanimous agreement is reached. The six delegations note that there is a divergence of views on what should be done in the event of a failure to reach complete agreement.

Should no such compromise be reached, France demanded compliance with the unanimity rule (i.e. giving the state in the minority a right of veto), while the five other partners held to the letter of the treaty. Noting this fundamental disagreement, the Six nevertheless decided that Community activities should resume. The document, which fundamentally altered the spirit of the EEC Treaty by creating a new mechanism by which states could exert pressure on the Council, did not, however, define what was meant by 'vital national interest'—this was left to the judgment of the state in question—or provide for an arbitration procedure in the event of dispute.

Charles de Gaulle welcomed the 'Luxembourg Compromise', which provided a means of containing the supranational aspects of European integration and reorienting it towards an intergovernmental approach. Thus, in a press conference held at the Élysée Palace on 21 February 1966, de Gaulle declaired:

> With regard to Europe, I shall tell you the point that we have reached and what my thoughts are in the light of the agreement reached in Luxembourg. We consider the agreement between the six governments to be felicitous, salutary even. For the first time since the beginning of the Common Market affair, we have openly walked away from the myth that the economic organisation of Europe was a matter for a body other than the states with all their power and responsibility. The matter was successfully dealt with by the Ministers for Foreign Affairs, away from Brussels, because we expressly acknowledged that political foundations and decisions were a necessary part of a successful economic order, because those foundations and decisions were the purview of states and states alone, and because it was for each government to determine whether the action they proposed taking jointly was compatible with the essential interests of its country. [...] Without overlooking the studies and proposals drawn up some time ago by the Commission in Brussels, it was only thanks to the intervention of individual countries — and, with regard to the common agricultural market, the intervention of France — that European economic integration was able to gradually overcome its difficulties. But the application of the majority rule and the associated extension of the Commission's powers threatened to do away with this reasonable practice through the permanent usurpation of sovereignty.

This successful mediation in European affairs at a difficult time and the prestige enjoyed by Pierre Werner in the Council of Ministers encouraged in the first half of 1967 the idea that the Luxembourg Prime Minister might one day stand for the presidency of the EC Commission. It was only a rumour, as the Luxembourg Prime Minister never really considered giving up his national electoral mandate.

Since then, the 1966 'Luxembourg Compromise' has frequently been invoked by Member States in order to block majority decisions. Contrary to the literal interpretation of the text, they have used the compromise in practice to make unanimity the normal decision-making procedure. The national delegations have therefore allowed the Luxembourg Compromise to degenerate into a right of veto with regard to sometimes minor issues. Under this arrangement, the Council agrees to continue discussions until such time as all the ministers are satisfied with the proposed solution. While the Luxembourg Compromise allowed the Six to break the deadlock, it created a situation which sometimes gave rise to a certain resistance to change, for fear that the negotiations might be blocked, and imposed a de facto limitation on the European Commission's right to propose legislation. This political loophole, which became progressively unmanageable as the number of Member States increased, was partially corrected by the application of the Single European Act, which, from 1 July 1987, considerably broadened the range of decisions that could be adopted by qualified majority.

10
Conclusion

As Prime Minister and Finance Minister of Luxembourg over several decades, Pierre Werner emerged to play a rare statesman-like role in the process of European unification in the second half of the twentieth century. He was all too aware of the particular geopolitical and historical situation of his country. For Luxembourg, adopting an outward orientation had always been a sine qua non. Werner was convinced of the need to preserve national sovereignty and vital interests by maintaining an international outlook. Accordingly, he placed the process of European integration at the centre of Luxembourg policy. Werner's foresight and his pragmatic approach enabled him to develop long-term strategies and focus on what was achievable. His political method was based on three main principles: anticipation, innovation, and consensus.

Werner has left an indelible mark on Economic and Monetary Union (EMU). He is rightly considered to be an architect of the euro for several key reasons. First, he possessed considerable expertise as a policy-maker and was able to translate this expertise into influence on

E. Danescu, *Pierre Werner and Europe*,
Archival Insights into the Evolution of Economics,
https://doi.org/10.1007/978-3-319-96295-5_10

agenda-setting and decision-making in EMU. Monetary policy was a major and sensitive bastion of national sovereignty, and the Member States were unwilling to make concessions. Werner was unanimously recognised as an 'honest broker' who helped to generate momentum and forward movement. He forged this consensus-builder reputation on three levels: the domestic level by promoting dialogue with both sides of industry, the 'social partners', which led to the Luxembourg model of social consultation; the regional level within the Belgium–Luxembourg Economic Union (BLEU) and the Benelux as a leading proponent of small-state diplomacy; and the EC level, above all in EMU. His name is closely linked with two key milestones in European integration: the 1966 'Luxembourg Compromise' which put an end to the 'empty chair' crisis and reconciled France with Europe; and the 1970 Werner Report which laid the foundations for the single European currency. Alongside his key mediator role, Werner provided a vital contribution to the substance of the plan in relation to both the parallelism principle and the concept of stages.

Secondly, Werner contributed his own vision of EMU. From the early 1950s onwards, Werner called for the establishment of a European monetary system based on a unit of account, for both official and private usage, and on a clearing house for central banks. He made monetary policy a pivotal part of his government's action. In addition, the burgeoning Luxembourg international financial centre, which experienced major growth in the early 1960s, served as a vanguard for a European currency unit. As early as 1962, Werner raised the idea of an EEC monetary cooperation fund, as the prelude to a common monetary policy. In 1968, his 'balanced monetarist' approach was evident when he delivered a clear roadmap to get to EMU and advocated the idea of gradualism and 'effective parallelism' in European integration. For Werner, economic union and monetary union had to work in perfect tandem, with political union as the ultimate aim. In his view, social Europe and the coordination of budgetary and monetary policies were intrinsic characteristics of EMU.

Thirdly, Werner developed a tradition of Luxembourg 'network diplomacy' and European integration leadership. He forged his ideas by cultivating long-term productive exchanges of views with other instigators of monetary innovation like Collin, Rueff and Triffin, as well as with financial technocrats like Ansiaux, Carli, Emminger and Zijlstra. There was also a notably strong Belgian dimension to these exchanges. In addition, Werner remained in close contact with the ACUSE, above all with Monnet, Brandt, Hallstein, and Marjolin. Although he never claimed to be an academic expert, Werner exerted his influence at various levels of Community decision-making and became a key figure in intellectual debates between monetary elites and in the efforts to establish consensual transnational guidelines on monetary matters. Werner also served as mentor and leadership trend-setter for other eminent political figures in Luxembourg who later became active on EMU matters. This process can be traced back to the time of Joseph Bech (Prime Minister from 1953 to 1958 and one of the key figures of the Messina Conference) and, besides Werner, included Gaston Thorn (Prime Minister from 1974 to 1979 and President of the European Commission from 1981 to 1985), Jacques Santer (Prime Minister from 1984 to 1995 and President of the European Commission from 1995 to 1999) and Jean-Claude Juncker, later long-serving President of the Eurogroup (2004–2013) and European Commission President from 2014. Luxembourg political leaders proved masters of the art of political consensus and the country was a rich source of 'men of providence' who were able to help find a way out of Europe's successive impasses. The influential nature of this leadership has given Luxembourg a role in the European integration process that far outweighs the country's socio-economic size.

To close this book which looks back at the European vocation of Pierre Werner, it seems only natural to give him the last word. In Werner's view:

> Europe is an essentially political, humanist enterprise. Our shared destiny calls for a new sentiment of Community-wide solidarity [...]. An increasing understanding of the particularities and diversity of the nations of Europe will pave the way for a sense of European pride in our common future. [...] Having ruled out fratricidal wars in this part of the world, the European project has now created an enviable climate of stability and growth, one which could never have been achieved with the alternative scenario of division and every man for himself. [...] Compared with the areas of discord, violent intolerance and merciless hatred elsewhere in the world, the humanist European Union can serve as an example and a model.[1]

In these troubled times for our continent, his analysis of the difficulties in 'building Europe' remains strikingly relevant. Pierre Werner's reflections, based on the principle of solidarity, the force of the law and the desire to move forward together for the common good, remain a source of inspiration for the course we should follow:

> Our own history has taught us that any economic union involves periods of flagging, of disaffection, of misunderstandings, of adjustment [...]. But we are also aware that, in these situations, we need to hold on to the progress made, to consolidate what has been achieved, to concentrate firmly on the formal commitments already entered into and to defend the substance of the treaties concluded—in other words, to persevere.[2]

Notes

1. Pierre Werner, *Itinéraires luxembourgeois et européens. Évolutions et souvenirs: 1945–1985*. (Luxembourg: Éditions Saint-Paul, 2 volumes, 1991–1992.) Quotation from volume 2, p. 171.
2. Pierre Werner, Address given in New York, 30 Sept. 1965. Source: Pierre Werner Family Archives.

Appendix A: Archival Insights

Part I: Photo Album

Thanks to Henri Werner for his invaluable efforts in preserving, selecting and interpreting these historical photos and preparing them for publication.

Source: Pierre Werner Family Archives

E. Danescu, *Pierre Werner and Europe*,
Archival Insights into the Evolution of Economics,
https://doi.org/10.1007/978-3-319-96295-5

4 September 1951—On board the *Liberté* ocean liner on the way to the meeting of the International Monetary Fund. Pierre Werner is at a table with Wilfrid Baumgartner, his former professor, now Governor of the Bank of France; Jean Van Houtte, Belgian Finance Minister; and André François-Poncet, French Ambassador to Germany. © Louis Hamon, Compagnie Générale Transatlantique.

29 December 1953, the day of Pierre Werner's 40th birthday; he has just been appointed Minister of Finance.

11–12 July 1960—At the Council of EEC Finance Ministers in Tivoli, Italy: Pierre Werner in conversation with Paolo Emilio Taviani, Italian Finance Minister (centre), and Emile van Lennep, Chairman of the EEC Monetary Committee.

17 September 1960—Pierre Werner, Luxembourg Prime Minister and Minister of State, is received by French President General de Gaulle.

24–25 October 1960—At the Council of EEC Finance Ministers in Luxembourg, Pierre Werner speaks to Wilfrid Baumgartner, French Finance Minister.

1960—Meeting between Pierre Werner, Luxembourg Prime Minister and Minister of State, and Robert Schuman.

21 November 1960—Pierre Pflimlin, Mayor of Strasbourg, speaks at the dinner he is hosting for the lecture given by Pierre Werner in Obernai, France, entitled: 'The contribution of European finance and currencies to economic integration and solidarity across the continent'.

6 April 1962—Pierre Werner is met at Rome station by Luxembourg Ambassador Pierre Majerus.

26 October 1964—20th meeting of the EEC Finance Ministers in Berlin. © dpa-Photo.

12 September 1966—Meeting of the EEC Finance Ministers in Luxembourg City. In the foreground: Antoine Wehenkel, Luxembourg Minister of the Economy and Budget; Anne Vondeling, Netherlands Finance Minister; and Pierre Werner. © Pol Aschman—Luxembourg.

12 June 1967—On the eve of the NATO Ministerial Meeting on 13 and 14 June 1967 in Luxembourg, German Federal Chancellor Willy Brandt meets Pierre Werner, Luxembourg Prime Minister and Minister of State. © Photothèque de la Ville de Luxembourg.

25–26 February 1968—Pierre Werner speaks to Roberto Tremelloni in the margins of the meeting of the EEC Finance Ministers in Rome. © Photo Service International—Roma.

1–2 December 1969—Summit of the Heads of State or Government of the Member States of the European Communities in The Hague; Pierre Werner is clearly visible in the bottom left-hand corner.

29–30 May 1970—The Finance Ministers of the European Community meet in Venice. At the centre of the photo: Karl Schiller, Minister of Economic Affairs of the Federal Republic of Germany; and Pierre Werner. In the background: Valéry Giscard d'Estaing, French Minister of Finance. © Ravagnan—Venezia.

9 September 1970—Pierre Werner speaks to Alfred Müller-Armack at the annual general meeting of the Board of Governors of the European Investment Bank.

September 1970—Discussions on monetary issues before the publication of the Werner Plan. Behind Pierre Werner: Rinaldo Ossola, Deputy Governor of the Bank of Italy and Chairman of the Group of Ten, a grouping of the Finance Ministers of the ten most industrialised world nations; in front of him: Gaetano Stammati, Chairman of the Budgetary Policy Committee in the Werner Group. Opposite Pierre Werner: Jean-Charles Snoy et d'Oppuers, Belgian Finance Minister; Mario Ferrari Aggradi, Italian Treasury Minister; and Johannes Hendrikus Witteveen, Netherlands Finance Minister.

24 September 1973—Pierre Werner and his wife Henriette Werner-Pescatore at the Annual Meeting of the International Monetary Fund and the World Bank in Nairobi. © Camerapix—Nairobi.

12 February 1974—The Board of Governors of the European Monetary Cooperation Fund (EMCF) meets in Luxembourg, provisional seat of the Fund following the decision taken in June 1973 by the Member States of the European Economic Community. Photo taken at the reception given by Grand Duke Jean and Grand Duchess Joséphine Charlotte at Berg Castle. © Jean Weyrich—Luxembourg.

9 November 1978—Celebration of Jean Monnet's 90th birthday by the Jean Monnet Foundation at the headquarters of the Bank of France in Paris. Pierre Werner with Guy de Muyser, Marshal of the Court of the Grand Duke of Luxembourg, and Paul Delouvrier, President of Électricité de France.

10 October 1979—Pierre Werner leaves his car and makes his way to the office of the President of the Commission of the European Communities in Brussels. © Photothèque CCE DG de l'Information.

10 October 1979—Pierre Werner (accompanied by Jean Dondelinger, Luxembourg Permanent Representative to the European Communities) attends talks in Brussels with Roy Jenkins, President of the Commission of the European Communities. The talks mainly focus on European issues ahead of the European Council due to be held in Dublin on 28 and 29 November 1979. © Photothèque CCE DG de l'Information.

19 December 1979—Pierre Werner is welcomed at the Élysée Palace by French President Valéry Giscard d'Estaing.

1979—UCL bank, founded in 1929 by Luxembourg railway workers, celebrates its 50th anniversary at the Holiday Inn with an event attended by Prime Minister Pierre Werner.

17 May 1982—Pierre Werner, Luxembourg Prime Minister, Joseph Luns, Secretary General of the North Atlantic Treaty Organisation (NATO), and Leo Tindemans, Belgian Minister for External Relations, meet at the NATO Ministerial Meeting in Luxembourg.

17–19 June 1983—The Prime Minister of Luxembourg, Pierre Werner, the British Prime Minister, Margaret Thatcher, and the Federal Chancellor Helmut Kohl, at the Stuttgart European Council.

25 June 1984—European Council in Fontainebleau: Pierre Werner and François Mitterrand.

21 June 1984—Pierre Werner closes his office door as Prime Minister of Luxembourg for the last time. © Jean Weyrich—Luxembourg.

29 September 1992—During the visit to Luxembourg of German Chancellor Helmut Kohl, Jacques Santer, Luxembourg Prime Minister, and Pierre Werner, Honorary Prime Minister and founder of the satellites project, take him to the headquarters of SES Astra in Betzdorf.

31 December 1998—Pierre Werner, flanked by Jean-Claude Juncker, Luxembourg Prime Minister, and Jacques Santer, President of the European Commission, on the eve of the launch of the euro at the Publications Office of the European Union, Luxembourg. © European Union.

Part II: Selected Documents

Handwritten note by Pierre Werner on the establishment of an economic and monetary union, in preparation for the meeting of the ad hoc group on 20 May 1970

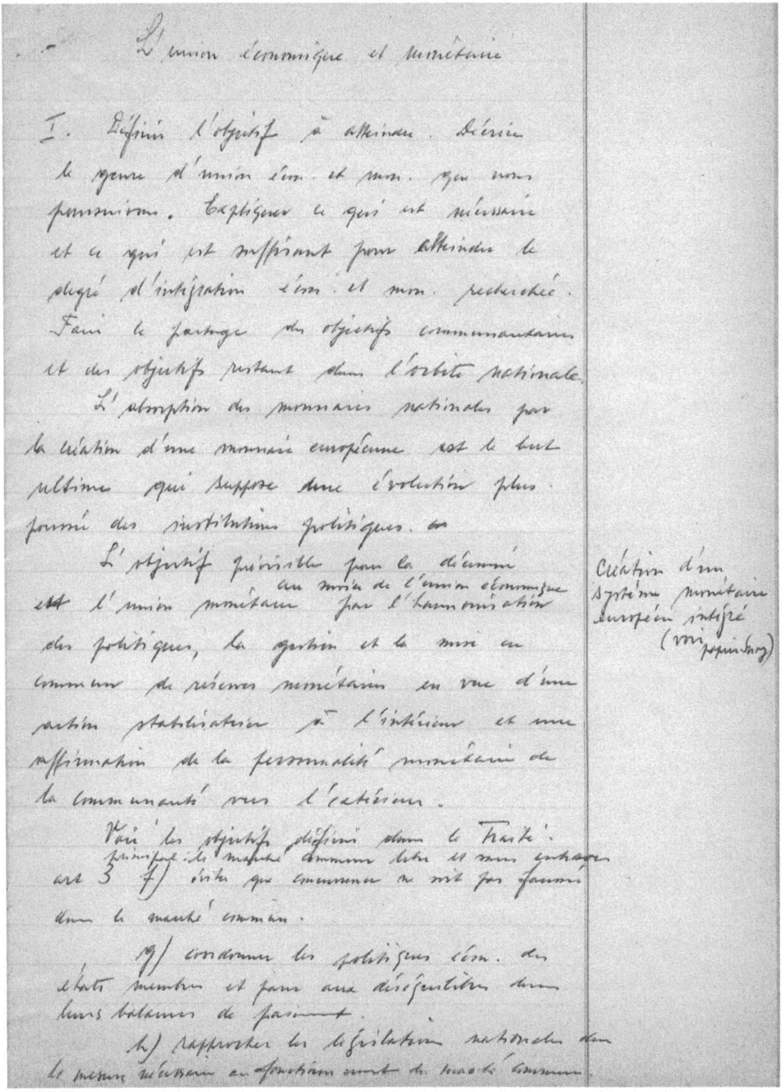
L'union économique et monétaire

I. Définir l'objectif à atteindre. Décrire le genre d'union écon. et mon. que nous poursuivons. Expliquer ce qui est nécessaire et ce qui est suffisant pour atteindre le degré d'intégration écon. et mon. recherché. Faire le partage des objectifs communautaires et des objectifs restant dans l'orbite nationale.

L'absorption des monnaies nationales par la création d'une monnaie européenne est le but ultime qui suppose une évolution plus poussée des institutions politiques.

L'objectif prévisible pour la décennie est l'union monétaire au sein de l'union économique par l'harmonisation des politiques, la gestion et la mise en commun de réserves monétaires en vue d'une action stabilisatrice à l'intérieur et une affirmation de la personnalité monétaire de la communauté vers l'extérieur.

Création d'un système monétaire européen intégré (voir papier Snoy)

Voir les objectifs définis dans le Traité: principal: le marché commun libre et sans entrave

art 3 f) [illegible] que concurrence ne soit pas faussée dans le marché commun.

g) coordonner les politiques écon. des états membres et parer aux déséquilibres dans leurs balances de paiement.

h) rapprocher les législations nationales dans la mesure nécessaire au fonctionnement du marché commun.

art. 67 suppression des restrictions aux mouvements des capitaux dans la mesure nécessaire au bon fonctionnement du marché commun. Paiements courants entièrement libres. voir aussi art 73

art. 103 politique conjoncturelle d'intérêt commun

art 104 Chaque État membre pratique la politique écon. nécessaire en vue d'assurer l'équilibre de sa balance globale des paiements et de maintenir la confiance dans sa monnaie art. 105 coordination des politiques écon

art 107 Chacun traite sa politique en matière de taux de change comme un problème d'intérêt commun

art 113 politique commerciale commune.

Dispositions de rapprochement des législations : art. 100 – 102.

art 235 —

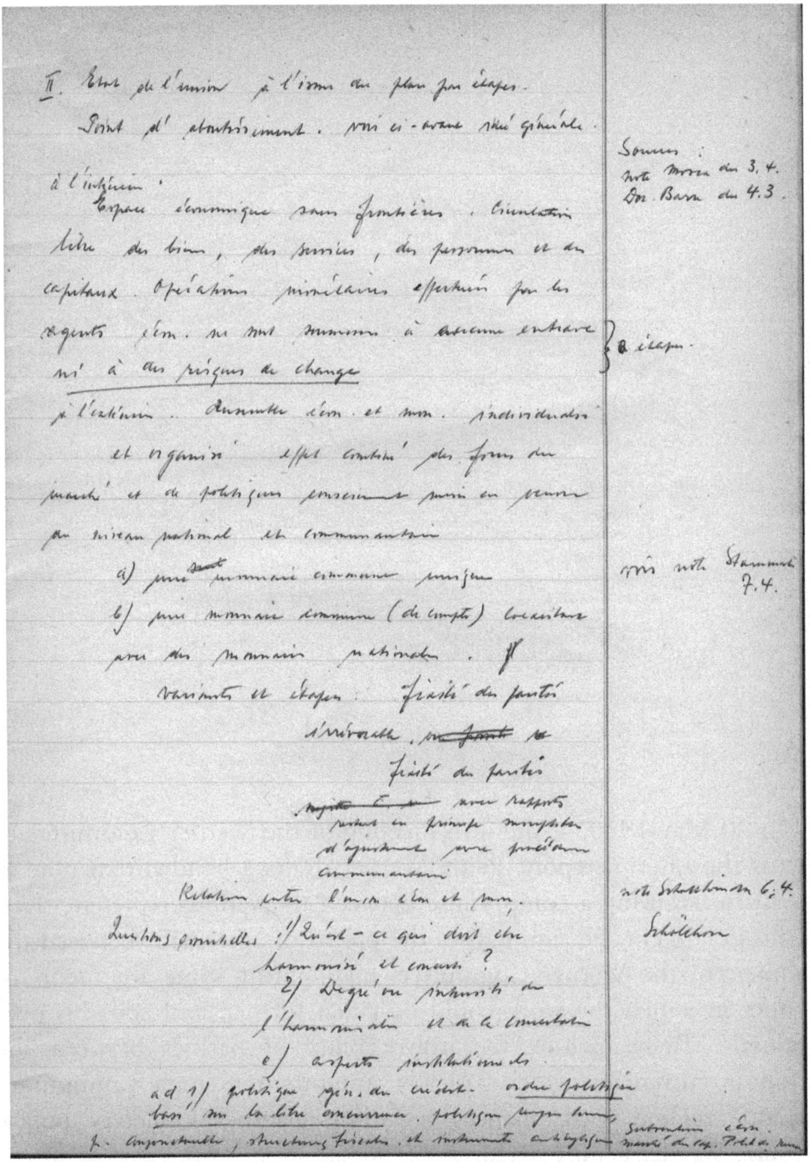

II. Etat de l'union à l'issue du plan par étapes.

Point d'aboutissement. voir ci-avant idée générale.

à l'intérieur.
Espace économique sans frontières. Circulation libre des biens, des services, des personnes et des capitaux. Opérations monétaires effectuées par les agents écon. ne sont soumises à aucune entrave ni à des risques de change

à l'extérieur. Ensemble écon. et mon. individualisé et organisé effet combiné des forces du marché et de politiques conscientes mises en œuvre au niveau national et communautaire

a) une ~~seule~~ monnaie commune unique

b) une monnaie commune (de compte) coexistant avec des monnaies nationales.

variantes et étapes: "fixité" des parités irrévocable, ~~ou parité~~ ou fixité des parités ~~...~~ avec rapports restant en principe susceptibles d'ajustement avec procédure communautaire

Relation entre l'union écon et mon.

Questions essentielles: 1) Qu'est-ce qui doit être harmonisé et concerté?
2) Degré ou intensité de l'harmonisation et de la concertation
c) aspects institutionnels

ad 1) politique gén. du crédit. ordre politique basé sur la libre concurrence. politique ... p. conjoncturelle, structures fiscales, et instruments ... Subordination écon. marché des cap. Politique ...

Sources: note Mosca du 3.4. Doc. Barre du 4.3.

} 1e étape.

voir note Stammati 7.4.

note Schöllhorn 6.4. Schöllhorn

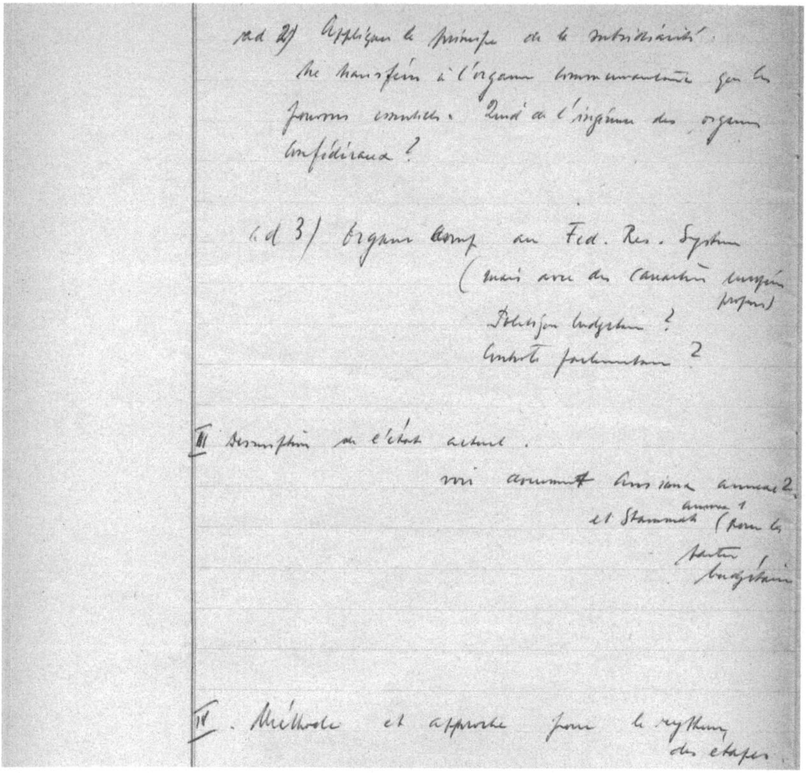
ad 2) Appliquer le principe de la subsidiarité: ne transférer à l'organe communautaire que les pouvoirs essentiels. Quid de l'ingérence des organes confédéraux?

ad 3) Organe comp. au Fed. Res. System
(mais avec des caractères européens propres)
Politique budgétaire?
Contrôle parlementaire?

III Description de l'état actuel.
voir document Ansiaux annexe 2, et Stammati annexe 1 (pour les [illegible] budgétaire)

IV. Méthode et approche pour le rythme des étapes.

On 20 May 1970, at the fifth meeting of the Werner Committee to discuss the interim report, Pierre Werner drafts a handwritten note as a basis for securing a compromise between the various representatives. In this document, he summarises the points of agreement between the members of the Werner Committee, highlighting some arguments or avenues in which the work could be taken further, and adds his own proposals. These include the irrevocability of parities between the European currencies, which basically amounts to a single Community currency regime with nuances regarding external monetary policy.

Letter from Jean Monnet to Pierre Werner (Paris, 26 May 1970)

On 26 May 1970, Jean Monnet, President of the Action Committee for the United States of Europe (ACUSE), sends a letter to Pierre Werner, Luxembourg Minister of State, Prime Minister and Minister for Finance, in which he shares his observations concerning the interim report to the Council and the Commission on the achievement by stages of economic and monetary union. © Pierre Werner Family Archives.

COMITÉ D'ACTION
POUR LES
ÉTATS-UNIS D'EUROPE

727 52-36
553 24-64

83, AVENUE FOCH, PARIS XVI

Personnelle.

le 26 mai 1970

Mon cher Président,

Je souhaite revenir sur notre conversation au sujet du rapport de votre Comité. J'en ai pris connaissance et ai discuté avec M. Clappier.

Je vous envoie ces quelques réflexions avant que nous parlions au téléphone mercredi après-midi.

Le rapport de votre Comité montre clairement une différence entre ceux qui veulent commencer une action monétaire de suite et ceux qui veulent reporter cette action monétaire après que l'union économique aurait été réalisée.

Le fait d'indiquer ces divergences profondes est très utile. Mais en même temps, je pense que pour surmonter cette différence il ne faut pas brusquer la discussion.

La suggestion que vous me faisiez l'autre jour de rendre visite au Chancelier Brandt est bonne. Vous devriez aller le voir le plus tôt possible et avoir une conversation avec lui avant le Conseil des Ministres les 8 et 9 juin.

Je pense que le mieux serait d'obtenir alors du Conseil des Ministres de la Communauté un nouveau mandat au Comité que vous présidez. Le Conseil demanderait à votre Comité des études plus complètes de la première étape tendant à préciser :

- les implications économiques et les modalités techniques d'un régime spécifique de change pour les pays de la C.E.E. appuyé sur un Fonds européen de stabilisation des changes ;

- les méthodes par lesquelles des progrès réels pourraient être faits dans la voie de l'harmonisation économique.

De cette manière, le nouveau rapport demandé à votre Comité pourrait concilier les deux points de vue qui s'expriment dans votre rapport préliminaire.

J'ai pleine confiance que vous pourriez ainsi dégager une solution unanime au sein de votre Comité.

Je vous prie de croire à mes meilleurs sentiments.

Jean Monnet

Jean Monnet

Monsieur Pierre WERNER
Ministre d'Etat
Ministre des Finances

LUXEMBOURG

Letter from Willy Brandt to Pierre Werner (Bonn, 1 February 1971)

BUNDESREPUBLIK DEUTSCHLAND
DER BUNDESKANZLER

Bonn, den 1. Februar 1971

Sehr geehrter Herr Ministerpräsident,

wenn ich Ihnen erst heute für Ihr freundliches Schreiben vom 29. Dezember 197o danke, so wollte ich zunächst meine Gespräche in Paris mit Staatspräsident Pompidou abwarten, um Ihnen zugleich zu dem Ihnen wie mir am Herzen liegenden Thema der weiteren Behandlung des Stufenplans etwas Näheres sagen zu können.

Sie haben mit Recht Ihre Wünsche zum Jahreswechsel, die ich herzlich erwidere, in Zusammenhang zu dem europäischen Aufbauwerk gebracht, um dessen Förderung wir uns im nächsten Jahr in gleicher Weise bemühen wollen. Ein sehr wichtiger Teil der Arbeiten des letzten Jahres ist mit Ihrem Namen verbunden und ich möchte diese Gelegenheit ergreifen, um Ihnen noch einmal den Dank der Bundesregierung abzustatten.

Ich betrachte den "Werner-Bericht" nach wie vor als grundlegend und richtungweisend. Das von uns in Den Haag proklamierte Ziel der Wirtschafts- und Währungsunion muß nunmehr in gemeinsame Entschließungen gefaßt werden, die uns die Gewähr dafür geben, daß der Prozeß irreversibel

Seiner Exzellenz
dem Großherzoglich Luxemburgischen
Ministerpräsidenten
Herrn Pierre W e r n e r

L u x e m b u r g

ist und daß die Währungsunion, deren Bedeutung Sie besonders hervorheben, zugleich eine Wirtschaftsunion mit gesicherter Stabilität und zufriedenstellendem Wachstum wird.

Bei unseren Gesprächen in Paris konnten und wollten wir nicht die Einigung zwischen den Mitgliedstaaten der Europäischen Gemeinschaft vorwegnehmen, aber ich hoffe, daß wir doch mitgeholfen haben, diese Einigung zu beschleunigen.

Präsident Pompidou und ich haben den politischen Willen bestätigt, in einem vernünftigen Zeitraum, etwa einem Jahrzehnt, die Union zu verwirklichen. Auf dem Weg zu diesem Ziel wollen wir realistisch und pragmatisch vorgehen. Nachdem wir uns in Brüssel über den Inhalt der ersten etwa dreijährigen Phase weitgehend geeinigt haben, sollte es nunmehr möglich sein, für die weiteren Phasen einige allgemeine Grundsätze aufzustellen. Dazu gehört der in Brüssel bereits anerkannte Grundsatz, daß der Gemeinschaft die zur Kohäsion der Wirtschafts- und Währungsunion und Wirksamkeit ihrer Aktion erforderlichen Befugnisse zugewiesen werden. Ich habe gegenüber meinen französischen Gesprächspartnern zum Ausdruck gebracht, daß die Organe der Gemeinschaft, einschließlich des Europäischen Parlaments, zu diesem Zweck selbstverständlich in die Lage versetzt sein müssen, jeder Zeit die ihnen übertragenen Befugnisse auszuüben; dazu gehört auch, daß die nationalen Zentralbanken in der Perspektive ihrer Zusammenfassung in einer europäischen Zentralbankorganisation einen unmittelbaren Beitrag zu der Realisierung der wirtschafts- und währungspolitischen Ziele der Union erbringen.

- 3 -

Die französische Regierung ist einverstanden, daß während der ersten Etappe der Rat mit Unterstützung der Kommission die zum Eintritt in die nächsten Phasen notwendigen Maßnahmen, sowohl auf wirtschafts- und währungspolitischem Gebiet als auch auf institutionellem Gebiet, untersucht. Dabei schließt die französische Regierung die Möglichkeit von Vertragsänderungen keineswegs aus, ohne daß sie es bisher für notwendig und wünschenswert erachtet, ausdrücklich darauf hinzuweisen, daß für die Maßnahmen, die in den weiteren Stufen nicht auf Grundlage der derzeitigen Vertragsvorschriften durchgeführt werden können, die Verfahren nach Artikel 235 bzw. Artikel 236 durchzuführen wären.

Um deutschen Sorgen wegen eventueller mangelnder Parallelität in den wirtschafts- und währungspolitischen Fortschritten entgegenzukommen, schlug Präsident Pompidou eine Vorbehaltsklausel vor, die es ermöglichen würde, einem Mitgliedstaat den monetären Beistand dann zu entziehen, wenn er nicht bereit sein sollte, einem Verfall seiner Währung durch geeignete Gesundungsmaßnahmen entgegenzuwirken. Dieser Gedanke wird noch im einzelnen zu prüfen sein. Im Laufe der Gespräche wurde von deutscher Seite ferner als zusätzliche Überlegung der Gedanke eingeführt, der Gefahr der Blockierung der Entwicklung zum Ende der ersten Stufe dadurch zu begegnen, daß alle monetären Maßnahmen, Institutionen und Mechanismen der ersten Stufe auf etwa vier Jahre oder etwas mehr begrenzt würden. Läßt sich im Laufe der ersten Stufe nicht die vereinbarte Parallelität zwischen wirtschafts- und währungspolitischen Fortschritten herstellen, so erhielten die Regierungen auf diese Art und Weise eine zusätzliche Spanne, um das Notwendige nachzuholen.

- 4 -

Der bevorstehenden Fortsetzung unserer Beratungen in Brüssel sehe ich vertrauensvoll entgegen. Sie können versichert sein, daß die Bundesregierung das Ihre tun wird, um das Werk, dem Sie soviel Ihrer Kraft gewidmet haben, in die Wirklichkeit umzusetzen.

Mit freundlichen Grüßen

On 1 February 1971, Willy Brandt, Chancellor of the Federal Republic of Germany (FRG), sends a personal letter to Pierre Werner, Luxembourg Prime Minister and Finance Minister, in which he reaffirms his support for the Werner Plan on the achievement by stages of a European economic and monetary union. © Pierre Werner Family Archives.

Appendix B: Chronology

Pierre Werner, Luxembourg and monetary Europe

1913
29 December
Pierre Werner is born in Saint-André, near Lille, France, to Luxembourgish parents.

1935–1938
Pierre Werner completes studies at the Law Faculty of the University of Paris and at the École libre des sciences politiques, Paris.

1937
Pierre Werner becomes vice-president of the 'Pax Romana' movement.

1938
Pierre Werner completes his doctorate in law and joins the Luxembourg Bar.

1944
5 September
The Benelux Customs Convention is signed in London by the governments in exile of Belgium, the Netherlands and Luxembourg.

E. Danescu, *Pierre Werner and Europe*,
Archival Insights into the Evolution of Economics,
https://doi.org/10.1007/978-3-319-96295-5

1938–1944
Pierre Werner is awarded an internship in a bank in Luxembourg, where he is assigned to the executive secretariat until October 1944.

1944–1945
Pierre Werner is recruited to the Ministry of Finance.

1945–1949
Pierre Werner is appointed banking supervisory commissioner and government adviser.

1945
14 April
Luxembourg's Grand Duchess Charlotte returns from exile.

26 June
Luxembourg signs the Charter of the United Nations (UN) in San Francisco.

1947
5 June
The US Secretary of State, George Marshall, gives an address proposing considerable financial aid to all European countries devastated by the war.

1948
17 March
In Brussels, Luxembourg signs the Treaty establishing Western Union (WU).
16 April
In Paris, Luxembourg signs the Convention establishing the Organisation for European Economic Cooperation (OEEC).

1949
4 April
In Washington, Luxembourg signs the North Atlantic Treaty.

5 May
In London, Luxembourg signs the Statute of the Council of Europe.

8 May
Foundation of the Federal Republic of Germany (FRG).

1950
9 May
French Foreign Minister Robert Schuman proposes a common market in coal and steel (the Schuman Plan).

1951
18 April
Belgium, France, Italy, Luxembourg, the Netherlands and the Federal Republic of Germany sign the Treaty of Paris establishing the European Coal and Steel Community (ECSC).

10 August
The ECSC High Authority holds its inaugural session in Luxembourg.

1952
27 May
Luxembourg signs the Treaty establishing the European Defence Community (EDC) in Paris.

25 July
Luxembourg City is chosen as the provisional seat of the ECSC institutions.

8 September
The first meeting of the ECSC Special Council of Ministers is held in Luxembourg.

10 December
The first session of the ECSC Court of Justice is held in Luxembourg.

1953–1959
Pierre Werner becomes Minister for Finance and Minister for the Armed Forces in the government headed by Joseph Bech.

1953
1 May
The first ECSC steel is cast at the Belval plant in Luxembourg.

1954

29 August

The French National Assembly refuses to ratify the Treaty establishing the EDC, sounding the death knell for the European Defence Community.

23 October

In Paris, Luxembourg signs the Treaty establishing Western European Union (WEU).

1957

25 March

Signing of the Treaty of Rome:

- Article 67 lays down that the 'Member States shall progressively abolish between themselves all restrictions on the movement of capital'.
- Article 105 provides for the setting up of a Monetary Committee with advisory status to promote the coordination of monetary policies.
- Article 107 lays down that each Member State shall treat its policy with regard to rates of exchange as a matter of common concern.

1958

27 December

Ten European countries restore the convertibility of their currencies as laid down in Article VIII of the Articles of Agreement of the IMF.

The European Payments Union (EPU) (set up in 1948) is replaced by the European Monetary Agreement (EMA), establishing a special European margin of fluctuation against the US dollar (± 0.75% instead of ± 1%) under the Bretton Woods agreements.

1959–1964

Pierre Werner becomes Minister of State, President of the Government and Minister for Finance.

1960

26 May

Joseph Bech, President of the Luxembourg Chamber of Deputies, receives the International Charlemagne Prize.

1960

21 November

Lecture on 'The meanings of monetary integration' delivered in Strasbourg by Pierre Werner, President of the Government of Luxembourg, Minister for Finance. The main points of his theory—based on the lessons learned from experience of the Benelux ('an economic union without a currency, but harking back to a monetary agreement of 1943') were as follows:

- 'economic cooperation and integration are more directly achieved through the use of the monetary instrument'; 'monetary rapprochement between sovereign countries can only be gradual and concomitant with the rapprochement of economic policies; the adoption of a single currency occurs at the end rather than the beginning of the process of integration';
- 'a common market among sovereign countries presupposes not only a financial order within the community but a financial order on a wider international, continental or global scale'. As for the 'financial area of the Six', it is not enough for it 'to be incorporated into a wider monetary system', but 'their financial policies must be given a more marked Community orientation'.

Werner proposed 'the progressive implementation of a European currency of account' capable of reducing the risks posed by speculative movements of capital associated with currency devaluations and/or revaluations. He believed that 'an accounting currency in the EEC's international relations, by supplying a standard of value unaffected by ups and downs in individual countries, would facilitate the expansion of international trade and encourage further saving'. He suggested that the currency should be called the 'Euror'—a name imbued with meaning—and noted that 'it will be possible to extend the use of this unit (or of another one, to be defined) and it need not necessarily be done by revising the treaties'.

1961

July

The Action Committee for the United States of Europe (ACUSE), chaired by Jean Monnet, calls for the setting up of a European Union of the monetary reserves of the six Member States of the EEC, as the prelude to a common monetary policy and a common European currency.

1962

24 October

Marjolin Report—Commission Memorandum defining monetary union as the third stage of unification. The report suggests that 'there needs to be a single currency, to ensure the success of the Common Market'.

27 November

'Problems with the financial integration of Europe': a talk is given in Brussels by Pierre Werner, President of the Government of Luxembourg and Minister for Finance, to the members of the *Association des amitiés belgo-luxembourgeoises* and the *Cercle royal gaulois*. Werner sets out his ideas on 'the monetary integration of the Six':

- restating his public proposal of 1960 for a European currency of account, 'the start of a European monetary system';
- stressing the need for 'fixed exchange rates' and monetary discipline and solidarity, in the specific institutional framework of a 'Monetary Institute';
- pointing out that 'the method thus recommended would make it possible for monetary integration to follow the same course of development as the tasks of the Community …', as 'economic policies will never be made absolutely uniform; at particular times, it may be necessary to take short-term action in one or other country'.

1964–1967

Pierre Werner becomes Minister of State, President of the Government, Minister for the Treasury, Minister for Justice and Minister for Foreign Affairs.

1964

8 May

EEC Council Decision setting up the Committee of Governors of the Central Banks of the Member States of the EEC.

EEC Council Decision on cooperation between Member States in the field of international monetary relations.

1965

25 February

'The foreign policy of the Grand Duchy of Luxembourg': speech by Pierre Werner, Minister of State, President of the Luxembourg Government, Minister for Foreign Affairs, Minister for the Treasury and Minister for Justice, to the Luxembourg Chamber of Deputies. Referring to relations between the Six, Werner calls for recognition of the need 'to establish as soon as possible the foundations for tighter monetary cooperation' in order to safeguard the Common Market 'from uncoordinated financial and monetary operations'.

8 April

Signing of the Treaty merging the executive bodies of the European Communities. Luxembourg City loses the seat of the ECSC High Authority but is chosen to house the European legal and financial institutions.

1966

17–18 January and 28–29 January

The Luxembourg Compromise:

'[…] where very important interests are at stake the discussion must be continued until unanimous agreement is reached.' Pierre Werner, President-in-Office of the Council during its meetings in Luxembourg, finds a compromise solution to the 'empty chair' crisis.

22 February

France leaves NATO.

5 June
Address on European monetary policy in Brussels by Pierre Werner, President of the Luxembourg Government and Minister for the Treasury, at the invitation of the American and Common Market Club.

1967

26 May
Speech by Pierre Werner, President of the Luxembourg Government and Minister for the Treasury, at the 20th Benelux Economic Congress. Werner reaffirms:

- the idea of setting up a European currency of account which will lead to the strengthening of monetary solidarity among the Member States. Such a currency will, among other things, have the virtue of 'resolving the problem of fixed exchange rates';
- 'the need for solidarity of action in a field which is still dominated by a very strong sense of national identity';
- 'the requirement to tighten up monetary discipline still further between countries so closely associated in the pursuit of their economic objectives as the Common Market countries'.

1968

26 January
'Prospects for European financial and monetary policy': address given in Saarbrücken by Pierre Werner, President of the Luxembourg Government and Minister for the Treasury, to the CDU economic congress. While referring to the prospects for European financial and monetary policy in an increasingly unpredictable international context, Werner puts forward 'a five-point action plan' for European monetary integration based on the creation of a European unit of account, consultation, fixed exchange rates between European currencies, and solidarity—internal and external.

1 April
'Benelux and the prospects for European financial policy': address given in The Hague by Pierre Werner, President of the Luxembourg Government and Minister for the Treasury, to the Benelux Committee.

In his speech, Werner returns to the 'five-point action plan' released at the beginning of the year, the success of which (ensuring stable financial relations between the Member States) would be guaranteed by 'making commitments similar to those made in the Benelux framework' (thereby proving their viability). 'We cannot make alterations to exchange rates except by common agreement.'

May–June
'Reform of the international monetary system'—article by Pierre Werner in *Academia—Nouvelle Revue Luxembourgeoise* 1968, No. 1.

9–10 September
At a meeting of the Ministers for Finance of the EC Member States in Rotterdam, Pierre Werner, President of the Luxembourg Government and Minister for the Treasury, once again sets out his 'five-point action plan', which he defends and discusses in detail in his official speech to his colleagues from the other Member States.

1969
12 February
First Barre Plan (Raymond Barre—Vice President of the Commission of the EC with responsibility for economic affairs). The Commission of the EC submits to the EC Council of Ministers a memorandum on 'appropriate policy in the Community on current economic and monetary problems', recommending an alignment of economic policies and the establishment of the machinery for short-term monetary support (STMS).

5 March
Memorandum from the Commission of the EC to the EC Council of Ministers identifying the need and procedures for action in the field of capital (in the context of a 'common market').

8 November
'European monetary prospects': lecture by Pierre Werner, President of the Luxembourg Government and Minister for the Treasury, to the Belgian Royal Institute for International Relations.

1 and 2 December
The Hague Conference. The Heads of State agree 'to take all necessary steps to achieve economic and monetary integration'. The summit of the 'Six' decides to set up a group of experts to investigate ways of making progress towards economic and monetary union by stages.

1970

2 January
Agreement between the central banks of the Six Member States of the EC on short-term monetary support (STMS).

12 January
The Belgian Plan (the Snoy Plan): at the instigation of Finance Minister Jean-Charles Snoy et d'Oppuers, Belgium puts forward its proposals on ways of making progress towards economic and monetary union by stages.

12 February
The Luxembourg Plan: Luxembourg puts forward its proposals on ways of making progress towards economic and monetary union by stages. The Luxembourg Plan incorporates in full—with a number of updates—the remarks made by Pierre Werner, President of the Government and Minister for the Treasury, in his public statement of January 1968.

23 February
The German Plan (the Schiller Plan): at the instigation of the Minister for Economic Affairs Karl Schiller, Germany puts forward its proposals on ways of making progress towards economic and monetary union by stages.

28 February
'Europe moves towards monetary union': new version of the paper drawn up by Pierre Werner and published as 'Prospects for European financial and monetary policy' in January 1968.

3 March
Pierre Werner takes office as chairman of the 'group of experts responsible for investigating ways of making progress towards economic and monetary union by stages' (the Werner Committee).

Étienne Davignon is instructed to investigate ways of taking more effective concerted action in the field of foreign policy.

4 March
The second Barre Plan. The Commission of the EC submits to the EC Council of Ministers a memorandum putting forward a plan for the establishment of an economic and monetary union in three stages, with a timetable for the period from 1970 to 1978.

20 March
The Werner Committee starts its work in Luxembourg. The group is composed of the President of the Committee of Governors of the Central Banks (Baron Hubert Ansiaux from Belgium), the Chairman of the Anti-Cyclical Policy Committee (Gerard Brouwers of the Netherlands), the Chairman of the Monetary Committee (Bernard Clappier of France), the Director-General of Economic and Financial Affairs of the EEC (Ugo Mosca of Italy), the Chairman of the Medium-Term Economic Policy Committee (Johann-Baptist Schöllhorn from Germany) and the Chairman of the Budgetary Policy Committee (Gaetano Stammati from Italy).

29 May
The Werner Committee publishes its Interim Report. Between 20 March and 29 May 1970, the Werner Committee meets five times.

9 June
The EC Ecofin Council approves the Interim Report and gives the go-ahead for deepening the reflection of the Werner Committee. A final report will be drawn up a few month later.

1 August
Ansiaux Report on the margins of exchange rate fluctuation between European currencies.

28–29 September
The Economic Affairs Committee of the European Parliament (EP) debates the 'Interim Report from the Werner Committee' on the attainment by stages of economic and monetary union (rapporteur Mr Bousch).

8 October
Report on the attainment by stages of economic and monetary union. Official submission of the Werner Report

- The Werner Report gives priority to the coordination of economic policies, the need for common decision-making bodies, the centralising of monetary policy through the establishment of a Committee of Governors of the Central Banks, the reduction of exchange rate variations as a first stage and the establishment of a European fund to support exchange rates. At the end of three stages spread over ten years, the Plan speaks of setting up a common central bank and, possibly, the introduction of a single currency.
- The Werner Report proposes moving by stages over seven to ten years, the order in which the stages are taken being interchangeable depending on the particular economic and financial situation in the participating countries and actual developments in European and international conditions.
- The Werner Report, based on convertibility, fixed parities, convergence and coordination, has similarities of substance with the 'five-point action plan' which Pierre Werner published in 1967 on the basis of his earlier monetary ideas (1960). It should be noted that the final objective set out in the Werner Report, having been put on ice following the world economic crisis of 1973, will come to fruition only 32 years later, with the introduction of euro coins and notes on 1 January 2002.

15 October
The Werner Report is officially delivered to the Commission of the EC and to the EC Council of Ministers.

On 15 October 1970 the *Agence internationale d'information pour la presse* mentions that '*in circles close to the Commission, no judgment is being expressed as to the substance, since responsibility for the document lies with the Werner Committee, which drew it up. It is felt, however, that a number of somewhat unenthusiastic, not to say negative, reactions that have been heard in this or that capital with regard to different aspects — a fear of over-hasty institutionalization, doubts as to the effectiveness of coordinating economic policies or the advisability of reducing exchange rate fluctuations — are due to partial familiarity with the document. Only in the next few days, when the content of the document is known in detail, will it be possible to gauge its importance and only then will the political options stand out more clearly.'*

17 October
The EC's Medium-Term Economic Policy Committee meeting in Brussels, with Walter Schölhorn in the chair, adopts the preliminary draft of the EEC's third medium-term economic policy programme, covering the period 1971–75. This programme is closely linked to the Werner Report, it being now agreed that the 'plan by stages' must be based on comprehensive quantitative guidelines which are valid for the whole of the Community and relate to the main features of economic development.

22–23 October
The Economic Affairs Committee of the EP adopts a draft report on the 'Interim Report from the Werner Committee' concerning the attainment by stages of economic and monetary union.

26 October
The Werner Report is presented during the Council of Foreign Affairs Ministers of the EC held in Luxembourg. Pierre Werner, chairman of the Werner Committee and also host of the Council meeting, makes an explanatory statement.

28 October
The EC Council discusses the Werner Report.

30 October
On the basis of the Werner Report, the Commission of the EC makes a Communication and proposals on the stage-by-stage implementation of economic and monetary union.

11 November
Lecture-cum-debate on the Werner Report at the EP, for the heads of Christian Democratic party groups, with Pierre Werner as guest.

18 November
Part-session of the EP—Exchange of views between the EP, the EC Council and the Commission of the EC on economic union and the prospects for a monetary union in the Community—stage-by-stage implementation of the economic and monetary union of the Community (debate on the Werner Report).

23–24 November
The Economic Affairs Committee of the EP adopts a draft supplementary report on the Werner Report (rapporteur Mr Bousch).

3 December
Part-session of the EP—Debate on the attainment by stages of the economic and monetary union of the Community (the Werner Report). Adoption, by unanimous vote, of the draft resolution on the Werner Report tabled by the Economic Affairs Committee.

14 December
The European Council approves the Werner Report.

1971
March
In recognition of his long-standing commitment to the European cause, particularly alongside Jean Monnet as a member of the Action Committee for the United States of Europe, Pierre Werner receives the Robert Schuman Gold Medal from the European Parliament.

22 March
Resolution of the EC Council and of the Representatives of the Governments of the Member States on the stage-by-stage implementation of economic and monetary union.
The Council adopts three decisions:

- Medium-term financial assistance (MTFA);
- Strengthening of the coordination of short-term economic policies;
- Strengthening of cooperation between the central banks.

15 August
Following the unilateral decision of the United States President Richard Nixon ending the US dollar's convertibility into gold, the fixed exchange rate system set up at Bretton Woods comes to an end. Currencies are left to float.

1972

21 March
Resolution of the EC Council and of the Representatives of the Governments of the Member States laying down the outlines for a European exchange system, the future 'monetary snake', with margins of fluctuation of ± 2.25% (as against the US dollar).

10 April
Basel Agreement between the central banks of the Member States of the Common Market (Banque de France, Deutsche Bundesbank, Banca d'Italia, Nederlandsche Bank, Banque Nationale de Belgique) and the candidate countries (Bank of England, Central Bank of Ireland, Norges Bank and Danmarks Nationalbank) stipulating that the spread between the exchange rates for any two EEC currencies at a given time must not exceed 2.25%, or half the authorised margin between any one of these currencies and the dollar (4.5%, 'the tunnel').This is the 'snake' in the 'tunnel'. This margin-shrinking mechanism enters into force on 24 April 1972.

23 June
The pound sterling leaves the 'monetary snake'.

12 September
EC Council Decision on the 'multilateralization of positions and regulations resulting from operations, consultation between central banks, very short-term financing (VSTF)'.

19–21 October
Paris Summit of the Heads of State of the (enlarged) Community concerning progress on a monetary Europe and providing for the creation

of the European Monetary Cooperation Fund (EMCF), as stipulated by the Werner Report.

1973

1 January
Denmark, the United Kingdom and Ireland join the EC.

12 March
The joint floating of six EC Member State currencies (Germany, France, Denmark and the Benelux countries) is confirmed. This is the 'snake in the tunnel', no longer supported by the US dollar.

14 March
Norway and Sweden join the 'monetary snake'.

3 April
EC Council Regulation setting up a European Monetary Cooperation Fund (EMCF), which begins operating on 1 June 1973.

1974

19 January
The French franc leaves the 'snake'. It will join it again from 10 July 1975 to 15 March 1976.

1974–1979

The Christian Social People's Party (CSV) leaves the Luxembourg Government and Pierre Werner, elected to the Chamber of Deputies, becomes leader of the parliamentary opposition.

1975

17 February
EC Council Regulation setting up loans.

21 April
EC Council Decision on the European unit of account (EUA) creating a basket of currencies on the basis of 'quantities' (applied to the EMCF by the EC Council Regulation of 18 December 1978).

16 September
Gaston Thorn, Minister of State and President of the Luxembourg Government, is elected President of the United Nations General Assembly.

1976
March
Belgium and the Netherlands give up the special 1.5% margin of fluctuation for their currencies (dating back to 1971).

June
Alongside Jacques Santer, leader of the CSV, Pierre Werner is involved in the creation of the European People's Party (EPP) in Luxembourg.

1–2 April
First European Council under the Luxembourg Presidency. The President-in-Office is Gaston Thorn, Minister of State and President of the Government.

1977
17–18 June
'Exploring the conditions for relaunching economic and monetary union in the European Economic Community': report by Pierre Werner, Honorary President of the Luxembourg Government, to the symposium on 'Economic union and the problem of the European currency' organised in Rome by the Union of European Federalists.

27 October
'Europe's Present Challenge and Future Opportunity—Jean Monnet Lecture'. Speech by Roy Jenkins, President of the European Commission, delivered at the European Studies Institute in Florence and regarded as 'relaunching a monetary Europe'.

17 November
Communication of the Commission of the EC to the Council on the prospect of economic and monetary union.

1978

7–8 April
Copenhagen European Council: the nine EC Member States reach agreement in principle on establishing a monetary stability zone in Europe.

6–7 July
Bremen European Council: agreement on the main lines of a European monetary system. Valéry Giscard d'Estaing (France) and Helmut Schmidt (Germany) propose setting up the monetary system to replace the 'monetary snake'.

5 December
Resolution of the European Council (known as the 'Brussels Resolution') setting up the European Monetary System (EMS) and creating the European Currency Unit (the official ECU). Parity: 1 official ECU = 1 EUA. It is decided that the European Monetary System (EMS) will enter into force on 13 March 1979.

1979–1984

Pierre Werner becomes Minister of State, President of the Government, Minister for the Treasury and Minister for Cultural Affairs.

1979

January
Pierre Werner masterminds the EPP's economic and social platform for the first elections to the European Parliament by direct universal suffrage.

12 March
Paris European Council: EMS scheduled to enter into force on 13 March 1979.

13 March
Agreement between the EC central banks on the operating procedures of the EMS (± 2.25% for all currencies, except the Italian lira at ± 6%). The object of launching the EMS is to stop the EC Member States having to resort to using the exchange rate weapon against their European

competitors. As soon as a currency approaches the limit set by the 2.25% margin, the government concerned has to intervene on the money market to bring the exchange rate for its currency back within the fixed margins.
The EMS also gives birth to the ECU (the European Currency Unit), a unit of account which serves as a reference point for the national currencies.

15 March
Luxembourg adopts a law which, for the first time, coherently defines the country's own particular monetary status. The law is a response to the demands for national legislation on Luxembourg's monetary status to be revised; this had become necessary following the international currency upheavals caused by the collapse of the Bretton Woods system.

31 March
Luxembourg adopts a Grand-Ducal Regulation laying down, in Article 1, that 'the exchange rate between the Luxembourg franc and the Belgian franc shall be one to one'.

24 September
The Deutschmark is revalued by 2% and the Danish krone is devalued by 2.85%.

30 November
The Danish krone is devalued by 4.76%.

1980
21 November
Gaston Thorn is appointed President of the Commission of the European Communities.

1–2 December
Second European Council under the Luxembourg Presidency. The President-in-Office is Pierre Werner, Minister of State and President of the Government.

9 December
Strasbourg European Council decides that the move to the institutional phase of the EMS will be carried out 'in due course'.

1981

1 January
Greece becomes a member of the EEC.

January
Creation of the private ecu on the money markets. Parity: 1 ecu = 1 ECU.
The European Investment Bank (EIB) launch the first bonds denominated in ecus.

22 March
The Italian lira is devalued by 6%.

4 October
The Deutschmark and the Dutch guilder are revalued by 5.5%. The French franc and the Italian lira are devalued by 3%.

1982

21 February
The Belgian franc and the Luxembourg franc are devalued by 8.5%. The Danish krone is devalued by 3%.

22 February
Luxembourg: The Belgian Government's decision to devalue the Belgian franc unilaterally seriously shakes Luxembourg's leaders. Pierre Werner, President of the Government of Luxembourg, sees the decision as 'an infringement of the principle of co-decision enshrined in the Belgo-Luxembourgish monetary protocols'.

12 June
The Deutschmark and the Dutch guilder are revalued by 4.25%. The French franc is devalued by 5.75%. The Italian lira is devalued by 2.75%.

1983

21 March
Parities within the EMS are adjusted: the Deutschmark is revalued by 5.5%, the Dutch guilder is revalued by 3.5%, the Danish krone is revalued by 2.5%, the Belgian franc and Luxembourg franc are revalued by 1.5%, the French franc and the Italian lira are devalued by 2.5% and

the Irish pound is devalued by 3.5%. France decides not to leave the system.

20 May
Luxembourg: creation of the Luxembourg Monetary Institute (LMI)—the embryo of the future Luxembourg central bank—responsible, among other things, for issuing banknotes and coins and supervising the financial sector. With the LMI, Luxembourg was able to assert its monetary identity, but, most of all, to be on an equal footing with the other states in the EMS. Although it was not yet an independent central bank in the strict sense, the LMI had all the powers it needed to discharge all the functions of a central bank in the event that Luxembourg's leaders decided to end the monetary union with Belgium.

1 June
Luxembourg: the LMI starts operating.

1984
24 February
The Luxembourg language law (*Loi sur le régime des langues*) is adopted.

July
Pierre Werner withdraws from political life. Jacques Santer succeeds him as Minister of State and President of the Government.

15 September
Five-yearly review of the weights of currencies in the ecu.

17 September
The Greek drachma joins the ecu.

1985–1987
After withdrawing from politics, Pierre Werner becomes Chairman of the Board of the Compagnie luxembourgeoise de télédiffusion (CLT).

1985
1 January
Jacques Delors (France) is appointed President of the Commission of the EC, succeeding Gaston Thorn (Luxembourg).

1 February
Greenland leaves the EC but retains associated status with it as an 'overseas territory'.

12 March
Palermo: amendments to the agreement of 13 March 1979, strengthening the status of the ecu (mobilisation, acceptance, remuneration, multiple holding).

10 June
Greece signs up to the agreement on the EMS.

14 June
In the Luxembourg town of Schengen, France, the Federal Republic of Germany and the Benelux countries sign the Schengen Agreement on the free movement of persons.

28–29 June
Milan European Council. The Heads of State or Government decide by qualified majority to convene an intergovernmental conference to reform the Rome Treaties (the 'Genscher-Colombo plan').

20 July
The ministers and the governors of the central banks of the EC Member States decide to modify the central rates within the EMS.

22 July
The Deutschmark, the French franc, the Dutch guilder, the Danish krone, the Belgian franc, the Luxembourg franc and the Irish pound are revalued by 2%; the Italian lira is devalued by 6%.

2–3 December
Third European Council under the Luxembourg Presidency. The President-in-Office is Jacques Santer, Minister of State, President of the Government and Minister for Finance.

1986

1 January
Spain and Portugal join the EC.

17 and 28 February
Conference of the Representatives of the Governments of the EC Member States—Decision to draw up a Single European Act. Signed in Luxembourg on 17 February and The Hague on 28 February 1986, the Single European Act inserts into the Treaty of Rome a reference to the experience acquired within the framework of the EMS, organising the 'monetary capacity' of Europe (Article 102A) and providing for the free movement of capital.

6 April
The Deutschmark is revalued by 3% and the Belgian franc, the Luxembourg franc and the Danish krone by 1%, and the French franc is devalued by 3%.

8 May
The International Charlemagne Prize is awarded to the people of Luxembourg, represented by HRH Grand Duke Jean, in recognition of their efforts for European unity.

2 August
The Irish pound is devalued by 8%.

17 November
Capital movements: the EC Council adopts a directive, amending that of 11 May 1960, imposing additional obligations on the EC in respect of capital movements.

1987

12 January
The Deutschmark and Dutch guilder are revalued by 3% and the Belgian franc and Luxembourg franc by 2%.

12 May
Spain joins the EMS.

1 July
The Single European Act enters into force.

12 September
The 'Basel-Nyborg' agreement: approval by the informal EC Ecofin Council of measures decided on in Basel by the central bank governors

and amending the agreement of 13 March 1979 (setting up of a supervision procedure and broadening of the very short-term financing mechanism to the advantage of intra-marginal interventions).

1988

8 January
France (the French Minister for Finance Edouard Balladur) submits a memorandum on 'European monetary integration' to the EC Ecofin Council.

20 January
Germany (the German Foreign Minister Hans-Dietrich Genscher) argues before the EP for the 'creation of a monetary union and of a European central bank'.

23 February
Italy (the Minister for the Treasury Giuliano Amato) backs 'the idea of a single currency'.

24 June
The EC Council Directive for the implementation of Article 67 of the Treaty of Rome for the deregulation of capital movements on 1 July 1990.

24 June

- Consolidation of medium-term financial assistance (MTFA) and Community loans in a single arrangement denominated 'medium-term financial support' (MTFS).
- Complete liberalisation of capital movements: the EC Council Directive for the implementation of Article 67 of the Treaty of Rome for the deregulation of capital movements on 1 July 1990.

28 June
Hanover European Council, following a proposal from Germany, mandates a committee of independent experts chaired by Jacques Delors with 'the task of studying and proposing concrete stages leading towards economic and monetary union' (the Delors Committee).

1989

12 April

The Delors Committee submits its report on Economic and Monetary Union (EMU).

Taking its lead largely from the Werner Plan, the Delors Report proposes attaining EMU in three stages, though without setting a calendar.

- The first stage will be devoted to strengthening economic and monetary cooperation and getting the currencies of all the Member States to take part in the EMS.
- The second stage will involve harmonising monetary policies and setting up a European central bank.
- The third stage fixes the exchange rates between the currencies irrevocably and brings in a single currency, the ecu, to take the place of the national currencies.

19–21 May

Informal EC Ecofin Council of S'Agaro: discussion and approval of the report from the Delors Committee for the study of EMU.

19 June

The peseta joins the EMS exchange rate mechanism (margin: 6%).

26–27 June

Madrid European Council: the Council approves the Delors Committee's report and decides to set the first stage in motion as from 1 July 1990. The final communiqué refers to the need to keep a balance between the social aspects and the economic aspects of the building of the Single Market.

17 July

Enlargement: the Republic of Austria applies to join the European Communities.

21 September

The peseta and the escudo are included in the ecu.

9–10 November
Fall of the Berlin Wall. Opening of the border between the Federal Republic of Germany (FRG) and the German Democratic Republic (GDR).

9 December
Strasbourg European Council:

- Convening of the intergovernmental conference on EMU for the end of 1990.
- The Heads of State or Government of the Member States adopt the Community Charter of the Fundamental Social Rights of Workers.

1990
5 January
The Italian lira is devalued by 4% and its margin of fluctuation within the EMS is reduced from 6 to 2.25%.

12 March
It is decided to assign extra functions to the Committee of Governors of the Central Banks of the EC Members States.

19 June
In the Luxembourg town of Schengen, France, the Federal Republic of Germany and the Benelux countries sign the Schengen Convention implementing the Schengen Agreement on the free movement of persons.

25–26 June
The Dublin European Council decides to hold two intergovernmental conferences (IGCs) in December 1990, one on EMU and the other on political union.

29 June
The EC Council lays down guidelines for the negotiation of an agreement with the EFTA countries with a view to the establishment of a European Economic Area (EEA).

1 July
Start of the first stage of EMU. The Capital Movements Directive enters into force. Monetary unification between the Federal Republic of Germany (FRG) and the German Democratic Republic (GDR) takes effect.

4 July
Enlargement: the Republic of Cyprus applies to join the European Communities.

16 July
Enlargement: the Republic of Malta applies to join the European Communities.

21 August
The Commission of the EC publishes its draft treaty on EMU.

17 September
German reunification: the EC Council adopts the provisional measures provided for in the framework of German reunification.

3 October
German reunification: the German Democratic Republic (GDR) and the Federal Republic of Germany (FRG) form the reunited nation of Germany. Berlin is reunited into a single city.

6 October
The pound sterling joins the EMS exchange rate mechanism (margin: 6%).

22 October
Norway pegs its currency to the ecu with a margin of fluctuation of $\pm$ 2.25%.

28 October
Rome European Council: 11 Member States announce that the second stage of EMU should start on 1 January 1994 and that a decision on moving on to the third stage should be taken before 1997. The UK rejects the very principle of a single currency.

15 December
Opening of the IGC on EMU.

1991

13 March

The Commission of the EC adopts the Community support frameworks for structural investment in the five new German Länder and East Berlin.

8 April

Informal European Council under the Luxembourg Presidency. The President-in-Office is Jacques Santer, Minister of State, Prime Minister and Minister for Finance.

9 April

Statement of principles regarding agreement prior to interventions in EC currencies.

17 May

Sweden pegs its currency to the ecu with a margin of fluctuation of ± 1.5%.

7 June

Finland pegs its currency to the ecu with a margin of fluctuation of ± 3%.

18 June

Draft Treaty on European Union presented by the Luxembourg Presidency.

28–29 June

Fifth European Council under the Luxembourg Presidency. The President-in-Office is Jacques Santer, Minister of State, Prime Minister and Minister for Finance.

1 July

Enlargement: Sweden applies to join the EC.

9–10 December

The treaty providing for the introduction of EMU is adopted by the Heads of State or Government at the European Council meeting in Maastricht. The 'Maastricht Treaty' makes the move towards a single currency irreversible. The UK and Denmark secure the right not to take part in the single currency (the opt-out clause).

1992

7 February
Signing of the Treaty on European Union (TEU) in Maastricht.

11 February
The Commission of the EC adopts proposals relating to the second package of structural and financial measures (Delors II Package).

18 March
Enlargement: Finland applies to join the EC.

6 April
The escudo joins the EMS exchange rate mechanism with a margin of fluctuation of 6% (decision of 4 April).

2 May
Signing of the Agreement establishing the EEA.

20 May
Enlargement: Switzerland applies to join the EC.

2 June
First Danish referendum on ratification of the TEU, rejected by 50.7%.

19 June
The Cyprus pound is pegged to the ecu with margins of fluctuation of ± 2.25%.

2 July
The Luxembourg Parliament ratifies the TEU.

8 September
The Bank of Finland removes the limits on fluctuation of the markka and allows its currency to float.

14 September
The Italian lira is devalued by 7%.

17 September
The peseta is devalued by 5%, the pound sterling and Italian lira leave the EMS exchange rate system.

20 September
Referendum in France on ratification of the Maastricht Treaty: approved by 51.05%.

19 November
Sweden unpegs the krona from the ecu and allows its currency to float.

23 November
The peseta and escudo are devalued by 6%.

25 November
Norway officially applies to join the EC.

6 December
By referendum, the Swiss decide against ratification of the agreement relating to the EEA.

10 December
Norway unpegs the krone from the ecu.

11–12 December
The Edinburgh European Council:

- approves the 'Delors II Package';
- sets 1 January 1993 as the date for the opening of accession negotiations with Austria, Sweden and Finland;
- allows Denmark derogations which enable it to put the TEU to referendum again.

1993

1 January
Entry into force of all the legislation required for the completion of the single market.

31 January
The Irish pound is devalued by 10%.

1 February
Opening of accession negotiations with Austria, Sweden and Finland.

5 April
In Luxembourg, opening of accession negotiations with Norway.

13 May
The peseta is devalued by 8% and the escudo by 6.5%.

18 May
Second Danish referendum on ratifying the TEU including the special status for Denmark (56.8% vote in favour).

21–22 June
Copenhagen European Council:

- Fixing of the criteria for accession to the European Union (EU) (the 'Copenhagen criteria');
- The Commission of the EC is instructed to draw up a white paper on a long-term strategy to promote competitiveness and employment;
- The EIB is asked to increase by 3 billion ecu the temporary loan mechanism decided upon by the Edinburgh Council;
- The EC Council confirms that Austria, Finland, Norway and Sweden will join the European Community as from 1 January 1995; and
- Countries of Central and Eastern Europe that wish to join the European Community will have to meet the accession criteria.

2 August
The margins of fluctuation are widened to 15% either way. The ministers and governors of central banks of the EC Member States reaffirm the validity of the current central parities.

29 October
The Brussels European Council:

- Adoption of a declaration on the entry into force of the TEU;
- The Council again states that the second stage of EMU will enter into force as from 1 January 1994.
- It is decided that the seat of the EMI, and therefore of the future ECB, will be Frankfurt.

1 November
The TEU, signed in Maastricht on 7 February 1992, enters into force and the composition of the ecu is frozen.
The Council of the EU adopts the first set of decisions and regulations on the secondary legislation required for the second stage of EMU.

5 December
The European Commission adopts the White Paper on 'Growth, Competitiveness, Employment: The Challenges and Ways Forward into the 21st Century'.

1994

1 January
Entry into force of the second stage of EMU. Establishment of the EMI in Frankfurt with the task of setting up the future ECB. The EMI takes over from the EMCF.

30 March
Conclusion of accession negotiations with Austria, Finland, Norway and Sweden.

1 April
Hungary applies to join the EU.

7 April
The European Commission sets up a think tank on the implementation of the single currency, consisting of private-sector experts and consumers' representatives (the 'Maas Group').

8 April
Poland applies to join the EU.

12 June
66.6% of Austrians vote in favour in a referendum on accession to the EC.

15 July
Jacques Santer, President of the Government of Luxembourg, is appointed President of the European Commission at an extraordinary meeting of the Council in Brussels.

18 July
Free-trade agreements are signed with Estonia, Latvia and Lithuania.

13 November
52.2% of Swedes vote in favour in a referendum on accession to the EU.

29 November
52.4% of Norwegians vote 'No' in a referendum on accession to the EU.

9–10 December
The Essen European Council approves the strategy of rapprochement with the countries of post-communist Central Europe.

1995

1 January
Austria, Finland and Sweden join the EU and the EMS. The act of accession of the three countries was signed in Corfu on 24 June 1994. Norway, which also signed, did not ultimately ratify the agreement.

9 January
The Austrian schilling joins the exchange rate mechanism (ERM).

20 January
Jean-Claude Juncker is appointed as Prime Minister and Minister of State, succeeding Jacques Santer, who becomes President of the European Commission.

23 January
Following a vote of approval by the EP on 18 January, the representatives of the governments of the Member States of the EU appoint President Jacques Santer and the new Members of the European Commission for the period from 1995 to 2000.

6 March
The peseta is devalued by 7% and the escudo by 3.5%.

10 May
Publication of the Maas Report on preparations for the introduction of the single currency.

18 May
The European Commission submits to the German Government its draft Green Paper on the scenario for the move to a single currency.

31 May
The European Commission adopts the Green Paper on the single currency, containing the proposals on the scenario for the move to the single currency and the legal framework for it, and on the communication policy to be pursued.

29–30 September
Informal Ecofin Council in Valencia. The Finance Ministers of the Fifteen:

- reiterate their agreement on the calendar and the criteria for the introduction of the single currency;
- agree to the principle of the stability pact and the Commission's scenario for the changeover;
- decide to drop the name 'ECU' for the single currency.

1 November
The EMI releases its report on the 'changeover to the single currency'.

15–16 December
Madrid European Council fixes the scenario for the practical steps and sets 1 January 1999 as the date for the changeover to Monetary Union. The Council adopts 'euro' as the name for the European single currency.

1996

13 April

Informal Ecofin Council in Verona: a clear majority of countries want an agreement on exchange rates between the countries in and out of the system. The principle of a 'stability pact' is accepted. The name 'cent' is given to the hundredth part of a euro.

21–22 June

Florence European Council: the broad outlines of the new exchange rate mechanism will be set by a European Council resolution; the operational procedures will be defined once the ECB has been set up in 1998.

21–22 September

Informal EU Ecofin Council in Dublin: agreement on the procedure for adoption of the legal framework for the introduction of the euro.

13 October

The Finnish markka joins the ERM.

24 November

The Italian lira rejoins the ERM.

13–14 December

Dublin European Council.

- Adoption of the legal status of the euro, the agreements on ERM II (a new European exchange rate mechanism) and the 'Stability and Growth Pact' (SGP). The euro will replace the ECU 1 to 1.
- Adoption of the agreement on the appointment of Wim Duisenberg (Netherlands) to head the EMI (though without prejudice to his appointment to head the ECB).
- Presentation by the EMI of the full range of banknotes in euros (Robert Kalina of Austria is the prizewinner in the competition to design the euro notes).

1997

7 January

The EMI publishes the report on the regulatory, organisational and logistical framework for the single monetary policy in stage III.

6 April
Informal Ecofin Council in Noordwijk. Agreement on the technical procedures for the 'Stability and Growth Pact' and on ERM II. The calendar for the selection of the countries to adopt the euro on 1 January 1999 is clarified.

8–9 June
Ecofin Council in Luxembourg. France expresses reservations regarding the signing of the SGP in its present state and asks for strengthening of the 'economic focus'.

16–17 June
Amsterdam European Council. Final adoption of the resolution on ERM II, the regulatory process for the SGP (France finally comes round to the Commission's proposals), and the regulation containing the most urgent provisions regarding the legal status of the euro. The design for the shared side of the euro coins is approved. A resolution on 'growth and employment' is adopted.

12–13 September
Informal Ecofin Council in Mondorf (Luxembourg). The irrevocable bilateral exchange rates of the currencies in the system will be announced in spring 1998. A start is also made on drawing up a code of good conduct in fiscal matters and on the coordination of economic policies.

2 October
Signing of the Amsterdam Treaty.

27 October
The British Chancellor of the Exchequer, Gordon Brown, officially announces that the UK will not take part in monetary union on 1 January 1999 and will therefore invoke the opt-out clause in the Maastricht Treaty. He also says that 'it is essential that the Government and business prepare intensively during this Parliament, so that Britain will be in a position to join a single currency, should we wish to, early in the next Parliament.'

20–21 November
Extraordinary European Council under the Luxembourg Presidency. The President-in-Office is Jean-Claude Juncker, Minister of State, Prime Minister and Finance Minister.

13–14 December
Seventh European Council under the Luxembourg Presidency. The President-in-Office is Jean-Claude Juncker, Minister of State, Prime Minister and Finance Minister.

13–14 December
Luxembourg European Council. Euro notes and coins will be introduced on 1 January 2002. Council adopts a resolution on the coordination of economic policies (establishment of informal meetings of Finance Ministers of the countries in the system) and on Articles 109 (exchange rate policy) and 109B (dialogue between Council and ECB).

1998
February
Eleven of the fifteen EC countries declare that they are willing and able to adopt the single currency. Greece does not meet the criteria, the UK and Denmark do not wish to join the single currency process and Sweden defers its decision on the question.

16 March
The Greek drachma joins the European ERM and the Irish pound is revalued by 3%.

25 March
Publication of reports on convergence by the EMI and the Commission. The countries concerned are the Fifteen minus the UK, Denmark, Sweden and Greece.

1–3 May
Brussels Council (known as the 'Jumbo Council').
1 May: Ecofin Council recommendation regarding the list of countries joining monetary union on 1 January 1999.

1 May: Opinion of the EP.
2 May: European Council Decision on the list of countries: beginning of the 'intermediate period'.
3 May: advance notice of the bilateral parities of the currencies in the system; Council recommendation on the appointment of the members of the ECB board.

26 May
Appointment of the members of the ECB board by the European Council.

1 June
Inauguration of the ECB and the European System of Central Banks (ESCB). The EMI thereby ceases to exist.

1 June
Creation of the Central Bank of Luxembourg (at the same time as the ECB).

15–16 June
Cardiff European Council. First review of the national action plans for employment.

26 September
Informal Ecofin Council in Vienna. Advance notice of participation by Greece and Denmark in ERM II and of the margins of fluctuation for their currencies (15% and 2.25% respectively); report to the Council on the external representation of monetary union.

8 October
Prince Felipe of Spain presents Pierre Werner and Jacques Santer with the Prince of Asturias Award, 'for [their contribution] to the process of European monetary integration that has culminated in the creation of the euro'.

1 December
Joint communiqué of the Council and the European Commission fixing the procedure for adoption of the conversion rates for the euro.

22 December
The ECB Council announces the interest rate for the first refinancing operation in euros, on 4 January (3%).

31 December
The Council of the EU adopts the irrevocable conversion rates of the currencies in the system in euros, as proposed by the European Commission after consulting the ECB and the EP. The central rates in euros for the Greek drachma and the Danish krone are adopted.

31 December 1998–3 January 1999
Weekend changeover to the euro in the financial sector (money markets, payment systems).

1999

1 January
The third stage of EMU enters into force with the establishment of monetary union and the creation of the euro (which becomes the currency of the countries participating in monetary union, with the national currency units becoming subdivisions of the euro). The single monetary policy is defined and put into effect by the ESCB, and new government securities are issued in euros.

26 February
Luxembourg signs the Treaty of Nice.

3–4 June
Cologne European Council: 'macroeconomic dialogue' is set up, involving, among others, the representatives of the Council of the EU, the European Commission, the ECB and the social partners, and encouraging economic policy coordination with a view to ensuring sustainable, non-inflationary growth.

Every two years from 1 January 1999 (or on the initiative of a country which is not yet a member of the monetary union), the competent EU authorities are to consider the position of countries which are not yet members of monetary union in the light of the convergence criteria (apart from the UK and Denmark, which are not taking part in stage 3 of EMU).

2000

17 January
Greek drachma revalued by 3.5% under ERM II.

23–24 March
Extraordinary European Council in Lisbon. Overall strategy for the transition to a knowledge-based society and economy. Implementation (by 2005) of the action plan for financial services. Adoption of the objective of bringing the employment rate to 70% by 2010.

May
Publication of the convergence reports for 2000 by the ECB and the European Commission.

8 May
Statement by the Eurogroup on the level of the euro, which does not reflect the economic fundamentals in the euro zone.

19–20 June
Feira European Council. Approval of the report on the 'tax package' (comprehensive report requested for the end of 2002).

22 September
G7 Decision. 'At the initiative of the ECB, the monetary authorities of the US, Japan, UK and Canada joined with the ECB on Friday, September 22, in concerted intervention in exchange markets, because of the shared concern of Finance Ministers and Governors about the potential implications of recent movements in the euro for the world economy.'

28 September
A referendum in Denmark on accession to monetary union is rejected by 53.1% of the population.

2001

1 January
Greece joins monetary union.

26 February
Signing of the Nice Treaty on the reform of the institutions with a view to enlargement (size and membership of the European Commission, weighting of voting rights in the Council of the EU, extension of qualified majority voting, relaxation of the procedures for recourse to enhanced cooperation, the 'enabling clause' for revising the voting rules in the Governing Council of the ECB).

8 June
Ireland refuses to ratify the Nice Treaty (53.87% vote against in a referendum).

1 September
Beginning of the phase involving frontloading of credit establishments in the euro zone with euro notes and coins (actual date depends on the country).

5 December
Laeken Declaration on the future of the EU—The Convention on the Future of Europe is launched, with Valéry Giscard d'Estaing (France) chosen to chair its work, which is to culminate in a draft Constitution for Europe.

2002
1 January
Euro notes and coins are introduced in the monetary union countries. All book payments have to be denominated in euros.

1 January
Luxembourg—Pursuant to the Grand-Ducal Order, the Netherlands Mint strikes—for use in Luxembourg—120 million euro coins, worth a total of more than 40 million euros, with the Luxembourg national side. The Luxembourg coins bear the effigy of Grand Duke Henri (born on 16 April 1955 and sworn in on 7 October 2000), using a design by the artist Yvette Gastauer-Claire in a classical style (on the 1-, 2-, and 5-cent coins), a traditional line-drawn style (on the 10-, 20-, and 50-cent coins) and a modern abstract style (on the 1- and 2-euro coins).

28 February
The withdrawal from circulation of notes and coins in national currency units in the countries belonging to monetary union ends. The Convention on the Future of Europe holds its inaugural session.

May
The convergence reports by the ECB and the European Commission are published (on 1 May and 22 May, respectively).

24 June
Pierre Werner dies in Luxembourg at the age of 88.

24 September
The European Commission postpones from 2004 to 2006 the established date for all the EU Member States to present 'budgets close to balance'.

October
Four countries in the EMU are in difficulties: Germany, France, Italy and Portugal. Only France refuses to agree, without reservations or any special conditions, to cut its structural deficit by at least 0.5% per year from 2003.

19 October
Ireland ratifies the Nice Treaty by referendum (making it the last country to ratify the Treaty).

24–25 October
Brussels European Council: the ten applicant countries chosen to join the EU in 2004 are Cyprus, the Czech Republic, Estonia, Hungary, Latvia, Lithuania, Malta, Poland, Slovakia and Slovenia.

19 November
As the commitments under the SGP have been infringed, the European Commission refers the matter to the EU Ecofin Council and launches:

- the 'early warning' disciplinary procedure against France;
- the 'excessive deficit procedure' against Germany.

27 November
Proposals from the European Commission designed to improve understanding of the SGP (for example, isolating the impact of the short-term economic situation on the budgetary position) and result in more effective implementation (particularly through a restatement of the political commitment to implement the pact).

13 December
Copenhagen European Council: accession negotiations with the ten applicant countries are concluded.

Appendix C: Index of Key Figures

Abs, Hermann (1901–1994): German banker. Chairman of Deutsche Bank (1957–1967).

Adenauer, Konrad (1876–1967): German statesman, Christian Democrat. Mayor of Cologne (1917–1933); Chairman of the CDU in the British zone (1946–1950); Chairman of the CDU (1950–1966); Chairman of the Parliamentary Council (1948–1949); Foreign Minister (1951–1957); Member of the Bundestag (1949–1967); first Chancellor of the Federal Republic of Germany (1949–1963).

Ansiaux (Baron), Hubert (1908–1987): Governor of the National Bank of Belgium (1957–1971); Chairman of the Committee of Governors of the Central Banks of the EEC (1967–1971); member of the Werner Committee (1970).

Barber, Anthony (1920–2005): British politician. Chancellor of the Exchequer (1970–1974).

Baffi, Paolo (1911–1989): Italian academic and banker. Employee then Head of Research at the Banca d'Italia (1938–1960); Director-General (1960–1975); Governor of the Banca d'Italia (1975–1979); Vice-Chairman of the Board of Directors of the Bank for International Settlements (BIS) (1988–1989); member of the Accademia dei Lincei.

E. Danescu, *Pierre Werner and Europe*,
Archival Insights into the Evolution of Economics,
https://doi.org/10.1007/978-3-319-96295-5

Barre, Raymond (1924–2007): Professor of Law and Economics. French politician. Vice-President of the European Commission with responsibility for Economics and Finance (1967–1973); Minister for External Trade (1976); Prime Minister of the French Republic (1976–1978, 1978–1981); UDF Member of the National Assembly for the Rhône (1978–2002); member of the Academy of Moral and Political Sciences (2001–2007).

Baumgartner, Wilfrid (1902–1978): French politician and senior official. Governor of the Banque de France (1949–1960); French Minister for the Economy and Finance (1960–1962); member of the Economic and Social Council (1969–1974); member of the Academy of Moral and Political Sciences (1965–1978).

Bech, Joseph (1887–1975): Luxembourg statesman, Christian Socialist. Member of Parliament for the Christian Social Party (1914–1964); Minister for the Interior, for Education and for Justice (1920); Foreign Minister (1926–1958); Minister of State; President of the Government (1926–1937, 1953–1958); President of the Chamber of Deputies (1959–1964).

Beyen, Jan Willem (1897–1976): Dutch banker, politician and diplomat. Employee then Treasurer-General at the Ministry of Finance (1918–1923); Executive Secretary of the company Philips (1924–1925); Manager of the Amsterdam office of the Bank of Java (1925–1927); member of the Executive Board of the Bank of Rotterdam (1927–1935); Vice-President then President of the Bank for International Settlements in Basel (1935–1940); financial adviser to the Netherlands Government in London (1940–1946); Executive Director of the International Bank for Reconstruction and Development (1946–1955); Executive Director of the International Monetary Fund (1948–1955); Minister for Foreign Affairs (1952–1956); Netherlands Ambassador to France (1958–1963).

Blessing, Karl (1900–1971): German economist. Employee at the Reichsbank (1920–1929), then assistant to Hjalmar Schacht, President of the Reichsbank (1929–1937); adviser to Hjalmar Schacht, Minister for the Economy (1937); member of the Board of the Reichsbank (1937–1939), ousted for criticising the Nazi regime; President of the Bundesbank (1958–1969).

Bloch-Lainé, Jean-Michel (born 1936): French senior official. Official in the Treasury Department of the Ministry of Finance (1967–1970, 1971–1974); alternate member of the Werner Committee (1970) as deputy to Bernard Clappier, Chairman of the Monetary Committee.

Borschette, Albert (1920–1976): Luxembourg diplomat and writer. Member of the European Commission with responsibility for Competition (1971–1976).

Brandt, Willy (1913–1992): German Social Democrat politician. Social Democrat Member of the Bundestag (1949–1957, 1961, 1969–1992); Mayor of Berlin (1957–1966); Chairman of the Social Democratic Party (SPD) (1964–1987); Foreign Minister of the Federal Republic of Germany (1966–1969); Chancellor of the Federal Republic of Germany (1969–1974); President of the Socialist International (1976–1992); Chairman of the 'North–South Commission' (1977–1983); Member of the European Parliament (1979–1982). Laureate of the Nobel Peace Prize (1971).

Brouwers, Gerard (1908–1991): Dutch senior official. Secretary-General of the Netherlands Ministry of Economic Affairs (1949–1973); Chairman of the EEC's Conjunctural Policy Committee and member of the Werner Committee (1970).

Burns, Arthur Frank (1904–1987): American economist. Chairman of the Council of Economic Advisers (CEA) under US President Dwight Eisenhower (1953–1956); Chairman of the Federal Reserve Board (1970–1978); United States Ambassador to Germany (1981–1985).

Carli, Guido (1914–1993): Italian banker and politician. Chairman of Mediocredito Bank (1953–1956); Chairman of the Italian foreign exchange institute (1956–1957); Minister for Foreign Trade (1957–1958); Chairman of the Banca d'Italia (1960–1975); President of Confindustria, the Italian employers' federation (1976–1980); independent Senator with the support of the Christian Democracy party (1983–1987); Treasury Minister (1989–1992).

Clappier, Bernard (1913–1999): French senior official. Inspector of Finance (1939–1947); head of the private office of Robert Schuman, who served as French Finance Minister, Prime Minister and Foreign Minister (1947–1950); Director of Foreign Relations at the Ministry of the Economy (1951–1963); Deputy Governor of the Banque de France (1964–1973); Governor of the Banque de France (1974–1983); Vice-Chairman of the Board of Directors of the Bank for International Settlements (1983–1991); Chairman of the EEC's Monetary Committee and member of the Werner Committee (1970).

Collin, Fernand (1897–1990): Belgian academic, lawyer and banker. Law Professor at the Catholic University of Leuven (1927–1952); President of Kredietbank Belgium (1938–1973). Known for his thinking on the definition and public and private use of the European unit of account.

Colombo, Emilio (1920–2013): Italian Christian Democrat politician. Christian Democrat Member of the Italian Parliament (1948–1994); Minister for Agriculture (1955–1958); Minister for Foreign Trade (1958–1959); Minister for Industry and Trade (1959–1963) and for Finance, the Treasury and the Budget (1967–1970); Prime Minister (1970–1972); Minister for the Treasury (1974–1976); President of the European Parliament (1977–1979); Member of the European Parliament (1977–1979, 1989–1992); Foreign Minister (1980–1983, 1992–1993). Winner of the International Charlemagne Prize in 1979. Advocate of European political cooperation (the Genscher–Colombo initiative) (1981).

Connally (Jr.), John Bowden (1917–1993): US politician, member of the Democratic Party then the Republican Party. Secretary of the Navy under President Kennedy (1961); Governor of Texas (1961–1969); Treasury Secretary under President Nixon (1971–1972).

Couve de Murville, Maurice (1907–1999): French diplomat and politician. Member of the French Committee for National Liberation (1943); Ambassador to Rome (1945); Director-General of Political Affairs at the French Foreign Ministry (1945–1950); Ambassador to Cairo (1950–1954); Permanent French Delegate to NATO (1954); Ambassador to Washington (1955); Ambassador to Bonn (1956–1958); Minister for Foreign Affairs (1958–1968); Prime Minister (1968–1969); Member of the French National Assembly, initially for the UDR, subsequently for the RPR (1973–1986).

Dahlgrün, Rolf (1908–1969): German Liberal Democrat politician. Member of the Hamburg *Bürgerschaft* (1952–1957); Member of the Bundestag (1957–1962, 1966–1969); Minister for Finance in the Federal Republic of Germany (1962–1966).

Davignon, Étienne (born 1932): Belgian legal expert and diplomat. Cabinet attaché at the Ministry of Foreign Affairs (1961); head of the private office of Ministers Spaak and Harmel (1964–1966, 1966–1969); Director of Political Affairs at the Ministry of Foreign Affairs (1969–1976); chairman of a committee of experts that drafted a report on the problems of political unification in Europe (the Davignon Report, 1970); Chairman of the Executive Committee of the International Energy Agency (1974–1977); member of the Commission of the European Communities (1977–1981); Vice-President of the European Commission (1981–1985); Chairman of the Association for the Monetary Union of Europe (1991–).

Debré, Michel (1912–1996): French statesman, member of the Resistance and Gaullist. Minister for Justice (1958–1959); Prime Minister of the French Republic (1959–1962); Minister for the Economy and Finance (1966–1968); Minister for Foreign Affairs (1968–1969); Minister for National Defence (1969–1973).

De Gaulle, Charles (1890–1970): French statesman. Elite military academy at Saint-Cyr, Paris; Under-Secretary of State for National Defence (1940); Brigadier General (1940); Chairman of the French Committee for National Liberation (1943–1945); President of the Provisional Government (1944–1946); Prime Minister (1958); President of the French Republic (1958–1969).

Delors, Jacques (born 1925): French economist and politician, Socialist. Head of department (1945–1962) and attaché in the private office of the Director-General for securities and the money market at the Banque de France (1950–1962); member of the section for planning and investments at the Economic and Social Council (1959–1961); Head of Social Affairs at the National Planning Board (1962–1969); Secretary-General of the Interministerial Committee for vocational training and social advancement created by Prime Ministers Jacques Chaban-Delmas and Pierre Messmer (1969–1973); adviser for Social and Cultural Affairs (1969) then special assistant to Prime Minister Jacques Chaban-Delmas (1971–1972); member of the General Council of the Banque de France (1973–1979); associate professor of business management at Paris IX University (1974–1979); national delegate for the Socialist Party on international economic relations (1976–1981); Member of the European Parliament, Chairman of the Committee on Economic and Monetary Affairs (1979–1981); Minister for the Economy and Finance (1981–1983) then Minister for the Economy, Finance and Budget (1983–1984); President of the Commission of the European Communities (1985–1995); Chairman of the UNESCO International Commission on Education for the Twenty-first Century (1994–1999); President of the Administrative Council of the College of Europe in Bruges (1995–1999); President, then Founder President, of the think tank Notre Europe (since 1996); President of the Council for Employment, Income and Social Cohesion (CERC) (2000–2009).

De Strycker (Baron), Cecil (1915–2004): Belgian economist and banker. Employee at the National Bank of Belgium (from 1945); Director at the NBB (1968–1971); Vice-Governor of the NBB (1971–1975); Governor of the NBB (1975–1982).

Drees (Jr.), Willem (Wim) (1922–1998): Dutch Socialist Democrat politician. Member of the Chamber of Representatives (1970–1971, 1972–1977); Minister for Transport and Waterways (1971–1972).

Duhamel, Jacques (1924–1977): French politician. Member of Parliament (1962–1973); Minister for Agriculture (1969–1971); Minister for Cultural Affairs (1971–1973).

Emminger, Otmar (1911–1986): German economist and banker. Member of the Board of the *Bank deutscher Länder* and then of the Bundesbank (1953–1969); Deputy Chairman and temporary Chairman of the Monetary Committee of the EEC (1958–1977); Deputy President of the Bundesbank (1969–1977); President of the Bundesbank (1977–1979).

Erhard, Ludwig Wilhelm (1897–1977): German politician, Christian Democrat. Christian Democrat Member of the Bundestag (1949–1977); Minister for Economic Affairs (1949–1957); Minister for Economic Affairs and Vice-Chancellor (1957–1963); Chancellor of the Federal Republic of Germany (1963–1966); leader of the Christian Democratic Union (CDU) (1966–1967).

Eyskens (Viscount), Gaston (1905–1988): Belgian academic and politician. Christian Democrat Member of Parliament for the Leuven constituency (1939); Minister for Finance (1945, 1947, 1965); Prime Minister (1949–1950, 1958–1960, 1960–1961, 1968–1972, 1972–1973); Minister of State (from 1963).

Eyskens (Viscount), Mark (born 1933): Belgian academic, economist and politician (son of Gaston Eyskens). Adviser to the Belgian Finance Minister, André Dequae (1962–1965); Professor at the Catholic University of Leuven/Louvain (KUL) (1965–1998); Member of the Chamber of Representatives (1977–2003); State Secretary for Regional Economy, Territorial Planning and Housing (1976–1977); State Secretary for the Budget (1978); Minister for Development Cooperation (1979–1980); Minister for Finance (1980–1981); Prime Minister (1981); Minister for Economic Affairs (1981–1985); Governor of the International Monetary Fund and the World Bank (1985–1989); Minister for Finance (1985–1987); Minister for External Relations (1989–1992); Member of the Parliamentary Assembly of the Council of Europe (1992–2003); Member and Vice-President of the Parliamentary Assembly of Western European Union (1992–2003); Minister of State (since 1998).

Fourcade, Jean-Pierre (born 1929): French economist and politician, member of the Union for a Popular Movement. Minister for the Economy and Finance (1974–1976); Minister for Equipment (1976–1977); Minister for Equipment and Regional Planning (1977); Senator (1976–2011). He is known for the 'Fourcade Plan', a stabilisation plan devised in June 1974 to tackle the inflationary impact of the first oil shock.

Frieden, Luc (born 1963): Luxembourg Christian Socialist politician. Barrister in Luxembourg (1989–1998); Member of Parliament, Chairman of the Finance and Budget Committee and Chairman of the Committee on Institutions and Constitutional Revision in the Chamber of Deputies (1994–1998); Minister for Justice, Minister for the Budget, Minister for Relations with Parliament (1998–1999); Governor of the World Bank (1998–2013); Minister for Justice, Minister for the Treasury and the Budget (1999–2004); Minister for Defence (2004–2006); Minister for the Treasury and the Budget,

Minister for Justice (2004–2009); Minister for Finance (2009–2013). Vice Chairman of Deutsche Bank (2014–2016); Chairman of the Board of Directors of Banque Internationale à Luxembourg (BIL) (since 2016); Chairman of the Board of Directors of the Luxembourg media group Saint Paul (since 2016).

Giscard d'Estaing, Valéry (born 1926): French politician. Member of the French National Assembly (1956–1959, 1962, 1967–1969, 1984–1989, 1993–1997, 1997–2002); Minister for Finance and Economic Affairs (1962–1966); founder and President of the National Federation of Independent Republicans (1966–1974); Minister for the Economy and Finance (1969–1974); Chairman of the OECD Council (1970); President of the French Republic (1974–1981); member of the French Constitutional Council (1981–); founder of the Association for Monetary Union in Europe (1987); leader of the Union for French Democracy (UDF) (1988–1996); Member of the European Parliament (1989–1993); President of the International European Movement (1989–1997); Chairman of the European Convention (2002–2003); member of the French Academy (2003).

Hallstein, Walter (1901–1982): German Christian Democrat politician. Rector of the University of Frankfurt (1946–1948); State Secretary in the Federal Chancellery (1950); head of the German delegation to the Schuman Plan negotiations (1950); State Secretary in the Foreign Ministry (1951–1958); President of the EEC Commission (1958–1967); Christian Democrat Member of the Bundestag (1969–1972); President of the European Movement (1968–1974).

Hansen, Albert: Luxembourg legal expert and senior official. Civil servant (1969–2002); Secretary-General of the Government (1979–1998); Head of Cabinet of HRH the Grand Duke (1998–2002); Private Secretary to HRH the Grand Duke (1999–2002); member of the Council of State (since March 2001); President of the Governing Board of the *Souvenir de la Résistance*, or Memorial of the Resistance (since 2004).

Heath, Edward (1916–2005): British Conservative politician. Conservative Member of Parliament (1950–2001); leader of the Conservative parliamentary group (1955–1959); Minister of Labour (1959–1960); Lord Privy Seal (1960–1963); President of the Board of Trade (1963); Secretary of State for Industry, Trade and Regional Development (1963–1964); leader of the Conservative Party (1965–1975); Prime Minister (1970–1974).

Israel, Edmond (1924–2011): Luxembourg economist and banker. Director-General of the Banque Internationale à Luxembourg (BIL) (1973–1989); President of the Board of Directors of Cedel International (renamed Clearstream International in 1999) (1970–1999); Luxembourg representative on the Board of Governors of ASEF (Asia Europe Foundation) (1997–1999); Chairman of the ASEF Board of Governors (1999–2011); Honorary Chairman of Clearstream International (2005–2011).

Jenkins, Roy (1920–2003): British politician. Labour Member of Parliament (1948–1976); Minister for Aviation (1964–1965); Home Secretary (1965–1967, 1974–1976); Chancellor of the Exchequer (1967–1970); President of the European Commission (1977–1981); Social Democrat MP (1982–1987); leader of the Social Democratic Party (1982–1983).

Juncker, Jean-Claude (born 1954): Luxembourg Christian Socialist statesman. State Secretary for Labour and Social Security (1982–1984); Minister for Labour, Minister with responsibility for the Budget (1984–1989); Minister for Finance, Minister for Labour (1989–1995); Governor of the World Bank (1989-1995); Chairman of the Christian Social Party (CSV) (1990-1995); Prime Minister, Minister of State, Minister for Finance, Minister for Labour and Employment (1995–1999); Governor of the International Monetary Fund (IMF) (1995–2013); Governor of the European Bank for Reconstruction and Development (EBRD) (1995–2013); Prime Minister, Minister of State and Minister for Finance (1999–2009); President of the Eurogroup, which brings together the Finance Ministers of all the Member States of the euro zone (elected as the first permanent president on 10 September 2004, in office until 2013); Prime Minister, Minister of State, Minister for the Treasury (2009–2013). Since 1 November 2014, he has served as President of the European Commission; his five-year term will come to an end in 2019.

Klasen, Karl (1909–1991): German banker. Chairman of the *Landeszentralbank Hamburg* (1946–1952); member of the Board of the Deutsche Bank (1952–1969), for which he was also the spokesman (1967–1969); Chairman of the Bundesbank (1970–1977); member of the Supervisory Council of the Deutsche Bank (1978–1984).

Lamfalussy, Alexandre (1929–2015): Belgian academic, banker and senior official. Economic Adviser, Member of the Board of Directors (1955–1972) then President of the Banque de Bruxelles (1972–1975); Economic Adviser, Head of the Monetary and Economic Department of the Bank for International Settlements (BIS) (1976–1985); Deputy General Manager (1981–1985) then General Manager (1985–1993) of the BIS; Founding President of the European Monetary Institute (EMI) (1994–1997); Chairman of the Committee of Wise Men on the Regulation of European Securities Markets (2000–2001).

Larosière, Jacques de (born 1929): French academic and senior official. Lecturer at Sciences Po and Inspector of Finance (from 1960); Assistant Director (1967–1974) then Director of the Treasury (1974–1978); Managing Director of the International Monetary Fund (IMF) (1978–1987); Governor of the Banque de France (1987–1993); President of the European Bank for Reconstruction and Development (EBRD) (1993–1998); Chairman of the Strategic Committee of Agence France Trésor.

Looijen, Anthony: Dutch expert, alternate member of the Werner Committee as deputy to Gerard Brouwers, Chairman of the Conjunctural Policy Committee.

Lulling, Astrid (born 1929): Luxembourg Christian Socialist politician. Secretary and editor at the Lëtzebuerger Arbechter-Verband (Luxembourg Workers' Union — LAV) (1949–1963); General Secretary for agricultural and food workers' trade unions at the European Trade Union Secretariat (ETUS) (1963–1971); Member of the Luxembourg Chamber of Deputies (1965–1989); Member of the European Parliament (1965–1974, 1989–2014); President of the European Movement Luxembourg (since 2016).

Luns, Joseph (1911–2002): Dutch politician and diplomat. Netherlands Representative to the UN in New York (1949–1952); Foreign Minister (1956–1971); Secretary General of NATO (1971–1984).

Machlup, Fritz (1902–1983): Austrian economist who played an important part in the development of economics (methodology, theory and policy aspects). A student of Friedrich von Wieser and Ludwig von Mises, he gained his doctorate in 1925 on the subject of *Die Goldkernwahrung* (The Gold Exchange Standard). He published a book in 1927 on the adoption of the Gold Exchange Standard. Machlup left for the United States on a Rockefeller fellowship and taught at Harvard, Columbia and Stanford Universities. He initially worked on the industrial economy and then focused on the international monetary economy. In 1963, he formed an organisation of academics, known as the Bellagio Group, to study this question, develop an academic consensus and propose practical solutions. His success in this venture attracted the attention of governments and central bankers and resulted in the publication of numerous books and articles on the international currency crisis and its solution. Robert Triffin dubbed him 'the unquestioned intellectual leader and mentor of our vain efforts to reform the crumbling international monetary system'. The Nobel Committee listed his name several times as a candidate for the Prize, although he was never awarded it.

Malfatti, Franco Maria (1927–1991): Italian politician, Christian Democrat. Christian Democrat Member of Parliament (first elected in 1958 and re-elected in 1963, 1968, 1972, 1976, 1979, 1983, and 1987); Minister for Posts and Telecommunications, Education, Finance and Foreign Affairs, Deputy State Secretary for Industry and Trade, Foreign Affairs, the Budget and programming activities in the successive governments between 1958 and 1980; President of the Commission of the European Communities (1970–1972). He resigned in 1972 to take part in the parliamentary elections in Italy that year.

Mansholt, Sicco Leendert (1908–1995): Dutch Socialist politician. Socialist Minister for Agriculture and Fisheries (1945–1958); author of the plan for a 'green pool' (1950–1953); Member of the EEC Commission (1958–1967); author of the Mansholt Plan for a reform of agriculture in the EEC (1968); member of the Commission of the European Communities (1967–1973); President of the Commission of the European Communities (1972–1973).

Marjolin, Robert (1911–1986): French senior official, academic and politician. Deputy Commissioner-General of the French National Planning Board (Monnet Plan for Modernisation and Equipment) (1946–1948); Secretary-General of the Organisation for European Economic Cooperation (OEEC) (1948–1955); Vice-Chairman of the French Delegation to the EEC and EAEC negotiations (1956–1957); Vice-President of the Commission of the European Economic Community with responsibility for the Economy and Finance (1958–1967); member of the Committee of the Three Wise Men (1978–1979); member of the Academy of Moral and Political Sciences (1984). In 1962, with Robert Triffin (Belgian–American economist and economic adviser to Jean Monnet's Action Committee for the United States of Europe), he drafted an Action Programme for the Second Stage of the European Economic Community. This programme proposed a reform of the Treaty of Rome with a maximalist interpretation of Article 108, paving the way for the establishment of an economic and monetary union.

Martens, Wilfried (1936–2013): Belgian statesman, Christian Democrat. Adviser to Prime Ministers Pierre Harmel and Paul Vanden Boeynants (1965–1966); President of the *CVP Jongeren* (the youth organisation of the Christian People's Party) (1967–1971); special adviser in the office of minister Leo Tindemans (1968); Chairman of the Christian People's Party (1972–1979); co-founder of the European People's Party (1976); Member of the Chamber of Representatives (1974–1991); Prime Minister (1979–1981, 1981–1992); President of the European People's Party (1990–2013); President of the European Union of Christian Democrats (1993–1996); Member of the European Parliament (1994–2004); Chairman of the Group of the European People's Party (1994–1999); Minister of State (1992–2013).

Maystadt, Philippe (1948–2017): Belgian academic and Christian Socialist politician. Assistant Professor (1970–1977) then Professor (1989–2017) at the Université catholique de Louvain; Minister for the Civil Service and Scientific Policy with responsibility for the coordination of Environment Policy (1980–1981); Minister for the Budget, Scientific Policy and Planning (1981–1985); Deputy Prime Minister and Minister for Economic Affairs (1986–1995); Chairman of the

G10 Finance Ministers (1990–1991); Chairman of the Council of Economics and Finance Ministers of the European Community (Ecofin) (1993); Chairman of the Board of Governors of the European Bank for Reconstruction and Development (1997–1998); President of the European Investment Bank (EIB) (2000–2011); Chairman of the Board of Directors of the Belgian Academy for Research and Higher Education (ARES) (2014-2017).

Mendès France, Pierre (1907–1982): French politician. Radical-Socialist Member of Parliament for the Eure Department (1932–1959); Commissioner of Finance in the French Committee of National Liberation (1943); Minister for the National Economy (1944–1945); French Governor of the International Monetary Fund (1946–1958); Prime Minister and Foreign Minister (1954–1955); Socialist MP for Grenoble (1967–1968).

Mersch, Yves (born 1949): Luxembourg academic and banker. Barrister in Luxembourg and Assistant Professor in Public Law at the University of Paris–Sud 11 (1974–1975); assistant in the Luxembourg Ministry of Finance (1975–1976); assistant at the International Monetary Fund, Washington DC (1976–1978); attaché in the Luxembourg Ministry of Finance (1978–1979); financial adviser to the Permanent Representation of Luxembourg to the United Nations, New York (1980–1981); adviser in international financial and monetary relations at the Ministry of Finance (1981); member of the Council of the Luxembourg Monetary Institute (1983–1999); government representative for the Luxembourg Stock Exchange (1985–1989); Director of the Treasury (1989–1998); President of the Banque Centrale du Luxembourg; member of the Governing Council and General Council of the European Central Bank (June 1998–September 2012); member of the Executive Board of the European Central Bank (ECB) (since September 2012).

Mertens de Wilmars, Jacques (1917–1986): Belgian academic and banker. Professor at the Université catholique de Louvain; adviser at the National Bank of Belgium; alternate member of the Werner Committee as assistant to Baron Hubert Ansiaux, Chairman of the Committee of Governors of the Central Banks (1970).

Molitor, Bernhard (1933–2007): German economist and senior official. Assistant at the Commission of the European Economic Community, Directorate-General for Economic and Financial Affairs (1958–1966); head of the department in charge of medium-term economic policy (1966–1968); Director for National Economies and Short-Term Economic Affairs in the Directorate for Economic and Financial Affairs of the EC Commission (1968–1975); Director in the Ministry of Economic Affairs of the German Federal Government (1979–1994).

Möller, Alexander (Alex) Johann Heinrich Friedrich (1903–1985): German politician, member of the Social Democratic Party of Germany (SPD); Member of the Bundestag (1961–1976); German Finance Minister (1969–1971); adviser to the Egyptian Government on behalf of the German Government led by Helmut Schmidt (1980–1985).

Monnet, Jean (1888–1979): French politician. Deputy Secretary-General of the League of Nations (1919–1923); member of the British Supply Council, Washington (provision of civil and military goods for the war effort) (1940–1943); Commissioner-General of the French National Planning Board (1947–1952); architect of the plan for a 'coal and steel pool' (1950); President of the ECSC High Authority (1952–1955); founder of the Action Committee for the United States of Europe (1955–1975).

Morel, Jean-Claude: official at the European Commission, deputy to Ugo Mosca, Director-General for Economic and Financial Affairs at the EEC. Alternate member of the Werner Committee (1970).

Morelli, Georges: official at the European Commission (DGII), technical secretary of the Werner Committee (1970).

Mosca, Ugo (1914–?): Director-General for Economic and Financial Affairs at the EEC (DGII). Member of the Werner Committee, representative of the EC Commission (1970).

Mundell, Robert Alexander (born 1932): Canadian academic and economist. Author of *A Theory of Optimum Currency Areas* in 1961 (also known as the 'Mundell–Fleming model'), which generalises Keynesian theory to monetary dynamics, exchange rates and capital markets in open economies. In 1970 he became a consultant to the EEC Monetary

Committee and, as such, in 1972–1973 he was a member of the EEC Study Group on Monetary Union. Professor at Columbia University in the City of New York (1974). Laureate of the Nobel Prize in Economics in 1999.

Nixon, Richard Milhous (1913–1994): US statesman. He was the 37th President of the United States (1969–1974).

Noël, Émile (1922–1996): French diplomat and senior official. Secretary of the General Affairs Committee of the Consultative Assembly of the Council of Europe (1950–1952); Director of the Secretariat of the Ad Hoc Assembly's Constitutional Committee (1952–1954); Chef de Cabinet for the President of the Council of Europe's Consultative Assembly (1954–1956); representative of the French Prime Minister in the delegation to the Conference on the Common Market and Euratom (1956–1957); Executive Secretary of the Commission of the European Economic Community (1958–1967); Secretary-General of the Commission of the European Communities (1967–1987); President of the European University Institute in Florence (1987–1993).

Nothomb, Charles-Ferdinand (born 1934): Belgian Christian Socialist politician and statesman. Christian Socialist Member of Parliament (1968–1995); leader of the Christian Social Party (1972–1979, 1996–1998); member of the Consultative Assembly of the Council of Europe (1968–1973, 1995–1999); Member of the European Parliament (1979–1980); President of the Chamber of Representatives (1979–1980, 1988–1995); Minister for Foreign Affairs (1980–1981); Deputy Prime Minister and Minister for the Interior and the Civil Service (1981–1985); Deputy Prime Minister and Minister for the Interior, the Civil Service and Decentralisation (1985–1986); Co-Chairman and General Rapporteur of the Conference of European Parliaments (1990); Senator (1995–1999); President of the Belgian Council of the European Movement (2001–2007); President of the European Institute for Research on Mediterranean and Euro-Arab Cooperation (2001–2007); Honorary President of the Pierre Werner European Circle.

Ortoli, François-Xavier (1925–2007): French politician and senior official. Minister for Information (1951); technical adviser to the private office of the Minister for Economic Affairs (1953); Director-General of the EEC Internal Market Directorate-General (1958); head of Georges Pompidou's private office (1962); Commissioner-General of the French National Planning Board (1966–1967); Minister for Equipment and Housing (1967–1968); UDR Member of the French National Assembly (1968); Minister for the Economy and Finance (1968–1969); Minister for Industrial and Scientific Development (1969–1972); President of the Commission of the European Communities (1973–1977); Vice-President of the Commission of the European Communities with special responsibility for Economic and Financial Affairs (1977–1984).

Ossola, Rinaldo (1913–1990): Italian academic (graduate of Bocconi University, Milan, and the London School of Economics) and banker. Employee at the Banca d'Italia (from 1938); Deputy Director-General at the Banca d'Italia (1962–1970); Chairman of the Group of Ten, which drafted the report on the establishment of SDRs (the Ossola Report) in 1964; Director-General of the Banca d'Italia (1975–1976); Senator (1976–1979); Minister for Foreign Trade (1976–1979).

Palumbo, Simone: expert, alternate member of the Werner Committee as deputy to Gaetano Stammati, Chairman of the Budgetary Policy Committee (1970).

Pescatore, Pierre (1919–2010): Doctor of law, Luxembourg diplomat and senior official. Legal Adviser, Director and subsequently Secretary-General with the rank of Minister Plenipotentiary at the Luxembourg Ministry of Foreign Affairs (1950–1967); Professor at the University of Liège (1952–1982); Judge at the Court of Justice of the European Communities (1967–1985).

Pleven, René (1901–1993): French politician. Finance Minister (1944–1946); Gaullist Member of the French National Assembly (1945–1973); member and Chairman of the Côtes-du-Nord General Council (1948–1976); Prime Minister (July 1950–February 1951, August 1951–January 1952); architect of the plan for a European Defence Community (1950); Defence Minister (1949–1950, 1952–1954); Foreign Minister (1958); Member of the European Parliamentary Assembly (1958–1969); Justice Minister (1969–1973).

Pompidou, Georges Jean Raymond (1911–1974): French academic (graduate of the École Normale Supérieure with an *agrégation* in literature) and statesman. General Manager of the Rothschild Bank (1956–1962); head of the private office of General de Gaulle (1958–1959); Member of the French National Assembly (1968–1969); member of the Constitutional Council (1959–1962); Prime Minister (1962–1968); President of the French Republic (1969–1974).

Reding, Viviane (born 1951): Luxembourg journalist, Christian Socialist politician and European senior official. Journalist at the Luxemburger Wort (1978–1999); Member of the Luxembourg Parliament and of the Benelux Parliamentary Assembly (1979–1989); President of the Christian Social Women organisation (CSF) (1988–1993); Member of the European Parliament (1989–1999, and (2014–2018); Member of the European Commission with responsibility for Education, Culture, Youth, Media and Sport (1999–2004); Member of the European Commission with responsibility for the Information Society and Media (2004–2010); Vice-President of the European Commission with responsibility for Justice, Fundamental Rights and Citizenship (2010–2014).

Rey, Jean (1902–1983): Belgian legal expert and Liberal politician. Liberal Member of Parliament for Liège (1939–1958); Minister for Reconstruction (1949–1950); member of the European Affairs Commission (1952); Minister for Economic Affairs (1954–1958); President and member of the ECSC Special Council of Ministers (1954–1958); member of the EEC Commission (1958–1967); President of the Commission of the European Communities (1967–1970); President of the European Movement (1974–1978); Member of the European Parliament (1979–1980).

Rist, Charles (1874–1955): French academic (Lecturer at the University of Montpellier and the Law Faculty of Paris) and economist. Author, with Charles Gide, of *Histoire des doctrines économiques* (1909); in 1926, he became Deputy Governor of the Banque de France and began a career as an international monetary and financial expert. Member of the Academy of Moral and Political Sciences (1928); founder of the Institute for Economic and Social Research (IRES) (1933).

Rohwedder, Detlev Karsten (1932–1991): German politician. State Secretary in the Federal Ministry of the Economy (1969–1978).

Rueff, Jacques (1896–1978): French economist and senior official. Special adviser to Raymond Poincaré, Prime Minister and Finance Minister (1926–1928); financial attaché to the French Embassy in London, then Director of the *Mouvement général des fonds* and Deputy Governor of the Banque de France (1939); Chairman of the War Reparations Conference in Paris (1945). He was a founder of the Mont Pelerin Society (1947). In the 1950s, he held several posts in European organisations, at the Court of Justice of the European Coal and Steel Community and at the Court of Justice of the European Communities. In 1958, he chaired the committee of experts tasked with consolidating public finances, resulting in the 'Rueff Plan'. The franc regained its convertibility and exchange controls became more flexible. Rueff anticipated the Common Market that was being created and recommending opening up to competition in a second study that he conducted with Louis Armand and an ad hoc committee of experts, the 'Rueff–Armand Committee'. When the study was published in 1960, journalists referred to it as the 'Rueff–Armand Plan', although the official title was 'Report by the committee on eliminating barriers to economic growth'. He became a member of the Academy of Moral and Political Sciences (1944) and the French Academy (1964).

Saccomanni, Fabrizio (born 1941): Italian banker and senior official. Head of the Office for International Monetary and Financial Issues (1975–1984) and Head of the Foreign Department (1984–1997) at the Bank of Italy; Managing Director for International Affairs at the Bank of Italy (1997–2003); Member of the committee set up by the Italian Government to manage the changeover to the single currency (1998–2002) and, in this capacity, chairman of the 'finance' subcommittee (2000–2002); Vice President of the European Bank for Reconstruction and Development (EBRD) (2003–2006); Member of the Governing Board and Senior Deputy Governor at the Bank of Italy (2006–2013); Italian Minister for Economic Affairs and Finance (2013–2014).

Santer, Jacques (born 1937): Luxembourg Christian Socialist statesman. Leader of the Christian Social Party (1974–1982); Member of the European Parliament (1975–1979, 1999–2004); Minister for Finance,

Employment and Social Security (1979–1984); Prime Minister, Minister of State and Finance Minister (1984–1995); Governor of the European Bank for Reconstruction and Development (1991–1994); President of the European Commission (1995–1999); member of the European Convention (2002–2003); President of the Board of Directors of the Fondation du Mérite européen.

Scelba, Mario (1901–1991): Italian politician. Minister for the Interior (1947–1952, 1952–1953, 1954–1955, 1960–1962); Prime Minister (1954–1955); President of the European Parliament (1969–1971).

Scheel, Walter (1919–2016): German Liberal Democrat statesman. Member of the Bundestag (1953–1961); Federal Minister for Economic Cooperation (1961–1962, 1962–1966); Vice-President of the Bundestag (1967–1969); Federal President of the Liberal Democrat Party (1968–1974); Vice-Chancellor, Federal Minister for Foreign Affairs (1969–1974); fourth President of Germany (1974–1979).

Schiller, Karl August Fritz (1911–1994): German academic and Social Democrat politician. Senator for Economic Affairs for the *Land* of Berlin (1961–1965); Social Democrat Member of the Bundestag (1965–1972); Minister for Economic Affairs (1966–1971); architect of a law on economic stability and growth (1967); Minister for Economic Affairs and Finance (1971–1972).

Schmidt, Helmut (1918–2015): German statesman, Social Democrat. Social Democrat Member of the Bundestag (1953–1961; 1965–1986); deputy leader of the SPD parliamentary group (1967–1969); deputy leader of the SPD (1968–1983); Defence Minister (1969–1972); Finance Minister (1972–1974); Chancellor of the Federal Republic of Germany (1974–1982); founder of the Association for the Monetary Union of Europe (1987).

Schmitz, Johnny: expert, alternate member of the Werner Committee as deputy to chairman Pierre Werner (1970).

Schöllhorn, Johann Baptist (1922–2009): German academic and politician. Researcher at the Munich-based IFO-Institut (economic research institute) (1952–1955); employee at the Federal Ministry of the Economy in the 'General European economic affairs' department (1956–1962); Director of the 'Short-term economic policy' sub-section (1962–1964); Director of the 'Basic questions on economic policy and international cooperation' sub-section (1962–1966); State Secretary (1967–1972); Chairman of the *Landeszentralbank Schleswig-Holstein* (1973–1989); member of the Board of Directors of the Bank for International Settlements (BIS) (1976–1989); Chairman of the EEC's Medium-Term Economic Policy Committee and member of the Werner Committee (1970).

Schröder, Gerhard (1910–1989): German Christian Democrat politician. Interior Minister (1953–1961); Foreign Minister (1961–1966); Defence Minister (1966–1969); Chairman of the Bundestag Foreign Affairs Committee (1969–1980).

Schuman, Robert Nicolas Jean-Baptiste (1886–1963): French Christian Democrat statesman, born in Luxembourg. Christian Democrat Member of Parliament (1919–1940); Finance Minister (1946–1947); President of the Council (1947–1948); Foreign Minister (1948–1953); founder of the European Coal and Steel Community (1950); Minister for Justice (1955–1956); President of the European Parliament (1958–1960).

Schumann, Maurice (1911–1998): French journalist and Christian Democrat politician. Founder member of the Popular Republican Movement (MRP) (1944); Member of Parliament (1945–1973); State Secretary for Foreign Affairs in the cabinets of Pleven, Faure, Pinay, Mayer and Laniel (1951–1954); Minister attached to the Prime Minister for Regional Planning (1962); Minister for Scientific Research and Atomic and Space Matters (1967–1968); Minister for Social Affairs (1968–1969); Minister for Foreign Affairs (1969–1973); UDF and RPR Senator (1974–1998); member of the French Academy (1974).

Schweitzer, Pierre-Paul (1912–1994): French economist and senior official. Director of the Treasury in the Finance Ministry (1953–1960); second Deputy Governor at the Banque de France (1960–1964); Managing Director of the International Monetary Fund (1963–1973). Initiator of special drawing rights (SDRs) and architect of the swift termination of dollar–gold convertibility and fixed exchange rates. He was criticised by the United States and resigned before the end of his second term.

Snoy et d'Oppuers, Jean-Charles (1907–1991): Count, Belgian politician and member of the Christian Social Party. As Secretary-General of the Belgian Ministry for Economic Affairs, he chaired the Belgian delegation to the Intergovernmental Conference on the Common Market and Euratom. He was one of the negotiators and signatories of the Treaty of Rome on 25 March 1957. He was elected as a Member of the Chamber of Representatives in May 1968 and became Minister for Finance in the Eyskens–Cools Government the same year, a post he would hold until 1972.

Snoy et d'Oppuers, Bernard (born 1945) (Baron): Belgian banker and high official. Head of the Financial Relations Department at the World Bank, Paris (1980–1986); Economic Adviser at the Commission of the EEC, DG EcFin (1986–1988); Head of the Private Office of the Belgian Finance Minister (1989–1991); Head of the Belgian delegation to the conference for the creation of the European Bank for Reconstruction and Development (EBRD) (1988–1991); Executive Director of the World Bank (1991–1994); Director of the EBRD (1994–2002); Coordinator of economic and environmental activities at the OSCE (2005–2008); President of the European League for Economic Cooperation (ELEC) (since 2008); President of Robert Triffin International (since 2008).

Spaak, Paul-Henri (1899–1972): Belgian Socialist statesman. Socialist Member of Parliament for Brussels (1932–1957, 1961–1966); Foreign Minister (1936–1939, 1939–1940, 1954–1957); Prime Minister (1938–1939, 1946–1949); President of the UN General Assembly (1946); President of the Consultative Assembly of the Council of Europe (1949–1951); President of the ECSC Common Assembly (1952–1954); Chairman of a working party established at the 1955 Messina Conference and entrusted with the preparation of a report on the creation of a common European market (Spaak Report) (1955); Secretary General of NATO (1957–1961); Deputy Prime Minister and Foreign Minister (1961–1966).

Spierenburg, Dirk (1909–2001): Dutch diplomat and senior official. Director-General for International Economic Relations in the Foreign Ministry (1949–1952); member of the ECSC High Authority

(1952–1962); Netherlands Permanent Representative to the European Communities (1963–1971).

Spinelli, Altiero (1907–1986): Italian politician. Co-author of the federalist Ventotene Manifesto (1941); co-founder and Secretary-General of the European Federalist Movement (1943–1962); member of the Commission of the European Communities (1970); Communist Member of the Italian Parliament (1976–1983); Member of the European Parliament (1976–1986); rapporteur of the committee tasked with the institutional reform of the European Parliament (1984).

Stammati, Gaetano (1908–2002): Italian academic, banker and politician. Finance Minister (1976–1978); Minister for Public Works (1978–1979); Minister for International Trade (1979–1981). Chairman of the EEC's Budgetary Policy Committee and member of the Werner Committee (1970).

Steichen, René (born 1942): Luxembourg legal expert and Christian Socialist politician. Mayor of Diekirch (1974–1984); State Secretary for Agriculture, Viticulture and Rural Development (1984–1989); Minister for Agriculture, Viticulture and Rural Development (1989–1992); member of the European Commission responsible for Agriculture and Rural Development (1992–1995); Director of SES ASTRA SA (originally known as the *Société européenne des satellites*) (1995); Chairman of the Board of Directors of SES ASTRA SA, SES WORLD SKIES and SES ASTRA Services Europe (1996–2016).

Thorn, Gaston (1928–2007): Luxembourg legal expert and Liberal statesman. Liberal Member of the Luxembourg Chamber of Deputies (1959–1975); Member of the European Parliament (1959–1969); Minister for Foreign Affairs and Foreign Trade, the Civil Service, Physical Education and Sport (1968–1974); Prime Minister, Minister of State and Minister for Foreign Affairs and Foreign Trade (1974–1979); President of the United Nations General Assembly (1975–1976); Deputy Prime Minister and Minister for Foreign Affairs, Foreign Trade and Cooperation, Minister for the National Economy and Small Businesses and Minister for Justice (1979–1980); President of the European Commission (1981–1985).

Thygesen, Niels (born 1934): Danish academic and international expert. Associate Professor (1964–1969) then Professor (1971–2004) of Economics at the University of Copenhagen; Economic Adviser to the Treasury of Malaysia, Kuala Lumpur, with the Harvard University Development Advisory Service (1969–1971); Head of Monetary Division and Studies at the OECD, Paris (1971–1973); Adviser to the Governor of the Danmarks Nationalbank (1973–1983); Chairman of the Danish Economic Council (1983–1985); Member of the Delors Committee (1988–1989); Member of the Swedish Government's Advisory Group on the economic crisis (1992–1993); Research Professor at the Danske Bank (1998–2003); Chairman of the European Fiscal Board (since 2016).

Tietmeyer, Hans (1931–2016): German academic and banker. Director of Research at Cusanuswerk, Bonn (1959–1962); official in the Federal Ministry of the Economy (1962–1982); head of the 'Fundamental questions on the economic system and economic policy' department (1962–1970); head of the 'European Common Market and relations with third countries' subdivision (during this time he was a lecturer at the Universities of Bochum and Cologne) (1970–1972); head of the 'Fundamental questions on economic, short-term and growth policy' subdivision (1972–1973); director and head of the 'Economic policy' department and also, in this capacity, chairman of the EEC's committee on economic policy (Brussels) and a member of the OECD committee on economic policy (Paris) (1973–1982); State Secretary in the Federal Ministry of the Economy with responsibility for fundamental questions on financial policy, international monetary policy and EEC matters (1982–1989); member of the Executive Board of the Bundesbank (1990–1991); Vice-President of the Bundesbank (1991–1993); President of the Bundesbank (1993–1999); Vice-Chairman of the Bank for International Settlements (BIS) (since 2003); alternate member of the Werner Committee as deputy to Johann Baptist Schöllhorn, Chairman of the Medium-Term Economic Policy Committee (1970).

Tindemans, Leo (1922–2014): Belgian statesman, Christian Democrat. Mayor of Edegem (1965–1976); Minister of Community Relations (1968–1972); Minister for Agriculture and Small and Medium-sized Businesses (1972–1973); Deputy Prime Minister and Minister for Finance responsible for coordination of institutional reforms (1973–1974); member of the Jean Monnet Committee for the United States of Europe (1960–1975); Prime Minister (1974–1978); Member of the European Parliament (1979–1981, 1989–1999); Minister for External Relations (1981–1989).

Triffin, Robert (1911–1993): Belgian–American academic and economist. Doctor of law and graduate in economics from the Université catholique de Louvain (Belgium). Appointed as an assistant at Harvard University, United States (1938). Member of the Board of the Federal Reserve System in Washington (1942), in charge of cooperation with the countries of Latin America. He was recruited by the International Monetary Fund in 1946 before moving to the European Cooperation Administration for the administration of the Marshall Plan in 1949, where he was one of the main architects and negotiators for the European Payments Union that was set up in 1950. In 1951, he joined the Department of Economics at Yale University. He then focused his attention on teaching and consultancy activities for various national and international organisations. His two major works were *Europe and the Money Muddle* (1957) and *Gold and the Dollar Crisis* (1960). His theory that would become known as the 'Triffin dilemma' confirmed his reputation as a leading expert. He was consulted at this time by both the US presidential administration and Jean Monnet's Action Committee for the United States of Europe. See: https://www.uclouvain.be/122304.html.

Unwin, Brian (born 1935) (Sir): British diplomat and senior official. Diplomat in the Foreign and Commonwealth Office (1960–1968); senior official in Her Majesty's Treasury (1968–1985); UK Director of the European Investment Bank (1983–1985); Chairman of the Board of Her Majesty's Customs and Excise (1987–1993); President of the European Investment Bank (1993–1999); Governor of the European Bank for Reconstruction and Development (1993–1999); Chairman of the Supervisory Board of the European Investment Fund (1994–1999); Member of the Board of the Centre d'Études Prospectives (CEPROS) (1996–2000); Chairman of the European Task Force on Banking and Biodiversity (2003–2009).

Von der Groeben, Hans (1907–2005): German economist and senior official. Director of the ECSC subdivision in the Federal Ministry of the Economy (1952–1958); spokesman for the German Government on the Coordination Committee of the ECSC Special Council of Ministers (1953–1958); head of the German delegation to the Intergovernmental Committee established by the Messina Conference (1955–1956); involved in the drafting of the Spaak Report (1956); Chairman of the Common Market Group at the Intergovernmental Conference on the Common Market and Euratom (1956–1957); member of the EEC Commission, chairman of the 'Competition' working group, deputy chairman of the 'Economy' working group, member of the 'Agriculture' and 'Overseas Territories' working groups (1958–1961); Deputy Chairman of 'Europa-Union' (1965); Director-General for Competition (1961–1967) then for regional policy, freedom of establishment and freedom to provide services (1967–1970).

Weicker, Alphonse (1891–1973): Luxembourg legal expert and banker. Managing Director of the Banque générale du Luxembourg (1919–1971).

Werner, Henri (born 1948): third son of spouses Pierre Werner and Henriette Werner-Pescatore. Higher education in Luxembourg City, Innsbruck and Liège. Magistère (similar to a Master's degree) in theology and civil and metallurgical engineering. Engineer in new products at Cérametal, Mamer (1979–1985). Since 1985, engineer at the DuPont de Nemours site, Contern (manufacture of polyester films; Personnel Superintendent; public relations management; Product Stewardship & Regulatory Communications Manager—Europe, Middle East and Africa). Chairman of the Walferdange Tourist Board, member of the committee of the Luxembourg Interfaith Association and of the Pastoral Community Council for the Catholic Church in Steinsel-Walferdange.

Werner, Marie-Anne (born 1943): Second child of spouses Pierre Werner and Henriette Werner-Pescatore. Higher education in Luxembourg City, Strasbourg and Paris. Trainee then teacher of French, history and Latin at the Lycée Robert Schuman (1967–1987), Director of the Lycée Robert Schuman (1987–2004, when she retired). Member of the Council of the Jean Monnet Foundation for Europe, Lausanne (since 1993).

Werner, Pierre (1913–2002): Luxembourg legal expert and Christian Socialist statesman. Minister for Finance and the Armed

Forces (1954–1959); Minister for Finance (1959–1964, 1969–1974); Minister for Foreign Affairs, Justice and the Treasury (1964–1967); Minister for the Civil Service and the Treasury (1967–1969); Chairman of the EEC study group for the establishment of economic and monetary union (Werner Report) (1970–1971); Member of Parliament and leader of the Christian Social parliamentary group (1974–1979); Member of the European Parliament (1979); Minister for Cultural and Religious Affairs (1979–1984); Minister of State; Prime Minister (1959–1974, 1979–1984).

Werner-Pescatore, Henriette (1914–1984): second daughter of spouses Ferdinand Pescatore and Cunégonde Heuertz. Married Pierre Werner on 11 April 1939. They had five children. Henriette Werner-Pescatore was devoted to her family and to bringing up her children, providing valuable support for her husband in all circumstances. She was closely involved in social and educational activities to help those in need (she founded the centre for fairground workers that was set up to create a kindergarten for the children of the fairground workers at the Schueberfouer, and was a pioneer of the International Bazaar) and encourage interfaith dialogue (she chaired the Interfaith Association of Luxembourg).

White, Harry Dexter (1892–1948): US economist. Director for monetary research and special assistant to Treasury Secretary Henry Morgenthau (1941–1945). In this capacity, he was the liaison officer between the Treasury and the State Department on all foreign relations questions (1941); he was also responsible for the management and smooth operation of the exchange stabilisation fund. He took part in the 1944 Bretton Woods Conference, where he dominated the conference and imposed his vision despite the objections of British representative John Maynard Keynes. He was involved in the establishment of the institutions that resulted from Bretton Woods, namely the International Monetary Fund (IMF) and the World Bank. He was Director and US representative at the IMF (1945–1947).

Wilson, Harold (1916–1995): British Labour statesman. Labour Member of Parliament (1945–1983); Parliamentary Secretary in the Ministry of Public Works (1945–1947); Minister for Overseas Trade

(1947); President of the Board of Trade (1947–1951); leader of the Labour Party (1963–1976); Prime Minister (1964–1970, 1974–1976).

Witteveen, Hendrikus Johannes (Johan) (born 1921): Dutch economist, academic and politician, member of the People's Party for Freedom and Democracy. Analyst in the Netherlands Bureau for Economic Policy Analysis, particularly under chairman Jan Tinbergen (1947–1963); Minister for Finance (1967–1971); (fifth) Managing Director of the International Monetary Fund (IMF) (1973–1978); chairman of the G30 think tank which aims to deepen understanding of economic and financial issues and to examine the consequences of decisions related to these issues made in the public and private sectors (international financial institutions, central banks, the exchange market and currency, etc.) (1978–1985).

Zijlstra, Jelle (1918–2001): Dutch economist and politician, member of the Anti-Revolutionary Party. Minister for Economic Affairs, then Minister for Finance (1952–1963); Senator (1963–1966); Netherlands Prime Minister and Finance Minister (1966–1967); Chairman of the Nederlandse Bank (1967–1981); President of the Bank for International Settlements (BIS) (1967–1981); Minister of State (since 1983).

Appendix D: Luxembourg in a Nutshell[1]

Situated in the centre of Europe and bordered by two major powers, France and Germany, the Grand Duchy of Luxembourg (with a total area of just 2586 sq km and, in January 2018, a population of 602,005 inhabitants, of whom 47.9% were foreigners with 170 different nationalities)—a multicultural, multilingual, and cross-border area *par excellence*—has always sought to maintain an openness to its neighbours, both for reasons of security and to give itself access to larger markets. The fact that the country did not have its own currency has increased this need for openness and made monetary policy a key factor for integration.

In the nineteenth century, Luxembourg was part of the German customs and trade union (Zollverein). Following the First World War, the country embarked on a process of economic and monetary integration with Belgium via the Belgium–Luxembourg Economic Union (initially set up in 1921 and regularly extended over the ensuing decades). It also played a driving role in the economic and political rapprochement of Belgium, the Netherlands and Luxembourg in the Benelux Economic Union (established in 1944 and restyled as the Benelux Union in 2008). Following the Second World War, it was ultimately with the European

E. Danescu, *Pierre Werner and Europe*,
Archival Insights into the Evolution of Economics,
https://doi.org/10.1007/978-3-319-96295-5

project that these integration efforts began to bear fruit and take on a new dimension. Luxembourg was one of the six founding members of the European Coal and Steel Community (ECSC) and the European Economic Community (EEC); in 1952 the country became the workplace and one of the permanent seats of the institutions of the European Community (later European Union—EU), and it played a pioneering role in the establishment of Economic and Monetary Union (EMU).

These achievements boosted the standing of this constitutional monarchy that was already renowned for its political stability and social consensus, for the foresightedness and pragmatism of its long-term leadership and for its ability to manage crises and adopt an innovative approach. In political terms, European integration and multilateral cooperation enabled Luxembourg to become an equal partner in the decision-making processes and leadership of European organisations. In economic terms, these features gave the country the tools it needed to forge a development model that could underpin the creative growth of its social market economy, while preserving the majority of its vital interests—particularly the steel industry and the financial centre—over the long term. With a gross domestic product (GDP) growth rate of 2.3% en 2017 and an average annual growth rate of 3.5% between 1990 and 2016, the highest GDP per caput among the Organisation for Economic Cooperation and Development (OECD) member states, a level of material well-being more than 37% above the European average, an unemployment rate of 5.3% and sound public finances, Luxembourg is currently one of the most innovative and prosperous countries in the world.

From Agrarian Economy to Knowledge Economy: An Outline of Successive Transitions

Throughout the twentieth century Luxembourg experienced several periods of transition. The largely agriculture-based economy became industrialised, driven by a powerful steel industry which remained the dominant sector from the immediate post-Second World War years to the mid-1970s. The country had a considerable competitive advantage in this respect owing to iron ore deposits in Luxembourg itself and in the neighbouring French region of Lorraine. The industrial flagship was Aciéries Réunies de Burbach-Eich-Dudelange (ARBED), founded in 1911, which developed its production in Europe and established a global network of sales outlets. Between 1953 and 1968 the steel industry contributed approximately 25% of the country's GDP growth, while steel production represented 50% of its added industrial value. Over the same period, the nominal wage grew by 29.3%. The improvement in living standards led to the emergence of the middle class and to an increase in urbanisation.

The Government improved the social security regime and extended it to all workers, thus helping to close the gap in social equality, raise living standards further, and boost social cohesion in the country over the long term. The asymmetry between steel output (e.g. 6.4m. metric tons of steel in 1974) and national requirements (approximately 5% of this output) meant that Luxembourg had to export its steel production, which made the country entirely dependent on the international economic climate. Most of Luxembourg's steel went to the EEC. Membership of the Community organisations had a positive impact on the country, multiplying its wealth and boosting living standards. At the same time, the contrast between Luxembourg's thriving steel industry and its small population prompted it to look beyond its borders to augment its workforce. This resulted in several waves of immigration, especially from Italy at the turn of the twentieth century and from Portugal in the late 1960s. The discrepancy between the required and available capital in the country meant that it needed to tap into foreign capital. Luxembourg also looked abroad for expertise.

Even as the steel industry reached its peak, the Government set about exploring possibilities for economic diversification, introducing a suitable legislative framework with the establishment of the Board of Industrial Development in 1959, the adoption of the framework law on economic expansion (1962) and the creation of the Société Nationale de Crédit et d'Investissement (SNCI, 1980). It managed to attract major multinational companies in other manufacturing sectors (glass, chemicals, and plastics) and in the service industry (trade, tourism, and public administration). Most of the new companies that came to the country were from the USA, such as Goodyear, DuPont de Nemours, and Guardian. Nevertheless, 60% of foreign direct investment into Luxembourg was from its neighbours Germany and Belgium. The early 1970s saw the rise of a new growth sector for Luxembourg: the international financial centre. This was the result of action taken by the Government as well as several external factors, including the interest equalisation tax introduced by the USA in 1963 and the German securities transfer tax (*Kuponsteuer*) introduced in 1965. US capital and German banks were attracted to Luxembourg. Germany was the main investor in the banking sector, with 53% of all investments. The international financial centre would also become a 'laboratory' for the single European currency, one of the architects of which was Pierre Werner (Prime Minister of Luxembourg in 1959–1974 and again in 1979–1984, and Chairman of the expert committee that drafted the 1970 Werner Report, which formed the basis of EMU). The Luxembourg Stock Exchange, Kredietbank SA Luxembourgeoise, the Banque Internationale à Luxembourg, the Banque et Caisse d'Epargne de l'Etat, Luxembourg (the latter two recognised as systemically important banks in the country), and Cedel (which became Clearstream Banking in 1999) also played a major role.

In 1974 the steel industry began to decline, marking the end of the 'Trente Glorieuses'. Luxembourg was forced to implement considerable structural changes and embarked on its second major transition, from an industrial economy to a service economy based on the financial sector. This was reflected by fundamental changes in the structure of the country's economic value added. Between 1970 and 2011 the share of industry contracted sharply from 47 to 8%, while the share of the steel industry shrank from 28 to 2%. From the mid-1980s the country's economic growth accelerated, driven by its financial centre. During 1985–2007 average annual GDP growth was 5.3%, twice as much as that of neighbouring countries and of the member states of the EC/EU. In 1998, the financial industry employed approximately 20,000 people (some 10% of the working population), generating 20% of GDP and directly providing between 30 and 40% of the country's public revenue. An indirect impact of this sector was the development of business in related specialist areas, including information technology, data processing, intellectual property, legal and accounting expertise, training and business services.

Luxembourg is an export-intensive economy and the trade deficit is a recurrent characteristic. Between 1988 and 2016 the balance of trade averaged €300m, reaching an all-time high trade deficit of €30m in February 1988 and a record low of €1060m in September 2012. In 2015 the deficit stood at €5800m, down from the previous year. The share of foreign trade in Luxembourg's GDP is higher than 30%. EU countries are by far the country's largest trading partner, accounting for about 84% of exports and 87% of imports. Its three main trading partners are Germany, France, and Belgium; its top customer is Germany (more than 27%) and its leading supplier is Belgium (nearly 33%). Luxembourg mainly exports iron and steel, chemical and rubber products, glass, electrical and electronic equipment, and financial services, its most profitable export. The country remains dependent on imports of energy (mineral fuels and oil) and most of its consumer goods. Luxembourg has successfully diversified its exports outside the EU and the country is now developing trade relations with countries in Asia and the Middle East.

The expansion of the financial industry resulted in the emergence of a new phenomenon in Luxembourg: in order to meet its workforce requirements, the country turned to cross-border workers. This new development was made possible only by labour mobility, the discrepancy in unemployment rates between Luxembourg and its neighbours, and a positive wage differential. In 1998 cross-border workers made up one-third of the country's workforce. Of the total workforce, 55% were non-Luxembourgers. Concerted state intervention (in the form of investing to boost productivity, controlling mass unemployment by introducing community projects, activating the ECSC's aid mechanisms, and developing a productive synergy with Belgium) and the spectacular growth of the financial sector enabled the country to avoid a painful socio-economic crisis. Political leaders improved the legislative and institutional infrastructure underpinning the financial centre in three main areas: implementing international regulations; setting low taxes; and establishing strict rules on banking secrecy. The leaders explored possibilities for further economic diversification in innovative, competitive areas such as audiovisual technologies and communications satellites, as reflected in companies such as the Compagnie Luxembourgeoise de Télédiffusion and the Société Européenne des Satellites (SES). SES is now the world's leading satellite operator, reaching 99% of the global population. As regards the steel industry, in 2001 ARBED merged with Usinor and Aceralia, thus creating Arcelor, which in turn merged with Mittal Steel in 2006. ArcelorMittal, which has its headquarters in Luxembourg, is currently the world's largest steel producer.

To reconcile economic interests and social stability, the Government opted for a proactive social policy, with key measures including an automatic wage indexation mechanism based on increases in the cost of living (1965), the 40-hour working week (1975), a guaranteed minimum income (1986) and the expansion of the health care system. Labour relations were strengthened. In 1977, during the steel crisis, a Consultative Tripartite Committee (comprising the Government, employers and the unions) was established, acting as a shock absorber for both sides of industry. The Committee complemented the Economic and Social Council set up in 1966 as well as the various trade organisations and unions; it formed the basis of the Luxembourg social model, which relies on democracy, social solidarity, and consensus to underpin social and economic development.

In 2007, during the emergence of the 'sub-prime' mortgage crisis stemming from low-income borrowers' inability to meet repayment obligations on lending, Luxembourg had the EU's largest banking sector and was a highly specialised, widely diversified global financial centre (with investment funds, insurance companies, and banks, most of which were branches of foreign-based establishments). Since Luxembourg's economy was strongly driven by this sector, the potential vulnerabilities were considerable. In 2008 the financial sector contributed 29% of the country's GDP, 12% of jobs, and 20% of total tax revenues—a significantly higher proportion than in any other OECD country. The global financial crisis resulted in a decrease of 20% on the aggregated balance sheet of Luxembourg's banks and a decline in GDP of 5.4%. The 2009 downturn was less severe than that of the steel crisis in 1975, which was an exception for European countries. The contraction of the financial sector led to a fall in tax revenues, which raised the risk of a long-term impact on the sustainability of the generous Luxembourg social security system, placed under growing pressure by an ageing population.

Another long-term problem was the country's ongoing structural unemployment, despite a rise in the overall employment rate. In 2015 GDP strongly increased by 4.9%, returning to its pre-crisis level (during 2000–2007 GDP rose by roughly 4.7% per annum). The Government bailed out two major cross-border banks, Dexia and Fortis, which were experiencing serious difficulties; both required recapitalisation equivalent to 6% of GDP. However, government aid, in the form of guarantees and injections of capital, was less extensive than in other OECD countries. Three small Icelandic banks were placed under the legal administration of the Financial Sector Supervisory Commission (CSSF). All these problems, which were caused by cross-border issues, were resolved without severe difficulties, and contagion to other establishments in the financial centre was avoided. Although Luxembourg fared better than its partners in the euro zone, the crisis had a lasting effect on the country's competitive advantage, particularly because it had to align its financial regulations with European and international initiatives (such as budget constraints, prudential supervision, and increased transparency).

To guarantee its future position in a competitive globalised environment, the country faced a major strategic challenge: it had to diversify its economy while preserving the competitiveness of the financial sector. Luxembourg took the decision to focus on innovation as the main driver of sustainable growth, embarking on its third major transition—from a financial economy to a knowledge-based economy.

Luxembourg's economy has come a long way since the Second World War, especially in recent years. The once bipolar agricultural/industrial society has become a competitive society largely based on knowledge-intensive services, characterised by high-performing human capital, political stability, prosperity, and a strong welfare system. The country is a driving force for the Greater Region in economic terms. Among the key growth factors for Luxembourg, five can be identified as particularly important: the country's integration into larger economic areas; the systematic development of infrastructures; a permanently available workforce (through migration and cross-border workers); the existence of growth niches, and high-value-added economic diversification (starting with the iron and steel industry, moving into the financial sector and arriving today at a service- and knowledge-based economy); and a high level of social protection. The country's proactive political leadership, a source of long-term continuity, has turned exogenous challenges into opportunities, integrating them into a creative economic policy. It was this approach that enabled Luxembourg's international financial centre to emerge in the early 1960s, aided by legislative and regulatory provisions in the USA and Germany; to become a 'laboratory' for a common European currency following the 1970 Werner Report; and to specialise in private banking in the wake of the debt crisis in Latin American countries in the early 1980s. The stability provided by the country's many longstanding prime ministers, leaders of successive coalition governments of varying compositions, has enabled the development of a sustainable and highly specific 'ordoliberal' model based on symbiosis between free competition and institutional order, with a strong social backbone. Within Luxembourg's long-term strategic vision, the economy has been the main area on which political platforms have converged, underpinned by two pillars: a balanced approach and a culture based on consensus and peaceful labour relations. The 'Luxembourg consultation model' and Luxembourg's specific brand of social stability largely reflect this: agreement is reached between the 'social partners' (within the Tripartite and the Economic and Social Council) before legislation is adopted by the Chamber of Deputies, thereby creating an environment conducive to social solidarity where any potential disagreements can be identified and resolved in advance. The country has consolidated its national identity by opening itself up to the international community. Looking to the future, if Luxembourg is to safeguard its welfare state and boost competitiveness, it will have to tackle three recurrent issues: an ageing population, unemployment (especially among young people and over the long term), and the sustainability of the social security system.

Note

1. This text is inspired by one of my recent publications: E. Danescu (2017) 'Luxembourg analysis' in Cathy Hartley (ed.), *Western Europe 2018* (London and New York: Routledge, Abingdon), pp. 475–486. Licensed material reproduced with permission of The Licensor through PLSclear.

Sources and Bibliography

Archives

Pierre Werner family archives, Luxembourg (PWLux)[1]
Archives Nationales de Luxembourg (ANLux)
German Federal Archives, Koblenz (BArch)
Archives historiques du Parlement européen
Archives of the European Central Bank in Frankfurt (AECB)
Archives of European Intergration, University of Pittsburgh (AEI) (http://aei.pitt.edu/)
Diplomatic Archive Center of the Ministry of Foreign and European Affairs, La Courneuve (FDAC)
Jean Monnet Archives, Fondation Jean Monnet pour l'Europe, Lausanne (FJME)

---

[1]Particularly the papers in the cases marked ref. PW 036, entitled '*1962–1971. La monnaie de compte. L'unité de compte. Le dollar comme monnaie de réserve*' [1962–1971. The currency of account. The unit of *account. The dollar as a reserve currency*]; *PW 046, entitled* 'L'intégration monétaire de l'Europe 1962–1969' [The monetary integration of Europe 1962–1969]; PW 047, entitled '*Groupe Werner: Antécédents, préparatifs et réunions 1968–1970*' [Werner Group: Antecedents, preparations and meetings 1968–1970]; PW 048, entitled '*Intégration monétaire de l'Europe. Le Plan Werner: 1970*' [Monetary integration of Europe. The Werner Plan: 1970]; and *PW 054, entitled* '*1972–1973. Union économique et monétaire. Fonds européen de coopération monétaire*' [1972–1973. Economic and monetary union. European monetary cooperation fund].

E. Danescu, *Pierre Werner and Europe*,
Archival Insights into the Evolution of Economics,
https://doi.org/10.1007/978-3-319-96295-5

Historical Archives of the European Union (HAEU)
Italian Historical Diplomatic Archives, Rome (IHDA)
Robert Triffin Archives (RTA)
Archives of Tommaso Padoa-Schioppa (TPSA)

Publications

M. Aglietta and N :Leron (2017) *La double démocratie. Une Europe politique pour la croissance* (Paris : Le Seuil).

G. Baer and T. Padoa-Schioppa (1989) 'The Werner Report Revisited', in *Committee for the Study of Economic and Monetary Union. Report on Economic and Monetary Union in the European Community*, April 1989 (Luxembourg: Office for the Official Publications of the European Community), pp. 53–60.

C. Balleix-Banerjee (1999) *La France et la Banque Centrale Européenne* (Paris: Presses Universitaires de France).

R. Barre (1968, I) 'Les problèmes monétaires internationaux et la politique monétaire de la Communauté', in *Bulletin des Communautés européennes*, 1 (November) (Luxembourg: Office for the Official Publications of the European Community).

D. Beach (2005) The Dynamics of European Integration: Why and When EU Institutions Matter (Basingstoke: Palgrave Macmillan).

J.-R. Bernard (1998) 'Georges Pompidou et l'effondrement du système de Bretton Woods', in *La France et les institutions de Bretton Woods 1944–1994. Colloque tenu à Bercy les 30 juin et 1er juillet 1994* (Paris: Comite pour l'histoire économique et financière de la France), pp. 121–125.

M.-T. Bitsch, E. Bussiere, and G. Lavezzi 'Entretien avec Raymond Barre. Transcription. Paris, 20 February 2004', in V*oix sur l'Europe: Histoire interne de la Commission européenne 1958–1973*. http://wwwarc.eui.eu/int/pdf/INT763.pdf, accessed on 6 March 2018.

M. Bordo and B. Eichengreen (1984) *A Retrospective on the Bretton Woods System: Lessons for International Monetary Reform*. National Bureau of Economic Research (London: The University of Chicago Press).

W. Brandt (1971) *Reden und Interviews*, Vol. I–III (Hamburg: Hoffmann und Campe).

W. Brandt (1990) *Mémoires* (Paris: Albin Michel).

M. K. Brunnermeier, H. James, and J.-P. Landau (2016) *The Euro and the Battle of Economic Ideas* (Princeton, NJ: Princeton University Press).

E. Bussière and O. Feiertag (2012) 'Triffin et la construction monétaire européenne: Une contribution à la rénovation du système monétaire international', in J.-C. Koeune and A. Lamfalussy (eds.), *In Search of a New World Monetary Order* (Brussels: P.I.E. - Peter Lang), pp. 73–96.

E. Bussière and E.Palermo (2014) 'La Commission européenne 1973–1986 [Texte imprimé]: histoire et mémoires d'une institution / Commission européenne' (Luxembourg: Office des publications de l'Union européenne).

M. Burgess (2000) *Federalism and European Union: The Building of Europe, 1950–2000* (London: Taylor and Francis).

G. Carli (1993) *Cinquant'anni di vita italiana* (Roma-Bari: Laterza).

Commission of the EEC (1958) Report on the Economic Situation in the Countries of the Community, September.

Commission of the EEC (1962a) Memorandum of the Commission on the Action Programme of the Community for the Second Stage, COM (62) 300 final, 24 October.

Commission of the EEC (1962b) Les perspectives de développement économique dans la C.E.E. de 1960 à 1970. Rapport d'un groupe d'experts.

Commission of the EEC (1963a) La coopération monétaire et financière au sein de la Communauté Économique Européenne (Communication de la Commission au Conseil), II/COM(63) 216 final, 19 June.

Commission of the EEC (1963b) Politique économique à moyen terme de la Communauté (Recommendation de la Commission au Conseil), II/COM(63) 271 final, 25 July.

Commission of the EEC (1964) Initiative 1964 for Speeding Up the Implementation of the Common Market, Community Topics 15. European Community Information Service.

Commission of the European Communities (1966) Le développement d'un marché européen des capitaux, Rapport Segré. Brussels.

Commission of the European Communities (1975) Report of the Study Group 'Economic and Monetary Union 1980', 8 March 1975.

Commission of the European Communities (1977) Report of the Study Group on the Role of Public Finance in European Integration.

Commission of the European Communities (1993) 'Stable Money—Sound Finances: Community Public Finance in the Perspective of EMU', *European Economy*, 53.

Committee for the Study of Economic and Monetary Union (1989) Report on Economic and Monetary Union in the European Community (Luxembourg: Office for the Official Publications of the European Community).

N. Crafts and G. Toniolo (1996) 'Postwar Growth: An Overview', in N. Crafts and G. Toniolo (eds.), *Economic Growth in Europe Since 1945* (Cambridge: Cambridge University Press), pp. 1–37.

CVCE.eu by UNI.lu *Oral history of European Integration Collection.* http://www.cvce.eu/en/oral-history (main page), accessed 6 March 2018.

E. Danescu (2011) 'Le comité Werner, nouvelles archives', in F. Clavert and O. Feiertag (eds.), *Histoire, économie & société*, 30 (4), pp. 29–38.

E. Danescu (2012a) *A Rereading of the Werner Report of 8 October 1970 in the Light of the Pierre Werner Family Archives* (Research corpus). https://www.cvce.eu/project/werner/ (front page), accessed on 6 March 2018.

E. Danescu (2012b) 'Summary of the Werner Committee's Schedule and the Main Issues Addressed (6 March 1970–22 March 1971)', in *A Rereading of the Werner Report of 8 October 1970 in the Light of the Pierre Werner Family Archives* (Research corpus). https://www.cvce.eu/project/werner/ (front page), accessed on 6 March 2018.

E. Danescu (2016a) 'Pierre Werner, a Visionary European and Consensus Builder', in K. Dyson and I. Maes (eds.), *Architects of the Euro. Intellectuals in the Making of European Monetary Union* (London: Oxford University Press), pp. 93–116.

E. Danescu (2016b) 'La construction européenne dans les années 1970: Pierre Werner et le couple franco-allemand', in S. Schirmann (ed.), *Le couple franco-allemand vu par les Etats tiers depuis 1963* (Paris: l'Harmattan), pp. 47–80.

E. Danescu (2017) 'Luxembourg Analysis' in C. Hatley (ed.), *Western Economy 2018* (London and New York: Routledge), pp. 475–486.

E. Danescu (2018) 'Through a century of change: Portrait of a pragmatic visionary' in *Journal of European Integration History (JEIH)*, 20, pp. 9–30.

A. De Saint Périer (2013) *La France, l'Allemagne et l'Europe Monétaire de 1974 à 1981* (Paris: Presses de la Fondation Nationale de Sciences Politiques).

M. Debré (1988) *Trois Républiques pour une France. Tome 3: Gouverneur. Mémoires 1958–1962* (Paris: Albin Michel).

J. Delors (1989) 'Economic and Monetary Union and Re-launching the Construction of Europe', in *Committee for the Study of Economic and Monetary Union, Report on Economic and Monetary Union in the European Community* (Luxembourg: Office for the Official Publications of the European Community), pp. 63–67.

J. Delors (1992) *Monetary Cooperation in the Building of Europe: The 1992 Jean Monnet Lecture* (London: London School of Economics).

J. Delors (1999) *Pierre Werner—Testimonies at the Threshold of the 21st Century*. Transcription, extract of oral account from the documentary, European Commission.

M. Dierikx (ed.), M. Smits, L. van Suijlekom, F. Clavert, E. Danescu, and M. Gabellini (2012) *Common Fate, Common Future: A Documentary History of Monetary and Financial Cooperation, 1947–1974* (The Hague: CVCE—Huygens ING).

H. Drake (2000) Jacques Delors: Perspectives on a European Leader (London: Routledge).

K. Dyson (2012) 'Maastricht Plus: Managing the Logic of Inherent Imperfections', *Journal of European Integration*, 35 (2), pp. 791–808.

K. Dyson (2015) 'Mastering Small-State Diplomacy: Pierre Werner in the History of European Monetary Union', in E. Danescu and S. Muñoz (eds.), *Pierre Werner and Europe: His Approach, Action and Legacy. Proceedings of the International Conference*, Luxembourg, 2013 (Brussels: P.I.E. - Peter Lang), pp. 19–26.

K. Dyson and K. Featherstone (1999) *The Road to Maastricht: Negotiating Economic and Monetary Union* (Oxford: Oxford University Press).

K. Dyson and I. Maes (2016) *Architects of the Euro. Intellectuals in the Making of European Monetary Union* (London: Oxford University Press).

K. Dyson and L. Quaglia (2010) *European Economic Governance and Policies: Commentary on Key Historical and Institutional Documents* (Oxford: Oxford University Press).

EC Commission (1968) 'Memorandum on Community Action in the Monetary Sphere'.

EC Commission (1969) 'Mémorandum de la Commission au Conseil sur la coordination des politiques économiques et la coopération monétaire au sein de la Communauté, 12 February', *Bulletin of the European Communities*, Supplement, 3. Brussels.

EC (1969) 'Communiqué of the meeting of Heads of State or Government of the Member States at The Hague (1 and 2 December 1969)', *Bulletin of the European Communities* 1/1970, pp. 12–15, Brussels.

EC (1970a) 'Interim Report on the Establishment by Stages of Economic and Monetary Union', Document 9.504/II/70-D in *Bulletin of the European Communities* 7/1970, Supplement, C94 (23 July 1970) (Luxembourg: Office for the Official Publications of the European Community).

EC (1970b) 'Report to the Council and the Commission on the Realisation by Stages of Economic and Monetary Union in the Community (Werner

Report)', Luxembourg, 8 October 1970 in *Bulletin of the European Communities* 11/1970, Supplement, 8 October 1970 (Luxembourg: Office for the Official Publications of the European Community).

EC (1975) 'Report of the Study Group "Economic and Monetary Union 1980" (The Marjolin Report)'. http://ec.europa.eu (main page), accessed on 6 March 2018.

B. Eichengreen (1996) *Globalizing Capital: A History of the International Monetary System* (Princeton, NJ: Princeton University Press).

B. Eichengreen (2011) *Exorbitant Privilege: The Rise and Fall of the Dollar* (Oxford: Oxford University Press).

European Commission (1990a) 'Economic and Monetary Union: The Economic Rationale and Design of the System', 20 March, IP/90/231 (Brussels: European Commission).

European Commission (1990b) 'One Market, One Money' in *European Economy*, 44 (Brussels: European Commission).

European Commission (1993) 'Growth, Competitiveness, Employment: The Challenges and Ways Forward into the 21st Century', COM(93)700 (Brussels: European Commission).

European Monetary Institute (1995) *The Changeover to the Single Currency* (Frankfurt: EMI).

O. Emminger and H. Giersch (1971) *Integration durch Währungsunion?/ Integration through monetary union? Symposium Juni 1970. Universität Kiel* (Institut für Weltwirtschaft. Tubingen: Siebeck).

M. Feldstein (1992) 'Europe's Monetary Union: The Case against EMU', *The Economist*, 323 (763), pp. 19–22.

C. Ghymers (2015) 'Une relecture du plan Werner par rapport à ses antecedents et ses successeurs', in E. Danescu and S. Muñoz (eds.), *Pierre Werner and Europe: His Approach, Action and Legacy. Proceedings of the International Conference*, Luxembourg, 2013 (Brussels: P.I.E. - Peter Lang), pp. 183–201.

C. A. Goodhart and S. Smith (1993) 'Stabilization', in *The Economics of Community Public Finance. European Economy Reports and Studies*, 5 (Brussels: European Commission), pp. 356–373.

C. Grant (1994) Delors. *Inside the House That Jacques Built* (London: Nicholas Brealey).

D. Gros and N. Thygesen (1998) *European Monetary Integration: From the European Monetary System to Economic and Monetary Union* (London: Longman).

C. Henning (1994) *Currencies and Policies in the United States, Germany, and Japan* (Washington, DC: Institute for International Economics).

C. Hiepel (2003) 'In Search of the Greatest Common Denominator: Germany and The Hague Summit Conference 1969', *Journal of European Integration History*, 9, pp. 63–81.

HM Treasury (1989) *An Evolutionary Approach to Economic and Monetary Union* (London: HMSO).

D. Howarth (2001) *The French Road to European Monetary Union* (Basingstoke: Palgrave Macmillan).

O. Issing (2008) *The Birth of the Euro* (Cambridge: Cambridge University Press).

H. James (2012) *Making the European Monetary Union. The Role of the Committee of Central Bank Governors and the Origins of the European Central Bank* (Cambridge, MA: The Belknap Press of Harvard University Press).

R. Jenkins (1977) *Europe's Present Challenge and Future Opportunity*. Jean Monnet lecture, 27 October (Florence: Institute of European Studies).

J.-C. Juncker (2011) '*Du plan Werner à l'Euro: 40 ans de succès et de crises*', in E. Danescu (ed.), *Pierre Werner et l'Europe. Actes de la présentation officielle du projet de recherche et de la conférence de Jean-Claude Juncker, Premier ministre, président de l'Eurogroupe*, 27 janvier (Luxembourg: CVCE), pp. 48–59.

W. Kaiser (2007) *Christian Democracy and the Origins of European Union* (Cambridge: Cambridge University Press).

J.-C. Koeune (2015) 'Challenges and Prospects of EMU', in E. Danescu and S. Muñoz (eds.), *Pierre Werner and Europe: His Approach, Action and Legacy. Proceedings of the International Conference*, Luxembourg, 2013 (Brussels: P.I.E. - Peter Lang), pp. 301–305.

P. Krugman (1993) 'What Do We Need to Know about the International Monetary System? in *Essays in International Economics*, 190 (Princeton, NJ: Princeton University Press, pp. 241–261.

A. Lamfalussy (1976) 'Monetary and Fiscal Integration', in F. Machlup (ed.), *Economic Integration Worldwide: Regional, Sectoral* (London: Macmillan), pp. 218–245.

C. Lamfalussy, I. Maes, and S. Péters (2014). *Alexandre Lamfalussy: The Wise Man of the Euro. A Conversation with Christophe Lamfalussy, Ivo Maes and Sabine Péters*. (Leuven: LannooCampus, February)

Maes, I. (1998a) 'Macroeconomic Thought at the European Commission in the 1970s: The First Decade of the Annual Economic Reports in *Banca Nazionale del Lavoro Quarterly Review*, 207, pp. 387–412.

I. Maes (1998) 'Projets d'intégration monétaire à la Commission européenne', in E. Bussière and M Dumoulin (eds.), *Milieux économiques et intégration européenne en Europe occidentale au XXe siècle* (Arras: Artois Presses Université), pp. 35–50.

I. Maes and L. Quaglia (2004) 'France and Italy's Policies on European Monetary Integration. A Comparison of "Strong" and "Weak" States', *Comparative European Politics*, 2 (1), pp. 51–72.

L. Magnusson and B. Stråth (eds.) (2004) *From the Werner Plan to the EMU: In Search of a Political Economy for Europe*, 2nd edition (Brussels: P.I.E. - Peter Lang).

R. Marjolin (1986) *Architect of European Unity: Memoirs 1911–1986* (London: Weidenfeld & Nicolson).

M. Marcussen (2000) *Ideas and Elites: The Social Construction of Economic and Monetary Union* (Aalborg: Aalborg University Press).

D. Marsh (1992) *The Most Powerful Bank: Inside Germany's Bundesbank* (New York: Times Books).

D. Marsh (2009) *The Euro: The Politics of the New Global Currency* (New Haven, CT: Yale University Press).

F. Masini (2014) 'European Integration: Contrasting Models and Perspectives' in R. Fiorentini and G. Montani (eds.), *The European Union and Supranational Political Economy* (Abingdon: Routledge), pp. 44–64.

K. McNamara (1998) *The Currency of Ideas: Monetary Politics in the European Union* (Ithaca, NY: Cornell University Press).

A. S. Milward (1984) *The Reconstruction of Western Europe, 1945–51* (Berkeley, CA: University of California Press).

A. Moravcsik (1998) *The Choice for Europe: Social Purpose and State Power from Messina to Maastricht* (Ithaca, NY: Cornell University Press).

E. Mourlon-Druol (2012) *A Europe Made of Money: The Emergence of the European Monetary System* (Ithaca, NY: Cornell University Press).

R. Mundell (1961) 'A Theory of Optimum Currency Areas', *American Economic Review*, 51 (4), pp. 657–665.

R. Mundell and A. Clesse (2000) *The EURO as a Stabilizer in the International Economic System* (Boston: Kluwer Academic).

P. Nora (1987) *Essais d'ego-histoire* (Paris: Gallimard).

T. Padoa-Schioppa (2000) *The Road to Monetary Union in Europe: The Emperor, the Kings, and the Genies* (New York: Oxford University Press).

T. Padoa-Schioppa (2004) L'euro e la sua banca centrale: L'unione dopo l'unione (Bologna: Il Mulino).

G. Pompidou (1975) *Entretiens et discours. Volume II: 1968–1974* (Paris: Plon).

J. Rueff (1950) 'L'Europe se fera par la monnaie ou ne se fera pas', *Synthèses* (revue), 45, Bruxelles. Reproduced in *L'âge de l'inflation* [The Age of Inflation] (Paris: Payot) 1963, pp. 123–129.

A. A. Sapir (2014) 'Financial Crises Under Two Monetary Regimes: EMU vs. EMS', in I. Maes and F. Moss (eds.), *Progress Through Crisis? Proceedings of the Conference for the 20th Anniversary of the Establishment of the European Monetary Institute* (Frankfurt am Main: ECB), pp. 33–67.

H. Scheller (2011) 'Le Comité des gouverneurs des banques centrales de la CEE et l'unification monétaire européenne', in F. Clavert and O. Feiertag (eds.), *Histoire, économie & société*, 30 (4), pp. 79–100.

H. Scheller (2014) 'The Design of the ECB's Toolbox: Fitting the EMI Blueprint into a Deeper EMU', in I. Maes and F. Moss (eds.), *Progress Through Crisis? Proceedings of the Conference for the 20th Anniversary of the Establishment of the European Monetary Institute* (Frankfurt am Main: ECB), pp. 113–128.

H. Scheller (2015) 'The Werner Plan and the Delors Report: One or Two Approaches to EMU?' in E. Danescu and S. Muñoz (eds.), *Pierre Werner and Europe: His Approach, Action and Legacy. Proceedings of the International Conference*, Luxembourg, 2013 (Brussels: P.I.E. - Peter Lang), pp. 277–298.

S. Schirmann (ed.) (2007) *Penser et construire l'Europe (1919–1992). États et opinions nationales face à la construction européenne* (Paris: Sedes).

G.-H. Soutou (2010) 'Raymond Barre et l'Europe in Académie des Sciences Morales et Politiques, FNSP, Aspen France, Raymond Barre, *Un homme singulier dans la politique française* (Paris: Éditions de Fallois), pp. 69–82.

A. Spinelli (1982) *Background Notes on the Collected Documents* in *Selection of Texts Concerning Institutional Matters of the Community from 1952 to 1982.* Luxembourg, European Parliament. Committee on Institutional Affairs.

M. Szenberg, (ed.) (1992) *Eminent Economists: Their Life Philosophies* (Cambridge: Cambridge University Press).

N. Thygesen (1989) 'The Delors Report and European Economic and Monetary Union', *International Affairs*, 65 (4), pp. 637–652.

H. Tietmeyer (1971) 'L'union économique et monétaire au centre du débat politique', *Hefte,* 1 (197) (Köln: Institut für Wirtschaftspolitik Press).

H. Tietmeyer (2003) 'Der Bericht der Werner-Gruppe von 1970 und der Bericht der Delors-Gruppe von 1989—Ein Vergleich', in W. Hankel, K. Schachtschneider, and J. Starbatty (eds.), *Der Ökonom als Politiker: Festschrift für Wilhelm Nölling* (Stuttgart: Lucius), pp. 345–359.

H. Tietmeyer (2004) *Herausforderung Euro. Wie es zum Euro kam und was er für Deutschlands Zukunft bedeutet* (Munich: Hanser).

H. Tietmeyer (2015) 'Der Werner-Bericht als Wegweiser für die Wirtschafts- und Währungsunion.' In Danescu, E. & Muñoz,S. (eds/dirs). *Pierre Werner and Europe: His Approach, Action and Legacy*. Proceedings of the international conference, Luxembourg, 27-28 November 2013 (Brussels: P.I.E. Peter Lang).

G. Toniolo and P. Clement (2005) *Central Bank Cooperation at the Bank for International Settlements, 1930–1973* (Cambridge: Cambridge University Press).

R. Triffin (1960) *Pour un Fonds européen de réserves* (Lausanne: Centre de recherches européennes), 1971.

R. Triffin (1977) 'A European Parallel Currency as a Shelter against Exchange-Rate Instability', *Bulletin de l'IRES*, 45.

R. Triffin and A. Swings (eds.) (1980) *The Private Use of the ECU* (Brussels: Kredietbank).

L. Tsoukalis (1993) *The New European Economy: The Politics and Economics of Integration*. 2nd edition (New York: Oxford University Press).

J. Van Yperseele and J.-C. Koeune (1988) *Le système monétaire européen* (Luxembourg and Brussels: Perspectives européennes).

A. Verdun (2004) 'The Political Economy of the Werner and Delors Reports: Continuity Amidst Change', in L. Magnusson and B. Stråth (eds.), *From the Werner Plan to the EMU: In Search of a Political Economy for Europe*, 2nd edition (Brussels: P.I.E. - Peter Lang), pp. 73–96.

S. Wall (2012) 'The Official History of Britain and the European Community' in Volume II: *From Rejection to Referendum, 1963–1975* (Abingdon: Routledge).

H. von der Groeben (1982) *Aufbaujahre der Europäischen Gemeinschaft: Das Ringen um den Gemeinsamen Markt und die Politische Union (1958–1966)* (Baden-Baden: Nomos Verlag).

R. Weintraub and E. Forget (2007). *Economists' Lives: Biography and Autobiography in the History of Economics* (Durham, NC: Duke University Press).

P. Werner (1960) 'Significations d'une intégration monétaire', *Documentation Bulletin*, 15 (December) (Luxembourg: IPS), pp. 3–11.

P. Werner (1962) *Problèmes de l'intégration financière de l'Europe.* Talk given in Brussels by Pierre Werner, Minister of State, President of the Luxembourg Government and Finance Minister, to the members of the Association des

Amitiés Belgo-Luxembourgeoises and the Cercle Royal Gaulois (Brussels: Cercle Royal Gaulois).

P. Werner (1966a) *Exposé sur la politique monétaire européenne.* A lecture given in Brussels by Pierre Werner, Minister of State, President of the Government and Minister for the Treasury and the Civil Service, at the invitation of the American and Common Market Club, Brussels, 5 June, *La Libre Belgique*, 6 June 1966.

P. Werner (1966b) 'Address by Pierre Werner, President of the Councils of the European Communities, to the European Parliament in Strasbourg, 28 June 1966', *Documentation Bulletin*, 9 (1 July) (Luxembourg: IPS), pp. 8–12.

P. Werner (1968a) 'Perspectives de la Politique Financière et Monétaire Européenne. Address given at the CDU Economic Congress in Saarbrücken on 26 January 1968', *Documentation Bulletin*, 2 (Luxembourg: IPS), pp. 3–9.

P. Werner (1968b) 'Benelux et les perspectives de la politique financière européenne'. Address given in The Hague by Pierre Werner, Minister of State, President of the Government and Minister for the Treasury, to the Benelux Committee, 1 April 1968', *Documentation Bulletin*, 6 (30 June) (Luxembourg: IPS), pp. 8–11.

P. Werner (1968c) 'Address given in Rotterdam by Pierre Werner, President of the Government, Minister for the Treasury, at the meeting of the Council of Finance Ministers of the EEC, 10 September 1968', *Documentation Bulletin*, 8 (September) (Luxembourg: IPS), pp. 4–6.

P. Werner (1969) 'Statement by Mr Pierre Werner, Minister of State, Prime minister of Luxembourg, at the conference of the Heads of State or Government, The Hague, 1 December 1969', *Documentation Bulletin*, 14 (10 December) (Luxembourg: IPS), pp. 3–7.

P. Werner (1970a) 'L'Europe en route vers l'Union Monétaire', *Documentation Bulletin*, 1 (28 February) (Luxembourg: IPS), pp. 5–12.

P. Werner (1970b) 'Statement by Pierre Werner to the Council of Ministers, Luxembourg, 26 October 1970', *Documentation Bulletin*, 6 (Luxembourg: IPS), pp. 4–5.

P. Werner (1972) 'L'union économique et monétaire en tant qu'étape vers l'Europe politique', in *Liber amicorum Fernand Collin* (Bruxelles: Kredietbank), pp. 263–268.

P. Werner (1980) '*Du Plan Werner au système monétaire européen* (*SME*)', *Studia Diplomatica*, 3 (Bruxelles: Egmont Institute), pp. 241–255.

P. Werner (1989) *L'Union économique et monétaire d'un rapport à l'autre*, Septembre 1989.

P. Werner (1990) 'Der Werner-Bericht und der Delors-Bericht zur Europäischen Wirtschafts- und Währungsunion im Vergleich', in O. Franz (Hrsg.), *Die Europäische Zentralbank* (Bonn: Europa Union Verlag), pp. 175–184.

P. Werner (1992) *Itinéraires luxembourgeois et européens. Évolutions et souvenirs 1945–1985*, 2 volumes (Luxembourg: Éditions Saint-Paul).

R. Wester (1992) 'The European Commission and European Political Union', in F. Laursen and S. Vanhoonacker (eds.), *The Intergovernmental Conference on Political Union: Institutional Reforms, New Policies and International Identity of the European Community* (Maastricht: Martinus Nijhoff Publishers), pp. 163–178.

M. Wolf, (2014) *The Shifts and the Shocks: What We've Learned—and Have Still to Learn—from the Financial Crisis* (London: Allen Lane).

Index

A

Abs, Hermann J. 21, 43, 297
Accession 101, 106, 210, 214, 238, 247, 260, 261, 274, 279
Achille-Fould, Aymar 289
Action Committee for the United States of Europe (ACUSE) 22, 25, 30, 39, 43, 49, 287, 357
Action Programme for the Second Stage of the EEC 44, 45, 79, 82, 297
Adenauer, Konrad 39
Ad hoc committee 68, 94, 97, 98, 130, 139, 204, 226, 234, 235, 260
Ad hoc group 93–95, 99, 102, 108, 109, 116, 118, 128, 134, 137, 204, 206, 227, 232, 270
Adjustment 54, 311, 312, 317, 328
Agriculture 66, 283, 294, 332, 350
Aigner, Heinrich 276, 277
Airey, Lawrence 339
Allemagne. *See* Germany
Allen, L. 279
All Saints Day Manifesto 340
American and Common Market Club 83
Ameye, Louis 295
Amsterdam 254, 279
Annual report 191, 209, 213, 231, 242, 264
Ansiaux, Hubert 43, 45, 70, 80, 94, 98, 102, 103, 106–109, 118–120, 123, 124, 127, 134, 135, 138, 139, 171, 176, 183, 185–188, 190, 196, 199, 200, 225, 226, 273, 283, 300, 344, 347, 348, 357
Anti-Cyclical Policy Committee 94, 102, 104

E. Danescu, *Pierre Werner and Europe*,
Archival Insights into the Evolution of Economics,
https://doi.org/10.1007/978-3-319-96295-5

Archiv der sozialen Demokratie der Friedrich-Ebert-Stiftung 90, 323
Archives Nationales de Luxembourg/ Luxembourg National Archives (ANLux) 15, 30
Archives of Tommaso Padoa-Schioppa 16
Archives of the Bank for International Settlements (BIS) 16
Archives of the Belgian Foreign Ministry 16
Archive of the Cabinet of the Prime Minister 134
Archives of the Netherlands Foreign Ministry 16
Archives of the European Central Bank (ECB) 16, 87, 282, 327
Archives of the European Commission Audiovisual Library 16
Archives of the French Ministry of Foreign and European Affairs (La Courneuve) 16
Archives of the Jean Monnet Foundation for Europe (Lausanne) 16
Armand, Louis 76
Arnhem 240
Arras 342
Association des Amitiés Belgo-Luxembourgeoises 81
Association for Banking History 76
Association of Catholic University Students ('Akademikerverein') 20
Atlantic 46, 55, 64, 126
Aubourg, V. 79
Audiovisual sector 23, 27, 28
Austria 34, 270, 313
Autostrade Eurobonds 279

B

Baden-Baden 30, 89, 91
Baer, G. 343
Baffi, Paolo 186, 232, 282
Bahr, Egon 90
Balance of payment(s) 35, 36, 38, 53, 58, 69, 78, 80, 82, 85, 136, 191, 211, 215, 216, 308, 323, 332
Banca d'Italia 49, 186, 199, 232, 258, 282, 312, 327
Bank Deutscher Länder 33
Bank for International Settlements (BIS) 78, 81, 184, 318
Banking 21, 23, 40, 52, 279
Banking Control Commission (CCB) 40, 52
Banks 37, 53, 73, 78, 82, 85, 124
Banque Centrale du Luxembourg (BCL) 14, 15, 453
Banque de Bruxelles 84
Banque de France 94, 97, 186, 199, 248
Banque et Caisse d'Épargne de l'État 21
Banque Générale 20, 29
Banque nationale de France 138
Barre, Raymond 28, 43, 56–58, 66, 68, 70, 75, 87, 90, 91, 96, 99, 101, 102, 114, 117, 127, 128, 131, 134, 137, 139, 140, 185, 186, 205, 206, 215–217, 219–221, 224–227, 230, 234, 239, 242, 252, 272, 280–283, 289, 299
Barre Plan 49, 56, 59, 70, 88
Barthel, C. 30, 49, 88
Bascoul, A. 199

Basel 78, 81, 87, 199, 282, 285, 311, 312, 327
Basel Committee of Banking Supervision 53
Baumgartner, Wilfrid 20, 40
Bech, Joseph 22, 24, 30, 357
Belgian 42, 43, 60, 65, 95
Belgian franc 307, 312, 325, 326
Belgian plan 70, 92, 292
Belgium 10, 26, 30, 34, 38, 43, 63, 66, 69, 80, 85, 97, 99, 102, 106, 130, 131, 136, 137, 161, 197, 201, 205, 226, 244, 256, 257, 260, 272, 273, 282, 292, 297, 302, 306, 314, 324, 326
Belgium–Luxembourg Economic Union (BLEU) 3, 16, 21, 27, 43, 45, 356
Belgium and Luxembourg Exchange Institute 52
Bellagio 39, 79
Belt, Haller 271
Benelux 3, 16, 21, 41, 43, 47, 49, 57, 60, 70, 71, 86, 106, 191, 195, 253, 255, 257, 307, 308, 311, 312, 324, 326, 356
Berg, Frédéric 295
Berger, G. 323
Bernard, J.-R. 89, 288
Biermans-Lapôtre Foundation 20
Bilateralism 78, 81
Bilderberg 79
Bilderberg Group 39
Bitsch, M.T. 89, 90, 281
Blessing, Karl 43, 44
Bloch-Lainé, Jean-Michel 102, 103, 123, 126, 248, 288, 348
Blondeel, Jean 27, 53
Blondel, D. 295
Blumenthal, E. 199
Boersma, E. 280
Bonn 66, 84, 86, 90, 98, 130, 132, 140, 243, 244, 272, 275, 285–287, 289, 290, 292, 293, 298, 301, 314, 323, 343
Bordo, M. 77, 87
Borschette, Albert 205, 351
Bossuat, G. 78, 81, 82, 90, 201, 287
Both sides of industry 115, 163, 168, 176, 210, 212, 213, 218, 222, 223, 228, 280, 332, 334, 356
Bourg, Georges 20
Bousch, J.E. 207, 277, 280
Boyer de la Giroday, F. 199
Brandt, Willy 64, 66, 67, 89, 90, 116, 192, 193, 202, 240, 244, 253, 285, 286, 289, 292, 309, 324, 349, 357
  archives 324
Bretton Woods Agreements 35, 37, 82, 84, 86, 87, 308, 313, 323
Bretton Woods System 37, 38, 44, 48, 52–56, 62, 77, 80, 253, 310–312, 336
Britain 43, 48, 65, 77, 88, 215
British accession 10, 46, 60, 64–66, 80, 106, 133, 214
British membership 48, 51, 54, 214, 215, 273
Brouwer, J.W. 290
Brouwers, Gerard 94, 102–105, 119, 122, 132, 138, 139, 171, 273, 291, 300

Brussels 30, 31, 45, 63, 76, 79, 81, 83, 84, 88, 90–92, 100, 104, 106, 110, 126, 131, 132, 134, 135, 137–140, 161, 185, 195, 196, 199–201, 234, 269, 276, 277, 280–282, 284–288, 292–299, 301, 302, 324, 325, 329, 341–344, 350, 352
Bruxelles. *See* Brussels
Bucharest 7, 13
Budget 197, 276, 288
Budgetary aspects 23, 105, 107, 115, 121, 163, 168, 169, 172, 320, 346, 350
Budgetary and fiscal policy 106, 107, 136, 210, 212, 292
Budgetary and monetary policy 117, 319
Budgetary and regional policies 268
Budgetary policy 73, 105, 113, 117, 136, 167, 170, 174, 181, 198
Budgetary Policy Committee 44, 94, 102, 108, 112, 121, 201, 258, 321, 322
Budgetary powers 224, 350
Budgets 176, 179, 197
Bundesarchiv Koblenz. *See* Federal Archives, Koblenz
Bundesbank 33, 44, 186, 194, 202, 232, 238, 243, 244, 249, 286, 288, 323
Bundesbankgesetz. *See* Bundesbank
Bundesministerium für Wirtschaft 285–287, 289, 293
Bundesrat 287
Bundestag 193, 202, 244, 290
Burns, Arthur 125, 348
Bussière, É. 30, 78, 88, 90, 288, 342
Butler, Harold 297

C

Cambridge 77, 79, 86, 87
Camdessus, Michel 14
Camu, Louis 84
Canada 136, 297
Capital control 306, 315–317, 319
Capital market 104, 106, 122, 132, 137, 162, 176, 207
Capital movements 166, 171, 180, 198, 213
Carli, Guido 43, 49, 85, 186, 187, 232, 258, 282, 348, 357
Carrerass, A. 79
Catholic Association of Luxembourg Students 29
Catz, P. 291
Central bank(s) 27, 35, 38, 41, 43, 44, 49, 52, 57, 60, 71, 73, 74, 78, 81, 85, 86, 112, 114, 116, 118, 123, 124, 133, 136, 172, 174, 182, 184–188, 191, 194, 198, 200, 202, 213, 215, 216, 219, 221, 231, 232, 238, 241–245, 248, 253, 255, 265, 267, 273, 274, 279, 309, 311–313, 316–318, 323, 325–328, 336, 340, 346, 347
Centre de recherches européennes 85
Centre for Documentation and Research into the Resistance 29
Centre of decision for economic policy 177, 178, 189, 334, 338
Centre Virtuel de la Connaissance sur l'Europe (CVCE) 7, 13–15, 17, 32
Cercle de l'Opinion 234, 272, 283, 299
Cercle historique (History Club) 20
Cercle Royal Gaulois 81

Chamber of Deputies 22, 24, 27, 31, 83
Chicago school 77, 78, 200
Christian Calmes 351
Christian Democracy 20, 25, 43, 280
Christian Social People's Party (CSV) 23–26
Clappier, Bernard 43, 94, 97–99, 102, 103, 112, 116, 119, 123, 124, 127, 134, 138, 186–188, 196, 225, 226, 248, 249, 347, 348
Clavert, F. 80, 201, 202, 339
Clearing house 45, 356
Collective currency 42
Collin, Fernand 27, 40, 42, 43, 47, 53, 84, 357
Colombo, Emilio 43, 95, 98, 114, 115, 219, 258, 292, 351
Comité pour l'histoire économique et financière de la France 82, 129, 201, 281, 288, 291
Commercial banks 85
Commission 10, 47–49, 52, 56–60, 62–65, 72, 73, 75, 81, 83, 93, 94, 96–99, 101, 103, 106, 108, 109, 112, 114, 117, 118, 120, 121, 128, 131, 132, 139, 140, 163, 166, 179, 185, 188, 192, 194, 197–199, 203–206, 208–210, 213, 217, 219–236, 238, 239, 241, 242, 245, 249, 252, 255, 259, 262, 263, 265–271, 273, 275, 277, 280–282, 284, 286, 287, 294, 295, 300, 305, 312, 314, 315, 317, 319, 320, 325, 329, 331, 333, 339–342, 344, 350–352
Commission européenne. *See* European Commission
Commission of the EC/European Commission 10, 15, 24, 26, 45, 92, 109, 131, 132, 134–137, 139, 140, 196, 199, 204–206, 208, 209, 213, 219, 250, 255, 258, 267, 271, 281, 284, 286, 288, 295, 300, 340, 341, 344, 350, 353, 357
Commission proposals 57, 102, 203, 225, 227, 232, 233, 236, 239, 245, 259, 262, 265, 266, 269, 270, 273, 275, 277, 301, 319
Committee for Finance and Budgets (CFB) 205, 207, 208, 217, 223, 276, 277
Committee for the Study of Economic and Monetary Union 342, 343
Committee of Alternates 112, 136
Committee of experts 34, 69, 76, 99–101, 109, 119, 127, 128, 134, 333
Committee of Governors of the Central Banks (CGCB) 10, 45, 58, 70, 81, 87, 94, 102, 114, 117, 118, 121, 123, 125, 138, 139, 176, 179, 180, 182, 183, 187, 188, 199, 208, 213, 219, 232, 241, 259, 266, 282, 283, 285, 300, 313, 317, 318, 321, 327, 328, 334, 341, 346, 347
Common agricultural policy 24, 47, 48, 54–56, 61, 62, 64, 83, 164, 274, 307, 350
Common European currency 38, 43, 51, 53, 71, 162, 176, 254, 287
Common financial policy 79

Common Market 30, 34, 39–41, 46–48, 53, 54, 81, 104, 118, 138, 164, 165, 167, 171, 180, 181, 183, 189, 192, 201, 214, 221, 234, 245, 249, 292, 294, 306, 339, 343, 345, 352
Common policy 67, 74, 162, 167, 212, 222, 263, 265, 268, 334
Common position 125, 165, 174, 180, 348, 349
Common reserve fund 103, 116, 346
Common/single currency 214, 271, 274
Common trade policy 44, 85
Commonwealth 65, 202
Communist Party 266
Community 35, 39, 41, 44, 45, 49, 50, 55, 56, 59, 61, 64, 66, 68, 70, 71, 73–75, 83, 84
Community authorities 166, 169, 181
Community banking system 71
Community bodies 111, 121, 122, 168, 170, 176, 178, 179, 207, 214, 233, 237, 238, 243, 245, 264, 269, 348
Community budget 44, 65, 80, 112, 177, 254
Community central bank 103, 255
Community cohesion 61, 173
Community currencies 109, 114, 162, 172, 174, 176, 184, 186, 189, 198, 311, 312, 317–319, 328, 347
Community decision-making 171, 275, 357
Community institutions 23, 35, 60, 64, 65, 71, 111, 131, 138, 139, 170, 194, 195, 203, 208, 227, 229, 231, 237, 247, 269, 294, 314, 329
Community instrument 85, 169, 170, 174, 181
Community method 206, 253
Community objectives 174, 181
Community of stability and growth 62, 67, 104, 233, 262
Community organisation of the central banks 313
Community policy 165, 168, 169
Community reserve fund 49, 75, 132, 163, 172, 179, 268
Community solidarity 55, 56, 162
Community system of central banks 177, 178, 180, 182, 189, 207, 220, 229, 267, 334, 338
Community system of internal and external monetary policies 332
Community monetary assistance mechanisms 133, 215
Compagnie Luxembourgeoise de Télédiffusion (CLT) 15, 27
Comparative overview 101, 102
Competition 34, 56, 103, 166, 168
Completion 61, 223, 270, 281, 335, 337
Compromise 125–127, 218, 223, 240, 242, 252, 255, 266, 272, 274, 349–353
Concerted action 60, 73, 198
Confederation 67, 82, 246
Confederation of Free Trade Unions in the Community 296
Confederation of German Trade Unions 135
Conference of Finance Ministers 96
Confidential documents 94, 97, 100, 104, 108–110, 118, 124, 125, 134, 135, 137
Congress of Europe 201

Conjunctural policy 104, 132
Conjunctural Policy Committee 291, 300, 321, 322
Connally, John 310
Consensus 24, 25, 32, 80, 115, 118, 120, 175, 188, 193, 204, 235, 252, 254, 256, 270, 348, 351, 356
Consultation 55, 58, 81, 84, 170, 187, 198, 212, 218, 222, 241, 260, 262, 264, 270, 279, 294, 295, 297
Consultation and coordination procedures 50, 84, 105, 115, 165, 170, 171, 174, 178, 180, 221, 260, 263, 267, 273, 346
Convention for European Economic Cooperation (CEEC) 36
Convention on Economic Union 328
Convergence 57–61, 115, 118, 120, 206, 210–213, 219, 223, 232, 238, 245, 259, 289, 322
Convertibility 34, 37, 38, 78, 79, 81, 273, 309, 312, 323
Cooperation 49, 64, 66
Cooperation between central banks 114, 172, 241, 242, 258, 267, 285, 347
Coordination 51–53, 56, 60, 61, 67, 162, 165, 169, 190
Coordination of economic policies 36, 47, 55, 68, 75, 111, 115, 117, 121, 138, 170, 178, 179, 184, 187, 189, 211, 221, 242, 258, 272, 273, 320, 326, 333, 347
Coordination of economic, monetary and budgetary policies 121, 181, 187, 220, 231, 273, 326, 335, 356
Coordination of national policies 169, 180, 181, 197, 212, 253, 289, 334
Coordination of short- and medium-term policy 58, 70, 115, 117, 346
Copenhagen 100, 120, 124, 125, 343
Coreper 236, 239–241, 257, 260, 281, 283
Corriere della Sera 300, 302
Council 10, 47, 50, 58, 59, 62, 63, 65, 69, 70, 76, 81–83, 86, 93, 95, 97, 100, 103, 110, 112, 116–119, 123, 128, 129, 132, 139, 157, 163, 179, 181, 183, 185–187, 191–195, 197–199, 203–206, 208, 211, 213, 217, 218, 220–222, 224–228, 231–235, 238–245, 251, 252, 256, 257, 259, 265, 266, 270, 277, 279–287, 292–295, 299, 301, 306, 308, 309, 311, 312, 315, 319, 320, 322, 325, 326, 328–330, 346, 349–353
Council for Economic and Financial Affairs of the Community (Ecofin) 333
Council of Finance Ministers 69, 86, 98, 325
Council of Foreign Affairs Ministers 128

Council of Foreign and Finance Ministers 302
Council of Ministers 22, 30, 50, 59, 63, 71, 72, 76, 84, 93, 99, 112, 115, 116, 118, 126, 127, 137, 140, 175, 191, 194, 195, 197, 234, 244, 245, 252, 256–258, 267, 269, 270, 274–276, 295–297, 301, 302, 309, 313, 314, 318, 350, 353
Council of Ministers for Economic Affairs 121
Council of Ministers for Social Affairs 296
Council of the EC 24, 47, 83, 185, 217, 262, 284, 285
Crafts, N. 79
Credit 21, 71, 82, 172, 198, 216, 232, 234, 267, 268, 318
Crédit Européen 53
Credit policy 34, 107, 122, 180, 216, 291
Crisis 2, 25, 26, 34, 38, 39, 47, 48, 247, 279, 306, 308, 310, 333, 335, 342
Currency 26, 33, 35–37, 41, 42, 44, 48, 52–54, 56, 59, 60, 62, 67, 69–72, 74, 77–82, 84–86, 96, 101, 107, 118, 162, 166, 172, 176, 183, 184, 189, 198, 200, 204, 207, 214, 215, 217, 219, 221, 223, 230, 234, 241, 250, 261, 267, 273, 274, 279, 291, 302, 305–307, 309, 310, 312, 313, 317, 318, 324–326, 328, 332, 334, 338
Currency and credit 169, 171, 174
Customs union 36, 39, 48, 53, 55, 57, 58, 62, 65, 164, 214, 245, 263, 281, 350

D

Danescu, E. 13–17, 31, 32, 80, 93, 131, 343, 344
Davignon, Étienne 15, 63, 131, 409
Davignon Report 63, 89
Debré, Michel 247
Debt in dollars 38
Decision centre for economic policy 82, 177, 207, 229, 237, 253, 255, 265, 267
Decision-making power 111, 163, 259, 314, 348
Decision-making process 52, 94, 111, 212, 227, 252, 294, 348, 351, 352, 353, 356
Deficit 35, 38, 42, 78, 79, 105, 115, 117, 216, 323
Deflationary policy 122, 269
De Gaulle, Charles 34, 38, 45, 46, 54, 76, 80, 82, 83, 89, 247, 288, 350, 352
Dell'Amore, G. 88
Deloncle, Michel-Habib 288
Delors, Jacques 15, 31, 333, 337, 342–344
Delors Committee 15, 333, 337, 338
Delors Report 10, 138, 333, 334, 336–338, 344
Democratic control 208, 210, 214, 222, 224, 228, 237, 262, 264, 266, 269, 270, 334
Democratic Party (DP) 24
Denmark 63, 193, 201, 311, 312, 314, 316
Deposits 266, 279, 295
Deputies' group 110, 111
Der Abend 301
Dessart, M. 80, 138, 200, 344
de Strycker, Cecil 185–187, 348

D'Estaing, Edmond Giscard 297
D'Estaing, Valéry Giscard 43, 69, 75, 95, 97–99, 112–114, 130, 226, 235, 247, 248, 293, 308, 309, 324, 330, 348
Deutsche Bank 21, 29, 43
Deutsche Bundesbank (German federal bank) 76, 136, 186, 199, 286
Deutscher Bundestag 202
Deutscher Gewerkschaftsbund 109, 135
Deutschmark (DM) 33, 55, 60, 62, 192, 273, 318, 323
Devaluation 38, 52, 54, 56, 62, 80, 133, 309, 310, 312, 326
De Wilmars, Jacques Mertens 102, 110, 126, 199, 327, 348
DG II Economic and Monetary Affairs 285
Dichgans, Hans 278
Dierikx, Marc 92, 134
Dinan, D. 339
Diplomatic Archives of the Ministry of Foreign Affairs of Belgium 292
Directorate for Economic and Financial Affairs (DGII) 94, 101, 110, 140, 290, 292, 294, 324, 325, 327, 329, 330
Directorate-General for Committees and Parliamentary Studies 276
Directorate-General for Economic and Financial Affairs 92, 132, 137, 139, 286, 339, 340, 342
Directorate-General for Personnel and Administration 139
Direct taxes 104, 180, 213
Direct universal suffrage 25, 208, 237
Di Vittorio, A. 79
Döry, S. 32
Draft report 110, 123, 124, 126, 139
Drees, Willem (Junior) 134
Ducci, R. 85
Duhamel, Jacques 247
Duisenberg, Wim 341
Dujardin, V. 91
Dumoulin, M. 30, 78, 79, 86, 88, 90, 91, 281, 342
Dupong, Pierre 21, 22, 30
Dupriez, L.H. 76
Du Réau, É. 90, 202
Dutch 44, 51, 60, 65, 94, 107, 130, 255, 291, 312, 318, 326
Dyson, K. 16, 31, 32, 80, 87, 342, 343

E

EC Commission 75, 127, 131, 161, 179, 307, 309, 318, 341, 353
EC Council of Ministers 63, 83, 97, 106, 128, 321
EC Finance Ministers 57, 137
Ecofin Council 235, 290, 308, 326, 330, 341
École libre des sciences politiques 20
Economic Affairs Committee (EAC) 205–207, 209–213, 217, 221–224, 231, 276–278, 280–282
Economic and Financial Affairs Committee 278
Economic and financial policy 93, 190, 194, 244, 246, 248

Economic and monetary aspects 40, 41, 53, 61, 93, 166, 169, 193, 201, 211, 227, 232, 237, 269, 272, 281, 336
Economic and monetary integration 62, 103, 174, 236, 257, 270, 307
Economic and monetary policy 37, 58, 62, 80, 111, 165, 166, 177, 178, 182, 191, 213, 221, 229, 233, 243, 261, 295
Economic and Monetary Union (EMU) 1, 2, 4, 9, 10, 13, 23, 25, 27, 28, 44, 50, 53, 56, 57, 61, 62, 65–69, 71, 75, 76, 81, 88, 92, 93, 97, 99, 101–104, 106, 107, 109–114, 116, 120, 121, 127, 128, 131, 132, 135, 139, 162–164, 166, 168–170, 172, 173, 175, 176, 178–183, 187, 189, 190, 192–200, 203–210, 213, 214, 217–222, 224–228, 230–233, 236–248, 250–254, 256–261, 263–271, 273–278, 280–282, 284–287, 289–302, 305–309, 315–327, 329–339, 341–344, 346, 347, 355–357
Economic and political union 57, 128, 235
Economic and social aspects 177, 219, 264, 288, 294, 321, 334
Economic and Social Committee (ESC) 179, 262–265, 294
Economic budgets 167, 198
Economic Committee of the European Parliament 140
Economic convergence 59, 113, 190, 256, 305, 334, 337
Economic cooperation 41, 190, 243, 259, 349
Economic Cooperation Department 290, 292, 294, 324, 325, 327–330
Economic coordination 60, 192
Economic crisis 340, 342
Economic growth 79, 212, 213, 223
Economic harmonisation 172, 191, 194, 245
Economic integration 40, 44, 46, 60, 103, 164, 192, 234, 244
Economic policy 33, 39, 45, 50, 51, 55, 58, 60, 76, 80, 98, 104–106, 109, 162, 163, 170, 173, 177–179, 181, 188, 191, 193, 194, 199, 206, 207, 209–212, 222, 237, 238, 240, 243–245, 253, 255, 261, 262, 264, 268, 272, 273, 288, 290, 305, 316, 317, 322, 332, 334, 335, 338, 341, 346
Economic Policy Committee 322
Economic policy convergence 138, 182, 188, 320, 335
Economic policy coordination 57, 119, 120, 122, 166, 178, 179, 318
Economic policy harmonisation 164, 173
Economic policy instruments 167, 170
Economisch-Statistische Berichten 300
Economist 42, 59, 103, 106, 107, 119, 138, 189–191, 200, 210, 219, 253, 271, 274, 298, 348
EEC Commission 81
EEC Council 46
EEC Council of Ministers 243, 302

EEC Finance Ministers 43, 286
EEC Member States 46, 53
EEC monetary cooperation fund 356
EEC Treaty 44, 290, 352
Ehlermann, C.-D. 329
Eichengreen, B. 77, 79, 86, 87
EMCF 200, 327–329
Emminger, Otmar 186, 188, 348, 357
Employers' and workers' organisations 258, 267, 270, 294, 297
Employment policy 26, 58, 80, 182, 267, 269, 339
Empty chair crisis 46, 47, 83, 350, 356
Enlargement 24, 63–65, 67, 72, 76, 89, 210, 214, 223, 247, 257, 281
Epunit 42
Equilibrium 80, 172
Équipes sociales 20
Erhard, Ludwig 33
Escape clause 251, 289, 320
Etzel, Franz 43
Euro 28, 29, 32, 87, 323, 335, 342, 343
Eurocurrency 134, 212, 215, 279
Eurocurrency market 134
Eurodollar market 38, 134, 323
Eurodollars 38, 55, 78, 134, 215, 216, 279, 308, 318, 323
Eurogroup 357
Euromarkets 49, 279, 341
Europaforum 48
Europe 22, 24, 29–31, 33, 35–39, 44, 46, 48–50, 55, 56, 58, 60, 64, 65, 68, 77–82, 85, 88–91, 109, 116, 129, 130, 138, 192, 194, 195, 199–202, 209, 215, 216, 224, 244, 246, 248, 250, 254, 261, 262, 271, 273, 276, 283, 288, 292, 293, 295, 297, 301, 306, 308, 309, 313, 321–323, 325, 327, 332, 339, 342–344, 347, 352, 356, 357
European Agricultural Guidance and Guarantee Fund (EAGGF) 83
European Atomic Energy Community (EAEC or Euratom) 23, 30, 39, 79
European Banking Federation 266
European Central Bank (ECB) 39, 70, 82, 173, 194, 202, 243, 254, 315, 328, 333, 343
European Coal and Steel Community (ECSC) 23, 39, 52, 79, 296
European Communities' Standing Committee on Employment (SCE) 296
European Community (EC) 10, 47, 56, 61, 65, 80, 81, 87–91, 203, 244, 260, 295, 297
European Confederation of Free Trade Unions (ECFTU) 135, 269, 296
European Council 31, 324, 325, 333, 334
European currency 28, 37, 42, 45, 47, 49–51, 59, 68, 74, 77, 172, 190, 213, 214, 244, 273, 287, 291, 302, 308, 310–312, 318, 341
European Currency Unit (ECU) 28, 31, 70, 341, 356
European Defence Community (EDC) 21

European Economic Community (EEC) 23, 39, 79, 135, 139, 193, 199, 201, 324, 327, 350
European exchange equalisation fund 108, 134, 135
European financial market 73, 79
European Free Trade Association (EFTA) 65, 202, 296
European integration 20, 22, 39, 46, 52, 60, 61, 64, 67, 79, 86, 89, 93, 128, 131, 338, 340, 341, 355–357
European Investment Bank (EIB) 14, 15, 52
European League for Economic Cooperation (ELEC) 25, 270, 297
European Monetary Agreement (EMA) 37, 78
European monetary authority 50, 216
European monetary bloc 220, 348
European Monetary Cooperation Fund (EMCF) 10, 37, 43, 48, 66, 68, 73, 74, 85, 87, 182, 183, 213, 230, 232, 244, 248, 253, 255, 265, 268, 305, 311, 313–319, 321, 322, 327–329, 332, 335, 346, 347
European monetary identity 43, 336
European Monetary Institute 328, 449, 482, 485
European monetary integration 29, 39, 41, 45, 48, 57, 201, 254, 293
European monetary policy 47, 57, 58, 87, 232, 245, 303, 316
European Monetary System (EMS) 10, 31, 45, 261, 332, 333, 340, 341, 356, 339
European monetary union 31, 32, 38, 40, 42, 46, 48, 71, 80, 87, 254, 276, 293, 298, 303, 331, 340–343
European Movement 297
European Organisation of Christian Trade Unions 296
European Organisation of the World Confederation of Labour (EOWCL) 269, 296, 297
European parallel currency 340
European Parliament (EP) 10, 25, 47, 57, 61, 63, 83, 128, 139, 177, 179, 188, 189, 204, 205, 207–210, 212–215, 217, 221, 222, 224, 226, 228, 231, 235, 237, 245, 255, 267, 270, 276–278, 280–282, 303, 334, 350
European Payments Union (EPU) 37, 42, 77, 78, 172
European People's Party (EPP) 25
European political union 301
European Recovery Program 23, 57, 77
European Regional Development Fund 320
European reserve currency 57, 68, 273
European reserve fund 44, 49, 62, 66, 69, 74, 78, 79, 81, 90, 101, 104, 106, 162, 347
European social model 335
European Social Secretariat (ESS) 296

European solidarity 171, 311, 321
European System of Central Banks (ESCB) 246, 333
European Trade Union Confederation 296
European Union (EU) 29, 80, 316, 320, 333, 339, 340
European unit of account 27, 44–48, 50, 59, 68, 73, 74, 84, 104, 314, 315, 321, 332, 341, 342
European University Institute (EUI) 341
Europe Daily Bulletin 275, 298
Euror 42
Exchange arrangements 34, 114, 117, 118, 180
Exchange market 85, 114, 116, 177, 182, 312, 313, 317, 346, 347
Exchange rates 35, 37, 40, 44, 45, 47, 50, 54, 55, 57, 59, 62, 72, 78, 80, 103, 104, 108, 132, 133, 136, 162, 166, 171–173, 176, 180, 198, 206, 210, 211, 216, 217, 223, 242, 244, 253, 261, 267, 268, 274, 291, 295, 306–309, 311, 313, 323, 325, 326, 333, 334, 337–339, 341
Exchange rate mechanism 31, 180, 186, 219, 220, 325, 333
Exchange stabilisation fund 107, 108, 113, 114, 116, 118–120, 126, 171–174, 183, 346
Excise duties 104, 137, 168, 334
Exorbitant privilege 38
Experts 27, 28, 94, 100, 102, 111, 118, 123, 125, 128, 131
External equilibrium 167, 311
External monetary policy 171, 177, 180, 209, 212, 254, 267, 347
Eyskens, Gaston 66, 257, 292, 349
Eyskens, Mark 15

F

Fabra, Paul 299
Federal Archives, Koblenz 130, 285–289, 293
Federal German Government 125, 243, 244, 249, 255, 259
Federal Minister for Economic Affairs 98, 130, 238, 242, 244, 272, 285, 299
Federal Ministry of Economic Affairs 99, 125, 130, 249, 286, 287
Federal Minister of Finance 288
Federal Republic of Germany 89, 244, 285, 286, 292, 301
Federal reserve system 71, 114, 123
Feiertag, O. 80, 202, 339
Ferdinand Lindebauer 271
Ferrari-Agradi, Mario 259
Fifth stage 73, 75
Final Communiqué 83, 88, 89
Final objective 101, 103, 104, 106, 107, 109, 164, 166, 169, 174–176, 181, 207, 220, 229, 230, 233, 256–259
Final report 109, 115, 116, 121, 122, 124, 126, 127, 173, 175, 176, 185, 188, 203, 204, 206, 218, 239, 255, 262, 271, 277, 346, 348, 349

Final stage 62, 71, 74, 75, 103, 113, 114, 120, 122, 138, 173, 180, 182, 189, 222, 237, 238, 245, 252, 253, 259, 264, 292, 333, 338
Finance Ministers 20–23, 26, 49, 59, 84, 86, 106, 112, 117, 118, 121, 125, 131, 137, 163, 164, 175, 187, 196, 225, 231, 234, 235, 240, 243, 254, 257, 282, 298, 306, 307, 333, 346
Finance Ministry 40, 51, 254, 307
Financial centre 27, 32, 42
Financial markets 174, 180, 273
Financial regulation 41, 61, 64, 347, 350
Financial stability 22, 35
The Financial Times 273, 300
First Barre Plan (Memorandum) 58–60, 70, 72, 131, 191, 282, 334
First stage 70, 73, 75, 106, 109, 110, 113, 116, 118, 122, 124, 127, 132, 137, 164, 170–176, 178, 179, 183, 187–189, 194, 195, 198, 209, 218, 220, 222–224, 226, 229–233, 236, 245, 251, 256, 260, 264, 270, 274, 275, 306, 311, 316, 329
First Werner Plan 49, 69, 101
Fiscal aspect(s) 26, 34, 75, 136, 168, 179, 238, 241, 266, 295
Fiscal harmonisation 113, 121, 206, 220, 238
Five-point Luxembourg Plan 49, 50, 57, 72, 101, 345, 347
Fixed exchange rates 49, 51, 55, 56, 68, 73, 81, 132, 166, 173, 176, 210, 217, 250, 267, 306–309, 333, 336
Floating exchange rates 107, 191, 274, 306, 307
Floc'h, R. 199
Florence 341
Fluctuation margins 172, 174, 189, 211, 212, 217, 230, 307, 308, 310–312, 315, 317, 318, 323, 325
Focke, Katharina 287
Fontainebleau 3
Foreign Affairs Council 23, 96, 235
Foreign exchange 46, 51, 74, 114, 174, 309, 311, 315, 323, 326
Foreign Ministers 58, 61, 63, 97, 238, 290, 299
Foreign Ministry 24, 249, 254, 283, 286, 290, 291
Foreign Office 260, 261
Forrestier, C. 32
Fourastié, J. 79
Fourcade, Jean-Pierre 339
Fourcade Memorandum 339, 341
Franc 21, 31, 34, 51, 54, 55, 60, 62, 192, 201, 247, 273, 310, 321, 326
France 10, 19, 28, 34, 35, 38, 43, 55, 59–61, 63–66, 80, 82, 83, 85, 87, 90, 98, 99, 102, 107, 113, 136, 175, 190–192, 194, 201, 202, 226, 236–240, 244, 246–252, 257, 272, 274, 287, 290, 293, 297, 299–301, 307, 309, 312–314, 319, 324, 350–352, 356
Frank, R. 78, 90, 201, 202
Frankfurt 87, 282, 327
Frankfurter Allgemeine Zeitung 287, 298, 301, 302
Franssens, Constant 53
Frasca, F. 199

Free movement 39, 79, 164, 165, 182, 206, 220, 294
French Communist Party (PCF) 250, 289
French Diplomatic Archives (La Courneuve) 290, 292, 294, 324, 325, 327–330
French-German summit 240, 251
French National Assembly 20, 308
French National Planning Board 79
French Republic 89, 241, 287, 290, 292, 294
Frieden, Luc 14, 32
Friedman, M. 78, 200
Friot, G. 279
Full employment 26, 39, 269, 320, 322
Fund 107, 127, 171, 172, 174, 184, 187, 213, 268, 305, 314–318, 322, 328

G

Gabriel du Chastain 283
Gallais, Hugues Le 22
Garric, Robert 20
Gasperi, Alcide de 39
Gazette de Lausanne 275, 301
Gazzo, Emanuele 301
General Agreement on Tariffs and Trade (GATT) 47
General equilibrium 167, 278
General German Trade Union Confederation 109, 164
General Secretariat of the Council of the EC 266, 341
German Central Bank. *See* Bundesbank
German Chancellor 66, 67
German diplomatic archives 97
German Federal Archives (Koblenz) 16, 249
German mark 33, 306, 312, 313, 323, 326
German plan for monetary integration 69, 190
Germany 10, 28, 35, 38, 43, 55, 57, 59, 64–66, 69, 85, 98, 99, 102, 105, 125, 131, 136, 137, 161, 190, 192, 193, 195, 200, 201, 202, 205, 216, 226, 238, 239, 242, 243, 251, 253, 256, 272, 282, 286, 297, 306, 309, 312–314, 319, 324, 349
Ghymers, C. 343
Giacone, A 327
Gillingham, J. 86
Girault, R. 82
Goldeur 42
Gold pool 54, 86, 87
Gold standard 35–38, 42, 45, 55, 56, 74, 77, 78, 82, 86, 87, 133, 136, 215, 248, 308–310, 312, 321, 323, 326, 327
Governors of the central banks 44, 84, 106, 185, 186, 219, 244, 333
Gradualism 36, 38, 42, 68, 69, 73, 74, 85, 114, 138, 168, 335, 346, 356
Gramor 42
Grand-Duché de Luxembourg. *See* Grand Duchy of Luxembourg
Grand Duchy of Luxembourg 46, 328
Great Britain. *See* United Kingdom (UK)
Gros, R. 199

Group of experts 93, 95–97, 109, 113, 163, 164, 168, 175, 187, 189, 190, 192, 193, 226, 271, 277, 335, 340, 341, 345, 346, 348, 349
Group of Ten 53, 112, 136, 258, 310, 326, 348
Growth 27, 32, 33, 39, 76, 79, 132, 133, 211, 215, 225, 247, 267, 272, 317, 320, 322, 323
Grygowski, G. 140
Guaranteed parallelism 219
Guggenheim, T. 76
Guieu, J.-M. 201
Guilder 307, 313
Guill, Joseph 20

H

Habsburg, Otto von 276
Hague communiqué 250, 284
Hague Conference 169, 189, 257, 263, 339
Hague Congress 297
Hague Summit 10, 60–62, 64, 66–68, 86, 88, 89, 90–93, 97, 108–109, 134, 192, 197, 201, 204, 209, 219, 221, 224, 227, 231, 235, 239, 254, 271, 272, 274, 277, 278, 291
Hallstein, Walter 48, 350, 357
Hankel, W. 342
Hanover Summit 333
Hansen, Albert 14
Harmel, Pierre 95, 244, 256, 257, 286
Harmonisation 165, 168, 169, 171, 174, 185, 187, 190, 191, 194
Harmonisation of economic policy 62, 74, 97, 165, 172, 175, 184, 207, 210–211, 212, 223, 245, 254, 255, 268
Harmonisation of fiscal and budgetary policies 69, 104, 137, 333–334
Harmonisation of monetary and budgetary policies 115, 117, 127, 167, 181, 206, 208, 210, 213
Harmonisation of monetary and credit policy 115, 117
Harmonisation of monetary policy 115, 117, 119, 124, 184, 210
Harryvan, G. Anjo 290
Heath, Edward 43, 260, 293, 348
Hennicot-Schoepges, E. 32
Hetzel, R.L. 323
Heyvaert, F. 199
Heyvaert Group 341
Historical Archives of the Council of the European Union (Brussels) 16
Historical Archives of the Deutsche Bundesbank 202, 286, 324, 325
Historical Archives of the European Union (Florence) 16, 131, 132, 135, 137, 139, 140, 270, 284–286, 292–297, 327
Historical Archives of the European Commission (Brussels) 16, 132
Historical Archives of the European Parliament (Luxembourg) 16
Hodson, D. 342
Hogan, M. 77
Howarth, D. 87

I

Imbalance 34, 38, 51, 54, 61, 71, 85, 268
Income policy 105, 115, 169, 269
Indirect taxes 179, 212
Inflation 26, 33, 34, 211, 273, 279, 315, 323, 332, 340
Information and Press Service (SIP) 14, 15, 31, 83, 84, 86, 90, 91, 199, 283
Institut Charles de Gaulle 82
Institut für Zeitgeschichte 286, 290
Institut Grand-Ducal 328
Institutions 24, 31, 79, 106, 107, 137, 138, 189, 229, 233, 240, 252, 254, 259, 268, 280, 281, 283, 292, 294, 314, 315, 332, 338
Institutional aspect 27, 45, 72, 75, 105, 113, 116, 117, 120–122, 172, 175, 198, 207, 222, 227, 229, 235, 237, 243, 249, 259, 263, 265, 266, 268, 273, 275, 277, 320, 336, 338, 339, 346
Institutional reform 168, 176, 181, 207, 255, 270, 350
Institutional structure 63, 103, 109, 177, 255, 261
Institut Pierre Werner 32
Instruments 61, 73, 104, 105, 115, 167, 179–181
Integration 36, 41, 51, 58, 60, 62, 64, 67, 106, 107
Inter-directorate working party 101, 104, 118
Interest rates 52, 85, 167, 171, 177, 216, 267, 279, 323
Intergovernmental 36, 63, 65, 84, 181, 206, 227, 237, 246, 270, 275, 352
Interim report 111–117, 119–123, 126, 128, 135, 137, 163, 168, 172, 175, 176, 195–197, 203, 204, 207, 210, 218, 239, 243, 254, 260, 277, 278, 348
Internal monetary policy 46, 171, 177, 179, 267
International Bank for Reconstruction and Development (IBRD) 22, 36, 77
International Confederation of Free Trade Unions (ICFTU) 296
International currency markets 37, 52, 79, 85, 174, 180
International Federation of Christian Trade Unions (IFCTU) 296
International Federation of Stock Exchanges 53
International financial markets 21, 23, 32, 53, 234, 267, 279, 347
International liquidity 38, 79, 215, 308
International Monetary Cooperation 87, 268
International Monetary Fund (IMF) 15, 21, 35, 40, 47, 49, 50, 55, 68, 73, 77, 84, 100, 116, 125, 133, 136, 171, 180, 215, 271, 306–308, 326, 347
International monetary relations 35, 45, 46, 57, 71–74, 82, 108, 162, 165, 174, 308, 309, 325

International Monetary System (IMS) 33, 38, 39, 42, 45, 48, 55, 56, 78, 82, 133, 136, 172, 174, 195, 206, 211, 215, 220, 251, 310–312, 317, 348
International Paneuropean Union 276
International trade 35, 42, 79, 85
International Trade Union Confederation 296
Investment 34, 179, 198
Ireland 63, 193, 201, 311, 314, 316
Irish pound 312
Irreversibility 103, 169, 333–335, 337
Israel, Edmond 14, 27, 28, 32, 53
Issing, O. 76
Italian banking association 49
Italian Finance Minister 131
Italian Foreign Ministry 137
Italian Historical Diplomatic Archives (Rome) 16
Italian lira 137, 307, 312, 326, 327
Italy 10, 34, 43, 61, 80, 85, 102, 131, 136, 200, 201, 216, 237, 244, 257, 258, 260, 272, 273, 302, 308, 312, 314, 327

J

James, H. 87
Japan 38, 39, 136, 297
Japanese yen 326
Jenkins, Roy 293, 341
Jennemann, G. 199
Joint consultation 53, 179, 244, 253, 256, 257, 268, 318
Journal de Genève 299, 300
Juncker, Jean-Claude 14, 26, 357

K

Kane, D. 279
Kasel, Jean-Jacques 15
Keller, Paul 301
Kennedy, J.F. 279
Kennedy plan 86
Kerstens, Pieter 297
Keynes, John Maynard 200
Kiesinger, Kurt Georg 89
Kirchberg European quarter 23
Kirschner, O. 77
Kirsch, Raymond 27, 53
Kirt, R. 31, 32
Klasen, Karl 186, 232, 286
Kleps, K. 324
Koblenz 130
Koeune, J.-C. 84, 344
Köln 342
Königstein im Taunus 200
Kohl, Helmut 14
Krause, B.L. 87
Kredietbank 42, 84
Kredietbank Luxembourgeoise S.A (KBL) 42, 47, 51
Kulakowski, Jan 297

L

La Libre Belgique 83
Lambert, L. 140
Lamfalussy, Alexandre 342
La Nation 299
La Quotidienne 298
La Roche-en-Ardenne 341
Larosière, Jacques de 15, 290
La Tribune de Lausanne-Le Matin 302
Lausanne 85, 342
Lavezzi, G. 90

Leboutte, R. 84
Le Dréau, C. 201
Lefèvre, S. 201
Le Figaro 272, 299, 302
Legal instruments 50, 198, 256
Le Monde 272, 288, 298, 299
Le Monde diplomatique 300
Lermen, G. 199
Leroy, Roland 250, 288, 289
Le Soir 300, 302
Leuven 344
L'Humanité 299
Liberalisation 36, 37, 49, 103, 171, 180, 319, 333, 334, 337
Ligue luxembourgeoise des prisonniers et déportés politiques 29
Liquidity 55, 82, 124, 167, 171, 176, 177, 215, 216, 267, 268, 274, 291, 308, 311, 317
Löhr, J. 280
London 21, 29, 32, 77, 79, 87, 88, 133, 200, 201, 215, 260, 279, 293, 294, 310, 339, 343
Looijen, Anthony 102, 123, 126
L'Opinion en 24 heures 283
Loth, W. 30, 78
Louvain-la-Neuve 90, 91, 130
Louw, A. 199
Luciolli, Mario 293
Ludlow, N.P. 30
Luns, Joseph 95, 351
Luxembourg 3, 4, 7, 10, 11, 19–32, 34, 40–42, 47, 51–53, 57, 66–69, 72, 80, 81, 83–87, 89, 94, 95, 97–100, 102, 108, 110–112, 116, 119–124, 126–129, 134, 135, 137, 138, 140, 161, 164, 175, 193, 196, 197, 199, 201, 204, 205, 226, 229, 234, 240, 257, 260, 271, 275, 276, 278, 279, 281–283, 289, 291–293, 297, 298, 303, 314, 317, 325, 326, 328, 329, 337, 342–344, 346, 347, 349–353, 355, 357
Luxembourg City Photo Library 15
Luxembourg Compromise 23, 24, 30, 47, 349–353, 356
Luxembourg financial centre 49, 52, 347, 349, 356
Luxembourg Monetary Institute (IML) 15, 27, 31
Luxembourg Plan 69, 72, 74, 164, 183, 206, 282
Luxembourg shipping flag 23
Luxembourg Socialist Workers' Party (LSAP) 24
Luxembourg Stock Exchange (LSE) 53
Luxemburger Wort 298, 303
Lyon 28

M

Maastricht Treaty 10, 335, 336, 338
MacDougall Report 341
Machlup, Fritz 110
Mackay, Paul 186
Macroeconomic governance 55, 335
Madrid 110
Maes, I. 16, 32, 80, 87, 88, 90, 201, 292, 293, 342, 343
Magna Carta 193, 244
Magnifico Report 339
Magnusson, L. 88
Majerus, J.M. 30
Majority rule 83, 352
Majority vote 350, 351, 353

Malfatti, Franco Maria 209, 217, 234, 241, 281
Maquil, M. 32
Margins for fluctuation 57, 59, 69, 71, 172, 190, 194, 219, 223, 230, 253, 265, 268, 305, 307, 328, 337
Maritain, Jacques 20
Marjolin Report 331–333, 336, 342
Marjolin, Robert 44, 45, 56, 81, 234, 272, 331, 343, 357
Mark 306, 307, 310, 313, 318, 323, 324
Marshall, George 36, 77
Martens, Wilfried 15
Martin network 21, 29
Masera, F. 199
Maystadt, Philippe 14, 197
Mechanism 25, 58, 63, 73, 106, 178, 311, 318, 328, 352
Mediation 25, 257, 348, 353, 356
Medium-term conjunctural policy 111, 109, 348
Medium-term economic policy 59, 60, 69, 71, 115, 170, 178, 181, 191, 211, 212, 285, 307, 324, 334
Medium-Term Economic Policy Committee 44, 58, 94, 99, 102, 105, 249, 321, 322
Medium-term assistance 58, 71, 108, 182, 195, 211, 242, 268, 285, 305, 314
Medium-term support 167, 179, 191, 206
Meiers, M. 32
Meisch, Adrien 15, 31, 32
Melchionni, M.G. 85
Member States 39, 56–58, 62, 63, 65, 70, 74, 81, 82
Memorandum 56–47, 62, 66, 69
Mémorial 31
Mendès-France, Pierre 275
Mersch, Yves 14, 342
Messina Conference 357
Method 24, 45, 74, 170, 174–177, 188, 206, 207, 226, 230, 247, 253, 256, 257, 345
Michel Debré 287
Michels, Ernest 16
Middle East 313
Mini-snake 313
Ministère des Affaires étrangères. *See* Ministry of Foreign Affairs
Ministers for Economic Affairs and Finance 97, 238, 290
Minister for Finance 124, 138, 316, 327
Ministers for Finance and Foreign Affairs 316
Ministers for Foreign Affairs 89, 327, 352
Ministry of Economic Affairs 130, 140
Ministry of Finance 30, 40, 91
Ministry of Foreign Affairs 138, 292
Ministry of Foreign Affairs and External Trade 292
Ministry of Foreign and European Affairs 290, 292, 294, 324, 325, 327–330
Ministry of State 31, 83, 84, 86, 90, 91, 140, 199, 283
Ministry of the Economy, Finance and Industry 82
Mischo, Jean 15

Mitzakis, M. 76
Molitor, Bernhard 95, 129
Möller, Alexander (Alex) 136, 235
Monetarists 59, 103, 106, 107, 119, 189–191, 200, 201, 210, 219, 272, 274, 348
Monetary and budgetary policy 104, 115, 167, 190, 306
Monetary and credit policy 26, 31, 106, 107, 176, 180, 188, 198, 232, 265, 335, 348
Monetary and financial cooperation in the EEC 34, 44, 81, 120, 167, 332
Monetary aspect(s) 39, 67, 93, 109, 115, 131, 229, 249, 264, 319, 339, 341
Monetary Committee 44, 73, 80, 84, 94, 97, 100–102, 106, 112, 187, 188, 191, 213, 232, 248, 285, 313, 315, 325, 327, 329, 342
Monetary cooperation 35, 37, 40, 46, 54, 55–58, 60, 62, 67, 74, 84, 85, 97, 111, 170, 188, 191, 192, 194, 197, 230, 234, 245, 245, 248, 254, 258, 258, 259, 261, 265, 268, 305, 319, 319, 331, 333, 335, 343
Monetary coordination 26, 284, 314, 346, 349
Monetary crisis 221, 306, 308–310, 323, 324, 342
Monetary discipline 45, 47, 48, 67, 273
Monetary disturbances 54, 60, 62, 309
Monetary Europe 35, 219, 283
Monetary identity 52, 116, 265, 315, 347
Monetary institute 45, 51
Monetary integration 41, 44–46, 50, 52, 60, 67, 69, 75, 113, 161, 183, 195, 208, 213, 223, 244, 247, 250, 283, 289, 298, 299, 346
Monetary measures 36, 39, 73, 74, 81, 84, 136, 211, 214, 226, 230, 237, 250, 252, 274, 357
Monetary mechanisms 107, 123, 253, 261
Monetary plans 75, 103
Monetary policy 27, 34, 41, 43–46, 50, 51, 72, 81, 113, 118, 119, 124, 137, 163, 167, 170, 176, 178, 183, 193, 194, 207, 210, 217, 233, 244, 254, 267, 278, 291, 293, 301, 309, 315, 327, 332, 334, 336, 356
Monetary policy instruments 42, 48, 105, 114, 117, 183, 185, 187, 248, 332
Monetary reforms 33, 35, 45, 52, 55, 67, 70, 72, 80, 247
Monetary relations 37, 55, 56, 171, 172, 180, 206, 232, 305
Monetary reserves 44, 177, 215, 312
Monetary snake 310, 311
Monetary solidarity 48–51, 58, 60, 61, 104, 106, 109, 166, 175, 176, 191, 209, 210, 223, 250, 291, 315
Monetary stability 39, 48, 62, 253, 313, 321
Monetary unification 33, 35, 40, 41, 49, 169, 171, 258, 299, 339

Monetary union 26, 37, 44, 57, 60, 61, 67, 68, 70, 72, 74, 105, 122, 128, 132, 134, 138, 139, 166, 189–191, 200, 203, 209, 223, 237, 242, 246, 247, 250–252, 254, 261, 271, 272, 275, 278, 300–302, 307, 322, 325, 333, 334, 337, 339, 341, 356
Money market 46, 54, 75, 180, 267
Monnet, Jean 22, 25, 30, 39, 43, 48, 49, 66, 67, 79, 81, 90, 116, 120, 122, 125, 192, 201, 253, 287, 343, 348, 349, 357
Monnet's Action Committee (ACUSE) 4, 30, 49, 66, 74, 81, 101
Montreux 39
Morel, Jean-Claude 102
Morelli, Georges 94, 118, 123, 126, 199
Mosca, Ugo 94, 102, 106, 112, 123, 132, 185, 187, 232, 258
Mourlon-Druol, E. 339
Mouvement européen 82
Movement of capital 165, 168, 318
Moyse, L. 32
Multilateralism 35, 36, 78, 314, 315
Munich 286, 290, 329
Murville, Maurice Couve de 350
Mutual assistance 57, 58, 68, 71, 73, 81, 85
Mutual intervention policy 268, 311
Muyser, Guy de 14

N

Nahoum, J.C. 85
Nappi, C. 325
Narrowing of margins 132, 172, 174, 183, 184, 186, 312, 317, 328
National Archives of the Netherlands 91, 134
National Assembly 249, 288, 289, 324
National Bank of Belgium (NBB) 45, 53, 70, 94, 98, 103, 108, 110, 134, 135, 138, 185, 199, 293, 300, 325, 328
National budgets 70, 168, 171, 222, 254, 267, 288
National Bureau of Economic Research 77
National Cultural Fund 26
National currency 41, 42, 52, 55, 73, 74, 133, 166, 177, 214, 254, 261, 267, 274, 312, 314, 317, 332–334
National interests 55, 61, 64
National Library of Luxembourg 15
National policies 171, 181, 308, 332, 336
National reserves 79, 314, 315
Nederlandsche Bank 115, 186, 199
The Netherlands 10, 34, 38, 43, 57, 59, 64, 80, 99, 102, 105, 107, 136, 200, 201, 216, 238, 240, 244, 253–255, 272, 273, 290, 292, 297, 306, 313, 314, 320, 324, 326, 349
Netherlands Ministry of Finance 134, 291
New Hampshire 35
New Haven 138
New York 30, 77
Nieuwe Europa 303
Nieuwe Rotterdamse Courant 302

Nixon, Richard 38, 308, 310
Noël, Emile 281
Nölling, Wilhelm 342
Non-Community countries 68, 167, 180
North Atlantic Treaty Organisation (NATO) 21, 46
Norway 34, 63, 193, 201, 313, 314, 316
Nothomb, Charles-Ferdinand 14

O

Oele, Adriaan Pieter (Ad) 280
Office for Official Publications of the European Communities (OOPEC) 83, 87–91, 129, 196, 197, 199, 278, 281, 282, 325, 328, 342–344
Official currency reserves 216, 122
Olivi, B. 327
Optica Report 340
Optimum Currency Areas 109, 340
Organisation for European Economic Cooperation (OEEC) 36, 77
Ossola, Rinaldo 112, 232, 258, 282, 327, 347, 348
Oxford 80, 87

P

Padoa-Schioppa, T. 77, 343
Palayret, J.-M. 82
Palumbo, Simone 102, 258
Pan-Europa Congress 39
Parallelism 50, 51, 60, 75, 95, 115, 120, 128, 174, 182, 190, 191, 206, 211, 213, 219, 222, 223, 234, 237, 242, 243, 245, 256, 263, 265, 268, 270, 272, 305, 309, 337, 340, 342, 349
Parallelism principle 219, 233, 251, 252, 258, 263, 317, 356
Parallel movement 119, 121, 188, 193, 222, 335
Parallel progress 120, 245, 268, 349
Paris 20, 30, 40, 65, 69, 77–80, 82, 89–91, 96, 99, 100, 120–122, 129, 130, 138, 164, 195, 201, 202, 234, 239, 246, 251, 274, 279, 281, 283, 287–292, 314, 316, 324, 325, 327, 329, 339, 340, 344, 350
Paris Summit 294, 320, 328, 340
Parity 35, 59, 69, 78, 182, 274, 291
Parliament 65, 203, 205, 208–210, 213, 214, 217, 218, 221, 224, 226, 227, 237, 277, 281, 293
Parliamentary control 177, 212, 241, 246, 252, 260
Pas-de-Calais 288
Pax Romana 20
Paye, J.-C. 281
Payments 172, 315, 316
Pengalou, Ch. 76
Permanent Representatives Committee (COREPER) 236, 283–285, 350
Pescatore, Pierre 23
Pescatore-Werner, Henriette 4, 28
Peyrefitte, Alain 82
Pierre Werner Family Archives 15, 81, 83, 84, 86, 87, 90–93, 110, 117, 129, 131, 132, 134, 135, 137–140, 196, 197, 199, 203, 270, 276–278, 280–285, 288, 289, 291–293, 295, 297, 325, 329, 343, 344
Pinay, Antoine 76

Plan by stages 34, 35, 48, 49, 58, 61, 62, 69, 70, 73, 75, 76, 80, 91, 92, 97, 101, 102, 104, 106, 109, 110, 117, 118, 123, 125, 129, 132, 134, 135, 137, 138–140, 162, 164, 175, 185, 188, 193, 195, 196, 204–206, 213, 226, 228, 230, 231, 234, 235, 239, 240, 242, 245, 247, 249, 251–253, 256, 258, 261, 262, 266, 271, 273–275, 287, 289, 295, 299, 300, 302, 331, 335–337, 345, 347
Pleven, René 247
Pöhl, Otto 244
Point of departure 164, 167, 169, 174
Policy coordination 195, 238, 251, 317, 321
Political Affairs Committee (PAC) 63, 205, 207, 208, 224, 277
Political commitment 218, 220, 221, 259, 300, 332
Political consensus 229, 357
Political cooperation 24, 61, 63, 112, 168, 176, 207, 218, 234, 246, 287, 289
Political decision 238, 250, 259, 263, 284
Political groups 205, 221, 224
Political negotiations 97, 235, 243
Political unification 63, 89, 224, 228, 259, 283
Political union 25, 63, 176, 194, 208, 218, 222, 224, 250, 263, 266, 270, 274, 289, 301, 335, 336, 338, 346, 356
Political will 50, 59, 68, 224, 251, 270, 335
Pompidou, Georges 64–67, 89, 90, 192, 194, 201, 227, 246–248, 252, 253, 285, 287, 288, 290, 309, 310, 316, 324, 325, 350
Pooling reserves 321, 317, 328
Postolache, Tudorel 7
Pound sterling 43, 51, 54, 56, 62, 65, 72, 86, 106, 133, 210, 213, 214, 215, 247, 260, 261, 274, 312, 317, 326
Powers 137, 252, 269, 305, 315, 317, 329, 338
Prate, A. 82
Preliminary report 100, 124
Preliminary stage 250, 258, 274
Price stability policy 34, 35, 268, 339
Prince of Asturias Award 29
Principle of unanimity 350
Problèmes économiques 298, 303
Public 25, 28, 34, 136, 203, 207, 221, 223, 233, 252, 262, 264, 266, 268, 270–274, 277, 288, 299, 320, 341

Q

Quaglia, L. 87, 201, 293
Quai d'Orsay 79, 247, 290
Qualified majority 70, 71, 81, 294, 350, 353
Queen Elizabeth II 293

R

Rasschaert, Theo 296
Realignment 310, 326
Reconstruction 35, 36, 77, 85
Reding, Viviane 14

Regional and structural policy 176, 182, 207, 212, 258, 264, 269, 339
Regulation 85, 280
Reichsmark 51
Report 204, 205, 207, 208, 210, 212, 213, 218, 219, 221, 223, 225–228, 230–232, 234, 239, 241, 243, 245, 248, 255, 256, 260, 262, 270, 271, 273, 275, 278, 282, 286, 287, 289, 291, 293–295, 298–300, 313, 315, 316, 318, 319, 327, 332–342, 343, 348
Reserve currency 54, 57, 80, 133, 213–215, 308
Reserve fund 73, 108, 183, 190, 265
Reserve instruments 34, 35, 38, 55, 59, 103, 136, 172, 215, 216, 254, 267, 314, 315, 317
Retinger, Josef 297
Revaluation 42, 52, 54, 56, 62, 216, 306, 310, 313, 318
Rey, Jean 109, 135, 209, 277
Ricquier, Jean-Claude 91, 130, 292
Right of initiative 63, 294
Rist, Charles 40
Rohwedder, Detlev 99, 130, 286
Rome 30, 56, 59, 85, 100, 107–109, 131, 137, 208, 244, 259, 310, 316, 327
Roosa Report 136
Roth, Lex 14
Rotterdam 50, 86
Rücker, K. 86
Rueff, Jacques 20, 34, 40, 76, 357
Ruppert, Charles 14

S
Saccomanni, Fabrizio 14
Salan, W. 87
Salzburg 271
Sanem 32, 342
Santer, Jacques 14, 25, 26, 28, 29, 32, 357
Satellites (Project) 32, 23, 28, 27
Savings Banks Group of the EEC 266, 295
Scelba, Mario 217
Schachtschneider, K. 342
Schaus, Eugène 30
Schaus, Léon 21
Scheel, Walter 238, 239, 256, 257, 295
Scheller, H. 344
Schiller, Karl 43, 49, 69, 84, 86, 95, 96, 99, 103, 113, 116, 130, 137, 138, 190–193, 202, 205, 217, 218, 226, 235, 238, 239, 242–245, 252, 272, 284–286, 289, 293, 299, 306, 308, 348
Schiller Plan 69, 76, 92, 101, 131, 137, 205, 243, 244, 253, 282, 299
Schirmann, S. 30, 78, 90
Schmidt, Helmut 323
Schmitz, Johnny 102
Schöllhorn, Johann 94, 99, 102, 103, 105, 112, 119, 127, 130, 132, 138, 171, 226, 243, 249
Schoutheete, De. Ph. 89
Schroeder, C. 30
Schuman Declaration 79
Schuman, Robert 3, 19, 20, 29, 39, 79

Schumann, Maurice 241, 248, 249, 294
Schuurmans, Constant 130
Schweitzer, Pierre-Paul 116, 271, 347
SDR transfer operations 108, 134
Second Barre Plan (Memorandum) 60, 75, 101, 205, 261
Second stage 81, 122, 127, 184, 194, 220, 224, 265, 320, 329, 336, 339
Seidel, K. 343
Short-term economic policy 45, 67, 71, 74, 75, 104, 105, 113, 122, 132, 133, 137, 165, 167, 169, 170, 177, 178, 181, 198, 211, 213, 230, 231, 241–243, 247, 268, 285, 295, 323
Short-term support 58, 59, 60, 182, 191, 200, 206, 212, 215, 231, 268, 311, 314, 315, 317, 318, 319, 321, 328
Sillem, J.A. 199
Single currency 27, 42, 43, 47, 50, 71, 72, 113, 116, 133, 166, 173, 176, 177, 189, 190, 195, 223, 246, 254, 261, 274, 305, 333–335, 338, 340, 356
Single European Act 353
Single market 332, 333
The Six 41, 43, 47, 48, 51–53, 55, 56, 58, 60, 61, 64, 68, 71–74, 84, 94, 97, 107, 133, 164, 165, 171, 180, 182, 191, 206, 209, 210, 217, 222, 223, 226, 230, 238, 242, 248, 256, 259, 261, 265, 267, 272, 273, 276, 278, 299–302, 306, 309, 311, 316, 346, 347, 352, 353
Small-state diplomacy 31, 356
Smithsonian Agreement 310, 326
Smithsonian Institute 310
Snake 274, 311–313, 319, 321, 326
Snoy et d'Oppuers, Bernard 15, 129
Snoy et d'Oppuers, Jean-Charles 43, 70, 91, 95–99, 101, 106, 113, 114, 129–131, 137, 205, 226, 235, 292, 307, 308, 349
Snoy–Giscard proposal 95
Snoy Plan 69–71, 101, 131, 205, 282, 292
Social Democratic group 280
Social Europe 25, 223, 356
Social partners 115, 213, 221, 262, 334, 356
Social policy 233, 265, 269, 270, 294, 317
Société Européenne des Satellites (SES) 28
Société Royale d'Économie Politique 300
Solidarity 45, 47, 49, 51, 66, 162
Sorbonne 201, 202
Sovereignty 41, 46, 55, 67, 190, 191, 222–224, 249, 250, 253, 261, 272–275, 299, 336, 350, 352, 355, 356
Soviet Union 297
Spaak, Paul-Henri 39, 351
Spaak Committee 95
Special committees 205, 283, 333
Special Drawing Rights (SDRs) 55, 68, 73, 74, 84, 108, 133, 134, 183, 215, 308
Special exchange system 84, 114, 184, 209
Specialist committees 225, 235, 238, 284

Speculation 38, 42, 56, 59, 80, 86, 212, 216, 308, 310, 312, 323
Spierenburg Report 341
Spinelli, Altiero 39
Stabilisation fund 114, 118, 127, 172, 230
Stabilitätgesetz 105, 236
Stability 27, 36, 37, 39, 55, 62, 66, 72, 80, 162, 166, 174, 191, 194, 209, 211, 215, 225, 228, 233, 246, 262, 267, 269, 272, 306, 313, 317, 320, 322
Stage(s) 35, 39, 57, 70–76, 82, 84, 101–103, 105, 121, 136, 139, 305, 313, 318–321, 333
Stage one 108, 129, 178, 180–182, 198, 236–240, 243–245, 247, 251–253, 256, 257, 259, 261, 264, 266, 268–270, 288, 305, 318–320, 333, 338
Stage two 182, 245, 247, 252, 253, 261, 265, 318–322, 333, 338
Stammati, Gaetano 94, 102, 103, 108, 112, 119, 121, 123, 171, 258
Starbatty, J. 342
Starting point 103, 109, 166, 175, 176
Steel crisis 24–26
Strammati, Gaetano 200
Strasbourg 41, 47, 83, 86
Stråth, B. 88
Strong currencies 190, 306
Structural and regional policy 105, 168, 180, 182, 198, 238, 252, 261, 265
Stuttgart 342
Stuttgarter Zeitung 298
Süddeutsche Zeitung 301
Summit 60, 64, 65, 67, 227, 252, 281, 316
Supranational aspect(s) 46, 65, 80–82, 191, 229, 238, 246, 247, 250, 254, 260, 274, 288, 336, 337, 332, 352
Sustainable growth 39, 162
Sveriges Riksbank 136
Sweden 313
Swedish krone 326
Switzerland 216, 270, 297, 313
Symmetrical EMU 256, 349
System 206, 207, 219, 220, 229, 245, 332
System of central banks 188, 251, 252, 253, 265, 336
Szasz, A. 199

T

Tageblatt 276, 302
Tagesnachrichten 91
Taxation 55, 67, 179, 180, 104, 106, 121, 162, 168, 171, 180, 266, 279, 280, 334, 336
Théron, M. 199
Think tank 28, 53
Third programme for medium-term economic policy 132
Third stage 69, 70, 71, 73, 81, 333, 334, 336, 338
Thorn, Gaston 15, 24–26, 30, 95, 96, 129, 357
Three-point working method 345

Thygesen, Niels 15, 343
Tietmeyer, Hans 91, 102, 103, 112, 123, 126, 135, 200, 201, 249, 289, 299, 342, 343, 348
The Times 273, 300
Timmerman, P.C. 199
Tindemans, Leo 316, 340
Toniolo, G. 79
Toulouse 31
Trade unions 203, 262, 266, 269, 296
Transfer of powers 168, 188, 208, 212, 220, 223, 224, 228, 233, 237, 239, 243, 246, 247, 255, 259, 261, 263, 278, 335, 337
Transfer of responsibility 111, 113, 169, 176, 181, 207, 289, 348
Transfers of sovereignty 248, 299, 333
Transnational governance networks 25
Transport policy 265, 294
Trausch, G. 31
Treasury 23, 26, 260
Treaty 30, 42–44, 63, 68, 79, 84, 85, 115, 123, 129, 170, 174, 178, 180, 181, 209, 210, 212, 220, 223, 227, 231–234, 237, 251, 252, 256, 260, 270, 294, 336, 352
Treaty establishing a single Council and a single Commission of the Communities 47
Treaty of Brussels 283
Treaties of Rome 30, 39, 43, 44, 56, 79, 81, 85, 95, 165, 194, 208, 223, 231, 233, 244, 252, 256, 294, 296, 302, 338, 350, 351
Triffin, Robert 25, 27, 38, 42, 44, 49, 53, 66, 78, 81, 90, 101, 110, 117, 120, 121, 138, 287, 342, 347, 349, 357
Triffin Archives 16, 90, 287
Triffin dilemma 74, 78, 79
Truman, Harry 77
Tsoukalis, L. 200
Two sides of industry 163, 179, 263, 264, 294

U

U.S. Federal Reserve System 255
UDF 289
Unanimity 57, 83, 100, 111, 115, 116, 127, 173, 252, 259, 265, 284, 336, 348, 351–353
Unemployment 33, 211, 332
Union 103, 129, 132, 135, 279
Union économique et monétaire 201, 276, 299
Union of Industries of the European Community (UNICE) 267, 295
United Kingdom (UK) 36, 38, 54, 63–65, 72, 80, 85, 89, 133, 136, 193, 201, 210, 213–215, 238, 247, 256, 260, 261, 273, 293, 294, 297, 307, 311, 312, 314, 316, 319
United Nations (UN) 35, 202
United States (of America) (US, USA) 4, 28, 36–39, 43, 45, 46, 52, 53, 55, 66, 71, 77, 78, 82, 85, 87, 109, 125, 136, 172, 195, 216, 248, 270, 271, 273, 279, 280, 287, 297, 306–310, 312, 316, 317, 323, 326, 338, 347

Unit of account 42, 43, 48, 49, 54, 57, 62, 74, 78, 315, 341, 356
Universal suffrage 269, 334
Université catholique de Louvain-la-Neuve 110, 287
Unwin, Brian (Sir) 15, 200
US dollar 35–38, 42–44, 50, 55, 56, 62, 71–73, 77, 78, 82, 85, 86, 107, 133, 172, 184, 186, 195, 198, 215, 216, 248, 250, 267, 273, 274, 279, 280, 306–314, 316, 317, 321, 323, 325, 326, 342
US Federal Reserve Board 125, 173, 177, 238, 348

V

Value-Added Tax (VAT) 104, 137, 168, 179, 334
Van Puyvelde, T. 295
van Yperseele, J. 84
Vaud Office for the Development of Trade and Industry in Lausanne 303
Vendroux, Jacques 288
Venice 112, 115, 117, 137, 163, 175, 196, 219, 231, 243, 286, 346
Verdun, A. 292
Very short-term support 311, 312, 314, 328
Veto 46, 54, 60, 82, 352, 353
Vietnam War 55
von der Groeben, Hans 136
Voting 73, 83, 350, 351
Vouel, Raymond 25
Vredenberg van der Horst, Jan Willem 91

W

Wages/salaries 58, 212, 269, 281
Washington 22, 310, 326, 348
Wegener, A. 139
Wehrmacht 21
Werner Committee 45, 51, 93, 100, 101, 104, 110, 111, 114, 118, 121, 125, 128, 131, 185, 189, 191, 192, 199–201, 203, 206, 207, 209, 219, 225, 230, 242, 245, 253–256, 258, 260, 262, 266, 273, 275, 282, 291, 298, 300, 301, 335, 337, 345, 349
Werner Group 42, 69, 100, 102, 106, 108, 109, 111–115, 118, 121, 123–125, 131, 135, 161–163, 166, 169–173, 175, 177–182, 185, 187, 190, 191, 193, 196, 197, 204, 205, 210, 214, 218, 223, 225, 226, 232, 233, 248, 265, 270–272, 278, 282, 291, 295, 300, 336
Werner, Henri 8, 13, 15, 32, 293
Werner, Marie-Anne 6, 7, 15, 32
Werner, Pierre 2–17, 19–32, 40–43, 45–52, 54, 57, 59, 66–68, 72, 74, 75, 80, 81, 83–87, 90, 91, 94–103, 106–109, 112–123, 125–129, 131, 134, 135, 137–140, 164, 171, 172, 175, 176, 182–185, 188, 190, 196, 199, 201, 202, 219, 225, 227, 235, 240, 241, 248, 251, 253, 255, 257, 260, 271, 272, 276, 277, 282, 283, 285, 288–293, 298, 303, 307, 324, 326, 328–330, 337, 343–345, 351, 355–357

Werner Plan 49, 75, 88, 92, 129, 204, 287, 288, 299, 301, 302, 339, 343, 344
Werner Report 4, 9, 10, 23, 27, 35, 50, 93, 111, 127, 131, 137, 138, 183–189, 193–197, 199, 203–205, 207–210, 212–215, 217–230, 232–236, 238–240, 242–252, 254–256, 258–263, 265–270, 272, 274, 275, 277, 282, 283, 287, 288, 290, 291, 298–303, 305, 311, 322, 331–339, 343–345, 349, 356
Western Europe 22, 37, 77, 85, 260
Western European Union (WEU) 21, 89
West Germany 33, 80, 323
Wigny, Pierre 42
Wilkens, A. 90, 201, 202, 324
Willaert, É. 30, 288
Wilson, J. 79
Wirtschaftsforschungsinstitute (Economic Research Institute) 324
Wirtschafts Revue 303
Witteveen, Johannes 95, 99, 107, 116, 130, 242, 253, 254, 291, 349
Woehrling, Francis 340
Working method 229
Working Party on Economic and Monetary Union 92, 163
World Bank 40, 47, 100, 125
World War II 21, 24, 33, 35, 39, 79, 85, 202, 310
Worm in the snake 311
Wormser, Olivier 186
Wortmann, H. 199

Y

Yale 78

Z

Zeeland, Paul Van 297
Zentralbankrat 194, 202
Zijlstra, Jelle 107, 114, 115, 142, 145, 147–149, 151, 153, 155, 157–159, 357
Zurich 279

The manufacturer's authorised representative in the EU is Springer Nature Customer Service Centre GmbH, Europaplatz 3, 69115 Heidelberg, Germany. If you have any concerns regarding our products, please contact ProductSafety@springernature.com

Printed and bound by CPI Group (UK) Ltd, Croydon, CR0 4YY
30/09/2026
02225439-0014